A History of Corporate Finance focuses on the role of institutions and organizations in the historical development of corporate finance. This book provides an overview of the evolution of practice in this field from the Italian merchant banks of the Renaissance through the conglomerates and leveraged-buyout partnerships of contemporary Wall Street. It also puts forth a compelling argument for the closer integration of historical and quantitative research methods in advancing finance theory. In addition, the Epilogue defines an original algorithm that explains the relationship between the short-term, firm-specific factors and longer-term environmental elements that have shaped the historical development of finance.

D0839257

A History of Corporate Finance

A History of Corporate Finance

Jonathan Barron Baskin
Baruch College

Paul J. Miranti, Jr.
Rutgers University

CAMBRIDGE
UNIVERSITY PRESS

PUBLISHED BY THE PRESS SYNDICATE OF THE UNIVERSITY OF CAMBRIDGE
The Pitt Building, Trumpington Street, Cambridge, United Kingdom

CAMBRIDGE UNIVERSITY PRESS
The Edinburgh Building, Cambridge CB2 2RU, UK   http://www.cup.cam.ac.uk
40 West 20th Street, New York, NY 10011-4211, USA   http://www.cup.org
10 Stamford Road, Oakleigh, Melbourne 3166, Australia
Ruiz de Alarcón 13, 28014 Madrid, Spain

© Cambridge University Press 1997

First published 1997
First paperback edition 1999

Printed in the United States of America

A catalog record for this book is available from the British Library

Library of Congress Cataloging in Publication data
Baskin, Jonathan Barron
A history of corporate finance / Jonathan Barron Baskin, Paul J. Miranti, Jr.
p.   cm.
Includes index.
1. Corporations – Finance – History. I Miranti, Paul J.
II. Title
HG4017.B37   1997
658.15 – dc20
96-19598

ISBN 0 521 55514 0 hardback
ISBN 0 521 65536 6 paperback

To the memory of Enid Baskin Fink
and
to Anne Phelan Miranti

Contents

Preface

This study of the role of institutions and organizations in the establishment of capital structures to finance the activities of large-scale business enterprises was begun by Jonathan Barron Baskin. My connection with the undertaking began when I was asked to review Baskin's original work. I was very favorably impressed by the approach of that work in explaining how the persistent problem of asymmetric information that divides the interests of corporate managers and investors shaped institutional arrangements in finance, a point brilliantly developed in Baskin's essay "The Development of Corporate Financial Markets in Britain and the United States, 1600–1914: Overcoming Asymmetric Information," which appeared in the *Business History Review* and won the Newcomen Society Prize in 1988.

My review suggested that the study might be strengthened if its focus was broadened by incorporating more examples of how particular firms or classes of firms historically resolved the capital structure puzzle. Besides bolstering the persuasiveness of the study's central findings, such an approach would provide support for Baskin's argument that theory building in finance could be enriched by a better blending of historical and quantitative research methods. A new synthesis could be achieved by reinterpreting the findings of a broad body of historical studies using the analytical constructs that guide contemporary financial research.

Baskin's revision was cut short by his untimely death. The project eventually moved forward again because of the loving commitment of Paul W. Fink, who, cherishing the memory of his gifted son, wished to see his major contribution to scholarship in financial history brought to fruition. At that juncture Paul Fink engaged me to complete the mission. I am grateful to him for his valued editorial assistance and for the financial support that he helped to arrange.

The new perspectives afforded by the introduction of firm-level histories to the study also led to a subtle, unanticipated modification of the framework of analysis. In evaluating the experience of the Medici Bank, the East India Company, the nineteenth century railroads, conglomerates and the other businesses that amplify this study, it became clear that institutional and organizational innovation in finance also served to enhance enterprise efficiency. As the study will demonstrate, financial innovation did this by facilitating the achievement of economies of scale and scope, by helping to surmount market imperfections, by making possible the successful adjustment to exogenous changes, as well as by reducing risk perceptions associated with informational asymmetries and other uncertainties confronting the firm.

Many contributed to the advancement of this study. Foremost were Lance Davis, H. Peter Gray and Richard Sylla, all of whom read the entire manuscript and offered many useful suggestions. Had Jonathan Baskin survived he would have wanted to acknowledge the guidance and support he received during his scholarly career from his friends and professional associates, including Robert Ariel, Paul Asquith, Dixon Chow, Benjamin Friedman, Richard Kalt, the late Jeffrey Liu, Stewart Myers, Howard Ross, James Stollar, Irving Stone, Vincent Su and Stavros Thomadakis, as well as from his dean at Baruch College of the City University of New York, Francis Connelly. I also profited from ideas about particular aspects of corporate finance offered by many others, including Nusret Cakichi, Alfred Chandler, Kevin Chen, Ernest Englander, Irene Finel-Honigman, Louis Galambos, Leonard Goodman, Jean Gray, Gikas Hardouvelis, Bikki Jaggi, Allen Kaufman, C. F. Lee, Kenneth Lipartito, Yaw Mensah, Barry Newman, Oded Palmon, Ed Perkins, Bill Taylor, Eugene White and Lawrence Zacharias. In addition, the study benefited from the many useful editorial suggestions put forth by Paul Fink, Gerry Kamber and Robert Racine, as well as from the diligent efforts of my research assistant, Eric W. Ostrager. Finally, I wish to recognize the encouragement and support of Dean Arthur Kraft, Dean John Burton and Dean George Benson, who have helped to make my current academic home, Rutgers University, an ideal location for scholarly endeavor.

Introduction

History and the Modern Theory
of Finance

I. The Two Lenses of Economic Theory

History and statistics have long been thought of as vital adjuncts in scholarly efforts to further the understanding of economics and allied fields such as corporate finance. In his classic work, *The Scope and Method of Political Economy* (1890), John Neville Keynes, for example, characterized the nature of the relationship between these two specializations as essentially complementary.[1] Inherent in this view was the belief that economic understanding could be brought into sharpest focus only by blending the unique perspectives afforded by each discipline, like the images cast by the separate lenses of a stereoscope.

Although in general accord with Keynes about the relevance of these two types of knowledge, Joseph A. Schumpeter later expressed, in his *History of Economic Analysis* (1954), the controversial opinion that historical studies were the more important. In his view economics was a uniquely historical process whose significance could be fully grasped only when viewed in a broader social context which incorporated events, institutions, individuals and organizations. In contrasting history with statistics and theory as a focus of scholarly endeavor, he wrote:

Of these fundamental fields, economic history – which issues into and includes present day facts – is by far the most important. I wish to state right now that if, starting my work in economics afresh, I were told that I could study only one of the three but could have my choice, it would be economic history that I would choose. And this is on three grounds.

---

[1] John Neville Keynes, *The Scope and Method of Political Economy* (London: Macmillan, 1890).

1

First, the subject matter of history is essentially a unique process in historic time. Nobody can hope to understand the economic phenomena of any, including the present, epoch, who has not an adequate command of historical *facts* and an adequate amount of historical *sense* or of what might be described as *historical experience*. Second, the historical report cannot be purely economic but must inevitably reflect also "institutional" facts that are not purely economic: therefore it affords the best method for understanding how economic and non-economic facts *are* related to one another and how the various social sciences *should* be related to one another. Third, it is, I believe, the fact that most of the fundamental errors currently committed in economic analysis are due to lack of historical experience more often than to any other shortcoming of the economist's equipment. History must of course be understood to include fields that have acquired different names as a consequence of specialization, such as prehistoric events and ethnology (anthropology).[2]

This study follows Schumpeter by employing historical methods to amplify an important contemporary paradigm, the "modern theory of finance," which evaluates two central questions: the first is the *financing question,* which identifies the determinants of optimal capital structure decisions; and the second is the *dividend question,* which explains the factors that control decisions about the distribution of residual income to shareholders.[3]

Although this study emphasizes the influence of changing institutional relationships, it recognizes the strong contribution of quantitative and statistical research in elevating the comprehension of finance. Since World War II, horizons of knowledge have been broadened by scholars who sought to place economics on a "positive" basis more akin to the physical sciences.[4] The intellectual constructs they set forth

---

[2] Joseph A. Schumpeter, *History of Economic Analysis,* Elizabeth Boody Schumpeter, ed. (New York: Oxford University Press, 1954), pp. 12–13.

[3] A third question that is not directly addressed by the modern theory of finance is concerned with how scarce financial resources are allocated between competing investment alternatives. For a discussion of the relationship of these fundamental questions, see James C. Van Horne, *Financial Policy and Management,* 10th ed. (Englewood Cliffs, N.J.: Prentice-Hall, 1994), chapt. 1 passim.

[4] During this era several proponents of these views wrote influential works about how economics might be placed on a more positive basis, including Milton Friedman, *Essays in Positive Economics* (Chicago: University of Chi-

were built up from a priori assumptions and were formalized and tested empirically. The importance of the insights rendered by the new scientism was evinced by the fact that four of its pioneers were awarded Nobel Prizes for economics during the 1980s. Their studies incorporated a distinctive methodological approach. They evaluated general problems by deductively specifying assumptions based on delineations of rational behavior that communicated the essential significance of the model. Although the model in its simplest form does not claim to reflect external conditions precisely, its consistency, completeness and implications can be evaluated through formal logic and mathematics. Its underlying suppositions, however, are expressed as rules that state how the model's elements correspond to circumstances in the real world.

This brings us to another purpose of this book, which is to demonstrate the need for greater recognition of path dependence and historical evolution in the modern theory of finance.[5] This does not mean that the modern theory is internally inconsistent or that practitioners, as distinct from theoreticians, do not amend the basic model according to the needs of their inquiries. It does mean that, as in all scientific research, there is a very real danger that the regnant model biases the approach of analysts and restricts the degree to which they are willing to incorporate or recognize relevant variables.[6]

---

cago Press, 1953); Andreas G. Papandreou, *Economics as a Science* (Chicago: Lippincott, 1958); and Lionel Robbins, *An Essay on the Nature and Significance of Economic Science* (London: Macmillan, 1932).

[5] A similar argument about the need for history to be incorporated into economic theory building has been made by Daniel M. G. Raff and Peter Temin, "Business History and Recent Economic Theory: Imperfect Information, Incentives and the Internal Organization of Firms," in Peter Temin, ed., *Inside the Business Enterprise: Historical Perspectives on the Use of Information* (Chicago: University of Chicago Press, 1991), pp. 7–35.

[6] For a discussion of some of the implications for research of a narrow concentration on positive economics, see Phyllis Deane, "The Scope and Method of Economic Science," *Economic Journal* 93 (March 1983): 1–12; H. Peter Gray, "Social Science or Quasi Science," *Eastern Economic Journal* 15 (October–December 1989): 273–86; and E. H. Phelps-Brown, "The Underdevelopment of Economics," *Economic Journal* 82 (March 1972): 1–10. See also the discussion of the consequences of scientism in management studies in Milton Leontiades, *Mythmanagement: An Examination of Corporate Diversification as Fact and Theory* (Oxford: Blackwell, 1989), chapt. 1 passim.

What role, then, is played by institutions and organizations in corporate finance? Following Lance E. Davis and Douglass C. North, institutions represent constraints that shape social interaction. In business and finance they are, in effect, the rules of the game for pursuing opportunity and thus define the range of possibilities open to entrepreneurship. Their value lies largely in their capacity to reduce uncertainty and to foster economic stability. They can be either formal, as in the case of contemporary long-term debt contracts, or informal, as in the case of the norms of probative behavior that guided traders in early financial markets.[7]

Organizations, which are groups unified to pursue a common objective, operate within social settings that are ordered by institutional constructs. Historically, organizations such as corporations, joint-stock companies and partnerships have been the primary social vehicles for exploiting economic opportunity. Institutions provided the cohesion for organizations to bind together their component elements and to define their relationships to the external environment. Moreover, institutions were crucial to organizations because they often embodied information that had been distilled from past experience about what are thought to be the "best" ways to achieve particular objectives. Among the leading business organizations that are the focus of this study, such institutional development came about through a path-dependent process of firm-specific learning about the most efficacious ways of accommodating a dynamic economic environment.[8]

In addition to questions of capital structure and dividend payment, this study's focus on institutional and organizational change makes it possible to analyze the ways that financial innovation historically contributed to the achievement of substantial efficiency gains. The sample of firms selected for evaluation is heavily biased in favor of those that proved highly adept during each epoch in securing a strong

[7] For a discussion of the role of institutions in economic history, see Lance E. Davis and Douglass C. North, *Institutional Change and American Economic Growth* (Cambridge University Press, 1971), pp. 6–10; Douglass C. North, *Institutions, Institutional Change and Economic Performance,* reprint ed. (Cambridge University Press, 1991), pp. 3–5; and idem, "Economic Performance through Time," *American Economic Review* 84 (June 1994): 359–68.

[8] North, *Institutions, Institutional Change and Economic Performance,* pp. 5–6; and Davis and North, *Institutional Change and American Economic Growth,* pp. 7–8.

position of economic leadership because of their ability to concentrate large amounts of financial capital. Thus, some of the chapters focus on assessing the contributions of great individual ventures such as the Medici Bank and the English East India Company. The remaining chapters, on the other hand, analyze the experience of important classes of business organizations such as railroads in the nineteenth century and giant, diversified manufacturing companies during the twentieth century.

Four sets of circumstances were preeminent in the drive of the firms evaluated in this study to bolster efficiency through financial innovation. First, there was the potential for realizing significant economies of scale and scope, a potential that was often contingent on a firm's capacity to devise effective ways of attracting substantial amounts of financial capital. In these cases finance was usually an ancillary activity that was vital for the acquisition of managerial and productive resources necessary to exploit untapped opportunities. By providing for the orderly disposition of liabilities, finance ensured that there was sufficient time available for the enterprise to learn how to incorporate new, efficiency-enhancing technologies and forms of management.[9]

Second, financial innovation could help corporate entities capture gains from exogenous events. For example, the rearrangement of financial commitments could facilitate the adjustment to major economic disturbances in the form of either sectoral shocks such as serious turbulence in the financial market or macro shocks such as significant changes in relative price or income levels. Moreover, modifications of financing practices could make possible the realization of gains from changes in tax or regulatory policies, political events such as wars or major environmental changes such as weather shifts that affected communications and agricultural output.[10]

---

[9] Davis and North, *Institutional Change and American Economic Growth*, pp. 12–14. For a discussion of how modern business organizations promote economies of scale and scope, see Alfred D. Chandler, Jr., *The Visible Hand: The Managerial Revolution in American Business* (Cambridge, Mass.: Harvard University Press, 1977); idem, *Strategy and Structure: Chapters in the History of the Industrial Enterprise* (Cambridge, Mass.: MIT Press, 1962); and idem, *Scale and Scope: The Dynamics of Industrial Capitalism* (Cambridge, Mass.: Harvard University Press, 1990).

[10] Davis and North, *Institutional Change and American Economic Growth*, pp. 14–19.

Third, gains could derive from financial innovations that reduced risk perceptions. A key problem was the asymmetric distribution of information about the enterprise and its prospects that separated managements from investors. Differences in goals and in access to knowledge frequently placed investors at a disadvantage in dealing with their corporate agents. Investor wealth, for example, could be threatened either by corporate agents' opportunism or, in the extreme case of moral hazard, by their dishonesty. Such risks could be diminished by more effective contracting: the securing of liens on enterprise assets could protect investors against default risk, and the goals of management could be made more congruent with those of shareholders in the negotiation of incentive compensation contracts. In addition, risk perceptions could be dissipated by more effective monitoring through the creation of boards of directors and the establishment of financial reporting requirements.[11]

Fourth, financial innovations could be effective in surmounting costly market imperfections.[12] Gains could result from the creation within the firm of information flows and managerial structures that reduced transaction costs below the level that would have been incurred by relying on market structures. In finance, as in other functional specializations, there were three levels of organizational development that gradually emerged from a path-dependent process of corporate learning.[13] The first involved the establishment of basic routines to ensure the efficient processing of recurring transactions such as procedures for controlling cash receipts from sales transactions. The second level was the development of methods for integrating and coordinating the financial requirements of major functional activities such as sales and manufacturing. The highest level was strategic planning, which was concerned with determining how the pool of enterprise resources might be optimally allocated to take advantage of anticipated changes in the environment of business.

Although costly, the creation of structures that increased the velocity and scope of knowledge transfers within the firm provided additional financial benefits. Accessibility to a greater abundance of reli-

---

[11] Ibid., pp. 19–20.   [12] Ibid., pp. 20–25.

[13] Alfred D. Chandler, "Organizational Capabilities and the Economic History of the Industrial Enterprise," *Journal of Economic Perspectives* 6 (Summer 1992): 79–100.

able information helped to reduce the costs of adverse selection and of insurance through more accurate assessments of risk. It also increased the potential returns from financial transacting by expanding the awareness of the range of exploitable market opportunities.

The remainder of this chapter provides background about some of the controversies surrounding the modern theory of finance. We begin by considering the factors that have contributed to the reinvigoration of positive economics since World War II. This is followed by four sections that highlight key issues in the scholarly debate over the findings of the modern theory of finance: the intellectual foundations of the modern theory, the findings of this theory with respect to debt policy, the role that dividend payments are purported to play in corporate financing and the problem of agency and information-related market inefficiencies. The chapter concludes with a brief overview of the organization of the subsequent sections of the book.

II. Sharpening the Focus of the Quantitative Lens

Before World War II several developments encouraged the greater quantification of economics and finance. Many scholars wanted to place these subjects on a more scientific plane by embracing the analytical approaches espoused by leading philosophers of science. This goal seemed plausible because of the greater computational efficiency made possible by advances in both statistics and data processing and because of the definition of new behavioral models that applied mathematical and logical processes in analyzing business decision making.

During the 1930s and 1940s many economists were favorably impressed by the ideas put forth by philosopher Karl R. Popper about what constituted the most valid approaches in scientific inquiry. Central to Popper's perspective was a deep misgiving about the reliability of knowledge derived from inductive reasoning, which he thought was incapable of verifying general scientific laws. The shortcomings of induction seemed most evident in the social sciences – for example, in the claims of Marxists that history, a subject whose comprehension was essentially extended through inductive studies, followed immutable laws. Popper considered this conclusion to be dubious for two reasons. First, the finite scope of human comprehension created uncertainty about generalizations developed by extrapolating from particular cases. In addition, induction was logically flawed because it violated the syllogistic prohibition against confirming consequent statements. Although he believed that empirical knowledge was incapable of verifying universal laws, Popper nevertheless thought that it was useful in identifying statements that were materially false. In his view the body of scientific knowledge at any point in time consisted of those statements that had successfully resisted rigorous tests of "falsifiability." In this schema, progress came about only through a continual process of conjecture, criticism and reformulation.[14]

After World War II this began to have greater appeal to many intellectuals, who were as impressed by the solid achievements of modern science as they were dismayed by the dim record of contemporary politics. The wars, depressions and cataclysms of this period doubtless seemed reflective of a fundamental failure to establish the social sciences on a firm intellectual footing. Milton Friedman, for example (who was favorably impressed by Popper's ideas), argued that more positive economics would ultimately promote greater social harmony, namely:

I venture the judgement, however, that certainly in the Western world, and especially in the United States, differences about economic policy among disinterested citizens derive predominantly from different predictions about the economic consequences of taking action – differences that in principle can be eliminated by the progress of positive economics – rather than from fundamental differences in basic values, differences about which men can ultimately only fight.[15]

The changing tenor of finance scholarship was also reflected in the formation in 1932 of the Cowles Commission, a pioneering organization based initially in Colorado Spring, Colorado, that was dedicated

---

[14] See Karl R. Popper, *The Poverty of Historicism* (Boston: Beacon, 1957); and idem, *Objective Knowledge: An Evolutionary Approach* (Oxford: Clarendon Press, 1972). For a discussion of Popper's impact on post–World War II research methodologies in economics, see Mark Blaug, *The Methodology of Economics, or, How Economists Explain,* 2nd ed. (Cambridge University Press, 1992); and idem, *Economic Theory in Retrospect,* 4th ed. (Cambridge University Press, 1985), chapt. 16. For a more general evaluation of Popper's theoretical thinking, see Robert John Ackermann, *The Philosophy of Karl Popper* (Amherst: University of Massachusetts Press, 1976).

[15] Friedman, *Essays in Positive Economics,* p. 5.

to the rigorous quantitative study of securities markets and price activity. Its founder, Arthur C. Cowles III, was the scion of a wealthy Chicago family who had become interested in determining whether price fluctuations were predictable as part of his estate management responsibilities.[16] Although econometric techniques had been already applied in the 1920s by scholars like Wesley C. Mitchell at Columbia University and Warren M. Persons at Harvard University, little emphasis had been placed on explaining security price fluctuations.[17] Moreover, one prescient statistical study of financial markets, prepared in 1900 by French mathematician Louis Bachelier and entitled *Theory of Speculation,* had remained largely forgotten for decades. Instead, the analysis of price movements had remained the province of financial journalists such as Charles Dow, the founder and editor of the *Wall Street Journal,* and his successor as editor, William Peter Hamilton, who popularized a method of stock price charting known as "Dow Theory." With the creation of the Cowles Commission, however, the opportunity for a more scientific study of price data greatly increased. The influence of the Commission's program on financial scholarship was soon reflected in its closer association with mainstream academic economics. In 1933, the Commission began to finance *Econometrica* (whose first editor was Joseph Schumpeter). In 1939 the Commission further cemented these relationships by moving initially to the University of Chicago and then in the 1950s, when it came under the direction of future Nobel laureate James Tobin, to Yale University, Arthur Cowles's alma mater.[18]

The quantification of economics and finance was also an outgrowth of developments that enhanced computational effectiveness and efficiency. During the 1930s, new statistical techniques perfected by R. A. Fischer, Jerzy Neyman and Egon Pearson for biological research eventually found outlets in analyzing economic aggregates. Success in resolving problems in cryptography, logistics, fire control and pattern

[16] Peter L. Bernstein, *Capital Ideas: The Improbable Origins of Modern Wall Street* (New York: Free Press, 1992), pp. 29–38.

[17] Guy Alchon, *The Invisible Hand of Planning: Capitalism, Social Science and the State in the 1920s* (Princeton, N.J.: Princeton University Press, 1985), especially chapt. 6; and Mary S. Morgan, *The History of Econometric Ideas* (Cambridge University Press, 1990), pp. 44–56 for discussion of Mitchell, and pp. 56–63 for Persons.

[18] Bernstein, *Capital Ideas,* pp. 17–29, 33, 37 and 67.

bombing during World War II augmented the prestige of statistics and operations research. The potential for more fruitful mathematical analysis was enhanced by the perfection of electronic data processing. The miniaturization of circuitry made possible by the invention of the transistor led to dramatic declines in the costs of analyzing vast amounts of information. Moreover, the quality and quantity of corporate financial data steadily improved through the further standardization of financial accounting. Finally, the rise of cybernetics and game theory assisted this transition by providing a logical framework for formulating testable hypotheses about business decision processes.[19]

During the 1950s many business disciplines sought to enhance their prestige by embracing the quantitative methodologies in vogue in the better-established programs in economics. Business education, since its inception near the turn of the current century, had remained isolated from many of the beneficial trends that had enriched other fields of scholarship. The body of knowledge in finance, for instance, had been largely descriptive, focusing on institutional and legal structures, modes of long-term corporate finance and pragmatic guidelines for investment analysis. The research literature remained sparse on such questions as the management of risk or working capital and the operation of the capital markets. Nor were there any attempts to unify these fragments through a comprehensive theoretical synthesis.[20]

The new trends in research and instruction were further advanced by the separate studies coming from the Ford Foundation and Carnegie Foundation calling for greater intellectual rigor in business studies.[21] There soon followed a major reorientation. In finance the subsequent reform was directed largely by economists who naturally followed the accepted pathways of their specialization. Finance be-

---

[19] John Von Neumann, *The Computer and the Brain* (New Haven, Conn.: Yale University Press, 1958); and Von Neumann and Oskar Morgenstern, *Theory of Games and Economic Behavior,* 3rd ed. (Princeton, N.J.: Princeton University Press, 1944, 1953).

[20] For a discussion of some of the factors changing the nature of education in finance, see R. Whitley, "The Transformation of Business Finance into Financial Economics: The Roles of Academic Expansion and Changes in U.S. Capital Markets," *Accounting, Organization and Society* 11 (1986): 171–92.

[21] See Robert A. Gordon and James E. Howell, *Higher Education for Business* (New York: Columbia University Press, 1959); and Frank Cook Pierson, *The Education of American Businessmen* (New York: McGraw-Hill, 1959).

came more intimately intertwined with neoclassical economic theory. Capital markets were analyzed in the context of equilibrium models of perfect product market competition. Market valuation processes provided the rationale for evaluating corporate finance decisions. This transformation was reflected in the growing number of quantitative studies that began to appear in what was finance's traditional leading periodical, the *Journal of Finance*. This trend was furthered in two later, highly regarded publications, the *Journal of Finance and Quantitative Analysis* (1966) and the *Journal of Financial Economics* (1974).

The application of the logical and mathematical methods that formed the core of the new approach to comprehending finance was not limited to the evaluation of the aggregate behavior of markets. As the following sections explain, these approaches also proved useful in theorizing about how business corporations financed their activities.

III. Foundations of the Modern Theory of Finance

The original research that eventually led to the promulgation of the modern theory of finance focused on two fundamental issues: (1) the predictability of stock price movements and (2) the minimization of portfolio risk. In 1953, M. G. Kendall published a study demonstrating that successive prices in both the stock and the commodity markets moved in random fashion. The failure to discover any systematic correlation in price movements over time was explained as evidence of the inherent efficiency and competitive nature of the financial markets. In this context efficiency specifically related to the capacity of the market to discount all relevant and known information about future dividends or capital values. Future price changes must necessarily reflect new and therefore unpredictable information. It is this uncertainty about future conditions that in turn dictates that share prices fluctuate in random fashion.[22]

The efficient market hypothesis, however, left unresolved several important questions. It did not, for example, define specifically what constitutes information relevant to evaluating share prices. Nor did it indicate the effect of variation in the quantity and quality of informa-

---

[22] Maurice Kendall, "The Analysis of Economic Time Series, Part I: Prices," *Journal of the Royal Statistical Society* 96 (1953): 11–25.

tion available to investors. The hypothesis also failed to establish a standard for assessing informational veracity or to discuss the implications of valuations based on inaccurate data. Moreover, it did not explain how information was used in decision making.

Soon Harry Markowitz addressed these problems as part of his work in portfolio theory. In his model the essential trade-off confronting investors was between risk and return. In this context rational behavior was associated with the desire to maximize return and minimize risk. The riskiness of investing in particular securities could be reduced by holding significantly diversified portfolios. Although diversification could not eliminate the risk associated with overall market fluctuations, portfolio managers could still choose portfolios that either accentuated or dampened the amplitude of these movements. The covariance of a particular company's shares to the overall market, or "beta," was the critical sensitivity measure for portfolio managers.[23]

During the next two decades, four scholars extended Kendall's and Markowitz's insights, thereby laying down the basic foundations of the modern theory of finance. First in 1958, Franco Modigliani and Merton H. Miller published their seminal paper on optimal capital structures in an economy that had perfect markets and was not burdened with either taxes or transaction costs.[24] This was soon followed in 1965 by John Lintner's extension of Markowitz's portfolio model.[25] Assuming perfect markets incorporating homogeneous beliefs and unlimited costless short-sales, Lintner derived his version of the capital asset pricing model (CAPM), which predicted a linear equilibrium relationship between risk and return. By 1970, the market rationality assumption inherent in these models seemed well founded when Eugene Fama confidently concluded that "the evidence in support of the efficient market hypothesis is extensive, and . . . contradictory evi-

---

[23] Harry Markowitz, "Portfolio Selection," *Journal of Finance* 7 (March 1952): 77–91.

[24] Franco Modigliani and Merton H. Miller, "The Cost of Capital, Corporation Finance and the Theory of Investment," *American Economic Review* 48 (June 1958): 261–97.

[25] John Lintner, "Security Prices, Risk, and Maximal Gains from Diversification," *Journal of Finance* 20 (1965): 587–615; and idem, "The Valuation of Risky Assets and the Selection of Risky Investments in Stock Portfolios and Capital Budgets," *Review of Economics and Statistics* 47 (1965): 13–37.

dence is sparse."[26] In this view, capital markets are perfect and frictionless, and price securities at the best estimate of their intrinsic value. Moreover, this view implies yet another assumption about human behavior. It follows from the efficient market hypothesis that corporations act in the interests of their securities holders and, therefore, are primarily committed to maximizing the value of their securities.

But the assumption that firms are seeking to maximize shareholder wealth seems unpersuasive and is at variance with the broad body of research in finance and other social sciences. An extensive literature on the development of professions, for example, emphasizes the lack of congruence in the objectives of practitioners and consumers for many types of specialized services. Nor do the findings of many historians suggest that politicians run governments solely for the benefit of the electorate. Beginning with Adam Smith, many economists have been sensitive to the inherent conflicts between the interests of owners and managers.[27] Adolf A. Berle and Gardiner C. Means in their classic *The Modern Corporation and Private Property* (1932) identified this dichotomy as a critical issue for those charged with the responsibility of reforming the financial markets.[28] Herbert A. Simon later embellished this notion by suggesting that management's actions were constrained by bounded rationality and could be better characterized as "satisficing" rather than optimizing.[29] These perceptions eventually influenced finance literature. In 1972, Armen A. Alchian and Harold Demsetz authored their seminal paper that sparked a new interest in studying the pervasive, but poorly understood problems of agency relations.[30]

The empirical evidence also calls into question the validity of the

[26] Eugene F. Fama, "Efficient Capital Markets: A Review of Theory and Empirical Work," *Journal of Finance* 25 (1970): 383–417.

[27] Adam Smith, *An Inquiry into the Nature and Causes of the Wealth of Nations*, 2 vols., reprint ed. (Chicago: University of Chicago Press, 1976), vol. 2, pp. 264–65.

[28] Adolf A. Berle and Gardiner C. Means, *The Modern Corporation and Private Property* (New York: Commerce Clearing House, 1932).

[29] Herbert A. Simon, *Administrative Behavior: A Study of Decision-Making Processes in Administrative Organization,* 2nd ed. (New York: Macmillan, 1957), chapt. 2 and pp. 241–42.

[30] Armen A. Alchian and Harold Demsetz, "Production, Information Costs and Economic Organization," *American Economic Review* 62 (1972): 777–

modern theory's efficiency assumption. While contemporary financial markets may be more functional than those of the past, even the most recent studies suggest major inefficiencies. Schiller, for instance, shows that stock prices appear too volatile to be consistent with rational valuation. He points out that U.S. stock prices during the period 1871–1979, varied five to thirteen times as much as would be rationally expected given the actual observed volatility in the dividend stream.[31] Schiller also confirms this in a second study, which evaluates long-term interest rate patterns. He concluded that long rates seemed more volatile than would be predicted from either observed short-term interest rates or the term structure theory.[32]

Recent evidence also suggests that price variation is not absolutely random. For example, large predictable (and occasionally exploitable) cycles in financial markets are now an established fact. Furthermore, tests that show that simple strategies do not always provide supranor-

---

95. See also the later studies of William H. Meckling and Michael C. Jensen, "Theory of the Firm: Managerial Behavior, Agency Costs and Ownership Structure," *Journal of Financial Economics* 3 (1976): 305–70; Eugene F. Fama, "Agency Problems and the Theory of the Firm," *Journal of Political Economy* 88 (1980): 288–307; Eugene F. Fama and Michael C. Jensen, "Agency Problems and Residual Claims," *Journal of Law and Economics* 26 (1983): 327–49; and idem, "Separation of Ownership and Control," in ibid., pp. 301–25.

[31] Robert J. Schiller, "Do Stock Prices Move Too Much to Be Justified by Subsequent Changes in Dividends?" *American Economic Review* 71 (June 1981): 421–36.

[32] Robert J. Schiller, "Causes of Changing Financial Market Stability," *Symposium on Financial Market Volatility – Causes, Consequences and Responses Sponsored by the Kansas City Federal Reserve Bank* (Jackson Hole, Wyo.: 1988). A number of other studies confirm Schiller's findings, including N. Gregory Mankiw, David Romer and Mathew D. Shapiro, "An Unbiased Reexamination of Stock Market Volatility," *Journal of Finance* 40 (July 1985): 677–87; and Andrew W. Lo and A. Craig MacKinlay, "Stock Market Prices Do Not Follow Random Walks: Evidence from a Simple Specification Test," *Review of Financial Studies* 1 (1988–89): 41–66. Moreover, James M. Poterba and Lawrence H. Summers, "Mean Reversion in Stock Prices: Evidence and Implications," *Journal of Financial Market Economics* 22 (1988): 27–60, provide striking prices in seventeen countries. A contrary opinion, however, is held by Eugene F. Fama and Kenneth R. French, "Permanent and Temporary Components of Stock Prices," *Journal of Political Economy* 96 (1988): 246–73, who argue that mean risk aversion is the "rational" outcome of changing fickle tastes as risk aversion abruptly shifts in each period.

mal returns have been deemed "proof" of market efficiency. But it requires a great leap of faith to believe that a time series, merely by virtue of its apparent randomness, represents the intrinsic value of anything. Random series can be generated by many processes that need not themselves be rational.

The nature and extent of market efficiency is an issue of consequence, and any clues provided by the historical evidence are worth considering. Kindleberger has recounted the periodic episodes in recent centuries during which asset prices rapidly rise far beyond the historical norm and then suddenly collapse. Statistical studies of recent data support Kindleberger's conclusion that these often violent fluctuations cannot be entirely explained by rational forces. The term "speculative bubbles" seems apt. When these episodes are compared, several recurrent patterns are apparent and there is a temptation to ponder the underlying mechanisms. One factor that often appears to burst speculative bubbles is an elastic supply of new securities that eventually satiates demand.[33]

It seems that various financial instruments have been subject to differential efficiencies. Traditionally, it has been easier to establish viable markets for debt, rather than equity, securities. In the past, corporations have mainly relied on borrowing to raise the bulk of funds from outsiders. The perfection of large-scale impersonal markets in common stock has been only a comparatively recent development.

But in spite of these controversies, the market efficiency assumption and its corollaries continued to be incorporated as central elements in further refinements of the modern theory of finance. In the following section we describe how these ideas influenced the theory of corporate debt policy.

IV. The Modern Theory of Debt Policy

A key question addressed by the modern theory with regard to capitalization is: What determines the optimal mix of debt and equity in financing a firm's operations? The answers that have been proposed have varied with the variables thought most relevant in resolving this

---

[33] Charles P. Kindleberger, *Manias, Panics and Crashes: A History of Financial Crises,* revised ed. (New York: Basic, 1989).

problem. Initially, the theory implied that managements should remain indifferent to this trade-off. In perfect markets in which managements act entirely in the interests of shareholders, the basic financial objective of the firm is the enhancement of the value of its securities. Thus, in completely efficient financial markets *without taxes,* all securities are priced to their intrinsic worth. Firms cannot increase value by issuing either debt or equity. Moreover, if both real and financial markets are perfect and frictionless, then all managerial decisions are irrelevant. In this schema firm value is unaffected by such factors as type of investment, a company's industry and the scope and scale of its operations. Risk-adjusted marginal returns are equal across the world economy.

Modigliani and Miller were the first to offer a theoretical proof for the conclusion that shareholder wealth was unaffected by capital structure changes in perfect markets not burdened by either taxes or bankruptcy costs. Their argument is based on arbitrage. It assumes that shareholders can borrow at the same cost as corporations and can substitute personal borrowing for that of a corporation. Under these circumstances shareholders can profitably exploit any value differences between leveraged and unleveraged firms. Buying either the leveraged or the unleveraged corporation and shorting the other equalizes the prices of securities with identical cash flows.[34]

In 1963, Modigliani and Miller modified this conclusion when they noted that taxes could not be readily dismissed. In this revision they concede that leveraged firms may be able to reduce their corporate tax liabilities. Accordingly, the value of their securities increases in frictionless capital markets by the discounted present value of the reduced tax payments. They prove that with taxes and deductible interest expense, a firm's value increases linearly with the amount of borrowing. Consequently, firms in their model will rationally choose to minimize taxable earnings through debt financing.[35]

But the theory would experience yet another refinement based on a greater appreciation of the effects of potential bankruptcies. In 1977, Miller proposed a general equilibrium model incorporating taxes and

[34] Modigliani and Miller, "Cost of Capital, Corporate Finance and the Theory of Investment."

[35] Franco Modigliani and Merton H. Miller, "Corporate Income Taxes and the Cost of Capital: A Correction," *American Economic Review* 53 (June 1963): 433–43.

bankruptcy costs. He showed that personal taxes may discourage debt finance if interest is more heavily taxed than equity income. At equilibrium a corporation's marginal tax benefit from borrowing is precisely equal to the marginal tax cost to investors. This, then, reaffirmed the belief that a firm's value is independent of capital structure.[36] Although it adds a nuance Miller's model rests on the notion permeating the modern literature on capitalization: firms borrow to achieve optimal debt ratios, which are determined by the countervailing effects of risk and taxes. The logic is unassailable. Corporate taxation encourages debt finance, and the risk of meeting fixed obligations creates prudent limits to leverage.

But there is little evidence that these models actually explain variation in borrowing behavior. For example, if taxes provide the primary motivation for borrowing, then presumably one would have expected little use of debt finance in the United States before the enactment of a corporate income tax in 1909.[37] This, as we shall see, is at variance with the actual heavy reliance on debt in financing the railroads, utilities and heavy industry starting in the late nineteenth century. Similarly, there ought to have been minimal borrowing in the United Kingdom before the onset of a separate company tax in 1947. Again actual practice contradicted the expectations of the modern theory. While corporate taxation during the period 1965–73 may have encouraged debt finance, it is not clear whether any material advantages remain under the prevailing imputation system and yet British companies continue to borrow.[38] This suggests that a descriptive theory of corporate debt policy must be more complex.

[36] Merton H. Miller, "Debt and Taxes," *Journal of Finance* 32 (May 1977): 261–75.

[37] Although the original impost was known popularly as the Corporation Excise Tax Law and had been enacted as part of the Tariff Act of 1909, it was in fact a tax whose liability was based on corporate net income. This was later superseded by a formal federal corporate income tax in 1913.

[38] The present U.K. corporation tax is minimal, partially due to liberal depreciation allowances. For example, in 1981–82, only 3.2 percent of tax revenues came from corporations and only about a third of the firms consistently paid taxes. Moreover, under the imputation system firms are allowed to deduct personal taxes on dividends from their overall tax liability. See J. A. Kay and M. A. King, *The British Tax System,* 3rd ed. (Oxford: Oxford University Press, 1983).

Modern theorists have also drawn on many of the same factors used in generalizing about debt structure to explain corporate dividend policy. But as we shall see in the next section, this approach still leaves some important questions unanswered.

V. The Modern Theory of Dividend Policy

As in the case of debt, Modigliani and Miller also were trailblazers in theorizing about corporate dividend policy. In 1961, they proved theoretically that with perfect capital markets and no taxes, the value of the firm is independent of dividend policy. They demonstrated that when a firm pays a dividend and obtains the required funds through issuing common stock at its intrinsic net worth, the value of each share falls by the amount of the payment. In effect old shareholders have sold part of the firm at its fair price and their wealth is unchanged.[39]

These conclusions have caused many theorists to ponder why firms bother to pay dividends. If dividends do not affect shareholder wealth, then it seems irrational that firms make these distributions in the face of discriminating taxation. In perfect markets, shareholders could always effortlessly liquidate their holdings at its fair price. They gain nothing from dividends except additional tax obligations. A few have even taken the extreme position that dividend payments reduce market value. But studies that hypothesize that high-dividend-paying firms provide greater risk-adjusted returns have proved inconclusive.[40]

But as with debt policy, the modern theory's explanation of the role of dividends is inconsistent with basic practice. In the United States, for instance, where dividends have been taxed since 1913, aggregate dividend payout ratios have remained relatively constant. Since the

[39] Merton H. Miller and Franco Modigliani, "Dividend Policy, Growth and the Valuation of Shares," *Journal of Business* 34 (1961): 411–33.

[40] Those scholars who have taken the extreme position that paying dividends reduces market value have thus sought to show that high-dividend firms provide a greater risk-adjusted rate of return. Despite the massive amount of data examined, the results of these studies were inconclusive, and if any effect exists, it would appear to be quite small. See, e.g., Merton H. Miller and Myron S. Scholes, "Dividends and Taxes," *Journal of Financial Economics* 6 (1978): 333–64.

end of World War I they have amounted to about one-half of net earnings, despite high personal income tax rates. In Britain, on the other hand, the dramatic fall in payout ratios after World War II may partially be explained by the fact that dividends were more severely taxed than retained earnings were during most of the 1947–73 period. But there is little evidence of much correlation with later changes in the Inland Revenue Code. Clearly, dividend policy must be understood as being something more than merely a tax avoidance scheme.

Historically, as we shall see, dividend policy had an important functional purpose in what initially were very imperfect markets. Investors viewed the cash flow provided by a security as an integral basis for its market valuation. These cash flows were useful indices when information about the true intrinsic value of a security was either unavailable or unreliable. Observed cash flows were one of the few ascertainable facts available to estimate intrinsic value. In fact, prudent investors preferred fixed-income instruments. Dividends also provided liquidity that may have been crucial in thin and erratic markets. Today, there is ample evidence that dividends communicate important information.[41] It has been shown, for instance, that high-yield stocks display much less price volatility, which is consistent with investors perceiving more reliable information.[42]

In the past there often was also an understandable reluctance to invest in equity securities. Common stock afforded little protection against either fraudulent or overly sanguine projections. Nor did it provide an adequate basis for effective valuation. Because of this, large-scale impersonal capital markets began by trading in low-risk public debt instruments. They only slowly adjusted to encompass the securities of quasi-public corporations. Even today debt instruments continue to be far more widely held than equity. Moreover, it seems that debtlike features, such as stable cash payments and liens on property, have generally enhanced the marketability of securities.

Other scholars who have focused on different aspects of financial

---

[41] Numerous "event" studies show statistically that announcements of changes in dividends are accompanied by like sign changes in stock prices. See, e.g., Paul Asquith and David W. Mullins, Jr., "The Impact of Initiating Dividend Payments on Shareholders' Wealth," *Journal of Business* 56 (1983): 77–96.

[42] Jonathan Baskin, "Dividend Policy and the Volatility of Common Stocks," *Journal of Portfolio Management* 15 (1989): 19–25.

market relationships have also found the paradigms derived from the perfect market assumption to be wanting in significant ways. In the following section we evaluate the findings of those who are primarily concerned with the effects that information has on moderating the relationship between investors and managers of corporate enterprises.

VI. Agency Problems, Information-Related Inefficiencies and the "Pecking Order" of Corporate Finance

Many of the central tenets of the modern theory also seem inconsistent with the findings of those scholars who primarily assessed the financial implications of the separation of ownership and control in the modern corporation. Unlike their perfect market brethren, they have not concentrated on analyzing aggregate financial market data. Instead, they consider a broader social context that emphasizes management roles and information dissemination. This research may be classified under two broad headings. The first, agency theory, assesses how managers' roles as agents of investors in corporate enterprises affect their motivation. The second, signaling theory, builds on the recognition that investors' access to information about the firm is asymmetric with respect to the more knowledgeable managers. Research into signaling has been concerned primarily with determining how information flowing from the firm shapes investors' expectations.

One important conclusion of this new scholarship, at variance with the efficient market model, is that the conflicting interests of owners and managers may actually discourage external financing. Jensen and Meckling, for instance, in their aforementioned theoretical piece argue that the crucial issue in financing is not so much capital structure as ownership structure. That is, to what extent does management own enterprise securities and how does this ownership influence the managers' attitudes about risk bearing and the maximizing of returns? Many of the answers they propose to these questions suggest that institutional arrangements such as well-conceived incentive compensation plans are critical in building mutually satisfactory relationships between owners and managers. Jensen and Meckling, for instance, assert that entrepreneurs become less diligent managers when they sell part of their equity. They also contend that high levels of outstanding debt may motivate managers to increase further the risk of the firm. In this latter case bondholders assume much of the downside risk due to the increased likelihood of default, while shareholders retain the full benefits of any future price appreciation resulting from successful operations.[43]

Barriers to corporate financing not anticipated by modern theory have also been discovered by scholars who were concerned primarily with assessing the implications of asymmetric information. Myers and Majluf, for example, show theoretically that an offer of new equity to outside investors generally conveys bad news. The idea is that the dilution of existing holdings motivates issues when the stock is overpriced. In fact, one might note that, quite generally, suspicions are rationally aroused whenever anyone tries to sell something of uncertain value. The implication is that when investors have poor information, firms may encounter difficulties selling securities of indeterminate worth. Accordingly, debt instruments with little likelihood of default may enjoy far greater marketability.[44]

Miller and Rock extended these notions by demonstrating that new security issues and reductions in dividends are rationally interpreted by outside investors as indicators of poor earnings. Investors use the observed flow of funds through the firm as a source of information. Miller and Rock note that, even today, financial reporting can be misleading and investors have imperfect knowledge of the true underlying profitability of a business.[45] If a firm needs to raise funds, then outsiders may legitimately infer that the firm is generating insufficient retained earnings. One prediction of the model is that security issues will depress valuation and that firms will become more dependent on internal sources. Although equity issues are empirically associated with subsequent declines in share prices, no such relationship has been observed with debt issues. Another prediction of the Miller and Rock model is that reduced dividends are viewed unfavorably and one indeed observes that reduction announcements are greeted by sharp drops in stock prices.[46]

---

[43] Meckling and Jensen, "Theory of the Firm."

[44] Stewart C. Myers and Nicholas S. Majluf, "Corporate Financing and Investment Decisions When Firms Have Information That Investors Do Not Have," *Journal of Financial Economics* 13 (June 1984): 187–222.

[45] Merton H. Miller and Kevin Rock, "Dividend Policy under Asymmetric Information," *Journal of Finance* 40 (September 1985): 1031–51.

[46] See, e.g., Joseph Aharony and Itzhack Swary, "Quarterly Dividend and Earnings Announcements and Stockholders' Returns: An Empirical Analysis,"

The idea that the dividend stream conveys information is consistent with the classic Lintner model. In contrast to dividend irrelevance – as later claimed by Modigliani and Miller – Lintner emphasizes that dividends represent the "primary and active decision variable." While he did not explicitly stress this point, Lintner implied that dividends are manipulated so as to influence shareholder beliefs and expectations. His statistical model of dividend policy incorporated several observations gleaned from interviews with executives and appears consistent with decision makers' views of their own actions. More important, the model's predictions have been amply corroborated in a number of empirical studies using both pre– and post–World War II data. Simply stated, the model predicts that current dividends are a weighted average of current earnings and the dividend in the past period. Thus, dividends reflect a process of adjustment toward some fixed payout rate of earnings. One implication is that the time series of dividends should be smoother than that of profits. This indeed appears to be the case. Firms seem to strive actively to provide shareholders with a dependable flow of steady cash payments. It is as if managers were trying to cloud investors' perceptions of the vicissitudes of the business and the true underlying risks of equity ownership.[47]

These research findings have yet another important implication for theory. If firms are constrained to provide a steady increasing dividend on their common stock, and if new equity issues have an adverse effect on market valuation, then borrowing may become the only practical means of raising additional incremental funds. This was the central idea in what previously was known as the "pecking order hypothesis."[48] It constituted the traditional explanation of funding decisions prior to Miller and Modigliani. Since then, the pecking order hypothesis has been largely ignored by contemporary theorists and even de-

---

Journal of Finance 35 (1980): 1–12; and Asquith and Mullins, "The Impact of Initiating Dividend Payments on Shareholders' Wealth."

[47] John Lintner, "Distribution of Incomes of Corporations among Dividends, Retained Earnings and Taxes," *American Economic Review* 46 (May 1956): 97–113; and Miller and Modigliani, "Dividend Policy, Growth and Valuation of Shares."

[48] The central tenets of the pecking order hypothesis are laid down by Gordon Donaldson in *Corporate Debt Capacity: A Study of Corporate Debt Policy and the Determination of Corporate Debt Capacity* (Boston: Division of Re-

leted from leading textbooks. Its verifications have probably not been widely accepted because of the profession's current infatuation with models that lend themselves to formal mathematical explication. But statistical evidence spanning the past fifty years and five countries demonstrates that the hypothesis corresponds closely to actual practice. The apparent reason why the pecking order hypothesis was ignored was the lack of a theoretical basis. In the context of perfect, efficient capital markets, pecking order behavior appears arbitrary. When confronting the problem of poor information, however, it may be rational to avoid actions that might convey bad news, and pecking order behavior would naturally seem to follow.[49]

A recent paper presents an intriguing complementary explanation consistent with the skewed reliance of corporations on debt finance. If some securities are subject to erratic price fluctuations, arising from what John Maynard Keynes called "animal spirits," then investors with finite time horizons may be reluctant to place their funds at risk. Even if investors have full information as to intrinsic value, they may rationally worry that it may be impossible to sell at a fair value when money is urgently needed. So informed investors may eschew the purchase of securities even at bargain prices and the arbitrage of mispricing is thus impeded. The effect is that the equilibrium price of these securities may be persistently depressed. The effect will be greatest for securities of uncertain value and long maturities. Consequently, there may be an incentive for firms to issue debt over equity securities and also to prefer short-term instruments to bonds. Dividend policy may also be influenced as firms strive to reduce the perceived duration

search, Graduate School of Business Administration, Harvard University, 1961). These issues are further explored in Gordon Donaldson, *Managing Corporate Wealth: The Operation of a Comprehensive Financial Goals System* (New York: Praeger, 1984), pp. 42–48; and Gordon Donaldson and Jay W. Lorsch, *Decision Making at the Top: The Shaping of Strategic Direction* (New York: Basic, 1983), pp. 49–59. See also the perceptive essay by Stewart C. Myers, "Presidential Address: The Capital Structure Puzzle," *Journal of Finance* 39 (1984): 575–92.

[49] Jonathan Baskin, "An Empirical Investigation of the Pecking Order Hypothesis," *Financial Management* 18 (1989): 26–35; and idem, "On the Financial Policy of Large Mature Corporations," Ph.D. dissertation, Harvard University, 1985.

of their common stock. The result is equivalent to pecking order behavior, as firms maintain liberal dividends and rely on debt for incremental finance.[50]

But these differing views about corporate financial theory remain unresolved. Although serious questions have been raised about important paradigms, no comprehensive alternatives have as yet emerged. In this book, however, we evaluate how the problems of risk and of informational asymmetry, which always beset the practical world of corporate finance, have been confronted in the past. Thus, this study will use history to amplify theory by indicating how explanatory constructs might either be extended or qualified by the analysis of the experience of leading business enterprises.

The following chapters will survey how risk, knowledge, organization and institutions interacted during various epochs to satisfy the requirements of business finance. Overall, the study has been organized into three parts, each comprising several chapters. Part I selectively surveys the problem of finance in the preindustrial world, where agriculture and trade were the most important forms of economic activity. The section's initial chapter considers the experience of merchant-bankers in the cradle of capitalism that was Italy in the latter Middle Ages and Renaissance eras. It is followed by a chapter that analyzes how business organizations and financial institutions were structured to respond to the global trading opportunities that emerged during the period of oceanic expansion, 1496–1720. The last chapter in this troika concentrates on the factors contributing to the rise of London as the world's first international financial market during the period beginning with the Glorious Revolution of 1688 and extending to the defeat of Napoleon at Waterloo in 1815.

Part II is concerned with finance during the era of industrialization, when the pace of change accelerated because of an increasing rate of innovation in technology and management. The first chapter in this part focuses on the financing of the transportation revolution of the

---

[50] J. Bradford De Long, Andrei Shleifer, Lawrence H. Summers and Robert J. Waldman address this in the following articles: "The Economic Consequences of Noise Traders," *Harvard Institute of Economic Research, Discussion Paper 1348* (November 1987); "The Size and Incidence of the Losses from Noise Trading," *Journal of Finance* 44 (1989): 681–96; and "The Survival of Noise Traders in Financial Markets," *Journal of Business* 64 (1991): 1–20.

nineteenth century. This involved the establishment of telegraphic communications, railroads and canals, which made possible the rise of urban-industrial economies. The last chapter in this part evaluates the financial practices of the industrial and utility corporations that provided much of the impetus of growth in the United States during the first three decades of the twentieth century.

Part III traces the evolution of finance into the contemporary era. Its initial chapter evaluates how the corporate financing puzzle was resolved by the great manufacturing entities whose strong economic performance contributed to the post–World War II prosperity in the United States and overseas. In contrast, the following chapter explains the functioning of two quite different business forms – the conglomerate firm and the leveraged-buyout association – each of which transformed corporate finance in different ways during the closing decades of the twentieth century. The Epilogue revisits the question of history's role in economics by setting forth a theorem that explains the differing temporal effects of firm-specific as well as broader environmental factors in corporate finance.

THE PREINDUSTRIAL
WORLD

CHAPTER ONE

Medieval and Renaissance Origins

I. Introduction

The influences that the perennial problems of information and risk have exerted on finance have been evident since the dawn of civilization. Beginning in Mesopotamia nearly five thousand years ago, the Sumerians and their Babylonian successors perfected rudimentary contracts for rationalizing commerce, finance and private property ownership. These basic and powerful ideas eventually spread far beyond the Fertile Crescent to become key elements in an intellectual diaspora carried by trade among the peoples of the Eastern Mediterranean. Later during the Greco-Roman era new financial institutions facilitated the expansion of economic activity. Coinage, bills of exchange and new modes of public finance were broadly transmitted through the expansion of the empires of Alexander and the Caesars.

These ideas, carefully preserved by ecclesiastics during the barbarian invasions of the seventh through ninth centuries A.D., again influenced Western thinking with the economic revival of the later Middle Ages. Economic recovery together with the formation of international trading linkages between Northern and Southern Europe gave rise to and was, in turn, facilitated by an expanding financial sector. A leading center for this development was the Italian city-states, which are the central focus of this chapter. Many of the practices emergent there were basic to what we know as modern international finance, including foreign exchange conversion, bills of exchange, specialized project financing, portfolio diversification and deposit acceptance. Improvements in the legal system also facilitated economic expansion. New contractual forms and financial instruments helped to reduce risk and to enhance the efficiency of international trade and finance. Particularly useful in this regard

29

were innovations that surmounted the impediments to business growth deriving from religious prohibitions against such practices as taking interest on loans. In addition, Italian entrepreneurs did much to enhance the operational capacities of their firms. They took steps to establish new methods for limiting liability and diversifying risk; to create effective administrative techniques for coordinating and controlling operations; and to maintain organizational continuity for facilitating the advancement of expertise in managing business affairs. Moreover, the unique types of commerce financed at particular cities gave rise to the creation of different corporate forms. This was most apparent in comparing the techniques employed at an inland, industrial town like Florence with those of a maritime entrepôt like Venice. The result of this experience was a breadth and diversity in financial and organizational practices that was to survive and be embellished throughout Europe in the next five hundred years.

This chapter evaluates how institutions and organizations were employed to surmount problems in finance during the medieval and Renaissance eras by leading businesses in two major Italian economic centers, Florence and Venice. The discussion is organized in four sections. The following section analyzes the factors contributing to the economic revival of Europe starting in the tenth century. The third section evaluates the commercial and financial institutions that Florentine merchant-bankers developed to capitalize on the growing opportunities in international trade. The fourth assesses the practices employed by the Florentines' counterparts in Venice. The concluding section considers what significance this varied experience has for the formulation of theories of corporate finance in the contemporary world. Appendix A (p. 313) highlights some of the ways in which these same problems were confronted in the ancient world.

II. The Medieval Commercial Revival

Although the Middle Ages was a rich period for the development of business and financial institutions, the most significant advances occurred during a general economic recovery beginning in the tenth century. After the collapse of the Western Empire in A.D. 476, Europe experienced a long period of anarchy. Barbarian, Saracenic and Viking invasions, local wars and the rise of brigandage and piracy all inhibited the free flow of trade and encouraged the abandonment of farms and urban centers. These trends ultimately resulted in population decline and economic decay.[1]

The worrisome problem of physical security encouraged the rise of the mutually supportive feudal and manorial systems. They first emerged in the Frankish Merovingian kingdom during the sixth century and rapidly spread across Europe. The manors were self-supporting agricultural communities that provided the economic basis for the feudal political order. These estates were usually headed by military leaders, who, in return for swearing fealty to a monarch, were granted suzerainty over particular lands. Besides governing localities, the nobles were obligated to raise retinues of armed horsemen and foot soldiers to support the sovereign in times of war. The elite, in turn, were sustained by the output of serfs who tilled manorial lands or practiced various crafts. Their surpluses, however, were usually meager. Since they lacked access to broader markets, the scale of their operations remained narrowly constricted, serving only the limited requirements of these small, isolated islands of safety. Contact with the outside world was sporadic, such as the occasional visits of itinerant Jewish or Syrian merchants.[2] These latter groups did not establish formal organizations. At best they formed loose coalitions for coordinating international trading activities, as was the case of the Maghribi traders who operated in the Mediterranean world during the eleventh century. They sought to increase the scope of their trade and to achieve transactional efficiency by engaging colleagues based in foreign mar-

---

[1] Robert S. Lopez, *The Commercial Revolution of the Middle Ages, 950–1350,* reprint ed. (Cambridge University Press, 1971, 1976), pp. 10–26; and R. H. C. Davis, *A History of Medieval Europe: From Constantine to St. Louis,* revised ed. (New York: David McKay, 1957, 1970), pp. 21–37 and 111–20.

[2] For the Merovingian dynasty, see C. W. Previté-Orton, *The Shorter Cambridge Medieval History,* 2 vols. (Cambridge University Press, 1966), pp. 150–67; and Davis, *History of Medieval Europe,* pp. 111–20. For an outline of the feudal system, see John L. La Monte, *The World of the Middle Ages: A Reorientation of Medieval History* (New York: Appleton-Century-Crofts, 1949), pp. 206–24 and 230–33; and also Guy Fourquin, *Lordship and Feudalism in the Middle Ages,* translated ed. (New York: Pica Press, 1976). For the role of Jewish and Eastern merchants, see Lopez, *Commercial Revolution of the Middle Ages,* pp. 60–62; and Gino Luzzatto, *An Economic History of Italy: From the Fall of the Roman Empire to the Beginning of the Sixteenth Century,* translated ed. (London: Routledge & Kegan Paul, 1961), p. 15.

kets as local agents. The functioning of such a system was highly dependent on the reputation of coalition members for honest service. As Avner Greif has persuasively argued, this required the definition of contracts that enabled agents to earn substantially higher income by providing long-term reliable service than the short-term gains achievable through opportunistic behavior.[3]

The first engines to drive the medieval economic revival were the concomitant growth during the tenth century in population and in agricultural output. Farm productivity benefited from the introduction of improved tools such as the heavy plow, which allowed the deep furrowing of Northern Europe's dense soils. More intense cultivation practices such as three-field rotation also increased yields. Improved husbandry of draft animals, the proliferation of grist mills driven by water or wind and the use of better-designed wheeled vehicles augmented labor efficiency. The resultant abundance contributed to better diets and an ever-increasing and healthier population. Moreover, the turnaround fueled a drive to recultivate lands previously abandoned to meadows and forests.[4]

Agriculture thus provided a tradable surplus that served as a basis for a revival of commerce with the Byzantine Empire and the Levant. Although Eastern merchants had earlier pioneered in fostering this interregional trade, it became the special province of certain Italian city-states, which had successfully asserted their independence from local feudal lords by the eleventh century. Initially, the leaders were Venice and Amalfi, which had traditionally maintained strong connections with Byzantium. They were later followed by other northern cities such as Florence, Milan, Pisa and Genoa which were well placed geographically to serve as channels of trade between the Mediterranean and the emerging markets of Northern Europe. From these points itinerant merchants could travel overland through a variety of mountain passes to the flourishing fairs of Champagne and Burgundy. There they came in contact with merchants from the new commercial towns bordering the Baltic and North Seas and from those located

---

[3] Avner Greif, "Reputation and Coalitions in Medieval Trade: Evidence on the Maghribi Traders," *Journal of Economic History* 49 (December 1989): 857–82.

[4] Lopez, *Commercial Revolution of the Middle Ages*, pp. 27–55.

on major navigable rivers including the Rhone, the Rhine and the Danube.[5]

Beginning about 1275, Italian merchants started to serve northern markets such as London and Bruges through permanent local offices. Improved methods of business administration made the coordination of international trade possible through resident rather than itinerant merchants. Better postal services and the perfection of new forms of trade documentation such as the invoice, bills of lading and shipping manifests also enhanced the capacities of sedentary merchants to conduct foreign trade. A new maritime route through the Straits of Gibraltar provided a less costly way to these markets than the overland alternative. Although less direct, galleys provided significant economies of haul in comparison to overland carriage. Water transport also allowed the merchants to avoid the new tolls and assessments imposed by Philip the Fair on the land route after Champagne became formally annexed to the Kingdom of France.[6]

Greater literacy and the perfection of new forms of measurement also contributed to commercial revival. Written documents facilitated communications with distant places and allowed more precise specification of contractual terms. In addition, as early as the thirteenth century many merchants relied on bookkeeping records for preserving continuity and control over their operations. There is evidence that double-entry bookkeeping was being used as early as 1340. Beginning with Lucca Pacioli's seminal work in 1494, formal treatises began to appear on this subject. Notarial services also became critical in bank-

---

[5] Ibid., pp. 63–70; and Luzzatto, *Economic History of Italy,* pp. 47–65 and 66–85 passim. See also Fernand Braudel, *Civilization and Capitalism, 15th–18th Centuries,* 3 vols., reprint ed. (Berkeley: University of California Press, 1979, 1992), vol. 2, pp. 90–94, for the later development and ultimate decline of the fairs. See also Harry A. Miskimin, *The Economy of Early Renaissance Europe, 1300–1460* (Cambridge University Press, 1975), pp. 116–29.

[6] Miskimin, *Economy of Early Renaissance Europe,* pp. 109–18; Lopez, *Commercial Revolution of the Middle Ages,* pp. 85–102; Raymond A. de Roover, *Money, Banking and Credit in Mediaeval Bruges: Italian Merchant Bankers, Lombards and Money Changers – A Study of the Origins of Banking* (Cambridge, Mass.: Mediaeval Academy of America, 1948), pp. 10–14 passim; and La Monte, *World of the Middle Ages,* pp. 362–75. For the role of Italian merchants in England, see M. M. Postan, *Medieval Trade and Finance* (Cambridge University Press, 1973), pp. 335–41.

ing. Official scribes were charged with the responsibility of maintaining accurate records of depository and lending transactions. Commercial arithmetic and algebra learned from the Moslem world made possible the computation of discounts, thus providing a basis for assessing the time value of money.[7]

The revival of coinage during the Carolingian era also facilitated trade growth. Drawing on the output of mines in England and southern Germany, many royal, feudal and civic governments earned seignorage by minting coins of a variety of weights and fineness either in silver or in vellom, a silver–copper amalgam. One outstanding example was the English silver penny, which contained 1.46 grams of silver of .925 fineness. Gold coinage followed later during the thirteenth century, first at Florence (1252) and then in the Kingdom of France under Louis IX (1266). Coins helped trade by providing standardized measures of economic value. They were also a convenient and easily portable store of value, which made business transacting easier to effectuate than the alternative barter. Moreover, the conversion of precious metal to coins also facilitated commercial development by helping to expand Europe's credit base.[8]

---

[7] For notarial services, see Abbott Payson Usher, *The Early History of Deposit Banking in Mediterranean Europe,* reprint ed. (New York: Russell & Russell, 1943, 1967), pp. 49–61. For accounting, see Luzzatto, *Economic History of Italy,* pp. 120–21; Raymond A. de Roover, "The Development of Accounting Prior to Luca Pacioli According to the Account Books of Medieval Merchants," in A. C. Littleton and B. S. Yamey, eds., *Studies in the History of Accounting* (Homewood, Ill.: Irwin, 1956), pp. 114–74; and Florence Edler de Roover, "Partnership Accounts in Twelfth Century Genoa," in ibid., pp. 86–90; and R. Emmett Taylor, "Luca Pacioli," in ibid., pp. 175–84. See also Geoffrey Alan Lee, "The Development of Italian Bookkeeping, 1211–1300," *Abacus* 9 (December 1973): 137–55; and Frederic C. Lane, "Venture Accounting in Medieval Business Management," in *Venice and History: The Collected Papers of Frederic C. Lane* (Baltimore: Johns Hopkins University Press, 1966), pp. 99–108. For the use of accounting in Venetian trades, see Frederic C. Lane, *Andrea Barbarigo, Merchant of Venice, 1418–1449,* reprint ed. (New York: Octagon Books, 1944, 1967), pp. 163–81; and for the practices of the Medici of Florence, see Raymond A. de Roover, *The Rise and Decline of the Medici Bank, 1397–1494* (Cambridge, Mass.: Harvard University Press, 1963), pp. 98–100.

[8] Lopez, *Commercial Revolution of the Middle Ages,* pp. 70–73; Previté-Orton, *Shorter Cambridge Medieval History,* pp. 699 and 715; and Usher, *History of Deposit Banking,* pp. 196–219.

New types of financial and business organizations also galvanized medieval economic life. Three distinctive types of banks flourished: (1) institutions providing foreign exchange services, accepting deposits and extending loans for local businesses; (2) large merchant banks combining foreign trade with dealings in bills of exchange used in financing international commerce; and (3) pawn banks that extended credit, secured by liens on personal assets, to consumers. In addition, medieval merchants and jurists proved skillful in devising new coventuring arrangements. Besides attracting capital from wider circles of investors, these new forms of exchange helped to improve returns and to minimize the risk of the business. Moreover, emergent maritime insurance underwriting provided another means for diversifying commercial risk.[9]

Although these developments sparked the growth of commercial centers across Europe, several towns in Italy were foremost in exploiting the expanding opportunities for wealth creation. Two in particular – Venice and Florence – formulated effective strategies for extracting high rents from the revival of international trade.[10]

Venice's success derived from its ability to use its substantial naval power to negotiate advantageous concessions for its entrepôt trade from its Asian trading partners. The city's large fleet of galleys, useful in both war and commerce, provided its diplomats with an effective lever in dealing with foreign powers. The galleys' large crews and ability to navigate in becalmed seas made them formidable in battle. The perfection of compasses and other navigational instruments enabled these Italians to navigate confidently far from the sight of land during all seasons of the year. By the eleventh century they were a major force on the Adriatic and the Ionian Seas. To counter the growing threat of Muslim sea power, the hard-pressed Byzantine regime eagerly granted the Venetians special trading privileges in their territories in return for military assistance. So too did the leaders of successive crusading expeditions, who relied on the Venetians to maintain sea connections between Europe and their Levantine fiefs. The

---

[9] Lopez, *Commercial Revolution of the Middle Ages,* pp. 73–79; and for insurance origins, see Luzzatto, *Economic History of Italy,* p. 113.

[10] For a discussion of the origins of commercial revival in Genoa, see Avner Greif, "On the Political Foundations of the Late Medieval Commercial Revolution: Genoa during the Twelfth and Thirteenth Centuries," *Journal of Economic History* 54 (June 1994): 271–87.

Venetians capitalized on their privileged status partly by exporting basic commodities including salt, meats, grains, wine, silver, metals, wool and lumber, which they exchanged for spices (particularly pepper), silk and precious jewels. Eventually, the imports were distributed throughout Europe either by the Venetians themselves or by German merchants who maintained a large *fondaco,* or warehouse, in the island community for commercial transacting.[11]

The Florentine strategy, on the other hand, capitalized on rectifying the chronic imbalance in the flow of funds between Italy and Northern Europe. Large credit balances accumulated in the branches of the Italian merchant banks in northern towns partly because the value of spice imports exceeded that of local exports. In addition, ecclesiastical deposits made to the papacy's accounts from such sources as the annual Peter's Pence collection or payments for benefices also contributed to the interregional disequilibrium.

Because local governmental restrictions made it difficult to export either specie or bullion, the Florentine merchants first turned to northern wool markets to provide a commodity of sufficient volume and value to restore trade balance. These exports were attractive because they bolstered the profitability of the merchant-bankers' dealings in bills of exchange. In addition, a few of these merchants were members of the influential Florentine wool manufacturers' guild, Arte della Lana, and needed this vital raw material for their Tuscan cloth conversion operations.

But because the growth of exportable woolen surpluses eventually failed to keep pace with demand, some Florentine bankers tried to ensure adequate supply by extending loans to local princes who regulated their sales in northern markets. Besides providing another outlet for underutilized resources, the royal loans could secure other privileges and immunities, which further bolstered the competitiveness of their trading operations in these markets. But these connections were often perilous. The critical problem was the lack of any means for

[11] For a discussion of Genoa and Venice, see Luzzatto, *Economic History of Italy,* pp. 146–55. See also Frederic C. Lane, "Venetian Shipping during the Commercial Revolution," *American Economic Review* 38 (1933): 219–39; and idem, *Andrea Barbarigo,* pp. 45–52. Previté-Orton, *Shorter Cambridge Medieval History,* pp. 344–50. See also Miskimin, *Economy of Early Renaissance Europe,* pp. 150–58.

liquidating these loans quickly during crises. Their lack of liquidity often led to ruinous runs on the lending institution.[12]

Nevertheless, the commercial policies formed in Florence and Venice served as instructive models for other European commercial centers. Seaports generally followed the Venetian pattern. Thus, large entrepôt trades developed at Pisa, Genoa, Naples, Palermo, Barcelona, Marseilles, London, Southampton, Bruges, Hamburg and Lubeck. Inland communities, on the other hand, were more apt to follow the Florentine example, which blended manufacturing and banking. Siena, Lucca and Prato also closely followed the example of their influential Tuscan neighbor. Other Italian towns, however, concentrated more narrowly on manufacturing, such as armaments in Brescia, fustian in Cremona, footwear in Bologna and a vast array of wares in Milan. Cloth manufacture was particularly important in the north, providing economic prosperity to many towns, including Ghent, Lille, Liege, Arras, Ypres, Paris, Rouen, Maastricht and Cologne.

The Italian cities also provided useful guides for the organizational and financial structuring of business enterprise. New practices developed there probably ensured the greatest flexibility and safety, both in raising capital and in accommodating changing economic conditions. The two following sections consider the experience of the two leading centers: first, industrial Florence, and then maritime Venice.

III. Finance and Organization of International Trade in the Florentine Republic

The growth of international trade during the medieval period provided a strong impetus for financial and organizational innovation. Although business was conducted through forms carried forward from

---

[12] For a general discussion of development in Lombard and Tuscan towns, see Luzzatto, *Economic History of Italy*, pp. 155–60. For Florentine merchant banking, see Edwin S. Hunt, *The Medieval Super-Companies: A Study of the Peruzzi Company of Florence* (Cambridge University Press, 1994), pp. 38–75; and de Roover, *Medici Bank*, chaps. 6–8 passim. For an overview of the wool trade from an English perspective, see Postan, *Medieval Trade and Finance*, pp. 342–52. See also Miskimin, *Economy of Early Renaissance Europe*, pp. 150–58.

Greco-Roman law, they proved insufficient for enterprises of substantial operational scope, scale and complexity. This section focuses on the steps taken by leading Florentine merchant banking partnerships in the fourteenth and fifteenth centuries to surmount these constraints. The influence of these multibranch organizations were felt in virtually every major European commercial center. Their achievement represented a high point of what was possible during this age in organization and institution building.

Under Greco-Roman law, the basic model for allocating the risks and the rewards in long-term ventures were found in the requirements of the *societas*. Equity in this form of partnership derived from the contribution of either capital or labor. Its main drawback, however, was that each member was potentially liable for the enterprise's debts. Since bankrupts were routinely imprisoned or even sold into slavery for their failures, it was critical that partners have high confidence not only in the ability of co-venturers, but also in their loyalty, honesty and diligence. Not surprisingly, many of these partnerships were essentially family ventures whose members were bonded through strong kinship ties.[13]

But during the twelfth century, a new form, the *compagnia,* started to displace the traditional *societas.* Although partner liability still remained unlimited, its more flexible capital structure attracted investors outside narrow family groups. For instance, the value and terms of each partners' contribution could be precisely stated. This made it easier for prospective investors to diversify their holdings among a variety of enterprises with different maturities. Besides equity, the *compagnia* were also financed by three classes of long-term liabilities, or *sopraccorpo* (above the capital). This included (1) partners' earnings retained in the business, (2) additional money contributed by partners beyond their basic equity, *fuori del corpo della compagnia* (outside of capital) and (3) time deposits accepted from outsiders, *depositi a discrezione* (discretionary deposits). Although each class was paid interest at rates, depending on circumstances, of between 5 and 10 percent, the payments were characterized as discretionary gifts made to lenders to avoid the church's strictures against usury. This enabled some of the Florentine merchant banks to leverage their finances and thus earn returns on capital of between 14 and 20 percent per annum.

[13] Lopez, *Commercial Revolution of the Middle Ages,* pp. 73–75.

The *sopraccorpo* of the merchant banks attracted investors who preferred creditor status. Besides the incremental contributions to *sopraccorpo* by partners who wished to limit their equity stakes, the larger merchant banks received deposits from grandees, nobles and leaders in religion, the military or politics. The deposits were generally more liquid than investments in real estate. Deposits with international bankers also provided those enmeshed in the uncertain political life of this period with a mechanism for rapid transfer of their wealth overseas. This was important to leaders whose personal fortunes might be confiscated because of political reversals.[14]

The leading Florentine companies were sufficiently well capitalized to engage heavily in international banking, especially in dealing in bills of exchange. These instruments emerged early in the thirteenth century as the sea routes connecting the Mediterranean with the trading towns of Northern Europe began to open up. During the next three centuries Italian merchant banks developed a dominant position in this market in all the major commercial centers in Europe. These contracts provided for payment of foreign currencies at future dates and thus combined a credit and exchange transaction. Because of religious prohibitions against usury, however, the interest implicit in these contracts remained disguised within the *agio,* or premium, the bankers charged for currency conversion. This latter fee was not viewed as usurious because the creditor bore the risk of any adverse change in exchange rates. Besides trade, these instruments could also be used to extend credit for other purposes. They were also vital in reducing the need for cumbersome specie transfers in clearing international transactions. Instead, bankers periodically assembled at the fairs of Geneva to clear their mutual claims through offsetting book entries. The development of effective capacities for international financing and funds transfer made these specialists invaluable not only to merchants but also to princes and to the church's hierarchy. Consequently, some of the largest, such as the Medici and the Pazzi, served at various times as fiscal agents for the papacy.[15]

---

[14] Ibid., pp. 74–75; de Roover, *Medici Bank,* pp. 100–107; idem, *Money, Banking and Credit in Mediaeval Bruges,* pp. 40–42; and Hunt, *Medieval Super-Companies,* pp. 110–14.

[15] De Roover, *Money, Banking and Credit in Mediaeval Bruges,* pp. 12–13 and 51–52; and idem, *Medici Bank,* pp. 10–14 and 110–14. See also Usher,

The Florentine merchant banks exploited the financial leverage potentials of the *compagnia* form to build market power by expanding
the scale and scope of their operations. The fifteenth century Medici
firm is a good example. Although the firm had an initial equity of only
10,000 florins, the magnitude of their operations was expanded by
substantial client deposits.[16] Its important branch in Rome, for example, which primarily served the requirements of the papacy, was in fact
financed entirely by deposits during its first years.[17] Similarly, large
deposits were maintained at other branches. At the Lyons branch, in
1489 Philippe de Commines, seigneur D'Argenton, maintained on
deposit a balance of 25,000 ecus sans soleil.[18] Operationally, the
additional capital enabled the leading companies to bear the high
shipping and holding costs incurred in consigning large inventories for
sale at distant places. The ability to shift deposits between branches
by means of bills of exchange provided bankers with arbitrage opportunities in both money and commodity markets.

The ample capitalization of the leading merchant banks enhanced
their capacity for diversifying risk. Diversification resulted from the
division of their basic business between complementary trading and
financing activities. They also reduced potential trading losses by dealing in a wide range of commodities. Moreover, the commitment of
some firms such as the Medici to wool trading also encouraged their
subsequent diversification into kindred businesses including cloth
manufacturing and the mining and marketing of alum, a key ingredi-
ent in dyeing.[19] In many cases the dealing in bills of exchange and
foreign commerce eventually drew large merchant banks into the dangerous practice of lending directly to princes. Finally, the establishment
of overseas branches reduced the sensitivity of their earnings to economic downturns in local markets.

Substantial capital enhanced the merchant banks' ability to substitute more efficient, internal administration capacities for the traditional dependence on less efficient market functions. Beginning in
the thirteenth century, new modes of communication and business

---

History of Deposit Banking, pp. 7–8 for bills of exchange and pp. 110–34 for
role of fairs as clearing mechanisms for interbank claims.
[16] De Roover, *Medici Bank,* p. 39.   [17] Ibid., pp. 53 and 73.
[18] Ibid., p. 103.
[19] Ibid., pp. 167–93 for cloth manufacture and pp. 152–64 for alum mining.

administration coordinated banks' representatives in distant cities. The Peruzzi Company during the fourteenth century, for instance, managed fifteen offices in locations as far-flung as Bruges, Barcelona, Avignon and Naples, while the Medici in the following century maintained banking branches in eleven cities.[20] Improved bookkeeping and accounting techniques provided information that strengthened management both at the branch and at the headquarters levels by providing the means to control and evaluate operations. A constant stream of interoffice correspondence kept branch managers apprised of conditions in foreign markets.[21]

The branches were also mutually supportive in transacting business. This was advantageous in competing with traders who had to rely on the goodwill and cooperation of correspondents or independent commission agents. Similarly, by providing reliable payment agencies for bills of exchange in distant lands, the affiliates enhanced the liquidity and the competitiveness of their common banking enterprise. This was critical because the bills could not be discounted, that being deemed a usurious taking of interest. A branch structure also helped in achieving greater efficiency in coordinating and managing industrial processes such as the Medici's extensive cloth-processing ventures. In this case the Bruges branch acquired the basic woolen raw materials, while the Florence branch, operating through a specialized local partnership, supervised the putting out of the various stages in conversion. Subsequently, the finished products were sold through the other branches of this merchant bank.[22]

The longer-term stability achievable through the *compagnia* enhanced Florentine competitiveness by facilitating the development of business expertise. Operational continuity over long periods was conducive to learning about the nuances of particular markets. During the course of their careers, managers built up knowledge through personal experience as well as through consultation with senior partners. This knowledge about past developments represented a valuable intangible asset that was difficult for less seasoned enterprises to replicate.

The inherent flexibility of the *compagnia* form enabled the great

---

[20] Ibid., pp. 86–95; and Hunt, *Medieval Super-Companies*, pp. 76–84.

[21] De Roover, *Medici Bank*, pp. 96–100; and idem, *Money, Banking and Credit in Mediaeval Bruges*, pp. 29–31.

[22] De Roover, *Medici Bank*, pp. 167–93 for manufacturing activities.

Florentine merchant banks to experiment with different business strategies. This is apparent in comparing the policies of the leading firms during the quattrocento with those of the following century. The changes introduced during the latter period sought to avoid the dangerous snares that trapped earlier generations of business leaders.

During the fourteenth century, decision-making authority in leading firms such as the rival Bardi and Peruzzi companies was highly centralized. A committee of senior partners, or *maggiori,* made most of the major policy and operational decisions for both the center and peripheral offices. The *maggiori* routinely issued their directives, or *ricordi,* to their salaried managers, or *fattori,* responsible for branch operations. The companies paid high salaries to recruit branch managers with steady judgment and good social connections. The Bardi, for instance, provided a £2,000 annual salary to their manager in Bruges. To further ensure high motivation, the *maggiori* also maintained close supervision through periodic visits and the audit of records.[23]

The highly centralized decision making in these firms seems to have been conditioned by the importance of political rather than market considerations in their business strategies. Basically, the leading firms enhanced their market power by securing trade preferences from influential political leaders, which also helped to insulate the Florentines from the efforts of local merchants to control their markets through guild regulation. The Bardi's loans to the kings of both France and Naples ensured the lenient supervision of their trading activities in these countries. This was also true in England, where the Bardi and the Peruzzi shared a virtual monopoly over wool exports after they made large but discreet loans successively to Edward II and Edward III. In these circumstances it was, perhaps, unwise to set up powerful local managers who could respond swiftly and independently to changing conditions in the market. Instead, their managers were more akin to diplomats who followed close instructions from the main office on how to deal with local potentates. Because of the primacy of political over market imperatives, decision making remained centered in Florence. In this way the politically active *maggiori* could carefully

---

[23] De Roover, *Money, Banking and Credit in Mediaeval Bruges,* pp. 32–34; and Hunt, *Medieval Super-Companies,* pp. 76–100 passim.

coordinate their business activities with the foreign policy of their city-state.[24]

Given their strategies, it was not surprising that these firms eventually failed because of political rather than business reversals. During the 1330s both companies grew steadily less liquid and more highly leveraged. Lower returns on equity, limited investment opportunities and a growing uncertainty about the solvency of their most important clients motivated the Peruzzi partners, for example, to withdraw their equity or to reinvest their capital as deposits paying fixed interest. By 1335, this company, like the hypothetical firms of Modigliani and Miller's theoretical model six centuries later, were entirely financed by debt. Soon the outbreak of the Hundred Years' War (1337) led to the banishment of the Bardi from France because of the financial assistance they had provided Edward III. Later in 1339, the English king defaulted on the loans extended by the London branches of the two banking companies. Although seriously impaired by the financial embarrassment of their royal client, the firms continued to operate for several years through moratoria granted by creditors and the Florentine state. In 1341, however, a serious run on these institutions developed when Florence failed to win control over the town of Lucca from its rival Pisa. In the aftermath of defeat, there emerged in Florence a new political leadership inimical to the interests of the great bankers. Unable to receive any further moratoria or other forms of cooperation from the state, the Peruzzi Company finally closed its doors in 1343. The Bardi held out for three more years.[25]

In contrast, the leaders of the Medici bank of the fifteenth century tried to avoid the errors that had earlier destroyed the Bardi and the Peruzzi. They, for instance, specifically prohibited their branch managers from making loans to princes, directing them, instead, to concentrate on their business endeavors. The Medici also minimized their exposure to loss by organizing each branch as a separate partnership in which a majority share was owned by the main partnership in

[24] Hunt, *Medieval Super-Companies*, pp. 38–48 and 57–62; and de Roover, *Money, Banking and Credit in Mediaeval Bruges*, pp. 30–33.

[25] Hunt, *Medieval Super-Companies*, chaps. 6–8 passim; Frederick Schevill, *History of Florence: From the Founding of the City through the Renaissance*, reprint ed. (New York: Ungar, 1936, 1961), pp. 194–225; and Postan, *Medieval Trade and Finance*, pp. 209–10.

Tuscany. During the early years of a new venture, they frequently used the *accommanda* (or *accommandita*) form, that is, a limited partnership that risked only their direct investment. Later, after the new business became better established, they reverted to the traditional *compagnia* form. This proved useful in preventing setbacks in one branch from imperiling other elements of the enterprise.[26]

The Medici relied on junior partners rather than salaried *fattori* to direct affiliates. The Florentine partnership typically provided most of the capital, while the local partners' contribution consisted primarily of their service. As partners the local managers also enjoyed greater autonomy than the hirelings of the previous century. Thus, they could respond quickly and decisively to sudden opportunities for making profits in their local markets. Through their profit sharing as partners, they had strong incentives to maximize returns. Conversely, their potential liability also encouraged prudence.[27]

Although the *maggiori* generally exercised their authority unobtrusively, they remained preeminent in ordering the affairs of their enterprise. Through the partnership agreements that were revised periodically, they placed legal restrictions on the types of activities open to local managers. Typically, the contracts prohibited imprudent business or personal practices such as lending to grandees or keeping mistresses. Headquarters also tried to limit the opportunities for collusion among branch employees by maintaining control over all personnel hiring. Through this patronage relationship, the *maggiori* could expect to be informed of any untoward developments at the branch through clandestine communications from their loyal informants. In addition, the leaders also relied on periodic financial statements and supporting schedules documenting the financial position of the branch. Besides providing a basis for audits, these documents were also used to evaluate performance, to define future operational goals and to determine profit distributions.[28]

But although these practices were often effective in limiting risk and in motivating managers, notable exceptions illustrated the inherent

[26] De Roover, *Medici Bank*, pp. 38 and 84; and idem, *Money, Banking and Credit in Mediaeval Bruges*, pp. 34–37.

[27] De Roover, *Money, Banking and Credit in Mediaeval Bruges*, pp. 34–35; and idem, *Medici Bank*, pp. 77–86.

[28] De Roover, *Medici Bank*, pp. 86–95.

limitations of administrative and financial controls in protecting owners from the venality or incompetence of their agents. This was a
problem encountered more by the later leaders of the Medici clan,
such as Piero di Cosimo (1416–69) and Lorenzo the Magnificent
(1449–92). They had been trained as humanists rather than as businessmen, and their interests were more directed toward politics and
diplomacy.

The decline of the London branch, for instance, began with the
outbreak of the War of the Roses (1455–85). The firm was unable to
collect their claims on noble clients who were casualties of the fighting.
The Medici's difficulties were further complicated in 1463 when the
local wool-dealers' guild based in Calais (then part of the English
kingdom) was able to have legislation passed restricting the rights of
foreign merchants to export English wool. To overcome these laws
Medici branch managers reversed the long-standing policy of not making loans to princes. They began extending loans to Edward IV in
return for special export licenses and immunities from export tolls. To
guard against future losses in this deteriorating environment, Piero de
Medici decided in 1465 to reorganize the London operation as an
accommanda, a prudent step because, by 1468, the king's receivable
had grown to £10,500, far in excess of any benefit the bankers could
expect to derive through the exercise of their special privileges. There
was also evidence that some of the active partners were diverting
business away from the Medici to their own enterprises. By 1472,
write-offs of bad debts and partner withdrawals had essentially wiped
out London's equity, the enterprise being financed solely by deposits
paying 12 to 14 percent annual interest. At that juncture the discour-
aged Piero decided to abandon London. But to avoid the stigma of
bankruptcy, and hoping eventually to recoup their claims, some of his
closest advisers persuaded Piero to transfer the net assets of London
to the books of the then more viable Bruges partnership.[29]

The transfer of the London business soon led in 1473 to a reorganization of the Bruges operations headed by the ambitious Tommaso
Portinari. This manager persuaded Florence to operate their affairs in

---

[29] Ibid., pp. 325–38 passim. For a discussion of the Staple of London, an early
regulated company, see Eileen Power, *The Wool Trade in English Medieval
History,* reprint ed. (Oxford: Oxford University Press, 1942, 1955), pp. 86–
103; and Postan, *Medieval Trade and Finance,* pp. 210–12.

the Low Countries through two separate partnerships. The first included the stable and profitable wool-trading activities. In this the *maggiori* agreed to accept a 55 percent profit–loss sharing ratio, while the active partners received 45 percent. The second partnership was more speculative, including the liquidation of London's net assets and a variety of enterprises stemming from Portinari's poorly conceived plans for developing closer financial ties to Charles the Bold, duke of Burgundy. Portinari evidently believed that the Medici could play a central role in helping this monarch build a powerful kingdom in northern France and the Low Countries. In this second business, the inactive partners' ratio was a much higher 62.5 percent, while their agents received 27.5 percent.[30]

But the Bruges operation also failed eight years later primarily because of the losses incurred in the speculative partnership. The firm, for instance, failed to manage profitably the rights to farm the tolls granted by Duke Charles in 1473 on wool imports entering the port of Gravelines. The branch also lost its one-eighth interest in two galleys it operated on behalf of the Burgundian monarchy in 1473–74. Losses were also incurred on an unsuccessful exploratory voyage around the west coast of Africa in 1475. The death of Charles the Bold at the Battle of Nancy in 1477 called into question the collectability of the loans extended to their august client. The shocked *maggiori* soon discovered that the total advance amounted to 16,500 groat, a balance that was nearly three times the amount they authorized the branch to extend. Nor was Bruges able to liquidate many of London's residual assets and thus reduce the onerous interest charges it had to pay depositors. Eventually, Lorenzo de Medici recognized that exposure to loss in these speculative ventures outweighed any benefits he expected from the more stable wool-trading activities. Consequently, in 1481 he closed down the partnership in order to cut his losses.[31]

Yet in spite of these serious setbacks and a major defalcation at their Lyons branch, the ultimate collapse of the firm that occurred in 1494, two years after the death of Lorenzo the Magnificent, resulted from political rather than economic causes. The decentralized structure enabled the Medici to seal off the impact of local catastrophes before they could drag down other elements in the group. But organi-

[30] De Roover, *Medici Bank*, pp. 338–46.
[31] Ibid., pp. 341–42 and 346–57 passim.

zational structure was of little consequence in light of the collapse of the Florentine state before the army of Charles VIII of France. The French monarch had invaded Italy to seize control of the Kingdom of Naples. On his march south, he captured Florence and confiscated all of the properties of the Medici clan, thus forcing the firm into bankruptcy.[32]

Yet in spite of the setbacks ultimately experienced by the Medici and other leading Florentine houses, merchant banking took strong hold in European finance, which continues today. The institutional relationships and organizational structures greatly facilitated the conduct of trade and finance in what by modern standards were very difficult economic circumstances. But Florence did not stand alone as an important center of innovation in business practices during this era. In the following section the unique contributions that Venice had at this time and that allowed it to develop a great entrepôt trade with the East will be considered.

IV. Finance and Organization of International Commerce in the Venetian Republic

Venetian prosperity, which derived from its position as a major entrepôt for the trade between the Mediterranean and Northern Europe, had long been contingent on that state's formidable naval power. Its economic leadership dated back to the ninth century when the republic had first been able to negotiate advantageous trade concessions from the beleaguered Byzantine Empire in return for military support. The leverage afforded by naval strength proved more effective and long-lasting than the financial power that the Florentines had relied on to advance their interests. A strong navy magnified Venetian power by enabling it to control vital channels of oceanic communication. Naval power did much to ensure the autonomy of the Venetian state, which was able to maintain its independence until the Napoleonic invasion of Italy during the late eighteenth century. Naval power facilitated Venetian overseas trade by reducing the risks of loss from attacks on its shipping or the exclusion of its merchants from important markets by unfriendly powers. Given this position, it is understandable why

[32] Ibid., pp. 358–75.

developments in finance and business organization in Venice should have been so sensitive to the imperatives of maritime trade.

The *compagnia* form, for example, which was popular at inland towns such as Florence, was not used as extensively in ordering business affairs at Venice. Although a hybrid of the *compagnia* known as the *fraterna* emerged there and enabled heirs to administer jointly inherited wealth for either commercial or personal purposes, its permanent duration was far from ideal for accommodating the risks associated with financing sea voyages. What was necessary for this latter class of activity were contracts that could be tailored more narrowly to the specific requirements of a specific venture.[33]

By the thirteenth century, Venetian merchants had come to rely increasingly on the *colleganza,* or *collegantia* (the Venetian term for what was known at other locations including Genoa as *commenda*), because it limited high risks of overseas commercial voyages. Under the *colleganza* one coventurer donated capital or goods and remained resident in the home port, while the other contributed his time and energy to transporting and selling the wares overseas. Like the sea loan of Greco-Roman law, this contract lasted only for the duration of a particular voyage, and the lender's liability was limited to the amount invested. It also enjoyed the primary feature of partnership, the sharing of any resultant gains or losses. Moreover, since these contracts specifically indicated that risk was borne by the coventurers, the returns earned by the sedentary party were not considered usurious. In addition to those of Venice, notarial records in Marseilles, Genoa and the Hanseatic towns testify to its widespread use throughout the twelfth and thirteenth centuries.[34]

The *colleganza* afforded other advantages to sedentary merchants. It was a contractual form that facilitated the diversification of risk over particular voyages, types of cargoes and time periods. These contracts also helped the sedentary merchant to avoid the opportunity costs as well as the expenses and risks of overseas travel. This flexibility furthermore enabled these businessmen to benefit from the new

---

[33] Lopez, *Commercial Revolution of the Middle Ages,* pp. 74–75. For a fuller discussion of the *fraterna,* see Frederic C. Lane, "Family Partnerships and Joint Ventures," in *Venice and History,* pp. 36–55.

[34] Lopez, *Commercial Revolution of the Middle Ages,* pp. 75–77. See also Frederic C. Lane, "Investment and Usury," in *Venice and History,* pp. 56–60; and idem, *Andrea Barbarigo,* pp. 94–95 and 202–205.

information about foreign markets gathered from colleagues based in a busy entrepôt like Venice.

Several factors, on the other hand, helped to constrain the opportunistic behavior of junior partners in these arrangements. The primary incentive for seeing the voyage through was the right to share in the profits of a successful venture. In addition, junior partners received a valuable educational benefit through the first-hand experience they gained of foreign markets. Finally, the desire to win acceptance from leading merchants was an additional incentive for traveling partners to maintain reputations of scrupulous honesty and reliability. Maintaining the goodwill of the merchant elite was vital for advancing one's career in business. This group controlled substantial capital as well as access to the maritime resources that supported Venice's leadership in trade.

The rise of maritime insurance underwriting also helped to spread the risk of commercial voyages. By the thirteenth century Venice had become an important center for this specialty. Since there were no actuarial guidelines or data for estimating the probability of loss, maritime insurance contracts remained highly speculative. Underwriters could reduce their risks only by maintaining portfolios of contracts or by coinsuring particular voyages.[35]

Eventually the *colleganza* was displaced in international trade at Venice and other entrepôts by the rise of commission agencies. There were several reasons for this change. First, some courts became reluctant to accept the limited-liability feature of these contracts and instead treated these arrangements as though they were simple debtor–creditor relationships. Second, the need for an active partner to accompany goods overseas diminished with improved postal services and better commercial documentation, such as the invoice and shipping manifest. Third, sedentary merchants by the fifteenth century also found it cheaper simply to pay a fixed commission of about 2 percent on sales or purchases to an overseas commission merchant than to share about a quarter of their profits with an active partner. Moreover, it was simpler to maintain accurate accounting records for a commis-

---

[35] For a review of marine insurance in this period, see Robert S. Lopez and Irving W. Raymond, *Medieval Trade in the Mediterranean World: Illustrative Documents Translated with Introductions and Notes* (New York: Columbia University Press, 1955), pp. 255–65 passim.

sion agency. Fees were simple to calculate on merchandise consigned for sale at specified prices. Under the *colleganza,* on the other hand, it was also often difficult to determine profit shares in a manner satisfactory to each partner. Disagreements could arise over the value of merchandise initially invested, as well as the true proceeds realized in the sales overseas by the active partner.[36]

The rise of commission agencies, however, did not lead to the complete abandonment of the *colleganza* at Venice. On the contrary, it was increasingly relied on for organizing local trading and manufacturing enterprises. These contracts were especially useful to passive investors who had few opportunities for purchasing real estate in the island community or who did not wish to hold public debt. Under the local *colleganza* contracts, the passive partner contributed capital, while his active coventurer managed the affairs of the business. The capitalist also bore the risk of loss due to either theft or fire. Although returns were not usually precisely stated, these contracts often provided yields of 5 to 8 percent during the fifteenth century.[37]

Venice, a leader in trade and insurance, also developed new financing for commercial sea voyages. These arrangements were of two types, the first of which was contracts for the operation of individual ships. In this case merchants in need of ocean transport formed temporary companies that bid for the lease of galleys owned by the Venetian state. Each voyage was financed through the issuance of twenty-four shares, or *carati,* among the coventurers, or *parcenevoli.* These stakeholders also appointed a *padrone* responsible for outfitting and managing the voyage. The Venetian state, however, remained responsible for the sailing schedule and ensuring the safe navigation of the trading fleet. Second, the interests of all stakeholders in the galley fleet were unified through a comprehensive contract known as a *maona,* thus diminishing the potential for destructive competitive bidding between the sponsors of these fleets. Through the *maona* the galley investors were able to exercise maximum leverage in negotiating favorable terms for basic supplies such as food, wine and ballasting materials. It was

[36] Frederic C. Lane, "Venture Accounting in Medieval Business Management," in *Venice and History,* pp. 99–108; and idem, "Investment and Usury," in ibid., pp. 59–60. See also Lane, *Andrea Barbarigo,* pp. 94–100.
[37] Lane, "Investment and Usury," pp. 60–68.

also effective in maintaining uniform prices for the common wares that the *parcenevoli* sold in foreign markets.[38]

These practices used for organizing and financing overseas trade, like the contemporary steps taken to place merchant banking on a sound footing, continued to shape Western economic life in important ways. As will be shown in a later chapter, many of the Venetian techniques continued to guide great trading enterprises during the subsequent age of oceanic expansion that began in 1492.

V. Conclusion

What significance then does the experience of the medieval and Renaissance periods have for the formulation of theories of corporate finance in the contemporary era? How did institutional innovations of this era contribute to the enhancement of operating efficiency of large business enterprises?

From the perspective of its primitive origins, it is clear that other factors than those considered in the modern theory as laid down by Modigliani, Miller and others had been foremost in defining early financial institutions. During the medieval period financial transactions could not be described as frictionless or efficient. Instead, these relationships were shaped by a sensitivity to the vulnerability of economic affairs to high risks of many types.

The combination of these high risks and the paucity of reliable information did not foster indifference among passive investors about the relative merits of debt versus equity instruments. The general tendency was to prefer creditor status. Nor did tax structures seem to have much influence on this choice. Of more importance were the stronger legal rights that were accorded to creditors. These legal rights provided some degree of protection against both the dishonesty or the incompetency of agents, as well as the reverses resulting from certain external circumstances. Moreover, such investors were further strengthened by guarantees both of fixed rates of interest and of specific maturity dates for their loans.

---

[38] See Lane, "Family Partnerships and Joint Ventures," pp. 44–52; and idem, "Merchant Galleys, 1300–34: Private and Communal Operation," in *Venice and History,* pp. 193–226.

Yet in spite of these inherent advantages, lending was subject to certain rigidities that increased risk. For one, the notion of installment financing never materialized. Instead, interest and principle both came due simultaneously, thus placing great pressure on the solvency of borrowers. In addition, secondary markets for debt remained poorly developed. For the most part they were local affairs specializing in state-issued instruments that were generally secured by the proceeds from particular taxes. The existence of broad markets for debt instruments would have facilitated their pricing and enhanced their liquidity. Had such markets existed in the fourteenth century, many of the pressures that forced the Bardi and Peruzzi banking houses into bankruptcy might have been greatly diminished.

Although equity investment was most usually limited to active rather than passive investors, there were several notable exceptions to this pattern. Partnerships that depended on the capital of inactive equity holders, for example, often unified the economic interests of family groups. In these cases the risks of equity, particularly with respect to the actions of agents, were offset by the deep personal loyalties of coventurers deriving from strong kinship bonds. Silent partnerships were common for local businesses and thus easily accessible to principals who could directly monitor their performance. Sedentary partners often hired active agents to conduct overseas trade. Besides profit sharing, another powerful incentive for constraining opportunistic behavior in these latter instances was the desire for agents to maintain the goodwill of leading merchants at home. Maintaining a reputation for honesty and reliability fostered greater assurances of cooperation from influential magnates. Such relationships promised over the longer term to yield more income than the short-term gains achievable by cheating a partner. But as improvements in insurance, transportation and documentation arose, the need for sedentary partnerships declined, and merchants began to rely, instead, on commission arrangements in foreign trade. The latter were popular because they were less expensive to operate and not as exposed to the potentials of adverse agency relationships as were partnerships.

Many medieval and Renaissance capitalists would have affirmed the underlying principles that support modern portfolio theory. A business environment characterized by high risk and poor information provided strong incentives for diversification. One example of this was the division of business affairs into self-contained partnerships. This practice enabled the Medici bank to survive all of the serious setbacks experienced at its branches. The demise of this firm came about only after the destruction of the Florentine Republic by invading armies. The diversification of risk was also implicit in the contracting chosen both to finance and to insure trading voyages. Investors and insurers alike could protect themselves against adversity by structuring portfolios that allocated their capital over multiple ventures, as well as different markets, time periods and types of merchandise.

Concerns about risk encouraged efforts during the Middle Ages and the Renaissance to connect the credit of the firm with that of the state. This could take the form of securing a trade monopoly and/or the proceeds from particular taxes in return for loans to a sovereign. This had been the procedure that the Florentines employed in dealing with their royal clientele. It enabled these businesses to earn monopoly rents in markets that might otherwise have been inaccessible. An alternative approach was for the state to finance a public good such as a navy to protect the overseas trading activities of its citizens. This latter approach, followed by Venice, lowered the high costs of security in foreign business and served as a lever for extracting trading privileges from foreign potentates.

Much was also achieved during the Middle Ages and the Renaissance to address the problems associated with agency relationships. Improved communications, better record keeping and new forms of contracts all helped to enhance the capacity of entrepreneurs to control and monitor their agents. The great expansion of international trade and finance during this era bears witness to the general success of these new methods.

The experience of the later Middle Ages and the Renaissance also showed how new enterprises of great scale and scope were capable of achieving substantial gains through operational efficiencies. Foremost in this regard were the leading Italian merchant banks. Because of their ability to concentrate large amounts of capital, these firms were able to handle a higher volume of business than the traditional small-scale partnerships, thus leading to substantial reductions in transaction costs. The extension throughout Europe of branches that employed improved administrative techniques enabled leading merchant banking firms to coordinate and control international finance and trade more effectively than would have been possible if they had relied solely on market structures. The establishment of internal administrative capacities reduced the costs of gathering vital information about conditions in widely dispersed markets; this enhanced the ability of these firms to exploit profitable arbitrage opportunities. Moreover, complementary financing and trading activities both augmented the returns earned on invested capital and helped to diversify risk. Finally, the unique capacities of these enterprises for successfully confronting economic vicissitudes attracted a choice clientele, who often assisted branch managers by informally sharing their expertise about business and political affairs.

Long operational continuity contributed to the ability of enterprises to develop pragmatic knowledge about the most effective ways to conduct business affairs. This was most evident with the Florentine merchant banks, which in some cases benefited from more than a century's experience. The gradual accretion of economic understanding within these organizations led to profound changes in the ways that capital was raised, risks were contained and business operations were administered.

The experience of the Medici Bank has also shown that there were limitations inherent in the elaborate administrative and contracting arrangements developed to control managerial action. The effectiveness of these measures depended heavily on the cooperation of management. But as the disastrous insubordination of Tommaso Portinari has indicated, such controls were too susceptible to being overridden by senior members of the firm. In the latter case the adverse consequences resulting from subversion of the system of controls remained localized only because the enterprise had structured its operations through separate partnerships with limited liability.

In the following chapter we consider the financial and organizational innovations that emerged after Europeans discovered new trading horizons in the Americas and Asia after 1492. In the new era, as we shall see in analyzing the experience of the English East India Company, success was also contingent on the ability of an enterprise to establish an organizational structure and to define institutional relationships that were viable in risky and poorly informed economic environments.

CHAPTER TWO

Corporate Finance in the Age of Global Exploration

Trading Companies and Oceanic Discovery, 1450–1720

I. Introduction

Although trade remained an important means for generating wealth, the primary channels of international commerce began to change radically in the fifteenth century because of oceanic discoveries. The advantages enjoyed by the Italian city-states as entrepôts for the trade between Europe and the East first started to decline as explorers charted new sea routes around Africa. The process started with the Portuguese, who, encouraged by Prince Henry the Navigator, opened trade with the African Gold Coast in 1448. By 1488, Bartholomew Dias anchored at the Cape of Good Hope, which served as the base a decade later for the voyage of Vasco Da Gama to Calicut on the Indian Malibar Coast. The frontiers of trade were further broadened by trans-Atlantic exploratory expeditions. In 1492, the Genoese captain Christopher Columbus found America while searching for a Western route to Asia on behalf of Ferdinand and Isabella of Spain. In 1498, the Venetian Sebastian Cabot, in search of a North Atlantic route to the Indies, laid claim to Newfoundland for the English Crown. In 1500, the Portuguese Pedro Alvares Cabral led a voyage that first landed in Brazil and then continued to India. The zenith was reached in 1519–22 with the Spaniard Ferdinand Magellan's global circumnavigation.[1]

The extended economic horizons opened by the increase in geographic knowledge created a favorable environment for the develop-

---

[1] A comprehensive overview of the patterns of discovery can be found in J. H. Parry, *The Age of Reconnaissance: Discovery, Exploration and Settlement, 1450 to 1650*, reprint ed. (New York: Praeger, 1963, 1969), chaps. 8–13 passim.

ment of innovative organizations capable of conducting large-scale, long-distance trading activities. Foremost in this regard was the joint-stock company, which, while appearing at many European commercial centers, reached maturity in England. Although such enterprises as the Royal African Company, the Hudson's Bay Company, the Levant Company and the Russia Company pioneered the use of this form in English foreign trade, this chapter focuses on the experience of the English East India Company in analyzing the impact of the joint-stock company on finance.[2] The achievements of the East India Company, which was chartered by Elizabeth I in 1600, were attested to by the fact that, by 1717, it ranked third (in terms of stated capital) among the largest businesses in Great Britain. The nominal value of its shares were £3.2 million, which was exceeded only by that of the ill-fated South Sea Company (£10 million) and the Bank of England (£5.6 million). It was also one of the most long lasting of the early English trading companies, continuing its operations for over two centuries until 1874.[3] Along with its counterparts in Holland, France and Portu-

[2] For the histories of some of the leading trading companies, see K. G. Davies, *The Royal African Company* (London: Longmans, Green, 1957; M. Epstein, *The English Levant Company: Its Foundation and Its History to 1640*, reprint ed. (New York: Franklin, 1908, 1968); T. S. Willan, *The Early History of the Russia Company, 1553–1603* (Manchester: University of Manchester Press, 1956); and Alfred C. Wood, *A History of the Levant Company* (Oxford: Oxford University Press, 1935). See also the studies of Ann M. Carlos and Stephen Nicholas, "Giants of an Earlier Capitalism: The Chartered Trading Companies as Modern Multinationals," *Business History Review* 62 (Autumn 1988): 398–419; and idem, "Agency Problems in Early Chartered Companies: The Case of the Hudson's Bay Company," *Journal of Economic History* 50 (December 1990): 853–75. Later economic aspects in the history of the Hudson's Bay Company are treated in Ann M. Carlos and Frank D. Lewis, "Indians, the Beaver, and the Bay: The Economics of Depletion in the Lands of the Hudson's Bay Company, 1700–1763," *Journal of Economic History* 53 (September 1993): 465–94. For a general overview of England's role in the development of international trade, see Ralph Davis, *English Overseas Trade, 1500–1700* (London: Macmillan, 1973). For an overview of the contribution of these entities to the advance of finance, see Jonathan Barron Baskin, "The Development of Corporate Financial Markets in Britain and the United States, 1600–1914: Overcoming Asymmetric Information," *Business History Review* 62 (Summer 1988): 201–206. See also Braudel, *Civilization and Capitalism*, vol. 2, pp. 443–45.

[3] For its founding, see William Robert Scott, *The Constitution and Finance of English, Scottish and Irish Joint-Stock Companies to 1720*, 3 vols., reprint

gal, it played a leading role in fostering European–Asiatic trade during the early modern era.[4]

The success of the English East India Company derived from a combination of organizational and financial advantages inherent in the joint-stock company form. The Company evolved effective means for concentrating substantial capital that consisted of liabilities of varying maturities supported by a permanent core of transferable equity shares. Its strong, permanent capital base in turn gave the firm sufficient financial flexibility to be able to exploit economies deriving from an increased scale of operations and a broader scope of trading activities. The creation of an effective administrative structure for coordinating and controlling far-flung business ventures yielded other competitive advantages, including the reduction of agency, information, transportation and other transaction costs. The business pros-

---

ed. (Gloucester, Mass.: Peter Smith, 1912, 1968), vol. 1, pp. 129 and 150, and for its relative size in 1717 see the table in vol. 1, p. 394. For the end of the East India Company after the Sepoy Mutiny in 1857, see Brian Gardner, *The East India Company: A History*, reprint ed. (New York: McCall, 1971, 1972), chaps. 17–18 passim; and Philip Lawson, *The East India Company: A History* (London: Longman, 1993), chaps. 6–7 passim.

[4] For the Dutch East India Company, see Kristoff Glamann, *Dutch–Asiatic Trade, 1620–1740,* 2nd ed. (Den Haag: Martinus Nijhoff, 1958, 1981); Femme Gaastra, "The Shifting Balance of Trade of the Dutch East India Company," in Leonard Blusse' and Femme Gaastra, eds., *Companies and Trade* (Leiden: University of Leiden Press, 1981), pp. 47–69; Larry Neal, "The Dutch and English East India Companies Compared: Evidence from the Stock and Foreign Exchange Markets," in James D. Tracy, ed., *The Rise of Merchant Empires: Long-Distance Trade in the Early Modern World, 1350–1750,* reprint ed. (Cambridge University Press, 1990, 1991), pp. 195–223; Larry Neal, *The Rise of Financial Capitalism: International Capital Markets in the Age of Reason* (Cambridge University Press, 1990), chaps. 6–7 passim; Neils Steensgaard, "The Growth and Composition of the Long-Distance Trade of England and the Dutch Republic before 1750," in Tracy, ed., *Rise of Merchant Empires,* pp. 102–52; and Jaap R. Bruijn, "Productivity, Profitability, and Costs of Private and Corporate Dutch Ship Owning in the Seventeenth and Eighteenth Centuries," in ibid., pp. 174–94. For France, see Pierre H. Boulle, "French Mercantilism, Commercial Companies and Colonial Profitability," in Blusse' and Gaastra, eds., *Companies and Trade,* pp. 97–117. For Portugal, see Sanjay Subrahmanyam and Luis Filipe F. R. Thomaz, "Evolution of Empire: The Portuguese in the Indian Ocean during the Sixteenth Century," James D. Tracy, ed., *The Political Economy of Merchant Empires: State Power and World Trade 1350–1750* (Cambridge University Press, 1991), pp. 298–331.

pects of this enterprise were further enhanced by the forging of mutually beneficial relationships with the nascent English national state.

The analysis of the experience of this unique institution is presented in three steps. The first describes the factors contributing to the rise of the joint-stock companies during the sixteenth and seventeenth centuries. Next is an evaluation of the managerial practices that the East India Company devised to reduce risk and augment efficiency. The last discusses the financial arrangements that sought to reconcile the financial interests of investors and management.

II. The Rise of Joint-Stock Trading Companies

Before the joint-stock company, the guild and the regulated company had been the organizational forms relied on in England for ordering major economic activities. In return for substantial monetary donations, the sovereign granted the guilds exclusive rights to practice particular trades or crafts at various locations and to exercise authority in adjudicating disputes and policing the conduct of affairs among its membership. Admission to practice was generally restricted to those who had successfully completed the requirements of an apprenticeship. Besides economic affairs, the guilds served as a primary focus for their members' social and religious lives. Some also provided welfare benefits, such as sickness, unemployment and burial insurance.[5]

The regulated companies that followed the guilds and were precursors of the joint-stock companies were, on the other hand, royally chartered associations of independent merchants who collectively enjoyed a monopoly of trade with particular foreign markets. These companies appeared in England in the thirteenth century and like the guilds, required prospective members to complete the terms of an apprenticeship. They enhanced their members' market power and operational efficiency by adopting many of the practices incorporated in the *maona* partnerships used at Venice to finance individual voyages. Like the *maona,* the combining of member capital enabled the regulated companies to organize large-scale ventures that significantly re-

---

[5] Scott, *Joint-Stock Companies,* vol. 1, pp. 1–8; and Eli F. Heckscher, *Mercantilism,* 2 vols., revised 2nd ed. (London: Allen & Unwin, 1931, 1955), vol. 1, pp. 392–98.

duced the average costs of transportation and protection for its members. The consolidation of purchasing power provided the company's merchants with leverage to negotiate favorable terms for supplies and merchandise. The mandating of uniform selling prices also enabled these enterprises to bolster the group's profits. But unlike the *maona,* the life of a regulated company was permanent and not limited to the time frame of a particular voyage. Thus, losses could be minimized by screening out the incompetent and the dishonest during apprenticeships or later through peer censure. Finally, the direct participation of all members in overseas voyages minimized the problems associated with asymmetric information because each venturer was directly responsible for managing his personal investments in trade.[6]

Like the guilds, the regulated companies received their special privileges because of the substantial financial assistance they rendered to the sovereign. One of the earliest regulated companies engaged in foreign commerce was the Staple of London, founded in 1248 to control the export woolen trade. With the collapse of the Bardi and the Peruzzi in 1343–46, Edward III turned to this association to provide financing for his military campaigns in France. After some interim funding, the king granted the Staple in 1357 the right to collect the customs on wool exports in return for additional loans. The royal financial dependency was long standing; for instance, in return for similar assistance in 1466 Henry VI granted the Staple authority over Calais, including the right to collect customs on woolen imports bound from that port to Continental markets. Beside providing for the military defense and civil administration, the Company protected the English Crown's interests by deflecting the scheme discussed in the preceding chapter, of the duke of Burgundy and the Medici's Tommaso Portinari to divert the wool trade from Calais to rival Gravelines. The Company remained the valued ally of the Crown until this bastion finally fell to the duke of Guise in 1558.[7]

Although many of the managerial and financial practices employed

---

[6] Heckscher, *Mercantilism,* vol. 1, pp. 373–92 and 394–99; and Scott, *Joint-Stock Companies,* vol. 1, pp. 7–14.

[7] For an analysis of the Staple, see Power, *Wool Trade,* pp. 96–103. See also La Monte, *World of the Middle Ages,* p. 660; Scott, *Joint-Stock Companies,* vol. 1, pp. 8–9; and Pierre Goubert, *The Course of French History,* translated ed. (New York: Watts, 1984, 1988), pp. 138–40.

by the joint-stock companies could be traced back to the guilds and regulated companies, the use of transferable shares of ownership was an idea that had long permeated many types of European business. Although their impact was limited and did not lead to the formation of giant, international enterprises, a miscellany of early entrepreneurial forms experimented with transferable shares. For example, the Genoese Republic issued *luoghi,* or shares, secured by public revenues through the quasi-official Casa di San Giorgio to fund its *compere,* or public debt, and for some military expeditions. Extractive and manufacturing ventures in other regions also relied on share financing. Mines in Siena, Styria and France sold shares during the thirteenth century; tradable *kuxen,* or shares, funded many Central European mines during the thirteenth century; and from the thirteenth to the eighteenth centuries cloth mills in Douai, Cologne and Toulouse were controlled through shares called *uchaux.*[8]

The conjoining of state-granted monopoly rights with transferable shares in the joint-stock form first emerged in England during the later Tudor and Stuart monarchies. The Crown granted letters patent (i.e., exclusivity) for many types of exploratory or risky undertakings. The colonization of overseas territories such as Bermuda, Massachusetts, Ulster and Virginia were initially carried out through joint-stock enterprises. Special patents for inventions encouraged such diverse manufactures as linen, paper, sword blades and saltpeter. One of the earliest attempts to use the form in large-scale foreign trade was the Russia Company organized in 1553 by Sebastian Cabot to exploit a monopoly over routes to Archangel.[9]

The reliance on joint stock introduced distinct advantages in mobilizing capital, in reducing transaction costs and in enhancing investor liquidity. The use of transferable shares enhanced the liquidity of their investment holdings that could be sold without incurring the costs and inconvenience of a formal liquidation of the enterprise. Liquidity was further augmented through the later growth of large and anonymous financial markets first in Amsterdam and later in London. Finally, share ownership provided an opportunity to invest capital without the

---

[8] Braudel, *Civilization and Capitalism,* vol. 2, pp. 323 and 439–40.
[9] For a general discussion of joint-stock companies, see Scott, *Joint-Stock Companies,* vol. 1, pp. 1–164 passim; and Heckscher, *Mercantilism,* vol. 1, pp. 326–455 passim.

need to participate in the business management, as was the case of partnerships and regulated companies.

For business promoters the joint-stock form was advantageous because it afforded greater financial flexibility. Transferable shares enabled promoters to tap more potential investors: their solicitations were not restricted to narrow kinship groups, as with partnerships, guilds and, often, with regulated companies. Such shares ensured greater operational continuity by eliminating the need to liquidate an entire enterprise in order to pay out withdrawing investors. Joint-stock enterprises could refinance in order to take advantage of improving economic circumstances after depressions or wars more quickly than alternative business forms could. These factors brought opportunities previously unattainable because of high capital requirements. Moreover, the lapse of ecclesiastical bans against usury after the Reformation expanded the capacities of these enterprises to raise funds by borrowing on their equity.[10]

Leading joint-stock companies prospered because they were able to achieve previously unattainable economies of scale and scope of operations by concentrating vast amounts of capital in a single enterprise. Size provided the opportunity to exercise strong market power and to negotiate advantageous contracts. It enabled these companies to reduce risk and to enhance the efficiency of transport by fitting out fleets consisting of large and well-protected sailing vessels. In addition, they could realize economies of scale and scope, as well as reduce risk by diversifying the products they traded and by shifting the focus of their overseas operations to the most promising foreign markets.

Joint-stocks companies were capable of reducing information costs. The establishment of more geographically dispersed administrative networks, while affected by difficulties in communicating over long distances, still provided more valuable proprietary flows of information about economic and political conditions in major markets than existed earlier. These internal sources of market knowledge were vital in establishing reliable estimates of the risks associated with particular business plans.

[10] See Scott, *Joint-Stock Companies*, vol. 1, pp. 44–46, as well as the discussion of the East India Company finances in vol. 1, pp. 163, 285, 340 and 443. See also Douglass C. North, "Institutions, Transaction Costs and the Rise of Merchant Empires," in Tracy, ed., *Political Economy of Merchant Empires*, pp. 22–40.

Joint-stock companies could also bolster efficiency by reducing agency costs. The development of administrative structures increased the capabilities of the most progressive firms for coordinating and controlling their far-flung business operations. A key aspect of this was the ability to establish techniques for monitoring performance in order to minimize losses deriving from agent incompetence or opportunism.

Joint-stock companies, like the older regulated companies and guilds, formed strong alliances with the state. They contributed to government revenues and their activities extended national power. During the Tudor and Stuart monarchies the periodic loans and cash grants made to the sovereign represented a crude effort to overcome limitations in contemporary taxation.[11] Although these transfers essentially represented a tax on enterprise income, contemporaries were less generous in their assessments, branding them, instead, as graft.[12]

However, after the Glorious Revolution of 1688, the English Parliament displaced the Crown as the key agency in the management of national fiscal affairs. Because it was broadly representative of the nation's predominant economic interests, Parliament emerged as a key forum for evaluating the ideas of many of the nation's most successful and experienced leaders in finance and trade. This became evident at the close of the seventeenth century, when England was engaged in prolonged military conflicts on the Continent. Parliament's leaders proved adept at developing instruments useful in financing national defense, some of which affected the funding practices of the nascent joint-stock companies.[13]

One such innovation was the "fund of credit," which sought to use

[11] The earnings of trade monopolies were not subject to direct taxation, the main sources of public revenues being trade tariffs and a mix of regressive imposts on personalty and consumption. The inherently more equitable and efficient system of income taxation was infeasible because of government's limited administrative capacities and the primitive state of accounting.

[12] See Scott, *Joint-Stock Companies*, vol. 1, pp. 238, 258 and 385 for examples of cash grants made by the English India Company to the sovereign. See also M. N. Pearson, "Merchants and States," in Tracy, ed., *Political Economy of Merchant Empires*, pp. 87–94 passim.

[13] For a discussion of the financial transition, see Charles H. Wilson, *England's Apprenticeship, 1603–1763*, 2nd ed. (London: Longman, 1965, 1984),

public finance as a means for reducing the risk of trading enterprises. Although direct grants to the Crown from private parties declined with the institution of the annual privy purse, Parliament compelled joint-stock companies to subscribe to the state's debt issues as a prerequisite for preserving their special privileges. These high-grade securities served as excellent collateral for loans to finance trading activities. Moreover, the interest earned on these holdings helped to defray the overall costs of borrowing.[14]

The joint-stock companies effectively enlisted the assistance of private capital to extend state power in other ways. Enterprises specializing in colonization and trade contributed to national economic growth and provided governmental administration and military protection in foreign territories. Joint-stock trading companies bolstered national power by stimulating the expansion of the merchant navy and its allied shipbuilding and domestic armament industries. They had information about overseas conditions, often unavailable to the state. This enabled corporate officials to advance national interests by negotiating more advantageous terms with host regimes than less knowledgeable government officials were able to negotiate.[15]

During the initial exploratory phase as the East India Company carefully assessed the potentials of Asian markets, its administrative practices were geared to the short-term requirements of particular voyages. Later, when they became more confident of overseas trade prospects, the Company's leaders sought to enhance operational efficiency by devoting more attention to problems of establishing a more permanent and elaborate organizational structure.

III. The East India Company and the Development of an Organizational Structure for International Trade

During the first decade of the seventeenth century the Company began to develop its administrative capabilities and to test the potentials of

chapts. 10 and 15. See also P. G. M. Dickson, *The Financial Revolution in England: A Study in the Development of Public Credit, 1688–1756* (New York: St. Martin's, 1967), chapt. 1.

[14] Scott, *Joint-Stock Companies,* vol. 1, pp. 396–98.
[15] Heckscher, *Mercantilism,* vol. 1, pp. 405–10.

Eastern trade. Initially, to serve these markets the Company organized separate terminable joint stocks to conduct single voyages. Twelve expeditions between 1601 and 1612 probed new markets extending from the Red Sea to the East Indian Archipelago. Subsequently, longer-term joint stocks – each sponsoring a cluster of consecutive voyages – extended the marketing and managerial infrastructure in the East (1612–42). During the last phase from 1642 to 1720, the Company adopted a permanent capitalization to support its vastly expanded scale and scope of operations.[16]

The Company's trade was structured around a complex sixteen-month voyage cycle worked out during the first decade. On the outward leg, scheduled in late winter to capitalize on favorable trade winds, it shipped metals and some manufactures. Foremost among the metal exports was silver from Spanish America which the Company's agents purchased at Amsterdam and other Continental markets. Smaller quantities of lead, tin and mercury were also exported along with such exotic materials as coral and ivory. The relatively high costs of European labor limited the range of exportable manufactures. War materials including armor and sword blades, as well as fine satins and broadcloths were among the few finished goods marketable in the East.[17]

The English venturers employed large convoys consisting of a dozen or more ships to exploit triangular trades that they had discovered in the East. The basic window of opportunity lay between India and Indonesia. The proceeds from the sale of European goods at Indian

[16] In his analysis of the business activities of the East India Company, Scott, *Joint-Stock Companies,* focuses primarily on organizational and financial issues. The more recent works of K. N. Chaudhuri, *The English East India Company: The Study of an Early Joint-Stock Company, 1600–1640,* reprint ed. (New York: Kelley, 1965, 1965), and *The Trading World of Asia and the English East India Company, 1660–1760* (Cambridge University Press, 1978), provide a broader scope of analysis, which incorporates trading and administrative activities. Neal, *Rise of Financial Capitalism,* focuses on factors that explain the contributions to the advance of modern finance made by both the Dutch and the English companies. The older work of Sir William Wilson Hunter, *A History of British India,* reprint ed. (New York: AMS Press, 1966, 1898), provides useful detail about both social and financial aspects of the East India Company's first century of activity.

[17] Chaudhuri, *East India Company,* pp. 111–39 passim; and idem, *Trading World of Asia,* pp. 67–71.

ports were used to purchase cotton textiles that were subsequently traded in Indonesia for spices including pepper, cloves and nutmeg. Side excursions to China, Japan, Persia, the Philippines or Cochin China brought in silk, indigo, sugar, coffee and tea. Finally, on the homeward run the fleet revisited India, where part of the spice cargo was traded for tea and calicoes, which were in demand in Europe.[18]

The Company gradually developed an administrative structure that was effective in controlling and coordinating operational activities. The ultimate source of executive authority was the General Court composed of all shareholders owning sufficient equity to qualify for voting (varying in the range of £500 to £2,000 of par value stock). The shareholders were broadly divided into two groups. In the first were many English and some foreign merchants who became active in management because of their previous experience in overseas trading. Prominent in this regard were such leading merchants as Sir Thomas Smith, Sir Morris Abbot and Sir Christopher Clitherow, who all had held high office in the Company. In the second group were nobles and private individuals who had been attracted by the prospects of earning large dividends and who were generally less active in management than the first group, although investors of the caliber of the earl of Cumberland and the lords of Worcester and of Southampton effectively supported the Company's interests at court and in Parliament. The General Court elected the governor, deputy governor and the twenty-four members of the powerful Court of Directors, who served as fiduciaries for their fellow shareholders and were responsible for strategic management. This team worked through seven subcommittees specializing in accounting, buying, correspondence, shipping, treasure (finance), warehousing and private trade. They were assisted by a staff of specialists, including accountants, auditors, clerks, cashiers and secretaries. In many cases directors and staff had previous, direct experience in Eastern trading.[19]

The governor and Court of Directors attempted to supervise the Company's overseas agents. During the period of the separate voyages (1601–12) they hired agents, the most important being the captains who were in charge of navigation and the fleet merchants who moni-

---

[18] Chaudhuri, *East India Company,* pp. 140–72 and 173–206 passim.
[19] Ibid., pp. 23–38 passim. See also Chaudhuri, *Trading World of Asia,* pp. 57–60 and 74–76.

tored trading activities. In this stage the Company's operations were similar to those of the old-style regulated company. Soon, however, the fleet merchants were displaced by resident factors who managed the local trading posts, or "factories." Permanent bases were initially established at Surat in India (1609) and at Bantam on Java (1603). By 1617, eighteen factories were scattered across the Eastern Hemisphere, from the Red Sea to Japan. That year the Company also established another level of management by elevating the resident merchants at Surat and Bantam to the status of presidents of the local territory, who were to be responsible for coordinating regional trading activities. These executives were assisted by local councils composed of staff personnel who were guided by directives from headquarters in London.[20]

Planning was conducted in London by the Court of Directors operating through functional subcommittees. The basic objective was to maintain the continuous flow of merchandise through its worldwide trading network. But this involved decision making about many subsidiary matters. One subcommittee, for example, had to estimate the supply and demand for a plethora of products as well as for the most profitable cargo mixes. This decision, in turn, required precise forecasts of the financial resources available to support such activities. Another dimension of planning was the scheduling of fleet movements. This had to coincide with the availability of textiles and agricultural commodities at overseas ports to minimize demurrage and financing charges and to optimize the use of cargo space. The voyage agendas went beyond merely listing arrival and departure dates. To take advantage of the lower prices, local factors had to quietly negotiate contracts for the supply of particular merchandise long before the arrival of trading fleets. Besides volumes, these instructions indicated the prices that London was willing to pay. To ensure adequate advance preparation, directives were dispatched overland prior to fleet embarkations to regional presidents responsible for coordinating the actions of local factors. Although they were highly specific, London's plans could be modified by local factors if the losses that would be incurred in following them exceeded some predetermined maximum.[21]

[20] Chaudhuri, *East India Company*, pp. 38–55.
[21] Ibid., pp. 31–33 and 74–88; and Chaudhuri, *Trading World of Asia*, pp. 57–77 passim and 131–33.

Planning effectiveness depended on the timeliness and reliability of information. Company strategy was to exploit the recurrent patterns of Eastern trade discovered during the first decade of operations. This understanding of trade flow was constantly being updated by a steady stream of reports from regional presidents and factors that contained a wealth of detail about prices, inventories and the trade prospects at various ports. The dispatches were carefully catalogued in a well-maintained filing system in London and were circulated for the edification of the operating committees.[22]

Besides qualitative information, the planners relied on quantitative data, especially accounting records. The recognition of the importance of accounting may have derived from the personal knowledge of many directors of Mediterranean commercial practice. During the early years the reporting had a managerial rather than a financial emphasis, focusing on particular voyages or operating segments instead of the global entity. Accounting records reported transactions and balances for merchandise and cash for both domestic and foreign operating units. They detailed the prices realized and the volumes of goods sold at the Company's quarterly cargo auctions as well as amounts remaining unsold. Voyage profitability was determined by netting revenues realized from the auction of its cargoes in London against the primary operating costs including labor, merchandise, supplies and insurance.[23]

Personnel practices strengthened management by seeking the services of factors who were competent, motivated and trustworthy. Like the medieval guilds, the Company preferred to engage the sons of merchant shareholders as apprentices. It also tried to regulate the professional and personal lives of its agents. Substance abuse, gambling and lavish personal consumption led to censure, fines or dismissal. Diligence and piety were inculcated through daily religious exercises. The use of terms such as "brethren" and "family" to describe various echelons within the Company reflected the conscious effort to form a strong sense of community identity among the field staff. A spirit of *Gemeinschaft* was especially important in isolated overseas outposts where the well-being and effectiveness of a small

---

[22] Chaudhuri, *Trading World of Asia*, pp. 57–61.

[23] For later accounting reforms, see ibid., pp. 436–52 passim. For early accounting, see Chaudhuri, *East India Company*, pp. 207–12; and Scott, *Joint-Stock Companies*, vol. 2, pp. 122–42 passim.

circle of traders depended on group cohesion and mutual support. These cadres were constantly vulnerable to attack by foreign rivals or to suppression by the adverse policies of host regimes.[24]

Compensation policy provided incentives for high-quality performance. Although it initially forbade factors from engaging in private trade for their own accounts, the Company eventually modified this policy by seeking, instead, to control rather than to eradicate this conflict of interest. Factors were paid relatively high salaries, which protected them from any personal risk of loss from unprofitable operations. The Company also made arrangements for factors to purchase shares, thus allowing them to benefit from any profits. So agents were licensed to conduct limited levels of private transactions. During the highly profitable formative years, this concession did little to diminish overall profitability. But it did provide an additional incentive for agents to work diligently for successful voyage completions.[25]

Although the Company's management encouraged high-mindedness, they suffered few illusions about the shortcomings of human nature and took steps to guard against agent malfeasance. Factor selection, for instance, depended in part on whether a candidate was sufficiently wealthy to post a performance bond that would indemnify the Company for losses resulting from misconduct. The bonding process afforded additional protection because insurers would not underwrite candidates with dubious reputations. Nor did the Court of Directors feel any compunction about fining or discharging poor performers – or suing those suspected of dishonesty.[26]

Information played a key role in controlling the activities of overseas agents. London asserted its control by communicating performance objectives through general and specific communications with the field agents. General rules were laid down in its *Laws and Standing Orders,* specifying the procedures to be followed for many routine activities. In addition, voyage plans served as a standard for evaluating the actual performance of employees. London directors scrutinized

[24] Hunter, *History of British India,* vol. 1, pp. 271–74; and Heckscher, *Mercantilism,* vol. 1, pp. 397–98.
[25] Chaudhuri, *East India Company,* pp. 74–88; and idem, *Trading World of Asia,* pp. 299–305.
[26] Chaudhuri, *East India Company,* pp. 76–77; and idem, *Trading World of Asia,* p. 81.

field reports for evidence of untoward events or of inconsistencies that might require closer management attention. Statistical and accounting data also provided useful insight into segment operations. Directors encouraged friends and relatives serving overseas to include confidential appraisals of the performance of colleagues in their private correspondence. Unsuitable behavior reported to headquarters was quickly corrected by blunt, even threatening, directives.[27]

The scale and scope of trade also helped London control the risks of opportunistic behavior. Since central leaders had a more comprehensive and accurate knowledge of world market conditions, they enjoyed an important advantage in dealing with local representatives. Moreover, headquarters generally had superior information about how resources might best be allocated to maximize returns. In addition, the Company could contain agent opportunism through its control of fleets capable of making the long voyage between Asia and Europe. The Company's quarterly auctions in London sold goods in greater volume than that of the individual merchants. Also, the scale of operations necessary to ensure high profitability always exceeded the capital of individual traders. Finally, many of the city's great merchants were shareholders who had little incentive for undermining the Company in which they maintained considerable investment interests.[28]

But the resolution of these problems required more than the development of effective administration. It also necessitated secure financial relationships that, as will be seen in the following section, also evolved with the growing understanding of the risks and rewards of international trade.

IV. The East India Company and the Development of a Financial Structure for International Trade

Five developments shaped the financial policies of the East India Company during its initial century of activity. First, the duration of enterprise financing shifted from the short term to the long term as the scale and scope of trading operations expanded. Second, corporate financial

---

[27] Chaudhuri, *East India Company,* pp. 27–79 and 86–88.
[28] Chaudhuri, *Trading World of Asia,* pp. 131–35.

arrangements became more responsive to investors' needs for signals, that is, information, useful in assessing enterprise financial condition. Third, besides enhancing the flexibility of corporate finance, the ending of ecclesiastical bans on usury allowed trading companies to concentrate capital more efficiently through financial leverage. Fourth, the liquidity of shareholder investments grew in tandem with the gradual but steady improvements in secondary markets for debt and equity instruments. Fifth, corporate and public finance were placed on a firmer footing by the development, late in the seventeenth century, of mutually supportive methods for funding its activities.

At the beginning of the seventeenth century, the English money markets – unlike those in Holland, where large public banks and permanent financial markets began to emerge first at Amsterdam, in 1609, and later at Middleburg, Delft and Rotterdam – remained highly fragmented and inefficient. In fact, England continued to be served by financial institutions dating from the later medieval period, and finance was still dependent on merchant-bankers and, later in the century, goldsmith-bankers. In addition, these groups provided a variety of banking services, such as accepting deposits, dealing in bills of exchange, converting currencies and lending unused credit balances. By midcentury they played an important role in the development of negotiable bank checks. This rudimentary banking community was served by lawyers as well as by specialized notaries, or "money scriveners," expert in conveying property, maintaining business and banking records and discovering safe and profitable outlets for the savings of wealthy patrons. These specialists played a key role in the highly personalized but irregular markets for allocating savings to such standard passive investments as mortgages on real estate, silent partnerships or the personal bonds of individuals, governmental entities or incorporated business enterprises.[29]

During the pioneering period of separate voyages that lasted from 1601 to 1613, the East India Company depended heavily on short-term instruments to finance its activities. Such commitments were necessary to attract capital because of limited knowledge about business and po-

---

[29] For Dutch banking, see Charles P. Kindleberger, *A Financial History of Western Europe* (London: Allen & Unwin, 1984), pp. 47–49, 50–51 (goldsmith-bankers) and 52–55 (antecedents of the Bank of England). See also Hunter, *History of British India*, vol. 2, pp. 277–305.

litical risks in the Indies. Moreover, there was always the possibility that a northwest passage to the Orient that would be shorter and cheaper to travel than the route around the Cape of Good Hope might be discovered. Also, some investors, including those previously associated with the Levant Company, were merely seeking temporary havens for their capital during a downturn in their primary trade. Others, drawn from the financing of privateering ventures, favored the self-liquidating voyages that the East India Company had organized. In addition, a short-term investment horizon seemed prudent because there was no guarantee that the Crown would continue the Company's monopoly privileges, which were scheduled for renewal in 1615.[30]

These investor concerns and the general problem of gathering reliable information led to the first dozen voyages being organized as terminal. The way this worked was that capital was raised by the sale of shares of £100 nominal value. Voyage capitalizations varied from a high of £80,000 (1609) to a low of £7,142 (1612), most being about £40,000–60,000. Proceeds were distributed to shareholders in the form of "divisions," which did not distinguish between income or the return of capital because they were doubtless viewed as elements in the total liquidation of a completed voyage.[31]

Although the Company at times negotiated bulk sales to wholesale dealers, especially in times of financial stringency, the main trend was to dispose inventories through auctions in London. Auctions allowed the Company to spread the distribution of a voyage's merchandise over a broad time horizon and thus avoid depressing prices severely by glutting the market. It usually took about four to six quarterly auctions to liquidate completely the cargo from one voyage. By 1650, the Company's quarterly auctions had become a well-established feature of London commercial life. Moreover, these periodic sales were vital to Company planners in formulating future trading programs. Customers benefited from the knowledge they gathered from these events about the quantities of goods available and the minimum bid prices the Company was willing to accept. Before the establishment of regular trading within London's emergent community of stockbrokers in the 1680s, the auctions served as a focal point for the sale and transfer of Company shares.

[30] Scott, *Joint-Stock Companies*, vol. 2, pp. 87–102.
[31] Ibid., pp. 98–101; and Chaudhuri, *East India Company*, pp. 207–12.

The dividends paid were calculated in the early years on the basis of a pro rata distribution of physical commodities. Shareholders, however, generally had the option of receiving payment either in cash or in particular commodities. Merchant shareholders frequently preferred to receive commodities, which could be resold at a profit in other European marts. The Company encouraged this practice by offering a 6.5 percent discount from auction sales for these distributions. Grandees, on the other hand, desired cash dividends, a preference the Company was usually able to accommodate, except in times of financial stress when only commodity dividends were paid.[32]

The early voyages were highly profitable, providing more attractive rates of return than those in other contemporary investments. The tenth voyage in 1611, for example, earned a return of 148 percent on its shareholders' capital of £46,092. A division equal to the entire shareholders' capital was paid in four years; this was followed by smaller payouts through 1617. The net income (total divisions minus original equity) provided an annual average return of 24.5 percent at a time when rates of interest in London fluctuated between 8 and 10 percent. The only unprofitable voyage in the set was the fifth in 1608, which lost £13,700.[33]

Trade was also financed through a variety of debt instruments. First, the Company relied on traditional bills of exchange to transfer funds internationally. Second, they issued fixed-interest debentures with maturities of up to six months. These liabilities increased the flexibility of corporate finance because they could be easily renewed or allowed to run down, depending on the fluctuations in business activity. In addition to being short term, the debentures were attractive to those creditors who could diversify risk by structuring portfolios with various maturity dates or by holding variable amounts of debentures and equity shares. Payment dates were eventually scheduled for either March 30 or September 30, coinciding with two of the quarterly cargo auctions. This provided greater assurance that the enterprise would be sufficiently liquid to pay down its maturing debt. Delays, on the other hand, warned of possible insolvency.

[32] Chaudhuri, *East India Company*, pp. 142, 147 and 151; and Hunter, *History of British India*, vol. 1, pp. 292–94.

[33] Chaudhuri, *East India Company*, pp. 208–11; and Scott, *Joint-Stock Companies*, vol. 2, pp. 95–102 and 123–27.

Third, shareholders were offered the option to subscribe to "bottomry" loans, or maritime insurance contracts, which were first developed during the medieval period and were still extensively used in the Mediterranean and at the Amsterdam financial market early in the seventeenth century. These contracts were payable only if the ships and their cargoes returned safely by a prescribed date. Because of their greater inherent risk, the bottomry loans were usually issued at steep discounts from par. The proceeds provided working capital in London while the fleets were in the East. This practice doubtless persisted even after the Company had reverted to leasing sailing vessels in the 1630s. These loans helped to ensure operational continuity, albeit on a more constricted scale, in the event of a shipping disaster. This form of finance went into decline only after well-capitalized casualty insurance companies began to emerge on the London financial scene late in the century.[34]

Several circumstances prompted the Company to shift to multiple-voyage finance beginning in 1613. First, the success of the separate voyages attracted more capital to support the expansion of trading activities. Second, lengthening the duration of the enterprise avoided the internal competition and conflicts from the overlapping terms of so many separate voyages. Ships chartered for one voyage, for example, had occasionally refused to carry the cargo owned by other voyages at foreign ports; similarly, the simultaneous arrival in England of ships sponsored by separate voyages created conflict when both tried to liquidate their cargoes at the Company's auctions. Consequently, many of the later joint stocks were planned to operate for a decade or more. Third, multivoyage arrangements promised greater operational efficiencies. They provided a broader base over which to allocate fixed overhead costs; they also minimized the costs of organizing and winding up ventures. Fourth, investors benefited by diversifying the

---

[34] Scott, *Joint-Stock Companies*, vol. 2, pp. 172–73. Although Scott first notes bottomry loans in the later seventeenth century, the practice was doubtless well established early in the Company's history. Although the documentary evidence for the Company's earliest years is incomplete, many of the early leaders would have been well aware of the substantial dealing in these contracts in Amsterdam; see Violet Barbour, *Capitalism in Amsterdam in the 17th Century*, reprint ed. (Ann Arbor: University of Michigan Press, 1950, 1963), p. 86. In addition, many of East India's founders had become familiar with Mediterranean practice through their earlier connections with the Levant Company; see Scott, *Joint-Stock Companies*, vol. 2, pp. 90–91.

risks of loss over a cluster of separate voyages. Fifth, for either religious or mystical reasons, the Company's management tried to base key aspects of its operations on the number 12 or its multiples. Given this belief, it was understandable that they transformed the business plan after the twelfth voyage.[35]

The greater capital requirements of the multivoyage joint stocks were financed through the innovation of share subscriptions payable in installments. The so-called First Joint Stock (1613) raised £416,000 through the sale of £100 par value shares in four equal installments. These arrangements assured committed investors and provided a schedule for structuring their personal cash flow so as to support the Company's expansion. This also signaled creditors that future cash infusions were likely from the payment of share installments even before the Company completed its initial voyages. Moreover, if the new enterprise proved successful, subscribers might plow back dividends received from earlier voyages. In the event of early failure, however, subscribers might limit their exposure by refusing to pay for subsequent installments.[36]

Although the four multivoyage joint stocks attracted considerable investment capital, their overall economic performance was uneven. The most successful were the initial ones, completed in the early 1630s. The Persian voyages from 1628 to 1630 provided the best average annual returns, yielding a total net return of 60 percent on an invested capital of £375,000 over three years. Next in success was the First Joint Stock of 1613 to 1623 capitalized at £418,691, which yielded a net return of 87 percent over a decade. The largest venture, the Second Joint Stock of 1617 to 1632 capitalized at £1,629,040, barely broke even. Its net return was a meager 12 percent after fifteen years of operation, and that took the form of a mandatory assignment of resources as seed capital for the subsequent Third Joint Stock in 1631 to 1642. Although the Third Joint Stock was somewhat more profitable, providing a net return of 35 percent on its capital of £420,000, its final reckoning was delayed until 1663.[37]

[35] Scott, *Joint-Stock Companies*, vol. 2, pp. 99–105; and Chaudhuri, *East India Company*, pp. 45–55.

[36] Scott, *Joint-Stock Companies*, vol. 2, pp. 102–105; and Chaudhuri, *East India Company*, pp. 45–55 and 215–18.

[37] Chaudhuri, *East India Company*, pp. 208–12; and Scott, *Joint-Stock Companies*, vol. 2, pp. 108–12.

By the 1640s complex economic, operational and political problems contributed to a deterioration in international trade. From an economic standpoint, the growing efficiency of the English company and its Dutch, French and Portuguese rivals undermined the prices of Oriental goods in Europe, thus leading to a worsening of the terms of trade with the East. The Company's imports of pepper, for instance, jumped from £419,000 in 1609 to a high of £2.9 million in 1626. Although import volumes moderated in subsequent years, supplies remained ample and prices moved downward at Company auctions from 28 pence per pound in 1613 to 16 pence in 1635. In fact, to alleviate the problem of mounting pepper inventories the Company's management began the practice of paying out some portion of the divisions in commodities after 1620.[38]

The increase in the scale and scope of operations overtaxed the loose administrative structure carried over from the single-voyage period. The conflicts arising from overlapping voyages persisted. Record keeping and accounting practices failed to keep up with the increasing complexity of operations. Company scribes were baffled by the problem of allocating joint costs of common facilities such as overseas trading posts to sets of simultaneous voyages. Venture liquidations were delayed by the difficulties of spreading operating losses or the deficits caused by defaults in paying for share calls. The Company required greater capital to support mounting fixed costs. Cadres of resident agents had to be maintained at numerous overseas factories; ships had to be leased or purchased for lengthy voyages; and the threat of attack led to the arming of ships and the fortifying of trading posts. This new financial burden forced the Company to borrow at high interest from creditors in Europe and Asia. Profits were diminished by interlopers who violated the Company's special trade privileges. More worrisome was the fact that some of the usurpers such as a consortium led by Sir William Courten, actually enjoyed for a time the support of King Charles I.[39]

Political and social disasters also undermined trade. England had two direct conflicts with the Dutch Republic, from 1620 to 1625 and again from 1652 to 1654. Also the English re-export trade of spices to the Continent was disrupted by the Thirty Years' War of 1618 to

---

[38] Chaudhuri, *East India Company,* pp. 140–60.
[39] Ibid., pp. 214–23; Scott, *Joint-Stock Companies,* vol. 2, pp. 110–23; and Hunter, *History of British India,* vol. 2, pp. 33–45.

1648. And in 1630, a severe three-year famine began in Gujarat, a primary market for the Indian trade; even events in England conspired against the Company's fortunes, namely, periodic outbreaks of plague in London and a destructive civil war from 1642 to 1646.[40]

These negative developments had serious repercussions on the profitability of the terminal joint stocks launched during the 1640s. The disarray of the import markets and a deterioration in firm liquidity encouraged a reliance on distributions of inventories to stakeholders in lieu of sales of excess inventories at auction. This practice probably led to an overstatement of the relatively modest profits recorded during this period. The commodity dividends were measured using nominal values rather than cash prices realized in competitive markets. Had these inventories been sold through normal auctions, the market-clearing prices very likely would have been much lower than the values assigned to these transactions. The experience of the Fourth Joint Stock (1642–62) is instructive. Although it yielded a gross return of 180 percent on its capital of £105,000, this return included one 30 percent division paid in indigo in 1647 and two 50 percent divisions paid in pepper in 1650; smaller cash dividends aggregating 50 percent of capital were paid through 1663.[41]

This poor performance led to the adoption of a more permanent capital structure. This was done at the behest of political leaders who were concerned about the Company's long-term viability and the implications of its survival for national power. The first change was mandated by Oliver Cromwell in 1657 as a prerequisite for the renewal of its charter. The lord protector wanted to preserve the enterprise, believing it to be a vital contributor to national economic strength. Although its charter required an equity of £739,782, uncertainties in the financial markets during 1658–59 limited the actual call-ups of subscriptions to half the total amount authorized.[42]

The new permanent capital structure shaped corporate finance in several ways. It was inherently a more stable arrangement than the earlier terminable stock financing because it did not require liquida-

---

[40] For conflicts with the Dutch, see Chaudhuri, *East India Company,* pp. 49–50 and 60–62. For famine in the Gujarat, see Hunter, *History of British India,* vol. 2, pp. 59–69. For domestic problems in England, see Wilson, *England's Apprenticeship,* pp. 46–47, 108–33 and 176–77.

[41] Scott, *Joint-Stock Companies,* vol. 2, pp. 119–20 and 127–28.

[42] Ibid., pp. 128–30.

tions of enterprise capital to fund the payments of divisions. This stability encouraged the expansion of debenture financing. To enhance the marketability of its shares, management introduced a new feature for bolstering their liquidity. Operating under yet another charter granted by the restored monarch Charles II (1661), the Company promised in 1664 to repurchase any of its shares that were tendered at their approximate book value as evidenced by triennial balance sheets. Management also modified its financing policies by declaring dividends only from net earned income. This change, however, had important implications for investors' information requirements. The critical issue in share valuation was the estimation of the present value of the discounted flow of future earnings available to finance dividends. This question became more important during the 1690s, when a financial market similar to ones found in Holland began to emerge in the vicinity of Exchange Alley in London.[43]

But the Company's external reporting capacities were insufficient to satisfy investors' new information requirements. Accounting capabilities had failed to keep pace with the increased scale and scope of operations after 1620. Although it used double-entry bookkeeping, the Company's accounting system was geared primarily to measure segment activities rather than those of the consolidated entity. Detailed periodic operating statements were not prepared; the triennial balance sheets often reflected estimated values rather than historic costs of assets; the depreciation of fixed assets was not routinely measured; audits of foreign branch accounts were not performed. The Company even lacked an account for analyzing whether sufficient income had been earned for paying a dividend. Instead, dividend decisions were based on the analysis of current cash balances in London and on rough estimates of prospective receipts and disbursements over the short term. Thus, dividend declarations, auction results and the news of fleet arrivals were all closely monitored signals of the enterprise's financial strength.[44]

---

[43] Ibid., pp. 131–35. See also the useful analysis provided by Chaudhuri, *Trading World of Asia*, pp. 417–26. See also E. Victor Morgan and W. A. Thomas, *The London Stock Exchange: Its History and Functions*, 2nd ed. (New York: St. Martin's, 1962, 1969), pp. 12–16 passim; and Neal, *Rise of Financial Capitalism*, chapts. 1–2 passim.

[44] Chaudhuri, *Trading World of Asia*, pp. 420–25.

During the period 1661–81, dividends also seemed to have had an impact on decisions about the proper mix of debt and equity. Management appears to have targeted the dividend return level at about 20 percent. The desire to sustain this ratio probably was a key factor dissuading management from calling the remaining unpaid subscriptions for the 1659 equity shares. Instead, increases in working capital were financed through the issuance of short-term debentures that were paid off as cargoes were liquidated or rolled over to support continuing operations. In addition, interest rates remained low during the latter half of the seventeenth century, with a mandatory ceiling of 6 percent imposed from the Restoration until the Revolution of 1688. The combination of these low rates on debt and high leverage augmented the returns earned on shareholders' equity.[45]

Despite the revival of prosperity after 1657, the Company was soon attacked by groups dissatisfied with its policies. Bullionists complained in Parliament that the Company exported too much precious specie in financing its purchases of Oriental goods. Others contended that unlike many of the regulated trading companies, it failed to promote English woolen exports and weakened the domestic fabric industry by importing cheap Indian cotton goods. Trade interlopers, who had been fined for trespass, and Levant Company merchants, whose business had been diminished after the opening of the Cape route to the East, demanded the end of special privileges. Moreover, some small shareholders complained that major investors selfishly engaged in private trade that reduced income available to fund dividends. Others simply resented the high dividends earned by the monopoly; in 1680, for example, a 50 percent dividend was paid and a share of stock sold for a high of £300.[46]

There was even a dissident faction within the Company led by Thomas Papillon, a Whig, who favored the end of monopoly and thus freer trade. Papillon and his adherents objected to the power wielded in Company affairs by Sir Josiah Child, who had dominated the office of governor because of his large stock holding. They were deeply disturbed by Child's drawing closer to James II to ensure the renewal

[45] Ibid., pp. 420–23.
[46] Scott, *Joint-Stock Companies*, vol. 2, pp. 135–40.

of the Company's charter. For instance, by 1687, the monarch had acquired £7,000 of Company stock for the royal portfolio.[47]

Child's response in 1681 was to broaden the capital base by issuing additional shares, which would provide more working capital and might draw in new shareholders of influence at court and in the city. The problem of the unpaid subscriptions of 1659 was resolved by the declaration of a 100 percent stock dividend, which reclassified much of its substantial earned surplus as capital. This action reduced the high market premium over par of the shares (quoted at £460 during 1681), which had deterred many prospective investors from purchasing new issues. The latter group worried that the eventual call of the earlier unpaid 1659 subscriptions might be made at par. This, they feared, would undermine the market price of any new share issues that had previously been distributed at higher values. Moreover, during January 1682 the Company paid a 50 percent cash dividend, which reduced the market price of the shares and enhanced the perception of financial strength.[48]

Child's scheme, however, soon aborted after Thomas Papillon and his circle suddenly sold out. This dramatic action was perceived as a negative signal inducing other less well informed share owners to liquidate their holdings in panic. The stock price plummeted even after taking into consideration the dilution of the stock dividend. During the Fall of 1682, it was quoted at £122½ (or £245 on the original basis). The resultant confusion led to a temporary drying up of credit, forcing the Company to default on its interest payments for three months. These events destroyed any hopes for launching a successful recapitalization. The Company, now drained of cash reserves by its large dividends, concentrated on rebuilding liquidity, and it deferred any subsequent divisions until 1685.[49]

The opposition to Governor Child's regime did not abate but grew more intense after the Revolution of 1688. The Company was in an awkward political position because of its earlier financial connections

---

[47] Ibid., vol. 2, pp. 144–46 and 149; and Chaudhuri, *Trading World of Asia*, pp. 426–29.

[48] Chaudhuri, *Trading World of Asia*, pp. 426–28; and Scott, *Joint-Stock Companies*, vol. 2, pp. 143–46.

[49] Scott, *Joint-Stock Companies*, vol. 2, pp. 146–48; and Chaudhuri, *Trading World of Asia*, pp. 428–29.

with James II. Equally worrisome was the formation of a rival financial syndicate led by Thomas Papillon, which continued to harass the Company in Parliament. Initially, the syndicate demanded the opening of the Company to more investment by outsiders and the deposing of Child; later, it insisted that the Company's monopoly privileges be ended and trade to the Indies be opened to free competition. These rivals also tried to weaken the Company by driving down the price of its stock whenever negative news broke. Serious runs started in 1692 after two disasters, a military defeat at the hands of the Moguls in Bengal and the loss of some of its ships to French privateers. The Company responded to the bear raids by supporting the price of its shares through issuing a 50 percent (of par value) cash dividend in 1691. It also built up its finances and tried to defuse the criticisms that its ownership was concentrated in too few hands by issuing enough additional shares to raise its paid up capital to £1,488,000. However, Child's clique was able to maintain its majority interest.[50]

The low point was reached in 1698, when the English government, engaged in a costly war with France, initiated public financing policies that ended the Company's monopoly and opened the Indian trade to its rivals. Since 1688, the English government had experimented with several new forms of public financing instruments to alleviate the burdens of taxation. One spectacular success was the formation of the Bank of England in 1694, which proved to be an effective agency for consolidating and financing much of the public debt. Another innovation that affected the East India trade was the development of the notion of a fund of credit, which sought to satisfy the financial requirements of both the government and the larger joint-stock monopolies. The aspect of this new arrangement most significant to any analysis followed the subscription of £1.3 million by the Papillon syndicate of a £2.0 million 8 percent government annuity loan. For this service the Crown chartered Papillon's New East India Company to enter the Indian trade.[51]

From the perspective of the government the fund of credit offered

---

[50] Chaudhuri, *Trading World of Asia*, pp. 429–33; and Scott, *Joint-Stock Companies*, vol. 2, pp. 147–63 passim.

[51] Scott, *Joint-Stock Companies*, vol. 2, pp. 163–68; and Chaudhuri, *Trading World of Asia*, pp. 434–35.

several potential benefits. It increased the funds for defense spending without driving taxes up by a corresponding amount. Moreover, by funding these expenditures through the creation of marketable debt, the British government expanded the national credit base and created a strong financial bond with the nation's economic elite.[52]

From the perspective of the firm, the new arrangement traded off the maximization of returns for the reduction of risk. The risks of bankruptcy and losing access to trade were diminished by investing in the government loan. On the other hand, overall returns were probably reduced under the fund of credit because the internal investment opportunities in the firm's primary trades offered greater profit potential than the interest earned on the government's securities. But the mandatory government loan stock investment provided an additional margin of safety that reduced risk for the Company's debentures. Although Parliament (at the beckoning of the Bank of England) had mandated that the debentures be issued for terms of at least six months, the fund of credit offset the risk of longer lending terms. Furthermore, the Bank of England accommodated the Company through the provision of an overdraft facility for transient borrowing of less than six months.[53]

Yet in spite of the apparent success of Papillon's New East India Company, the older enterprise was not dislodged because it was able to exploit significant first-entrant advantages in overseas trade. Although its business had fallen off sharply during the Nine Years' War and it was only able to subscribe to £744,000 of the government loan of 1698, the Old Company reasserted its dominance in the Eastern trade by 1701. In refinancing, its leaders called on the shareholders to increase their capital by 25 percent. They also sold bonds at a 3 percent discount from par and negotiated large loans from Bengali bankers. The revival of the Old Company's financial prospects resulted largely from its ability to retain the loyalty and cooperation of its overseas agents. These echelons were able to earn high profits quickly by managing the expansion of the product flow through its well-organized trading infrastructure in Europe and the Far East. By 1701,

[52] For a discussion of the fund of credit, see Scott, *Joint-Stock Companies*, vol. 1, pp. 396–98.
[53] Chaudhuri, *Trading World of Asia*, pp. 434–35.

the Old Company's finances had improved so much that its management offered to refund the entire government loan of 1698 at 5 percent and its share quotation rose from a low of 33¼ in 1698 to 142.[54]

Finally in 1702, the leaders of the New Company, recognizing their vulnerability in trade, decided to compromise their differences and to merge with their former rivals. Under the terms of the Indenture Tripartite of 1702 and the Award of Godolphin of 1708, the rivals consolidated their affairs in a surviving entity, the United East India Company. Under the Indenture the companies also assented to a joint administration for a term of seven years, during which their operations were integrated and the capital accounts of shareholders were appropriately adjusted. Moreover, the Company established a capital structure that remained stable until 1745. The share capital was set at £3.163 million and the government loan was increased from £3.0 million in 1710 to £4.2 million in 1744. This level of equity capital and of investment in government obligations provided a safety buffer for purchasers of its debentures, whose total value fluctuated in the range of £2.6–3.4 million during the period 1710–45.[55]

The merger also led to a strengthening of financial management. The complex allocations required under the terms of the Indenture Tripartite induced management to improve the enterprise's accounting capacities. In addition, the Company laid down new financial guidelines to avoid the crises experienced earlier. Arrangements were made for regular audits of overseas account balances. Managers were now instructed as to the optimal levels for debt, interest rates and the ratio of cash to liabilities. Dividend payments also became more regularized, although at much lower levels than during the heady days of Josiah Child's regime. These payments gradually declined from a high of 12.6 percent of capital (1711) to a low of 5.8 percent (1758–60).[56]

---

[54] Ibid., pp. 435–36; and Scott, *Joint-Stock Companies*, vol. 2, pp. 166–69.
[55] Scott, *Joint-Stock Companies*, vol. 2, pp. 169–88 and 189–206 passim; and Chaudhuri, *Trading World of Asia*, pp. 435–36 and 436–40.
[56] Chaudhuri, *Trading World of Asia*, pp. 436–52 passim.

V. Conclusion

In what ways, then, does the experience of the English East India Company amplify corporate finance theory? How did the financial-institutional innovations of this era contribute to the efficiency of large-scale business enterprises?

The formation of close and abiding relationships with the state was one effective means used by promoters to assuage the concerns of prospective investors about the risks of large-scale trading ventures in the seventeenth century. Such an approach was followed by the East India Company's organizers, who sought to overcome the reluctance of investors to commit their capital to an inherently risky undertaking by associating it with the charisma of national power. Initially, this took the form of grants of monopoly rights over specific business activities. This signaled to prospective investors that the venture would remain insulated from despoliation by domestic competitors. Later, as financial markets became better established, these connections took on a more financial character with the establishment of such devices as the fund of credit to unify the interests of government and private groups.

The East India Company's experience evidenced how critical the establishment of effective administrative processes were to the achievement of enterprise financial objectives. Although grants of monopoly power provided strong incentives for prospective investors, in the long term it was not as important as sound administration. The promise of monopoly power served as a strong inducement to attract investment capital to what initially seemed a highly uncertain venture. Strong administrative capabilities, however, became essential to preserve and expand the advantages accruing to international trade after its formative phase. The development, by the East India Company, of a well-conceived organizational structure proved more effective for ordering trade than placing reliance on independent market mechanisms. Information and contracting costs for recurrent transactions, for example, were reduced when they were internalized and routinized. In addition, decision making about resource allocations was rendered more effective by the regular transfer, through well-defined internal channels, of reliable information about attractive trading opportunities worldwide. The potential for profit maximization was enhanced by the greater effectiveness of the Company's hierarchical management structure for coordinating its physical and human resources.

Strong administration reduced the overall riskiness of the firm. Effective internal channels of communication were crucial in relaying performance objectives and providing evidence for monitoring and evaluating managerial actions. Compensation plans, the development of a group ethos, reliance on accounting information and the education of employees to preserve the corporation in order to safeguard their living standards all served as incentives for maintaining goal congruence between owners and operators. Finally, besides enhancing the power of the enterprise, administrative capabilities helped to ensure the permanence of the Company by making it able to survive recessions and to recover quickly with upturns in the business cycle.

Although monopoly power was a crucial precondition for raising capital to finance the East India Company's initial, uncertain ventures, this was less important to the mature firm whose success derived from operating efficiencies gained from the development of strong administrative capabilities. The benefits of effective organization necessarily came subsequent to the guarantee of preferred market status because it derived from a path-dependent process in which management gradually learned how to coordinate and to control the enterprise in a complex global business environment. Moreover, the eventual selection of a permanent capital structure was propitious because it afforded sufficient time for management to apply this firm-specific learning about the requirements of the international commodity trade in the development of effective organization, procedures and strategies. In 1698, such first-mover advantages enabled the mature Company to neutralize the efforts of Thomas Papillon's less experienced New East India Company to encroach on its markets after the Crown suspended for a time the monopoly on Indian trade.

The East India Company's debt policies were generally in accord with the predictions of the pecking order hypothesis. First, debt seems to have been used because it was relatively cheap and thus maximized returns on equity, provided greater financial flexibility and sustained the control of dominant owner-managers. As we have noted, interest rates during this period were generally at lower levels than equity returns, which provided an opportunity for enhancing profits through leverage. In addition, short-term debenture balances could be more readily adjustable than equity capital to accommodate fluctuations in the business cycle. Moreover, the largest shareholders were reluctant to broaden the equity base and so dilute their power to control enterprise affairs. This latter motive was most clearly reflected in the experience of Child's regime. But even after the 1709 reorganization, when a new group of leaders took the helm, these concerns persisted, and the Company did not increase its capitalization substantially through 1760.

Unlike the case of the modern corporation, however, the effect of taxation on the East India Company's cost of capital was due to other factors than the deductibility of interest charges. Although payments made to the king and the required holding of government debt in the fund of credit represented de facto taxes on enterprise income, the Company did not benefit from any augmentation of its cash flows deriving from the deductibility of these transfers. Instead, the benefit in these arrangements that reduced the cost of capital was the monopoly power accorded to the Company from these payments. The monopoly of trade to the East reduced investors' perceptions of enterprise risk, which was translated into an overall reduction of the cost of capital. In this regard the most significant advantage from the perspective of the firm was the fund of credit. Besides monopoly rights, the latter arrangement additionally conveyed a regular stream of interest payments as well as a claim against the government that could be collateralized.

Although the trade monopoly also functioned in effect as a tax on consumers by creating the potential for raising the prices of Eastern goods, several factors moderated its impact during this period. Pricing was constrained by the basic elasticity of demand for what were essentially luxury goods. The monopoly was also threatened by additional supply brought to market by interloping English ventures and by rival trading companies operating on the Continent. Moreover, the East India Company's growing efficiency contributed to a deterioration in its terms of trade. Although the tightening of the imperial trading system through such steps as the passage of the Navigation Acts eventually strengthened the Company's position, the economic distortions brought about by these actions over the longer term led to heightened political tensions. It was such frustrations with an overly rigid trade system that motivated the destruction of Company property during the Boston Tea Party of 1773.

Debt financing was also placed on a more stable basis during a period when financial markets were not well developed by forming strong financial bonds between the Company and the state. Before the 1690s, the Company was exposed to high potential risk because it relied on short-term debentures to finance its long-term operations. Creditors, who had to contend with great uncertainties about trade and were unable to hypothecate valuable assets lodged overseas, understandably tried to protect themselves by holding short-dated portfolios.

After 1790, on the other hand, the perfection of the fund of credit arrangement strengthened corporate finance in two ways. First, it provided a high-quality asset in London, which served as a safety buffer for protecting creditors in the event of business failure. Second, it signaled that the government intended to preserve the valuable privileges which were so important to the Company's continued prosperity. Although the terms of debenture financing lengthened under the fund of credit, they never approached the long-term maturities characteristic of modern corporations. The key factor in ensuring greater financial stability at this juncture, however, was not the term of the debentures, but the quality of the assets insuring creditors against potential losses.

The need to assuage concerns about business risk, particularly among equity investors, led to the establishment of limited liability status for shareholders in the larger foreign trading companies, including the East India Company in 1662.[57] This protection was restricted to these particular enterprises and did not become a general condition in corporate finance until the nineteenth century. Although this represented a strengthening in the legal protection afforded to shareholders, creditor interests were still protected in these large and risky ventures by other financial buffers. One such device was the aforementioned fund of credit, which was based on the holding of a large portfolio of low-risk government obligations. Another technique involved the use of calls on incompletely funded share subscriptions. In financial emergencies company directors could require shareholders to make additional payments to reduce their share subscription receivables. This approach was most effective when leading shareholders were individuals with great fortunes.

The findings of this study, with respect to the role of dividends, are

[57] Scott, *Joint-Stock Companies,* vol. 2 , p. 270.

more consistent with those of scholars of agency relationships than with those of scholars concerned with market efficiency. In an age when the sources of information about enterprise performance or condition were severely limited, dividends, or events that might be reasonably interpreted as signals for future declarations, were seemingly important objective clues about profitability and solvency. The frequency and size of these payments were used early in the firm's history as a gauge for assessing its basic economic vitality. As will be seen in the following chapter, these perceptions continued to influence the outlooks of investors long after financial accounting and reporting practices became standardized and well established.

The composition and payment patterns of dividends changed markedly in response to the requirements of government, passive investors and emergent markets for financial assets. During most of the first century of its existence, there was a serious conflict over dividend policy within the Company between merchant-investors and passive shareholders. The dominant merchant faction preferred to use the dividend to adjust their own stock levels for personal trading activities. The rundown of the private inventories of these key intermediaries, who distributed the Company's imports to end consumers, created strong pressures for the declaration of dividends taken in the form of salable commodities. On the other hand, if their supply levels became surfeited these leaders preferred to have the Company continue to warehouse excess levels of goods. Although cash dividends were paid, their importance was secondary in the thinking of the controlling merchants, who were more concerned with satisfying the product requirements of their own customers. Under these circumstances passive investors were sorely inconvenienced during liquidity crises when they were forced to accept payment in the form of bags of pepper or bolts of calico, which were not easily liquidated.

After the 1709 reorganization, dividend policy changed markedly in ways that enhanced the viability of the fund of credit relationship. One aspect of this transformation was to make share ownership more attractive in comparison to the alternative investments available through London's now burgeoning financial market. In order to compete successfully with regular interest payments available from government stock issues that predominated in this market, the Company's leadership had to promise regular cash dividends. In addition, the Crown may have wished to rely on the capital of a broad class of passive investors rather than on that of a merchant clique. The protracted attacks on Child's regime demonstrated to government leaders the political problems that arose when the ownership of a valuable public franchise was concentrated in too few private hands. In any event, the Company soon embarked on a policy of paying annual cash dividends, which, as Defoe has pointed out, enhanced the marketability of its shares in Exchange Alley.

The financial arrangements adopted by the East India Company, however, had inherent limitations, as we shall see in the following chapter, which deals with the South Sea Company in the eighteenth century. The problem involved the use of the fund of credit mechanism in consolidating and retiring vast amounts of public debt. The solution was eventually discovered to lay in the development of broad, anonymous financial markets rather than reliance on a circle of privileged enterprises.

CHAPTER THREE

The Emergence of Public Markets for Investment Securities, 1688–1815

I. Introduction

The development of large-scale trading enterprises (discussed in Chapter 2) was an essential part of the growth of national economies. Similarly, the financial requirements of nascent nation-states nurtured the growth of broad, anonymous financial markets. Although the prototypes of modern public debt instruments first appeared in the Italian city-states of Genoa and Venice and in the Low Countries in Antwerp and Bruges, the markets for these obligations reached great efficiency in England between 1688 and 1815.[1] The primary impetus for innovation was in financing the heavy economic burdens in the form of high taxes and huge public debts that stemmed from the warfare between the island kingdom and France as they vied for European political leadership. In this competition English political and business leaders proved resourceful in forming economic institutions that helped to achieve political stability and to ensure their nation's leadership in international markets: The Bank of England was formed in 1694 and the Board of Trade was revived in 1695.[2]

Several factors placed British public finance on a much firmer basis. Foremost were the political reforms, resulting from the Revolution of

---

[1] See Fernand Braudel, *Capitalism and Material Life, 1400–1800* (New York: Harper & Row, 1973), pp. 357–72, for an overview of factors affecting the development of money, banking and credit. See also Kindleberger, *Financial History of Western Europe*, pp. 35–54; and Usher, *History of Deposit Banking*, Part 1 passim.

[2] Dickson, *Financial Revolution*, pp. 3–11; Wilson, *England's Apprenticeship*, pp. 58 and 167 for the Board of Trade and pp. 219, 314 and 332–33 for the Bank of England.

1688, that established Parliament as the key agency in managing national fiscal affairs. This substitution of the rule of law for the divine right of a monarch made investor interests more secure. The guarantee of the nation-state was better protection than the personal promise of the sovereign. The standardization of contractual details for governmental debt obligations allowed for their uniform market pricing and rationalized the relationship between lenders and the state. The new markets thrived because they provided liquidity for investor portfolios. Moreover, they enabled state leaders to concentrate much greater financial power through borrowing than had hitherto been possible. State finance became more flexible after effective methods were devised to service debt and thus avoid the potentially crushing demands for the liquidation of outstanding obligations that had undermined earlier monarchical regimes.[3] Britain's ultimate leadership derived partly from the slowness of its archrival France to establish more viable institutions. The parliamentary assembly of the Etats Generaux, which imposed fiscal and monetary reforms, had not convened since 1570. Also, in contrast to England, the French monarchy had resisted efforts to create a central banking mechanism or to draw a clearer line of separation between public and private finance.[4]

This chapter analyzes these transformations in four sections. The following section focuses on the conjoining of four factors that set the stage for the development of broad and anonymous financial markets

[3] Dickson, *Financial Revolution,* pp. 10–14. See also Wilson, *England's Apprenticeship,* chapt. 5 for a discussion of the chronic financial problems of the later Stuart monarchs and chapt. 10 for an analysis of the financial reforms introduced late in the seventeenth century. For an analysis of the connection between the problem of informational asymmetry in finance and the rise of public debt markets in Britain, see Baskin, "Development of Financial Markets," pp. 206–208. For a history of the Bank of England, see Sir John H. Clapham, *The Bank of England: A History,* 2 vols. (Cambridge University Press, 1945), pp. 1–53 passim, on origins; and the more recent work of John Giuseppi, *The Bank of England: A History from Its Foundation in 1694* (Chicago: Regnery, 1966), pp. 1–32 passim.

[4] See John Lough, *An Introduction to Seventeenth Century France,* (New York: McKay, 1954, 1955), 2nd impression, pp. 152–59, for problems of national economic and financial ordering during the regime of Colbert. See also Dickson, *Financial Revolution,* pp. 13–14; and A. J. Grant, *A History of Europe: From 1494 to 1610,* reprint ed. (London: Methuen, 1931, 1967), pp. 432–33 and 471–73.

in London after 1688. This includes (a) the high degree of physical security and social stability prevailing in England; (b) the perfection of quantitative techniques useful in comprehending and ordering financial affairs; (c) the greater financial flexibility and credit growth attendant on the rise of new banking institutions, new forms of public debt and negotiable credit instruments that served as quasi-money; and (d) the transfer of knowledge about the functioning of financial markets in the Low Countries.

The third section, covering the period from the Revolution of 1688 until the culmination of the South Sea Bubble in 1720, explains how contemporary institutional arrangements in the emergent market assuaged investor concerns about risk and agency relationships and also provided the state with an efficient means for drawing in international capital to support its operations.

A peculiarity in official thinking during this early stage was the belief that debts incurred during wartime had to be paid off rapidly in order to preserve state power. Because of the difficulty in paying off these debts so quickly, this notion induced governmental leaders to capitalize much of the national debt burden as part of the equity of the great joint-stock companies. As the fourth section, covering the period 1721–1815, makes clear, the managers of public finances eventually found a more desirable alternative when they discovered that the gradual amortization of a vast debt was an achievable objective that did not undermine the state's executive capacities. Because the new financial markets provided liquidity for investors in government debt obligations, treasury officials could afford to focus on the problem of servicing interest without running much risk of precipitating a financial crisis. It was this insight about the ability to defer loan principal repayments that enabled Britain to magnify its financial power in its long competition with France. This section also concludes with a consideration of how the experience of this epoch relates to contemporary theories about the nature of corporate finance.

II. England's Financial Apprenticeship, 1688–1720

The primary preconditions for the advance of corporate finance – such as the rise of mathematical economics, the growing flexibility of banking and credit and the emergence of financial markets – were general and affected much of Europe. These preconditions found a particularly attractive outlet in England after 1688 because of its secure geopolitical position, its strategic insularity and its known military strengths. Also the reduction of risks of disruptive shocks facilitated the process of financial innovation, thus making possible a more effective mobilization of capital than elsewhere.[5]

After 1688, English financial management benefited from new ideas that redefined the relationship between the individual and society and that, fifty years before Rousseau and Voltaire, established guidelines for political and economic institutions. The rationalist free market philosophy of John Locke, Thomas Hobbes's diatribes against absolute monarchy demanding government protection against humanity's natural tendency toward despotism and Daniel Defoe's pragmatic mercantilism defined the purpose of government as the preservation of individual liberties, property and a competitive marketplace.[6]

Policies more responsive to a broader constituency, specifically the merchant class and newly rich landed gentry, vindicated this social group's claim to political and economic power. Combined with an Anglican guilt-free ethic toward gain and commerce, the English merchant class became fully enfranchised morally and politically. This transition also involved the establishment of a new framework of law and governance that reduced the potential for the arbitrary exercise of state power. The traditional royal governmental system based on the belief of the divine right of kings was reformed to give Parliament greater power especially over fiscal matters, including the authorization of new taxes and the monitoring of Crown expenditures. A reorganization of the legal system effectively curtailed royal prerogatives, strengthened the independence of the judiciary and provided common law guarantees for the protection of both political and economic rights. By enhancing the credibility of the state's commitment to the preservation of these rights, the Revolution of 1688 contributed,

[5] Dickson, *Financial Revolution*, pp. 5–14.
[6] Thomas Keith Meier, *Defoe and the Defense of Commerce* (Victoria: University of Victoria Press, 1987); Leo Strauss, *The Political Philosophy of Hobbes: Its Basis and Its Genesis* (Oxford: Clarendon Press, 1936); and Mark Blaug, ed., *The Later Mercantilists: Josiah Child and John Locke* (Brookfield, Vt.: Elgar, 1991).

as this chapter demonstrates, to a revitalization of both public and private finance.[7]

Economic thought was influenced by seventeenth century advances in mathematics that extended beyond the bounds of Renaissance algebra and geometry. John Napier and Henry Briggs illustrated the functioning of logarithms, Pierre de Fermat and Blaise Pascal laid down the basic framework for statistics and probability theory and Isaac Newton and Gottfried Leibniz separately defined the calculus.[8] These ideas spread rapidly because of the general availability of books and pamphlets made possible by the invention of movable type in the fifteenth century and the rise of cheap paper manufacturing in the eighteenth century.[9] New measurement techniques assisted in the management of complex business activities. English thinkers such as William Petty, John Graunt and Edmund Halley (discoverer of the comet) applied probability theory to the practical problem of calculating life expectancies in the marketing of annuity contracts.[10] Accounting knowledge spread through the formation of instructional academies and the publication of specialized texts. Accounting was recognized as a critical function by architects of mercantilism; Colbert believed that a uniform system of accounting encompassing all business activities and tied into the national system of taxation was vital in attaining national economic goals.[11] Mathematics was also enlisted in the search for solutions to macroeconomic problems. Petty and Graunt began to prepare estimates of national income and to evaluate the impacts on business activity of changes in the supply of money.[12] Two other English writers, Gregory King and Charles Davenant, became concerned with the problem of assessing the macroeconomic effects of changes in the international balance of trade. A growing interest in

---

[7] See Douglass C. North and Barry R. Weingast, "Constitutions and Commitment: The Evolution of Institutions Governing Public Choice in Seventeenth-Century England," *Journal of Economic History* 49 (December 1989): 803–32.

[8] Wilson, *England's Apprenticeship*, p. 226.

[9] Braudel, *Capitalism and Material Life*, pp. 295–300.

[10] Wilson, *England's Apprenticeship*, pp. 227–29 and 334–36.

[11] See G. R. R. Treasure, *Seventeenth Century France* (London: Rivingtons, 1966), pp. 298–320 passim; Heckscher, *Mercantilism*, vol. 1, pp. 102–105 and 345–51; and Lough, *Seventeenth Century France*, pp. 152–53.

[12] Wilson, *England's Apprenticeship*, pp. 227–31.

this latter issue eventually led to the formation of both the Board of Trade and a specialized statistical reporting unit in the Treasury to determine England's foreign trade position.[13]

Finance and commerce benefited from an expansion of credit and from greater flexibility in contracting. Three developments ranked foremost in this important transformation: the creation of rentes, long-term annuities and funded debt contracts for municipalities and national governments; the perfection of negotiable commercial paper, which functioned as quasi-money; and the formation of large banking institutions to facilitate credit expansion. Although the issuance of funded debt first occurred in the Italian city-states, this practice had spread to the free towns of Germany, Switzerland, France and the Low Countries by the fifteenth century; two centuries later they were also being floated by leading kingdoms including Castile and France.

Toward the end of the seventeenth century the law of negotiable instruments had become well defined in most of the major European business centers. The use of negotiable demand notes supported by precious metals, coins, or notes drawn on other banks represented a less costly means for clearing interbank balances than the older, cumbersome system of offsetting book entries. As early as 1596, the Bank of Saint George in Genoa had extended the earlier practice of the Venetian *banci di scritti* by issuing *biglietti* backed by gold or silver. Later during the mid-seventeenth century, English goldsmiths began to issue notes backed by their own and depositors' stocks of precious metals. By the end of the eighteenth century the Banks of England, Amsterdam and Stockholm had emerged as major note issuers in their respective regions. Besides facilitating commercial transacting, increases in the amount and turnover, or velocity, of the new forms of money and quasi-money were believed by many contemporaries to be powerful stimulants of economic activity.[14]

English business leaders learned much about finance by dealing in the markets of the great entrepôts that had emerged in the Low Countries. For instance, the Merchant Adventurers Company, al-

---

[13] Ibid., pp. 228–30.

[14] See Kindleberger, *Financial History of Western Europe,* pp. 19–34 and 35–70 passim; Braudel, *Capitalism and Material Life,* pp. 325–72 passim; and Usher, *History of Deposit Banking,* chaps. 1–7 passim.

though organized as a regulated company like its counterpart, the Staple based at Calais, specialized in a different type of trade in the late fifteenth century. Through the fairs in Holland and Bruges, it distributed semifinished cloths to local dyers and converters rather than raw wool to weavers. Cloth sales financed the purchase of indigenous commodities as well as wares and exotic Indian spices imported by Italian merchants. Through these contacts English tradesmen learned the commercial techniques of credit and bills of exchange.[15]

Bruges's leadership as a commercial center was, however, relatively short-lived. It was displaced by Antwerp by 1482 because of the silting of the River Zsin, which provided access to the port of Sluys, and because of the town's unsuccessful alliance with the Hanseatic League in its conflict with the dukes of Burgundy.[16]

Antwerp had been an active commercial center since the 1460s, which saw its prosperity bolstered by greater Oriental trade resulting from the Portuguese discovery of a route around the Cape of Good Hope to the Indies. The Portuguese began dispatching through Antwerp substantial portions of their spice cargoes brought to Lisbon for redistribution to Northern European markets. Later, the port's product mix broadened to include imports of Spanish bullion from the Americas, fustian from various German towns and copper from Hungary. Despite these breakthroughs in trade, strict government monopolies did not allow independent or state-subsidized merchant companies to flourish.[17]

---

[15] Heckscher, *Mercantilism*, vol. 1, pp. 326–455 passim. See Power, *Wool Trade*, chapt. 5 passim, for the Staple. For the Merchant Adventurers Company, see Wilson, *England's Apprenticeship*, pp. 69–70 and 270–71; and D. R. Bisson, *The Merchant Adventurers of England: The Company and the Crown, 1474-1564* (Newark: University of Delaware Press, 1993), especially chapts. 1–2. For a discussion of Antwerp, see Richard Ehrenberg, *Capital and Finance in the Age of the Renaissance: A Study of the Fuggers and Their Connections*, reprint ed. (New York: Augustus Kelley, 1928, 1963), pp. 233–80 passim.

[16] Ehrenberg, *Capital and Finance*, pp. 233–34; and de Roover, *Money, Banking and Credit in Mediaeval Bruges*, p. 351.

[17] De Roover, *Money, Banking and Credit in Mediaeval Bruges*, pp. 349–50; Ehrenberg, *Capital and Finance*, pp. 236–44; and G. D. Ramsay, *The Queen's Merchants and the Revolt of the Netherlands: The End of the Antwerp Mart* (Dover, N.H.: University of Manchester Press, 1986), pp. 1–15. For shifting patterns of international trade, see Parry, *Age of Reconnaissance*, pp. 38–52.

The local bourse was an institutional innovation at Antwerp that enhanced the efficiency of trade and finance by hedging transaction costs. Besides cash settlements, the bourse handled options contracts for commodities, which could be used either for speculation or to hedge against adverse price fluctuations. Furthermore, a secondary market emerged for trading rentes, annuity contracts and bonds issued by the Portuguese and English crowns and leading towns in the Low Countries.[18] Its operations so favorably impressed Sir Thomas Gresham, Queen Elizabeth I's ambassador to the Netherlands and England's future economic advisor, that after successfully speculating in short-term Spanish gold contracts, he returned to London and opened the Royal Exchange in Change Alley.[19] By 1609 when Shylock in the *Merchant of Venice* speaks of speculating in ducats and debt transactions in Florence, Antwerp, Venice and Seville, his audience is familiar with these markets and forms of transactions.

But political and religious strife abruptly ended Antwerp's reign as Northern Europe's primary international trade entrepôt. In the last quarter of the sixteenth century, tensions mounted as militant Calvinists confronted crusading Catholics supported by Philip II of Spain (successor through his mother's line to the Burgundian dukedom). The passionate disagreements over cosmology led to the sacking of Antwerp by troops under the command of the Spanish viceroy, the duke of Alva in 1574. This action motivated many in the town's religiously diverse merchant community to migrate gradually to the more tranquil environs of Amsterdam.[20]

The Amsterdam Bourse, created in 1530, was one of the most sophisticated centers for the trading of shares from all regions of the Low Countries. It specialized in shares, options and futures, with a huge volume until the 1636–37 Tulip Mania provoked a major crash. The Dutch vindication for creating joint-stock companies came about when they forced the Portuguese out of the Moluccas and gained control over the Indonesian Archipelago. The Dutch East Indies Company, although initially established as a regulated company in 1599, was reformed in 1602 at the behest of the Republic's government,

---

[18] Ehrenberg, *Capital and Finance,* pp. 244–50.
[19] Ibid., pp. 252–55.
[20] Ramsay, *The Queen's Merchants,* pp. 153–90 passim.

correctly believing that this step would facilitate capital concentration and enhance the Company's capacity to compete overseas.[21]

One factor helping to ensure the success of the Dutch trading enterprise were the steps taken to reconcile the interests of shareholders and managers. The Dutch Company's charter, for instance, promised dividends as soon as goods were sold in order to encourage subscriptions in this unprecedented long-term venture. To allay fears about agent honesty the Company was required to sell all its assets and distribute its proceeds once every decade. But by 1612, a finer appreciation, on the part of management and government officials, of the heavy capital requirements of their great venture led to an exemption from the decennial liquidation mandate. Instead, recognition of the need to maintain a substantial, permanent investment induced these leaders to restrict the payment of dividends during the period 1610–20 to 150 percent of the original equity invested. Although many shareholders were dissatisfied, the company's overseas successes attested to the wisdom of these measures. Moreover, this experience had clearly demonstrated that high returns were achievable through the formation of complex administrative organizations capable of managing operations of great scale and scope.[22]

The privileged status of the East India Company and formal steps taken to diminish uncertainties about its affairs also calmed the anxieties of some investors with high aversions to risk taking by the purchase of shares traded on the Amsterdam Exchange. Like its English counterpart, the Dutch Company maintained an important public franchise, which, besides its endowment with monopoly rights, operated with the presumption that its interests would be protected in the highest councils of state. Investors benefited from mandatory periodic accounting that provided information about its financial position. The English and the

---

[21] Charles H. Wilson, *Anglo-Dutch Commerce and Finance in the Eighteenth Century,* reprint ed. (New York: Arno, 1941, 1977), pp. 3–16; Neal, *The Rise of Financial Capitalism,* pp. 118–40; Glamann, *Dutch–Asiatic Trade,* pp. 1–11; and Femme Gaastra, "The Shifting Balance of Trade of the Dutch East India Company," in Blusse' and Gaastra, eds., *Companies and Trade,* pp. 47–69. See also Braudel, *Civilization and Capitalism,* vol. 2, pp. 100–106, for the formation of Amsterdam exchange.

[22] Glamann, *Dutch–Asiatic Trade,* pp. 2–6; Gaastra, "Dutch East India Company," pp. 49–53; and Heckscher, *Mercantilism,* vol. 1, pp. 368–70.

Dutch policies allowing public access to auction sales of landed merchandise provided unambiguous signals about corporate financial performance. However, it is important to note that although English shares
were transferable, a secondary market for these securities similar to the
one in Amsterdam did not begin to thrive in London until the 1680s.

The existence of a secondary market in Amsterdam also encouraged
speculation. Ironically, the problem of asymmetric information about
firm affairs or world conditions may have emboldened some to pursue
speculative profits. Corporate managers and the overseers elected to
monitor firm operations in the interest of regional shareholders had
access to privileged information, which they may have used personally
or shared with close associates or important constituents. In addition,
the town's large community of Portuguese Jewish merchants, who,
through their private correspondence with relatives or business associates overseas, were knowledgeable about foreign political and economic developments, capitalized on this information by market speculation. Finally, unscrupulous individuals tried to manipulate the
market by fabricating false information through bogus missives from
foreign agents or through untruthful reports from scout boats about
the impending arrival of trading fleets.[23]

The development of hedging techniques for financial assets could
help diminish risk. In Amsterdam, shares could be traded on margin
or by the use of put and call options. This enhanced market liquidity
and reduced transactions costs by providing the means to trade securities and to avoid the expensive and time-consuming registration procedures required of cash sales. In addition, the risk of holding a share
portfolio could be reduced by hedging in the forward markets. Finally,
forward contracts were easily liquidated at quarterly contango days
by offset or by cash payments for any uncleared balances.[24]

Although the Dutch had laid a strong foundation for forming viable
markets, shifts in the geopolitical balance of Europe by the 1680s led
to the emergence of London as the premier center, and of public

---

[23] For corporate governance, see Glamann, *Dutch–Asiatic Trade*, pp. 2–5; and
Gaastra, "Dutch East India Company," pp. 49–58. For speculation, see Wilson, *Anglo-Dutch Commerce*, pp. 13–16. For market information and quota-
tions, see Neal, *Rise of Financial Capitalism*, pp. 21–22; and Dickson, *Financial Revolution*, pp. 486–89.
[24] Wilson, *Anglo-Dutch Commerce*, pp. 13–14.

debt instruments as the primary investment vehicle. The vast overseas empire of the Dutch Republic was threatened first by Spain, and later by French–English alliances.[25]

The pressures on the Dutch Republic abated with the acceptance in 1688 of William of Orange as the consort of James II's Protestant daughter Mary by parliamentary leaders who feared the restoration of Catholicism as the state religion. This union began a strong and abiding alliance between the two countries that lasted through most of the eighteenth century. The extension of English naval and military power helped to ensure the preservation of the Dutch state and to protect its overseas colonies from attack by powerful rivals. The English also accorded special status to the Dutch merchant marine by their Navigation Acts, which had severely restricted access of foreign shippers to its ports. The Dutch reciprocated and so supported England's growth as a world power by becoming a major purchaser of English debt issues, which were traded on both the London and the Amsterdam markets. In the following section it is shown that these debt instruments soon surpassed corporate shares as the primary securities that spurred the continued development of impersonal financial markets.[26]

III. The Rise of Public Debt Market in London: First Phase, 1688–1720

The rise of the London financial market was intimately connected with the extraordinary funding requirements of the English government in its prolonged competition with France. This section focuses on four developments that redefined the financial interrelationships between the state and the great "monied" companies during the period 1688–1720. First, successive governmental administrations diversified the national revenue base by broadening the range of taxes. Second, these regimes experimented with the marketing of new types of debt obligations to attract capital from wider circles of investors and to achieve a smoother synchronization of the inflow of tax receipts with the out-

---

[25] Ernest John Knapton, *Europe, 1450–1815* (New York: Scribner, 1958), pp. 312–13 and 317 for Anglo-Dutch conflicts and pp. 244 and 343 for war with France.

[26] Heckscher, *Mercantilism*, vol. 1, pp. 34–44; and Wilson, *England's Apprenticeship,* pp. 163–65 and 263–67.

flow of interest and principal payments. Third, the standardization of public debt contracts and the vast expansion of the outstanding amounts provided a strong basis for robust market growth. Served by a growing host of jobbers, brokers, underwriters and other financial specialists, these emergent markets supplied liquidity and provided uniform pricing for these investment securities. Finally, the national leadership was convinced that state power could be preserved only if, during periods of peace, substantial amounts of war debt were paid off. Thus, self-liquidating borrowing schemes or plans for converting public debt into private equity received great attention. In fact, it was the failure of the South Sea Company to attain this latter objective in 1720 that marks the end of this first epoch in finance and the transition to new ideas about how best to fund affairs of state.

The revenue sources of the English monarchy before 1688 were generally insufficient to meet its expenditures. For most of the seventeenth century the primary sources of funds came from rents and sales of royal lands, customs duties and a variety of excise and personalty taxes. In addition, the Crown exacted substantial fees from managing the estates of minors and from the imposition of fines. Money was also raised from the sale of peerages, of dispensations from particular regulations and of monopolies. Moreover, the state could exercise the power of purveyance, which allowed its agents to seize goods deemed vital for effective governance at prices below those prevailing in the market. However, periodic deficits resulting from the failure of these channels to provide sufficient funds induced the Crown to resort to the coercion of forced loans from the monied interests.[27]

The failure of the Stuart regimes to service adequately their outstanding debts created additional financial and political problems. Periodic insolvencies resulted from the failure to arrange manageable debt amortization schedules; the ability of the Crown to repay was often undercut by the rapid compounding of both principal and interest. The tendency of the monarchy to alter unilaterally the terms of its borrowing contributed to the mounting alienation of many within the nation's propertied classes.[28]

By the end of the seventeenth century some relief from these chronic

---

[27] North and Weingast, "English Institutional Evolution," pp. 808–12.

[28] See the discussion in Chapter 1, this volume, concerning the financial problems encountered by Edward III. For problems of Stuart monarchs, see Wil-

and dangerous deficits had come from the widening of the tax base and the introduction of new short-term debt obligations. As early as 1636, a temporary land tax to satisfy the critical financing requirements of the navy was revived during the Dutch wars and made permanent by the Land Tax Act of 1677. In addition, excise taxes first imposed by the Parliament during the Civil War in 1643 were continued by subsequent regimes. The excises on staples, clothing and industrial raw materials were earmarked for the payment of specific debt obligations. After the Restoration, government officials tried to lessen the state's reliance on the powerful tax farmers by forming administrative commissions to collect tax receipts and by issuing tax anticipation obligations. These debts took the form of Exchequer tallies (i.e., assignable receipts of indebtedness imprinted on wood) and bills and debentures issued by various departments such as the army and the navy and their ancillary services. Although these arrangements did bolster the Treasury's financing capacities, the developing system experienced a severe setback in 1672, after Charles II's regime had exceeded a serviceable level of short-term borrowing. This led to the embarrassing "Stop of the Exchequer," which bankrupted many of the goldsmith-bankers who held much of this debt.[29]

After 1688, the burdens of state finance induced English leaders to follow the Dutch practice of financing by long-term debt instruments. During the two decades after 1690, Britain borrowed long-term £24 million through self-liquidating tontines, lotteries and annuity contracts. In contrast, although during this period the short-term debt of the Exchequer and the administrative departments rose sharply from £452 thousand to £11.467 million (exclusive of the £3.349 million in current borrowing by the East India Company), the short-term debt came to about half of the long-term total.[30]

---

son, *England's Apprenticeship*, pp. 84–107. For financial difficulties associated with the policies of Louis XIV, see Treasure, *Seventeenth Century France*, pp. 431–42. For a comparison of England and France in the seventeenth century, see Dickson, *Financial Revolution*, pp. 39–40.

[29] Dickson, *Financial Revolution*, pp. 42–46 and 341–43; Wilson, *England's Apprenticeship*, pp. 89–107 and 206–16; Kindleberger, *Financial History of Western Europe*, pp. 50–51.

[30] Dickson, *Financial Revolution*, pp. 39–75, and for the volume of outstanding short-dated securities, see also pp. 526–27. Wilson, *England's Apprenticeship*, pp. 216–25.

The new finance affected the state in many ways. This experience encouraged the cultivation of cooperative relationships between the Treasury and the City's monied interests. Lacking substantial administrative resources and a large cadre of knowledgeable bureaucrats, the voluntary service of seasoned and patriotic merchants and bankers proved invaluable. Furthermore, extensive experimentation with various types of debt yielded valuable insights to Treasury officials about consumer preferences for particular contractual terms, interrelationships between long- and short-term borrowing and the importance of a stable currency in attracting foreign capital. Moreover, the government was able to avoid insolvency by establishing manageable debt-servicing plans while at the same time concentrating unprecedented amounts of capital in selected areas. The high volume of debt was sufficient to support the formation of viable financial markets. Government debt represented a central core of liabilities that was above suspicion – or effectively risk-free. The debt served as a base that allowed riskier issues to be dealt with. In addition, because these credit instruments were readily salable in markets, such as London and Amsterdam, that attracted foreign investors, they were effective vehicles for drawing in foreign wealth and thereby bound the economic interests of overseas investors with those of the English state. Finally, since these obligations could be used to collateralize borrowing, they also had the potential to serve as financial stimuli to national economic growth.[31]

The new finance was also successful because it resolved investor concerns about risk and agency relationships. The riskiness of the Exchequer's long-term and most of its short-term borrowing remained low because of the assignment of the receipts from particular excises and tariffs to the servicing of these issues. In addition, the unsecured debentures and bills of the administrative departments, although riskier, were supported by the guarantee of the state rather than the personal credit of a particular monarch. The promise of fixed income payments diminished uncertainties about prospective income streams that confronted investors in private enterprises. The standardization of debt contracts and the mounting outstanding balances facilitated

---

[31] Wilson, *England's Apprenticeship*, pp. 219–25 and 313–36; and Dickson, *Financial Revolution*, pp. 57–58 and 304–11. See also Braudel, *Civilization and Capitalism*, vol. 2, pp. 542–49.

the formation of secondary markets capable of ensuring uniform pricing and providing investment liquidity. Fixed-interest governmental obligations represented a more attractive store of value than the coinage, which was so debased that it had to be reminted in 1696.[32] Moreover, securities issued by a large and powerful island state like England may have seemed more attractive as safe havens for Continental investors than centers that were more vulnerable either to domestic political upheavals or to the threats of external aggression by bordering states. The leadership of commercial and banking interests in directing state fiscal policy made England more attractive for the placement of savings than France or Spain, whose absolutist regimes adhered more to chivalric than to mercantile imperatives. After Spain's decline and France's political instability in the aftermath of the wars of religion and the revolt of the nobility – the Fronde of 1648 – England represented not only security but a far sounder and more mature, knowledgeable center for banking, fiscal and monetary practices.[33]

The magnitude of outstanding debt and the worrisome prospect that state prerogatives might be curtailed by foreign creditors at a moment of great national stress motivated government leaders to devise new means for enlisting the great monopoly companies as allies in ambitious schemes for debt retirement. The primary practice, known as "engraftment," involved the trading of state debt obligations held by the public for the equity shares of these companies. The swap provided the accommodating company with a substantial fund of credit, which, as we have seen in the case of the East India Company, could be collateralized to support business expansion. The state benefited by concentrating debt in a single institution that could be induced to accept lower interest rates and less stringent repayment schedules in return for the grant of particular privileges that bolstered its ability to make profits.[34]

The pioneer in this new approach to debt clearance was the Bank

[32] Braudel, *Civilization and Capitalism*, vol. 2, pp. 57–58; and Wilson, *England's Apprenticeship*, pp. 220–21.

[33] Treasure, *Seventeenth Century France*, pp. 187–99 for the Fronde and pp. 369–442 for the effects of that period's foreign wars. For early stock trading in London, see Braudel, *Civilization and Capitalism*, vol. 2, pp. 106–110.

[34] Scott, *Joint-Stock Companies*, vol. 1, pp. 396–97.

of England, which launched its initial engraftment operation in 1697, the final year of King William's War. At this point the English government had exceeded its capacity to service its short-term debt from its tax funds. To avoid a repetition of a crisis similar to the Estoppel of 1672, the Whig chancellor of the Exchequer, Sidney Godolfin, persuaded Parliament to allow the Bank to increase its share capital and to trade its additional equity interest for short-term government debt and the financial institution's own notes (in a ratio of 4:1); about £800,000, or 17 percent, of the existing short-term debt was quickly taken off the market. Those who had accepted this arrangement received a permanent equity in the Bank and the prospect of future dividends. The Bank benefited (a) from its expanded role as a repository for tax and loan receipts, (b) from fees earned for assisting the government in transferring funds overseas and for the payment of interest on various debt issues and (c) from the knowledge it often gained of future Treasury intentions. The timing of this novel plan was propitious, coming as it did before the signing of the Treaty of Ryswick, which ended the war (and its extraordinary demands on the English Treasury).[35]

The Bank's success soon encouraged more ambitious conversions. Toward the end of the costly War of the Spanish Succession (1701–14), the subsequent Tory regime of Prime Minister Robert Harley, later earl of Oxford, and chancellor of the Exchequer Henry St. John applied the engraftment technique to clear the market of a heavy burden of government short-term obligations. However, the refinancing of 1711 was undertaken by the South Sea Company which had been organized by leading Tories with this purpose in mind. John Blunt's scheme was to take over a part of the national debt by exchanging government obligations, bonds and debentures for shares of stock in the Company, promising to pay large dividends in the short term.[36]

---

[35] Clapham, *Bank of England,* vol. 1, pp. 46–50; Dickson, *Financial Revolution,* pp. 56–57; and Scott, *Joint-Stock Companies,* vol. 1, pp. 349–52, and vol. 3, pp. 208–20.

[36] Dickson, *Financial Revolution,* pp. 90–121; Scott, *Joint-Stock Companies,* vol. 1, pp. 389–99; John Carswell, *The South Sea Bubble,* revised ed. (Stroud: Sutton, 1960, 1993), chaps. 3–4 passim; John G. Sperling, *The South Sea Company: An Historical Essay and Biographical Finding List* (Boston: Harvard Graduate School of Business Administration, 1962), pp. 1–14.

To induce creditors to trade their claims on the government for South Sea shares, the Company was granted a monopoly over English trade with South America. Its prospects brightened when the right to operate the Asiento, the African slave trade to Latin America, was granted to the Company as a provision of the Treaty of Utrecht which ended the war. In addition, the government agreed to pay a £8 thousand annual management fee and £586 thousand in annual interest for the £9.5 million of debt it had exchanged for shares. Although economic circumstances compelled the Company to declare only stock and bond dividends to conserve cash, eventually the conversion operation proved successful. Like the Bank of England's earlier engraftment, this effort benefited greatly from the incipient armistice and from the diminishment of pressure on the national Treasury.[37]

After the signing of the Treaty of Utrecht, England and France escalated their efforts to retire their war debts. They feared that excessive debt would undermine state sovereignty and lead inexorably to the subordination of important national interests to the dominion of major foreign creditors. This specter made many leaders in these two nations receptive to new plans for employing the innovative engraftment techniques of the Bank and the South Sea Company on a grander scale.[38]

Although the English had been first in the field, the French, guided by the Scottish financier John Law, began a gigantic experiment to retire war debt in 1719–20. John Law was the son of a wealthy goldsmith-banker and a distant cousin of the financially astute John Campbell, second duke of Argyll. As a young man Law was apparently tutored in monetary affairs by his London landlord and mentor, Thomas Neale, who, besides serving as a master of the mint, was a confidential adviser to Charles Montagu of the Bank of England. Neale's acumen was evidenced by his roles as an architect of the "Million Adventure," the first national lottery in 1694, and possibly as a developer of the Exchequer bills that, beginning in 1696, served as the first form of national paper currency. Law learned Continental

<hr>

[37] Dickson, *Financial Revolution,* pp. 65–71 and 93–94; Carswell, *South Sea Bubble,* pp. 40–41 and 54–57; and Sperling, *South Sea Company,* pp. 14–26 passim.

[38] Carswell, *South Sea Bubble,* chapt. 5 passim; Scott, *Joint-Stock Companies,* vol. 1, pp. 397–400; and Dickson, *Financial Revolution,* pp. 91–92.

financial practice firsthand in 1695, when he was forced to flee to Amsterdam after participating in a fatal duel. There he prospered by amassing a substantial personal fortune through shrewd speculation. A brilliant economist and mathematician, Law wrote a pamphlet in 1705 extolling the use of paper money entitled "Money and Trade Considered," in which he equated money in circulation with the country's prosperity.[39]

In 1716, Law persuaded the regent, Philip, duke of Orleans, to grant him permission to set up a Banque Generale, a plan that had previously been proposed by Colbert and the banker Samuel Bernard but that had proved unacceptable to Louis XIV. After the death of the king in 1715, France was in desperate financial straits, plagued by chronic shortages of specie in circulation, high inflation, an unstable currency, the louis d'or, which was prone to speculative fluctuation, and a lack of domestic investment. Law's plan called for paper money converted into bank notes to help reduce the huge war debts, refill the depleted treasury and increase the money supply in circulation. The ultimate objective of these monetary reforms was to reduce French interest rates to about 2 percent, a level that Law reasoned would ensure the full utilization of national economic resources and prosperity. The public's acceptance of Law's bank notes was due to their convertibility into fixed quantities of gold, which stabilized the debased French coinage. Within a few months Law received a mandate that required the *fermiers generaux,* the wealthy landowner tax collectors, to pay their taxes to the treasury in bank notes. Since 1704 the louis d'or had suffered a series of devaluations that provoked heavy speculation (*agiotage*) in gold and paper currency. The famine of 1709 and subsequent inflation in grain prices had depleted the state's revenues. The French merchant class tended to hoard gold and silver and, feeling marginalized, refused to invest in state ventures.[40]

---

[39] H. Montgomery Hyde, *John Law: The History of an Honest Adventurer* (London: Home & Van Thal, 1948), pp. 7–56 passim; and Kindleberger, *Financial History of Western Europe*, pp. 96–97.

[40] Hyde, *John Law,* pp. 79–86; Kindleberger, *Financial History of Western Europe,* p. 97; and Carswell, *South Sea Bubble,* pp. 68–70. See also Antoin E. Murphy, *Richard Cantillon: Entrepreneur and Economist* (Oxford: Clarendon Press, 1986), pp. 68–73. For a discussion of *fermiers generaux* and a background to state finance in seventeenth century France, see Braudel, *Civilization and Capitalism,* vol. 2, pp. 537–42.

The significance of Law's scheme lay in demonstrating the limits of joint-stock equity conversions as a means for reducing onerous public debt levels. Reviving the poorly managed and insolvent Compagnie des Indes (also known as the Mississippi Company), Law sought to sponsor emigration to the Americas, acquire control and monopoly of all tobacco concessions and control trade in the East Indies, China and Senegal. The French trading company founded in 1664 by Colbert, unlike its English and Dutch counterparts, never succeeded. Between the 1660s and the 1680s the company lost its state-granted monopoly and suffered from a lack of cooperation between the monarchy and the merchants, as well as a lack of a regulatory system like the English Board of Trade to protect the merchant's interests.[41]

Law continued to consolidate a strong position in French finance. In 1718 he extended his influence by gaining the exclusive rights to mint coins and to collect taxes on behalf of the state. He also ingratiated himself with the corrupt regent by converting his private bank to the Banque Royale and became the Controller of the Realm. From this powerful position Law sought to create a new financial order to release the untapped potential that he believed existed in the French economy.[42]

Law's plans for rationalizing the French public debt moved ahead in the fall of 1719. Under this scheme the government agreed to pay 3 percent interest annually on that portion of its 1,500 million livres in outstanding debt that the Compagnie des Indes was able to trade for its equity. Any government securities acquired, besides providing a steady source of interest income, could be collateralized to support loans to finance the Compagnie's overseas expansion. Simultaneously, Law sought to build up the enterprise's capital surplus account by manipulating the market value of its shares so that it sold at a premium over the par value of the debt acquired. The Bank of England and the South Sea Company had earlier made use of this sort of arbitrage. Because of his dominance over much of French finance and commerce, Law was better positioned to inflate the value of the Compagnie des Indes's stock. He relied on the relatively simple expedient of margin sales, a drastic

---

[41] Hyde, *John Law*, pp. 86–89 and 101–102; Murphy, *Richard Cantillon*, pp. 67–79; and Carswell, *South Sea Bubble*, pp. 70–71.
[42] Hyde, *John Law*, pp. 96–100; Kindleberger, *Financial History of Western Europe*, p. 97; and Carswell, *South Sea Bubble*, pp. 71–72.

expansion of the money supply and the production through effective propaganda of what Keynes later termed "animal spirits" among shareholders from all social classes, from aristocrats to valets, who swarmed into the Rue Quincampoix, where Law resided, to buy shares and make quick fortunes. Paris was overcome by a speculative frenzy that broke down class and rank barriers.[43]

Purchasers were required to advance only a 10 percent margin, the balance payable in nineteen monthly installments. The potential dilutive effects of issuing several consecutive classes of shares in stages to finance the conversion were diminished by requiring that prospective purchasers first establish predetermined positions in existing issues before buying into any new subscriptions. In addition, the Banque Royale, dominated by Law, assisted by expanding the money supply through the issuance of 800 million livres in notes during the first half of 1719. The impact of these actions on equity values was spectacular; the price of 500 livre par value shares of the Compagnie des Indes rose to 10,100 livres by November 1719.[44]

Law's success prompted British political leaders, who feared that France might be catapulted ahead by its refinancing, to support similar proposals advanced by their own South Sea Company. In 1719, after a second modest success in exchanging annuity contracts paying £135 thousand per annum in interest for its shares, South Sea's directors began to promote an ambitious plan to convert three large classes of long-term debt obligations with a value of £31 million. Most problematic to state finance were two classes of irredeemable annuities issued during wartime with interest rates much higher than the 4–5 percent prevailing in 1720. One annuity, aggregating £15 million, matured in 72–87 years and paid 7 percent per annum; the other, aggregating £1.5 million, matured in twenty-two years and paid 9 percent per annum. Besides the annuities, there was outstanding £16.5 million in redeemable loan stock that was less burdensome because its interest rates were periodically adjusted to declining market levels.[45]

---

[43] Scott, *Joint-Stock Companies,* vol. 1, pp. 399–403; Murphy, *Richard Cantillon,* pp. 127–32; and Hyde, *John Law,* pp. 102–109.

[44] Scott, *Joint-Stock Companies,* vol. 1, pp. 404–405; Murphy, *Richard Cantillon,* pp. 127–31 and 151; and Hyde, *John Law,* pp. 109–31.

[45] Dickson, *Financial Revolution,* pp. 80–89 and 90–105; Scott, *Joint-Stock Companies,* vol. 1, pp. 405–408; Carswell, *South Sea Bubble,* pp. 75–76 and 85–90; and Sperling, *South Sea Company,* pp. 26–29.

108

The refunding plan offered substantial advantages to the English government and to the managers and shareholders of the South Sea Company. From the government's perspective there were five principal benefits. First, the refunding would consolidate £31.5 million in various long-term debt issues into the hands of a single enterprise whose management maintained intimate ties with the Tory administration. Besides creating a powerful corporate ally for the incumbent regime, a vigorous South Sea Company would provide valuable assistance to the state in advancing any future plans directed toward extending overseas trade or colonizing activities. Indeed, the enterprise used this opportunity to lay claim (unsuccessfully) to the privileges previously accorded to the Whig-sponsored Bank of England and the East India Company as a precondition of its debt-refunding proposal. Second, the recasting of the public debt promised to reduce the government's interest charges by a projected maximum of £542 thousand per annum. This was especially appealing to Tory landowners who had long borne a heavy property tax burden. Third, the South Sea Company contracted to pay substantial fees for the right to manage the refunding, agreeing to remit from £4–7.4 million, depending on how much of the total debt was exchanged and to maintain a permanent investment of £1 million in Exchequer bills. Fourth, the refunding was to serve as a stimulant to the British economy by accelerating a reduction in interest rates and taxes and by creating a pool of governmental securities to serve as collateral in financing future business expansion. Finally, the proposal reduced the administrative costs of servicing the national debt by allowing the government to deal with one large creditor rather than many small ones.[46]

The primary advantage of the refinancing for the South Sea Company was that it provided a new lease on its economic life. The hopes raised in 1711 about the potentials for trade had never materialized. The Company's penetration of the Latin American markets had been frustrated by uncooperative Spanish colonial administrators. Consequently, the Company eagerly pursued the new opportunity to establish a sizable fund of credit that could bolster profits through interest and fee income and gains on debt conversion. Such a prospect would

---

[46] Dickson, *Financial Revolution*, pp. 93–105; and Carswell, *South Sea Bubble*, pp. 85–90.

enhance the enterprise's financial flexibility and its capacity to diversify into more promising businesses.[47]

But the uncertainties about the Company's future influenced the definition of the formula to be applied for inducing the exchange of high-quality annuities and bonds for more dubious equity shares. The stratagem the Company selected was to inflate the market value of its equity and to structure an exchange that would yield an immediate and substantial capital gain for contract holders. To enhance the attractiveness of the conversion, the Company agreed to purchase long-term annuities at thirty-two years' purchase and short-term annuities at seventeen years' purchase rather than the twenty- and fourteen-year terms that Parliament believed was fair recompense. Moreover, if the market value of the shares issued to finance the conversion was at a high premium over their £100 par value, the Company would have to issue only a fraction of the total authorized by Parliament. A market price of £400 would require the exchange of only one-quarter of the total authorized shares. The remaining unissued shares could be used to pay stock dividends or be sold to the public for cash. The potentially dilutive effects of this latter policy, however, did not rank foremost among the concerns of the Company's principals.[48]

The inflation of share values was necessary for other reasons. Rising prices ensured the successful outcome of the secret share purchase compacts the Company entered into with members of the royal circle and of Parliament, whose influence was thought crucial in maintaining state support. In addition, the opportunity to sell additional shares from the capital surplus created by the exchange would increase the Company's ability to pay the high fees it had promised the government.[49]

To effect a successful conversion, the South Sea's leadership used many devices to inflate share prices. Like John Law, they placed a heavy reliance on margin sales; in four subscriptions during the period from April to August 1720, they sold shares on 10–20 percent margins, requiring the balances to be paid off in two to nine monthly installments. Second, the Company accepted shares and scrip on new

---

[47] Carswell, *South Sea Bubble*, pp. 54–57 and 64; Sperling, *South Sea Company*, pp. 20–24; and Scott, *Joint-Stock Companies*, vol. 1, pp. 408–409.
[48] Sperling, *South Sea Company*, pp. 28–30.
[49] Ibid., pp. 28–29.

subscriptions as collateral for loans to speculators. Third, management encouraged exaggerated reports about future profitability in newspapers, journals and broadsheets. One example of this was the promise made (when the share price was beginning to falter during August 1720) that a 50 percent dividend would be paid in each of the next twelve years. Fourth, with the support of their political allies, the Bubble Act (11 June 1720) was enacted and placed severe restrictions on the formation of new joint-stock companies and on disenfranchised business entities no longer engaged in activities authorized under their original charters. The intent of this was to reduce the number of enterprises that would compete with the South Sea Company in the London market for investment capital.[50]

Setbacks encountered by John Law in implementing his ambitious plans motivated many speculators to abandon the Compagnie des Indes during the spring of 1720 and to move their treasure to the bull market gaining momentum in London. Law, who had become concerned about the inflation caused by his monetary policies, had tried unsuccessfully to check speculation by temporarily closing the Paris bourse in February and by restricting gold trading. Although he was soon forced to relax these measures by the regent, many interpreted this as a signal of impending crisis and began to liquidate speculative balances in Paris. By the spring of 1720 it became clear that the speculators had no intention of actually taking part in the emigration to the Mississippi region sponsored by the Compagnie des Indes. Emigration to the American southwest had remained largely limited to forced deportations of convicts and undesirables, as described in Prevost's *Manon Lescaut* and Daniel Defoe's *Moll Flanders*. By early summer of 1720, two of the most influential shareholders, the Prince de Conti and the Prince de Conde, asked to be reimbursed in full in gold, causing a desperate run, since the Banque Royale had paper shares for 3 million covered by reserves of less than 500,000 in gold. By June 1720 the plague hit Marseilles, and a general sense of fear and loss of confidence forced the prices of shares to tumble.[51]

---

[50] Ibid., pp. 26–32; Scott, *Joint-Stock Companies,* vol. 1, pp. 405–16; Dickson, *Financial Revolution,* pp. 123–49; Carswell, *South Sea Bubble,* pp. 108–16; and Neal, *Rise of Financial Capitalism,* pp. 77–80.

[51] Hyde, *John Law,* pp. 125–47 passim. See also Daniel Defoe, *Moll Flanders* (New York: Dutton, 1977); Murphy, *Richard Cantillon,* pp. 132–39 and 148–

The interplay of these factors led to a spectacular run up in South Sea's share value and to the conversion of much of England's long-term debt. Share prices rose from £128 on 1 January 1720, to £335 by 2 May, peaking at £1,050 on 24 June. In all, 85 percent of the redeemables and 80 percent of the irredeemables had been tendered. This operation increased the nominal capital of the South Sea Company by £26 million, of which £17.5 million represented the surplus resulting from the high premium on shares sold. £10 million of this capital surplus was later reissued in the form of new shares at higher prices, which when fully paid would have drawn in £75 million. This handsome bounty was more than enough to pay off the £17.5 million promised to the government in fees and purchase of short-term securities.[52]

But the South Sea's financing plans began to crumble in the summer of 1720 in the midst of a growing financial panic. A deterioration in the credit markets was first evidenced by the rise in the price of gold and a fall in the exchange rate for the pound. Gold exports increased as speculators transferred funds overseas when the enforcement of the Bubble Act threatened to reduce the number of joint-stock enterprises whose shares could be traded in England. Share prices declined in London as speculative balances were drawn to the new joint-stock flotations being sponsored on the less restrictive Amsterdam bourse. In addition, pressure mounted on London shares as the Paris bourse began a short-lived rally on the disturbing misinformation that John Law's financial designs had achieved their ambitious objective of reviving the French economy. The faltering London market contributed to the erosion of the price of South Sea Company shares during late summer as speculators anticipated that a continued decline would have an effect on the Company's overextended finances. At that time it had substantial subscription receivables whose collection was doubtful because the contract price was higher than the market value of the shares. To stave off a liquidity crisis, the South Sea Company arranged for the Bank of England to support its stock at £400 per share and to

53; and Abbé Prevost d'exiles, *The Story of Manon Lescaut and the Chevalier des Grieux* (New York: Heritage, 1935).
[52] Dickson, *Financial Revolution,* pp. 121–44; Neal, *Rise of Financial Capitalism,* pp. 89–112; and Sperling, *South Sea Company,* pp. 30–32.

hold a large issue of its bonded indebtedness. This line of defense, however, collapsed on 24 September when the Bank of England reneged after the closure of the Sword Blade Bank, the South Sea's primary funds repository. At this point the shares dropped to £190 per share and the growing public uproar forced Parliamentary leaders to begin an extensive investigation and to intervene in management of the Company.[53]

The crisis in the London share market was soon transmitted to other European financial centers. During October, after much effort to check inflation by systematically withdrawing its bank notes from circulation, the Banque Royale became insolvent and closed its doors. This shocking event led to the crash of the Paris share market and to the end of the national currency that France had hoped would create stability for its state finances. In November the bubble burst in Amsterdam, bringing to an end an epoch in which corporate enterprises were viewed as logical and useful adjuncts to state finance.[54]

IV. Aftermath of Crisis: The Second Stage of Financial Development, 1721–1815

The watershed of 1720 had different repercussions on the development of finance in France and England. In France this disruption delayed the growth of broad, impersonal securities markets until the 1830s and installed a profound distrust of all speculative activities due to the combined impact of the collapse of the national currency and the inability of major trading companies to maintain their market value. Under Law's attempt to control the system, it was virtually impossible for French investors looking for gains in domestic financial

[53] Dickson, *Financial Revolution*, pp. 144–53; Carswell, *South Sea Bubble*, pp. 151–53; Neal, *Rise of Financial Capitalism*, pp. 112–17; and Sperling, *South Sea Company*, pp. 31–34.

[54] Dickson, *Financial Revolution*, pp. 153–56. See also Kindleberger, *Manias, Panics and Crashes*, pp. 134–35, for international transmission of the shock caused by the collapse of the South Sea's bubble. See also Murphy, *Richard Cantillon*, chaps. 8–9, for the experience of a successful speculator who capitalized on the rise of share prices and the financial crises it eventually engendered in Paris, London and Amsterdam.

assets to reduce risk through diversification. Thus, when currency devalued and shares crashed simultaneously, France felt a much more severe repercussion than England, where investors had greater opportunities to reduce risk by allocating their capital among investment securities of many business institutions. Although the Bank of England, the East India Company and other great enterprises were shaken by this crisis, they survived and thereby preserved the wealth of many investors. Nor did the debacle in England seriously undermine the viability of the national currency. Whereas the English Parliament intervened to uphold sterling, the French government did not provide any monetary guidelines or support.[55]

France remained locked into a quasi-feudal economic system of rank, rights and privileges for its nobility but did not have a tradition of mutual responsibility toward the state. Rendered powerless and excluded from all commercial activities by the dictates of Louis XIV, France's nobility continued to live off the public treasury. While the dynamic merchant class remained frustrated and disdained, French commerce through the eighteenth century remained in the hands of small family firms and limited partnerships, whose members were by reason of their birth able to perpetuate their wealth. In France joint-stock societies and large merchant companies did not take hold until the 1840s. The basis of wealth was ownership of land rather than financial assets, which remained tainted with Catholic interdictions and societal contempt. The few private banks were often of non-Catholic and even non-French origins. The French treasury had to turn to Swiss financiers and Geneva bankers to float bond issues and rescue the economy. After the Law fiasco, France turned antitrade and antimarket, reflected in the Physiocrat economic school of thought, where philosophers and writers like Quesnay and Mirabeau advocated protectionist policies, rejecting trade, corporations and market speculation as contrary to the interests of the state. Thus, because of the

---

[55] Hyde, *John Law,* pp. 134–47; Dickson, *Financial Revolution,* pp. 157–76 and 177–98 passim; Sperling, *South Sea Company,* pp. 33–38; and Carswell, *South Sea Bubble,* chapt. 12 passim. Kindleberger, *Manias, Panics and Crashes,* pp. 232–38, argues that the successful role played by the Bank of England as a lender of last resort lessened the dislocation resulting from the collapse of the bubble and that the more severe adjustment experienced in France was due to the lack of a strong national financial institution that was capable of dissipating the shock experienced from the collapse of the Compagnie des Indes.

relative underdevelopment of financial institutions, the costs of capital remained generally higher in France than in Britain.[56]

Although the French financial market (the bourse was established in 1726 in Paris) would never equal the scope of London's, by 1860 France became England's sole competitor in global money markets, foreign investment and shareholder enterprises. But France had to suffer total dismantling of its political and economic base before accepting economic modernization and establishing a strong, well-defined synergy between industry, finance and government. Between 1789 and 1814 France saw a large portion of its liquid assets smuggled out of the country. The French Revolution of 1789–95 came about in part because the monarchy and the legislative assemblies did not respond to the economic crisis and refused to correct fiscal abuses. Through the 1750s finance ministers who espoused different monetary policies all called for a central bank. From Necker to Calonne to Mirabeau, French economists understood the need to centralize the financial and monetary policies, yet they never succeeded in creating such a mechanism. As late as the winter of 1790, Necker, Louis XVI's last finance minister, desperately tried to establish credit facilities and

---

[56] Treasure, *Seventeenth Century France,* pp. 431–34 and 437–42; and Kindleberger, *Financial History of Western Europe,* pp. 96–103. For discussion of the ideas of the Physiocrats, see John H. Randall, Jr., *The Career of Philosophy,* 2 vols. (New York: Columbia University Press, 1962–65), vol. 1, pp. 940–84 passim; and Roland N. Stromberg, *An Intellectual History of Modern Europe,* 2nd ed. (Englewood Cliffs, N.J.: Prentice-Hall, 1975), pp. 167–71. For the later emergence of joint-stock enterprises in France, see John E. Freedeman, *Joint-Stock Enterprises in France, 1807–1867: From Privileged Company to Modern Corporation* (Chapel Hill: University of North Carolina Press, 1979). For the role of notaries as agents of financial intermediation in private finance, see Philip T. Hoffman, Gilles Postel-Vinay and Jean-Laurent Rosenthal, "Private Credit Markets in Paris, 1690–1840," *Journal of Economic History* 52 (June 1992): 293–306; and idem, "Redistribution and Long-Term Private Debt in Paris, 1660–1726," in ibid., 55 (June 1995): 256–84. For the problems of finance, governmental administration and politics, see Francois R. Velde and David R. Weir, "The Financial Market and Government Debt Policy in France, 1746–1793," in ibid., 52 (March 1992): 1–40; David R. Weir, "Tontines, Public Finance, and Revolution in France and England, 1688–1789," in ibid., 49 (March 1989): 95–124; Eugene Nelson White, "Was There a Solution to the Ancien Regime's Financial Dilemma?" in ibid., 49 (September 1989): 545–68; and idem, "The French Revolution and the Politics of Government Finance, 1770–1815," in ibid., 55 (June 1995): 227–55.

a central bank, only to be vetoed again by the first Legislative Assembly. In 1790 the country had a deficit of 300 million louis d'or and throughout the revolution continued to accrue vast war debts. Ironically, France was a very wealthy country that in part went bankrupt funding the American Revolution and maintaining an unproductive royal welfare state. In 1780 the upkeep of Versailles (with over 15,000 courtiers on its payroll) required a budget equal to half the total budget of all other European courts combined. France had to wait for Napoleon and the establishment of an entirely new economic and political coda to finally achieve a consolidation of credit, commercial and government policies with the creation of the Banque de France in February 1800.[57]

The response to the financial crisis was different in England, where the panic led to state intervention to reorganize rather than liquidate the endangered financial institutions. The South Sea Company was saved from complete liquidation by its portfolio of low-risk governmental securities. The solution imposed was a modification of the terms of sale for the debt tendered, which provided a better matching of the rates and the maturities for assets and liabilities. Investors who had been drawn to the great speculation had reason to carp about the unattractive conversion ratios that the new administration of Prime Minister Robert Walpole forced them to accept; this draconian finance restored order in the credit markets and placed the South Sea Company on a sound financial footing. Although the reorganized entity continued a lackluster foreign trade until 1740, its primary function, henceforth, was to manage a large portfolio of governmental securities, much like a modern-day mutual fund. It operated in this manner until 1855, when its affairs were finally wound up.[58]

---

[57] Knapton, *Europe, 1450–1850*, pp. 566–67; Gordon Wright, *France in Modern Times: From the Enlightenment to the Present*, 2nd ed. (Chicago: Rand McNally, 1960, 1974), pp. 321–37 passim; and Kindleberger, *Financial History of Western Europe*, pp. 100–102. For a discussion of the reasons for Britain's superiority in raising war finance during the Napoleonic period, see Michael D. Bordo and Eugene N. White, "British and French Finance during the Napoleonic Wars," in Michael D. Bordo and Forrest Capie, eds., *Monetary Regimes in Transition* (Cambridge University Press, 1994), pp. 241–73.

[58] Dickson, *Financial Revolution*, pp. 158–76 passim; and Sperling, *South Sea Company*, pp. 38–49.

Although the Parliamentary investigation of the South Sea Bubble focused on incidents of venality among corporate and political leaders, this experience provided instructive insights about the limitations of contemporary institutions to undertake complex financing. What was most striking about this affair was the dearth of well-defined channels of communication and control for coordinating this mammoth task. Investors, for example, had been seduced by rumors, in that details of the conversions were announced after the debt obligations had been tendered for shares; the government's role had been shaped through private dealings that suborned important officials; no effective constraints had been placed on the unstable methods applied to inflate share prices. This is not surprising given the administrative thinness of the British state at this time. Lacking adequate regulatory bodies with clearly defined roles, responsibilities and powers, the relegation of this great authority to private groups clearly ran the risk of being misused through a combination of greed and, perhaps, incompetency due to uncertainty as to what they were dealing with (as it had been in 1720).

Public policy toward joint-stock enterprises became more restrictive after 1720 for reasons that are still being debated by scholars. One aspect of this was doubtless the recognition on the part of British governmental leaders of the shortcomings of state administration in preventing the use of joint stocks as vehicles for promoting fraud, as described earlier. Effective monitoring of corporate finance would have required the elaboration of commercial law and the formation of regulatory bureaucracies – objectives that exceeded the capabilities of a diminutive national executive state that had been willing to sponsor joint-stock formation in the past to augment its own limited power. Instead, government leaders reverted after 1720 to dealing in the old informal ways with a small, manageable circle of enterprises led by individuals of proven reliability. Witness, for example, the establishment of a duopoly in marine insurance in 1720 that was shared by the Royal Exchange Assurance and London Assurance, and the continuance of the Bank of England's monopoly over short-term bill issuance that dated back to 1708.

Recent historiography has cited other reasons for more restrictive governmental policies toward joint-stock formation during this era. Some scholars have argued that the curtailment in company chartering stemmed from a desire of Parliament to protect the significant income that derived from this activity and to safeguard the interests of firms that had previously been endowed with this status. Another scholar, who takes exception to the parliamentary interpretation because it places too much emphasis on the significance of the Bubble Act, argues that the change in policy was conditioned more by the administration of common law. In this latter view the strongest opposition to joint-stock chartering came from the lords justices, acting as regents, who in the summer of 1720 started "to dismiss further petitions, limit the granting of charters in the following years and prosecute abusing charters by *scire facias.*" In any event, whatever the precise proximate causes, the opportunities to form joint-stock companies declined substantially after the collapse of the South Sea Bubble.[59]

The devolution of power to a limited circle of trusted agents was also the pattern followed in establishing a structure of governance for the financial markets. Here there were two fundamental problems. The first was the need for rules to ensure probity among jobbers, brokers and other specialists who maintained market continuity and liquidity. The other was the need to contain disruptive speculative dealing that, during crises, threatened to destroy the stability of the government debt market.

Three steps were taken to regulate the probity of agents in the market. First, legislation in 1697 required brokers to sign written pledges to deal honestly and avoid conflicts of interest with clients. This was coupled with what proved an ineffective mandate requiring the registration of sales and stock transfers with the Bank of England. In 1708, these rules were more sharply defined, and responsibility for market oversight was vested in a committee appointed by the mayor, alderman and sheriffs of the City of London. This legislation tried to ensure fair dealing

---

[59] Dickson, *Financial Revolution,* pp. 147–49; and Bishop Carlton Hunt, *The Development of the Business Corporation in England, 1800–1867* (Cambridge, Mass.: Harvard University Press, 1936), chapt. 1 passim. See also Morgan and Thomas, *The London Stock Exchange,* pp. 29–40 passim. The argument relating to parliamentary prerogatives is put forth in Margaret Patterson and David Reiffen, "The Effect of the Bubble Act on the Market for Joint Stock Shares," *Journal of Economic History* 50 (March 1990): 163–71; and Henry N. Butler, "General Incorporation in Nineteenth Century England: Interaction of Common Law and Legislative Processes," *International Review of Law and Economics* 6 (December 1986): 169–87. For the role of common law in restricting joint-stock company growth, see Ron Harris, "The Bubble Act: Its Passage and Its Effects on Business Organization," *Journal of Economic History* 54 (September 1994): 610–27.

by licensing brokers. But in an ascriptive society whose Parliament was sensitive to the views of the dominant landed aristocracy, good character was often equated with social background. Thus, although this law seems to have been most effective in restricting access to the market by foreign aliens, Jews and members of nonconforming Christian sects, its utility for ensuring honest practice was less certain.[60]

Although concerns about speculation that threatened to disrupt the equilibrium of the financial markets had led to restrictive legislation on particular practices, its impact was minimal. In 1734, after the financial collapse of the York Building Society, option dealing was prohibited, but a legal loophole allowed the continuation of margin sales. But with this sole exception, no further attempts were made to restrict the application of particular market practices. Instead, by the 1770s, a new view emerged that market participants should not be fettered by official monitors but rather should regulate themselves through the rules of the Stock Market. In a market specializing in low-risk securities issued by government and powerful monopolies, the costs of private group self-regulation seemed lower to national leaders than to those in favor of greater state intervention. The growth of broad and flexible markets during the years that followed suggests that these intuitions about regulatory costs were well founded.[61]

The South Sea Company crisis marked a turning point in thinking about the efficacy of trying to retire large amounts of public debt and the usefulness of fund of credit arrangements in public finance. This experience convinced Walpole and his successor that high debt levels could be reduced only gradually. Because the financial markets provided liquidity for the debt holdings of investors, the key to effective public finance depended on efficient policies for servicing rather than retiring debt. In this new context, conversions on a heroic scale, like the ones mounted earlier by the Bank of England and the South Sea Company, seemed less crucial. The vital issue, instead, was to establish an adequate revenue base for paying current interest and the gradual amortization of principal amounts.

The new attitudes toward debt administration were reflected in the

[60] See Dickson, *Financial Revolution,* pp. 486–520, for a detailed discussion of maturation of new stock exchange. See also the discussion of the origins of the markets and the rise of trading in governmental debt in Morgan and Thomas, *The London Stock Exchange,* pp. 58–77 passim.
[61] Dickson, *Financial Revolution,* pp. 516–20.

actions of the chancellor of the Exchequer, Henry Pelham, at the end of the War of the Austrian Succession (1740–48). The national debt had reached £70 million, primarily in ordinary loan stock rather than annuity contracts. In the peace that followed, Pelham concentrated on negotiating a gradual reduction of interest rates and the development of efficient ways for debt servicing. By 1750, he had structured a refunding arrangement that by the end of 1757 lowered Britain's annual interest charges by 25 percent. In addition, debt management was rationalized in 1752 by the creation of "consols," which consolidated into perpetuities over £17 million in various issues that had previously been separately serviced by both the Bank of England and the Exchequer. Besides simplifying record keeping, the consolidation of the debt issues and their associated tax funds enhanced the flexibility and liquidity of the government's debt management.[62]

New fund-raising techniques replaced the practice of engrafting debt in joint-stock companies. One alternative was to rely more on specialized intermediaries like underwriters, who were capable of raising large amounts of capital from wealthy investors at home and abroad; one was Samuel Gideon, who had strong connections both in London and in Amsterdam. By the 1790s prominent underwriting families (such as the Rothschilds) began to play an important role in international finance because of their ability to mobilize large amounts of capital in the major money markets of Europe.[63]

In addition, the Exchequer, usually with the assistance of the Bank of England, began making direct sales of government debt securities to individual investors. This practice was preferred because it insulated government from the demands of powerful underwriters; the government was often able to secure better terms by dealing with many unorganized investors with little negotiating leverage. But this alternative was not always available, especially during times of crisis when the underwriters represented the only certain sources of much-needed funds.[64]

The South Sea Company experience improved the position of those in the British government who believed that full disclosure of prospective financing plans was essential for effective financial markets. Lead-

---

[62] Ibid., pp. 229–45.

[63] Ibid., pp. 222–24, 286, 289, 294 and 450. See also Wilson, *Anglo-Dutch Commerce*, chaps. 4–7 passim, for a discussion of financial interconnections between these nations in the eighteenth century.

[64] Dickson, *Financial Revolution*, pp. 224–28 and 289–90.

ers like Godolfin and Pelham eschewed the practice of withholding information about future refinancing, which had enabled the South Sea Company's sponsors to excite speculative passions. These leaders recognized that the short-term advantages accruing to the state would only destroy public confidence in the government and the markets. Such disclosure did curtail the Exchequer's freedom of action by allowing market participants to react to precise indications of future actions. But these responses were useful gauges of the tolerable limits of fiscal policies, which was crucial information for government ministers who wanted to fund state operations through the financial markets. In these and other ways, national leaders sought to preserve an emergent financial sector that had been highly effective in advancing the interests of the state.[65]

The new restrictive policies toward joint-stock formation also functioned as a powerful mechanism for capital rationing in support of costly national defense priorities. The preponderant economic doctrine of the early eighteenth century was mercantilism, with its emphasis on the symbiotic nexus between home countries specializing in manufacturing and colonial territories specializing in supplying raw materials and staples. But the drive to establish these self-contained regimes continued to draw the leading European powers into conflict throughout the century. Although it was infeasible to erect the administrative structures necessary to direct the sort of command economies that have arisen during wartime in the twentieth century, policy could be implemented in ways that channeled private resources to support national security objectives. Thus, to control the formation of joint-stock companies, government could indirectly limit the ability of private interests to compete for scarce financial capital during a period when heavy costs were being incurred in defending Britain's expanding territories. It is also noteworthy that one highly visible manifestation of government's changed attitude about company formation, the Bubble Act, was not repealed until 1824 well after the defeat of Napoleon and the onset of the great European peace of the nineteenth century.[66]

For one and a half centuries after the Bubble Act new businesses in Britain were organized primarily as either partnerships or joint venture

---

[65] Ibid., pp. 197–98.
[66] Hunt, *The Development of the Business Corporation in England*, pp. 37–45; and Kindleberger, *Financial History of Western Europe*, pp. 196–98.

associations. These forms did not facilitate the concentration of capital into single economic units as had the larger joint stocks (although joint venture associations could issue transferable shares of ownership). Besides lacking the protection of limited liability and the charisma of state-granted monopolies that some joint stocks enjoyed, partnerships and joint ventures found it more difficult to overcome investor foreboding about risk and about the problems of agency relationships. Consequently, they were only moderately successful vehicles for raising capital (which may have slowed the progress of industrialization). A notable exception to the general prohibition was the use of the joint-stock form for carrying on canal building and related enterprises during the mid-eighteenth century. For example, the duke of Bridgewater completed a canal in 1761 that connected the collieries of what then was the small mill town of Manchester with the port of Liverpool. Such deviations were tolerated because of the quasi-public nature and size of the enterprise, as well as the impeccable background of its chief sponsor. Between 1791 and 1794, 81 acts were passed allowing the construction of canals and other aids to navigation in addition to the more than 100 acts that were ratified in the latter half of the century for incorporating various mining and extractive ventures.[67]

V. Conclusion

In what ways does this experience amplify corporate finance theory? How did the financial-institutional innovations of this period contribute to the efficiency of large-scale business enterprises?

Contrary to the underlying assumptions of the modern theory, the financial markets of the eighteenth century were neither perfect nor frictionless. To a greater extent than present-day markets, they had to contend with the problem of high risk in economic affairs and poor information. These imperfect circumstances had a major influence on the types of securities that could form the basis for the establishment of broad, impersonal markets. In this context of uncertainty, government obligations provided the most favorable mix of qualities for market building.

[67] Kindleberger, *Financial History of Western Europe*, pp. 197–98.

The primary advantage of these securities was their insulation from credit risk. The nation-state was endowed with a permanence not usually characteristic of most businesses. Moreover, Britain's size, power and favorable government attitudes toward business and finance contributed to London's reputation as a safe haven for investment balances.

The second advantage of government obligations was their fixed interest payments, which facilitated their pricing. The amounts and terms of cash payments were specified, enabling holders to determine the value of their portfolios in light of changes in money market conditions. This coupled with low risk, ease of transfer and a growing quantity of outstanding issues throughout the eighteenth century provided the impetus for the establishment of London as the premier market for these securities for many years.

In contrast, equity shares were much more difficult to evaluate accurately. The key problem was that returns were not guaranteed, but were contingent on a host of often poorly understood circumstances affecting the economics of the firm. Such conditions could contribute to mispricings. Witness the tenuous bubbles created through speculation in the shares of the South Sea Company and the Compagnie des Indes. Misleading expectations were encouraged by the managements of these companies in their drives to convert large amounts of public debt.

Taxes had a significant impact on the development of the London financial market due to the tax-exempt status of interest income. Business interest expense provided no particular advantage for enterprises operating under a regime whose main sources of revenues derived from land, excise and customs imposts. Conversely, interest income earned by individuals remained untaxed except for a brief period during the Napoleonic Wars when a national income tax was temporarily imposed. Joint-stock companies, on the other hand, were required to pay a small assessment of the interest they earned from the securities they maintained in their funds of credit.

The experience of the South Sea Company and the Compagnie des Indes illustrates the problems associated with agency relationships in large enterprises during this period. Although the managers of the ill-fated companies had maintained close relationships with the political leadership of their respective nations, this was not enough to ward off financial disaster. In France the reaction to the financing debacle was a general retreat from any further experimentation with giant business institutions. In England, although the joint stocks were not prohibited, tight restrictions severely constrained the formation of any new entities for over two centuries.

The steps taken to limit the growth of joint stocks in Britain also reflect a sensitivity among British leaders to the administrative capacities of the state to oversee the financial markets. Government may have simply recognized that it lacked the expertise and the resources to undertake this mission properly. The traditional approach in promoting large-scale economic activities had been to blend the objectives of private groups and the state. The South Sea Company and the Compagnie des Indies debacles revealed how vulnerable a developing financial market that was crucial to state finance could be to shocks caused by the failure of a major entity.

Although it labored under difficult conditions, the emerging financial community in London would learn much about the potential of finance for a wide range of public and private purposes over the course of the following two centuries. The new financial markets established during years of international strife and dedicated to funding the activities of the national state were transformed in the nineteenth century to support a great industrial expansion. New investment opportunities centering primarily in manufacturing and transportation required vast agglomerations of capital. This need, as will be seen in the following chapter, was effectively satisfied through the extension of the useful institutions that had been slowly perfected in London in the years after 1688.

THE RISE OF MODERN INDUSTRY

CHAPTER FOUR

Finance in the Age of Canals and Railroads, 1775–1900

I. Introduction

The last quarter of the eighteenth century saw the start of a great economic expansion that changed corporate finance in fundamental ways. The age of global exploration was waning and the discovery of new lands in the Western Hemisphere brimming with untapped resources was no longer to be counted on to provide economic growth. Boundaries imposed by the closure of geographic horizons underlined the need for the conservation of dwindling natural stocks. Robert Malthus, for example, thought that the ultimate survival of the human race depended on a sharp restriction of population growth.[1] Sensitivity to demographic pressure emanated from a high, constant birth rate, lowered death rates and the alienation of a growing portion of the population whose connections with the land were severed by estate enclosure. Others, such as David Ricardo, responded to the problem by arguing that a greater abundance could be achieved by allocating scarce resources more efficiently. This latter reaction took several forms. First, a growing body of scientific knowledge was used to develop improved products and manufacturing processes.[2] Second, new forms of business organization and management were created to

---

[1] T. R. Malthus, *An Essay on the Principle of Population*, reprint ed. (Cambridge University Press, 1992); and Donald Winch, *Malthus* (Oxford: Oxford University Press, 1987).

[2] For Britain, see Phyllis Deane, *The First Industrial Revolution*, 2nd ed. (Cambridge University Press, 1965, 1979), pp. 119–41; and idem, "The Industrial Revolution in Great Britain," in Carlo M. Cipolla, *The Emergence of Industrial Societies, Part 1* (New York: Harvester, 1976), pp. 174–88; Witt Bowden, Michael Karpovich and Abbott Payson Usher, *An Economic History of Eu-*

enhance productivity by more effective coordination and control of economic affairs.[3] Third, new beliefs were emerging about the gains to be realized by eliminating distortive impediments to freer trade.

A major technological advance, the substitution of coal for wind and water as the energy source for industry, was maximized in Britain. Major improvements in steam engine design, introduced by Thomas Newcomen and James Watt, transformed two leading manufacturing sectors, textiles and iron, and catapulted Britain into the position of the world's leading industrial economy during the first half of the nineteenth century. The increases in industrial output made possible by these innovations in industrial output were impressive. Coal consumption expanded from 11 million tons in 1800 to about 100 million tons by 1870; pig iron production jumped from a mere 0.2 million tons in 1806 to 6.6 million tons in 1873; the number of power looms used in the textile industry increased from 2,400 in 1813 to 250,000 by 1850; and steam power–generating capacity rose from 0.6 million horsepower in 1840 to 13.7 million horsepower in 1896.[4]

Steam energy also revolutionized transportation. The extension of railroad and telegraph service contributed to the rise of great urban-industrial economies. The advent of regular, all-season rail service made possible the establishment of high-volume manufacturing units capable of distributing their output efficiently to consumers concentrated in growing cities. An early milestone in this transformation was

rope since 1750 (New York: Fertig, 1970), pp. 105–26; and David S. Landes, *The Unbound Prometheus: Technological Change and Industrial Development in Western Europe from 1750 to the Present* (Cambridge University Press, 1969), pp. 41–123. For the influence of technology on U.S. development, see W. Elliott Brownlee, *Dynamics of Ascent: A History of the American Economy,* 2nd ed. (New York: Knopf, 1974, 1979), pp. 271–80.

[3] See, e.g., Chandler, *The Visible Hand,* for the U.S. experience. For early European impacts on industrial organization, see Bowen et al., *Economic History of Europe,* pp. 127–45; and for the effects on firm organizational change, see Chandler, *Scale and Scope,* chaps. 7–9 passim regarding Britain and chaps. 10–14 passim regarding Germany.

[4] For a general discussion of these patterns, see Bowden et al., *Economic History of Europe,* pp. 125–26 and 306–307; and T. S. Ashton, *The Industrial Revolution, 1760–1830,* revised ed. (New York: Oxford University Press, 1964), pp. 42–65. For specific details with respect to output, see Landes, *Unbound Prometheus,* p. 86 (power looms), pp. 96 and 194 (pig iron), pp. 97 and 194 (coal) and p. 221 (steam power).

the completion of the rail line connecting Liverpool and Manchester in 1830. The success of this early venture led to a vast expansion in British railway mileage, jumping to 2,000 by 1840 and to 12,000 by 1867.[5]

Progress in both transportation and manufacturing accelerated the pace of investment in productive assets in Britain. The estimated annual rate of fixed capital formation amounted to about 7 percent of gross national product at the dawn of the nineteenth century. By the 1840s, with the expansion of railways, cities and industry, this rate jumped to 10 percent and eventually reached 11 percent during the period 1869–78.[6]

New patterns of economic thought in Britain also facilitated change: belief in the efficacy of mercantilism was eclipsed by laissez-faire and free trade doctrines. A new paradigm, known as "political economy," was shaped in part by three contributors. Adam Smith was an early proponent of free trade and international economic specialization to ensure maximum output. He abjured the great trade monopolies as wasteful and corrupt, arguing that small enterprises controlled by owner-operators would guarantee greater efficiency. David Ricardo amplified Smith's basic conceptions in a more formalistic "law of comparative advantage," which contended that a more efficient allocation of the world's economic resources would derive from the liberalization of global commerce. In addition, John Stuart Mill extended these and other ideas to social philosophy in the form of a new creed of liberalism whose ideal was the attainment of the greatest economic utility for the greatest number.[7]

[5] Deane, *First Industrial Revolution,* pp. 171–75; idem, "Industrial Revolution in Great Britain," pp. 215–16; and Morgan and Thomas, *London Stock Exchange,* pp. 105–10.

[6] Deane, "Industrial Revolution in Great Britain," pp. 199–202.

[7] For a general discussion of changing patterns of thought, see Deane, *First Industrial Revolution,* pp. 186–201; and Ashton, *The Industrial Revolution,* pp. 88–97. For a cogent analysis of the thinking of Smith, Ricardo and Mill on trade, see H. Peter Gray, *International Trade, Investment and Payments* (Boston: Houghton Mifflin, 1979), pp. 10–31 passim. For a discussion of the connections between thought and politics, see Donald Winch, "Economic Knowledge and Government in Britain: Some Historical and Comparative Reflections," in Mary O. Furner and Barry Supple, eds., *The State and Economic Knowledge: The American and British Experiences* (Cambridge University Press, 1990), pp. 41–46; B. J. Gordon, *Political Economy in Parliament,*

It was against this intellectual background that major reforms creating greater opportunity were introduced to the British system of economic governance. In 1819, the currency was again made convertible to gold. In 1824, the Combination Acts, which had previously imposed restrictions on the organization of labor, were relaxed. In 1833, Parliament abrogated the trade monopoly privileges earlier granted to the East India Company. In 1834, the revision of the Poor Laws facilitated the free movement of labor by loosening residency restrictions for those receiving poor relief. In 1844, the Bank Charter Act strengthened the position of the central bank. The process of economic liberalization culminated in 1846 with the repeal of the Corn Laws, thus advancing free trade and curtailing protectionism.[8]

Industrialization was further advanced by the more efficient concentration of capital in business units made possible by the liberalization of laws controlling the formation of joint-stock companies. Beginning in 1825, legal prohibitions restricting the use of joint-stock companies, imposed by the Bubble Act of 1720, were abrogated, a reform that assisted pioneers in the dynamic sectors of the economy to draw funds from a broader constituency of investors. The Companies Act of 1856 provided an even more conducive atmosphere for marketing of corporate securities by limiting liability in the event of bankruptcy for those who purchased equity shares of incorporated businesses.[9]

The patterns of change that first emerged in Britain had important reverberations overseas, especially in the United States. British ideas about business ordering were readily accepted because of common cultural and legal traditions. This influence also grew because of the heavy British portfolio investment made in this country, which grew to $1.1 billion by 1876 and to over $4.0 billion by 1914. Moreover, the British example seemed highly relevant because the three sectors

---

1819–1823 (London: Macmillan, 1976); idem, *Economic Doctrine and Tory Liberalism, 1824–1830* (London: Macmillan, 1979); and F. W. Fetter, *The Economist in Parliament, 1780–1870* (Durham, N.C.: Duke University Press, 1980).

[8] See Bowden et al., *Economic History of Europe*, pp. 341–61. See also Deane, *First Industrial Revolution*, pp. 186–201 and 202–19.

[9] Hunt, *The Development of the Business Corporation in England*, chaps. 3–5 passim. For a general discussion of the impact of incorporation reform, see Kindleberger, *Financial History of Western Europe*, pp. 202–205.

that had sparked industrial development – iron, textiles and railways – were also prominent in America's takeoff.[10]

In the United States, however, the working out of national economic policies varied in important ways from the British experience. Although many Americans were receptive to laissez-faire notions, strong political coalitions were able to erect high tariff barriers to protect "infant" industries. Moreover, because the United States was independent of foreign sources for vital food and fuel staples and its growing internal markets were enormous, its national leadership was less sensitive to arguments for more liberal international trade policies. Instead, public policy was directed more toward regulating the market power of railways and of the emergent industrial oligopolies that had flourished in a protectionist cocoon.[11]

This chapter considers how the basic institutional relationships supporting the modern structure of corporate finance emerged during this epoch of industrial flux. The analysis centers on the railroads, which were then the world's most capital-intensive industry. The discussion is restricted to Britain and the United States, which independently became strong bastions of finance capitalism. The chapter begins by evaluating the factors that led to the establishment of anonymous markets for corporate debt. Next, it explains how the early fragmented corporate securities markets gradually became more cohesive and lays out an explanation of the purposes of corporate debt that emphasizes how corporate leaders had, in their pursuit of managerial and technological efficiency, to be sensitive to investor concerns about risk and informational asymmetry. It then shows how the emergence of preferred stock financing was sensitive both to investor concerns about risk and to management concerns about leverage and corporate control. It concludes with a comparison of the predictions of modern theorists with the salient patterns evident in nineteenth century finance.

---

[10] Mira Wilkins, *The History of Foreign Investment in the United States to 1914* (Cambridge, Mass.: Harvard University Press, 1989), pp. 155–67, 298–99 and 704–10. For the role of an important international banking firm in supporting this financial nexus, see Vincent P. Carosso, *The Morgans: Private International Bankers, 1854–1913* (Cambridge, Mass.: Harvard University Press, 1987), especially chapt. 5.

[11] Brownlee, *The Dynamics of Ascent*, pp. 354–58; and F. W. Taussig, *The Tariff History of the United States*, 8th revised ed. (New York: Capricorn, 1931).

II. The Quasi-Public Nature of Early Canals and Railroads

Although broad, impersonal financial markets had emerged to facilitate the sale of government debt obligations, they slowly became accessible to corporate securities during the early nineteenth century because of the quasi-public nature of the first issuing entities – canal and railroad companies. Before 1800, many corporate bodies, such as municipalities and universities, had been formed to carry on particular public functions. In the case of the great trading companies in Britain, corporations were also effective mechanisms for blending the economic interests of the state and of private groups in mutually beneficial ways. The distinction between public and private corporations was not sharply defined until later.[12]

The early railroads and canals in Britain and in the United States were viewed as public improvements whose establishment was vital to enhancing local economic fortunes. These were vital links connecting world markets to what hitherto had been remote communities. This recognition frequently motivated prominent local leaders to encourage promoters of new lines to serve their towns and to persuade their neighbors to support these projects by purchasing the securities of these companies. Moreover, in Britain substantial local financial commitments were crucial preconditions before promoters were allowed to acquire Parliamentary charters for establishing railroads.[13]

Governments played key roles in helping to establish early railroads and canals. Although in Britain the first roads built to serve the populous southern counties were privately financed, the strict preconditions imposed by Parliament for acquiring a charter augmented public confidence. This was supplemented by the tradition of informal but active

---

[12] Joseph S. Davis, *Essays in the Earlier History of American Corporations*, 2 vols. (Cambridge, Mass.: Harvard University Press, 1917), vol. 2, p. 3, reports: "To the end of the eighteenth century, however, not only had no classification of business corporation been developed, but no sharp line was drawn between these and corporations of other sorts." For a general discussion of the patterns of finance for railroads and canals and the problem of informational asymmetry, see Baskin, "Development of Corporate Financial Markets," pp. 208–22.

[13] M. C. Reed, *Investment in Railways in Britain, 1820–1844* (New York: Oxford University Press, 1975), pp. 76–98; and Frederick A. Cleveland and Fred Wilbur Powell, *Railroad Promotion and Capitalization in the United States* (New York: Longmans, Green, 1909), p. 201.

governmental oversight of corporate affairs dating back to the South Sea Company scandal. In the United States, government provided assistance to the early canal and railroad construction. Between 1815 and 1860, for example, about three-quarters of the $188 million invested in canals were financed through the flotation of state and municipal debt obligations.[14] Besides providing support through the purchase and the guarantee of securities, many state and local governments assisted particular railroads through land grants.[15] Moreover, since railroads and canals were often natural monopolies sanctioned by the state, their securities were viewed as akin to those of government. Consider, for example, the description of railroad securities by one contemporary writer:

Railway bonds had much resemblance to government securities; the railways did not appear, at first blush, to be dependent on the efforts of individuals, but rather on the condition of the tributary country, and their income was quite similar to the taxes paid to the government. The investor in railroad bonds seemed to be putting his faith not in [Cornelius] Vanderbilt or [Jay] Gould, but in the manufacturers, producers, and consumers of the tributary territory upon which the railroads depended for their success.[16]

Railroad regulators were sensitive to the strong market power of this industry. Henry Carter Adams, who served as chief statistician (1887–1910) for the Interstate Commerce Commission (ICC), believed that the problem was not so much the risk of enterprise failure as that of extracting too high rents because of monopoly power. Adams

---

[14] Chandler, *Visible Hand,* p. 90.

[15] George Heberton Evans, Jr., "The Early History of Preferred Stock in the United States," *American Economic Review* 19 (March 1929): 43–58, reports loans to state governments; Arthur M. Johnson and Barry E. Supple, *Boston Capitalists and Western Railroads* (Cambridge: Mass.: Harvard University Press, 1967), documents early investment in railroad finance by the state of Massachusetts. Also see Leland H. Jenks, *The Migration of British Capital to 1875* (New York: Knopf, 1927), p. 74; Paul Studenski and Herman E. Krooss, *Financial History of the United States,* 2nd ed. (New York: McGraw-Hill, 1963), p. 131; William Z. Ripley, *Railroads: Rates and Regulation* (New York: Longmans, Green, 1912), pp. 37–43; and Davis and North, *Institutional Change and American Economic Growth,* pp. 139–43.

[16] Quoted in Frederick A. Cleveland and Fred Wilbur Powell, *Railroad Finance* (New York: D. Appleton, 1912), p. 55.

compared railroad tariffs to a tax imposed on local communities for vital transportation services.[17] This association with the public good created an aura of economic stability and thus helped these railroad companies gain acceptance among investors during a period when the primary opportunities for holding financial assets remained limited to public debt, to mortgages or, in Britain, to the securities of a few joint-stock companies in trade, banking or insurance. Some measure of the vast scale of the railroad enterprise that had to be financed is reflected in the track mileage laid down in the United States. By the 1870s, U.S. railroads operated over 70,000 miles of trackage; the grid grew to almost 200,000 miles by 1900 and almost 250,000 miles by 1911.[18]

The later extension of the railroads to more remote and thinly populated locales would have been rendered infeasible if reliance had been placed solely on local financing sources. This was especially true on America's western frontier, which remained sparsely inhabited. Construction of rail facilities in these regions depended on the transfer of substantial amounts of capital from more densely settled districts. This financing was made possible by the development of broader and more cohesive capital markets.

III. From Fragmentation to Cohesiveness

A prerequisite for the formation of markets capable of attracting capital from wide geographic areas was the need to develop procedures enabling investors to evaluate the underlying worth of traded securities. As previously noted, a paucity of reliable information sources had been a major difficulty for outside investors in the East India Company, the South Sea Company and other early joint-stock companies. Poor information heightened the risk of loss due to adverse selection. The problem centers on the difficulty of distinguishing between the price paid for a financial asset and some truly informed discounted net value of the asset. This is less problematic for riskless

[17] Paul J. Miranti, Jr., "The Mind's Eye of Reform: The ICC's Bureau of Statistics and Accounts and a Vision of Regulation, 1887–1940," *Business History Review* 63 (1989): 478–80.

[18] Chandler, *Visible Hand*, p. 88; and Ripley, *Railroads: Rates and Regulation*, pp. 34 and 78.

bonds held to maturity but virtually impossible for other classes of financial assets.

One solution to the problem of informational insufficiency was to base the valuation of a unique item on standardized commodities for which continuous pricing information was available to knowledgeable market participants. This approach had been followed by John Law when he made the bank notes issued by the Banque Generale convertible into fixed quantities of gold; it is the same technique used today to value the shares of closed-end mutual funds. This technique, however, may be ineffective in cases where trading volume is light and pricing information is often stale, thereby providing opportunities for manipulation. Reliance on the pricing of comparable issues as proxies for thinly traded securities is also limited to those cases where external factors produce similar effects. Given these constraints it is understandable that large-scale markets first emerged for public debt. This security class had low default risk and its pricing was responsive to interest rate expectations.

Poorly informed investors may alternatively rely on the guidance provided by more knowledgeable participants. In the fragmented markets prevailing early in the nineteenth century, prospective investors sought the counsel of local professionals or business associates with a reputation for competency and honesty. The scope of early capital raising was broadened by personal contacts. Respected financiers were often able to fund their new ventures by mobilizing the savings of well-to-do friends and associates. As Johnson and Supple have noted in analyzing the early financing of western roads by Boston capitalists:

In an age when institutional arrangements to facilitate the flow of capital into new ventures were embryonic, the role of the individual mobilizer of capital and his place within a social group were crucial. Hence the tendency of Boston investment to "bunch" in particular sectors and enterprises. The C. B. & Q. and Atchison were Boston ventures because investment tended to be a cumulative social process in an environment lacking an impersonal, national money market.[19]

Early investment banking enterprises only gradually began to market corporate securities. The first entrants were usually drawn from other market specializations. The banking houses of Cooke, Baring,

[19] Johnson and Supple, *Boston Capitalists,* p. 338.

Rothschild and even Mitsui in Japan, for example, originally concentrated on government finance. In the United States many pioneering railroad financiers were drawn from the ranks of the foreign-exchange dealers and included such firms as Winslow, Lanier, DeCoppet and Company, and De Launay, Islin and Clark. The group undertook this function to assist European clients wishing to transfer some of their wealth to the United States, which had a more stable political environment than that which existed in Europe after the revolutions of 1848.[20] In contrast, the general reluctance of bankers to establish a position in the forefront of revolutionary progress earlier in the century was probably explainable by their conservative predilections – a quality crucial for bolstering public confidence.

Even after the investment bankers began to develop these markets in earnest, public trust in their activities was often eroded by suspicions about the self-serving use of privileged information and relationships to build personal fortunes. Moreover, the lack of reliable and timely information inhibited the formation of broad and anonymous markets for corporate securities.[21] Instead, the main focus, particularly for equity, remained highly localized. In England, canal and railroad securities were primarily marketed locally until the 1840s. Consider the opinion reported in an 1835 "Circular to Bankers":

It is a remarkable fact that the Railway system advanced and became established in the public confidence without the assistance of the Stock Exchange. The support accorded to it was derived almost exclusively from the capitalists and men of thrift and opulence, in the mining and manufacturing districts in the North of England. We will venture to assert that taking into account all the railways [north of Manchester]. . . not one twentieth part of the capital was provided by members of the stock exchange.[22]

---

[20] Chandler, *Visible Hand*, pp. 91–92.

[21] Vincent P. Carosso, *Investment Banking in America: A History* (Cambridge, Mass.: Harvard University Press, 1970), chapt. 3, describes the informal practices that were common in financing syndications prior to the 1912 Pujo investigation. Syndicators wanted to avoid disclosure of their profits, relying often on oral rather than written contracts.

[22] Quoted in Morgan and Thomas, *London Stock Exchange*, p. 107, who indicate that the latter claim was exaggerated. See also George Heberton Evans, Jr., *British Corporation Finance, 1775–1850* (Baltimore: Johns Hopkins University Press, 1936), p. 10; Hunt, *Development of Business Corporation in*

Just as local property owners were intrigued by the potential benefits the railroads afforded their regions in Britain,[23] early railroad financiers showed a keen interest in the railroads in New England.[24] Besides being a more efficient means of transportation, the railroads gave local investors an opportunity to maintain their funds in a tangible venture whose operations could be observed daily. These investors often had direct knowledge of key determinants of railroad profitability. They could observe how well roadbeds and equipment were serviced, the intensity of traffic flows and the quantities and types of cargoes hauled.

Although proximity had provided local investors with rough gauges of enterprise performance, this knowledge was often ambiguous and its dissemination haphazard. The primary barrier impeding the growth of large-scale markets was not physical distances but rather the insufficient flow of reliable and timely information; this was partially overcome by reliance on an understanding of the potential of railroad investment derived from previous experience. Successful investors in early ventures may have had sufficient confidence in their valuative capacities to accept the risks inherent in investing in distant enterprises. In England, investors in the highly profitable line from Manchester to Liverpool were prominent in financing rail extensions to other parts of the country.[25] Moreover, a rising ability among British investors to analyze and manage railroad affairs was a skill that proved advantageous in their extensive promotion of rail projects in Europe, the Near East, India and South America.[26] In the United States before the Civil War, Boston had a head start on New York as the domestic center of railroad finance because local investors recog-

England, p. 108; Reed, *Investment in Railways in Britain,* p. 104; and William A. Thomas, *Provincial Stock Exchanges* (London: Cass, 1973), p. 31.

[23] Reed, *Investment in Railways in Britain,* analyzes the geographic distribution of stock ownership in the early railroads. As we shall see later, it is understandable that Liverpool and Manchester investors contributed substantially to distant rail projects. See also Kindleberger, *Financial History of Western Europe,* pp. 199–200.

[24] Arthur Stone Dewing, *The Financial Policy of Corporations,* 2 vols. in one, 4th ed. (New York: Ronald Press, 1920, 1941), p. 64. For a similar pattern in France, see Freedeman, *Joint Stock Enterprises in France,* p. 30.

[25] This is a primary finding of Reed, *Investment in Railways in Britain.*

[26] Jenks, *Migration of British Capital*; and Kindleberger, *Financial History of Western Europe,* pp. 219–25.

nized the need to overcome the problems associated with their city's poor access to navigable inland waterways.[27]

The uncertainties associated with doing business over time and distance were partially mitigated by the rise of specialized railroad underwriters – banks with reputations for honesty and competency. These bankers had firsthand knowledge of the financial capabilities of client railroads from having served as members of railroad boards of directors. Two U.S. banking houses were the leaders in railroad finance by the 1890s. They were J. P. Morgan & Company, which also maintained strong connections with the London and Paris financial communities, and Kuhn–Loeb & Company, with contacts in Amsterdam, Paris and Frankfurt. Wealthy investors in both the United States and Europe relied on the professional counsel of such leading firms in deciding where to commit their capital.[28]

New forms of managerial control over railroad companies reduced the perceived risks of these investments. The ordering of corporate affairs was made more effective by modern professional management techniques that were perfected in the railroad industry beginning in the 1860s. These included innovations and improvements in existing techniques and involved the definition of hierarchical structures that strengthened managerial capabilities for coordinating and controlling widely dispersed operations. Moreover, new forms of statistical and accounting information also augmented administrative capacities. Balance sheets and operating statements succinctly highlighted for management the salient details of operating performance and financial condition. The information summarized in these statements was amplified by an array of supplementary schedules yielding further insights into corporate activities, and beginning with Albert Fink's definition of the ton-mile as the measure of traffic density in the 1860s, railroad managements increasingly relied on analytical ratios in order to monitor performance.[29]

The introduction of limited liability provisions in corporate law in

[27] Johnson and Supple, *Boston Capitalists.*
[28] See Dorothy R. Adler, *British Investments in American Railways, 1834–1898* (Charlottesville: University Press of Virginia, 1970), pp. 170–89 passim; and Wilkins, *Foreign Investment in the United States,* pp. 536–47.
[29] Chandler, *Visible Hand,* pp. 109–21.

both Britain and the United States facilitated the process of raising capital to support giant undertakings like the formation of the railroads. Limited liability was advantageous to equity holders because, unlike partnerships, where all principals were jointly and severally liable for the entity's debts, the total potential exposure in the corporation was confined to the sums actually invested. Limited liability also shifted some of the risk of loss due to business failure to creditors, who could now seek recovery only from the assets of the borrowing corporation and not from those of its owners. This deterioration in the position of creditors, however, was offset by the increased opportunities for profitable lending made possible by institutional reform, which increased levels of economic activity.

But these changes that encouraged corporate formation also created new needs for financial and operating information for investors. Equity investors required more information to monitor management performance because of the asymmetries in knowledge of the firm that emerged in large, growing entities with a high degree of separation of ownership and control. In addition, lenders now became more sensitive to the need for more reliable information to assess corporate credit risk because of the limitations placed on the scope of liability assessment in bankruptcy.

Until the mid-nineteenth century, limited liability protection for corporate shareholders was granted in Britain only through acts of Parliament, which were restricted in this regard to entities involved in undertaking large-scale public improvements such as canal or railroad building. There was a reluctance among public leaders to extend this protection to other businesses because it was feared that it might facilitate the defrauding of investors. Although limited liability strengthened the ability of railway companies to concentrate equity capital, the transitional financing required during the period of incorporation could present barriers to business formation. The problem involved parliamentary rules requiring substantial subscriptions to share capital before the process of charter ratification could be completed. In these cases wealthy individuals were often reluctant to subscribe because the purchase of subscription scrip made them partners in the promotional venture, with full liability for losses if it failed. Brokers tried to overcome this dilemma by serving as nominees for their clients until incorporation was completed. But this expedient was not entirely satisfactory because it encouraged manipulative speculation in scrip, which contributed to the perception of risk about railroad financing.[30]

Progress was slow in extending corporate status with limited liability to other types of British businesses. In 1825, the ability to form joint-stock companies with unlimited liability was reestablished through recision of the Bubble Act of 1720. To gain control over the many joint-stock entities created in the subsequent two decades and to place incorporation on a firmer footing, Parliament passed the Joint-Stock Companies Registration, Incorporation and Regulation Act in 1844. The unregulated joint stocks had become problematic because unscrupulous financiers had used this form as a vehicle for launching fraudulent business promotions. The 1844 legislation sought to curtail such abuses by requiring the disclosure of minimum levels of subscribed capital and the filing of semiannual, audited balance sheets with the Board of Trade. Similar reporting requirements were also imposed on the banking industry that same year under the Joint-Stock Bank Act. The Companies Clauses Consolidations Act of 1845 extended the reporting responsibility by mandating the preparation of a balance sheet fourteen days prior to any ordinary meeting of shareholders.

Revisions of the companies acts between 1855 and 1862 eliminated the need for acts of Parliament to incorporate and extended limited liability protection to all corporations. Although many members of Parliament were sensitive to the importance of financial disclosure, the mandatory reporting provisions of the 1844 law were set aside and registrants were encouraged to continue these practices on a voluntary basis. This latter objective was covered by appendixes to the 1855 and 1862 legislation, which included model articles of incorporation that called for periodic audits and standardized balance sheets. This new laissez-faire approach to financial disclosure was strengthened by the passage of the Fraudulent Transactions Act of 1857, which protected investors against defalcations by managements, and the Punishment of Frauds Act of 1857 and the Larceny Act of 1861, both of which prohibited financial misrepresentations.

This system of voluntary disclosure was eventually found to be wanting in the protection it afforded investors. The need for the

---

[30] Reed, *Investment in Railways in Britain*, pp. 3–14 and chapt. 3 passim.

periodic transmission of higher-quality financial information than available through the voluntary action of corporations was first recognized in industries requiring the most intensive investment of capital. New detailed accounting reports were mandated by the Board of Trade under the Regulation of Railways Act of 1868, the Gas Works Clauses Act of 1871 and the Electric Lighting Act of 1882. In addition, the failure of the City of Glasgow Bank in 1878 because of managerial malfeasance led to the reimposition of requirements for the certification of bank financial statements in the Companies Act of 1879. And finally in 1900, all companies registered under the companies acts were required to file audited balance sheets annually with the Board of Trade.[31]

In the United States, on the other hand, while corporate limited liability laws were not the rule early on, they became widely accepted in the commercial law of leading states by the 1830s. Although grants of limited liability had been made to commercial enterprises as early as 1786, legal opinions on this practice remained sharply divided in many states well into the 1820s. Some had shared the misgivings of British officials, noted earlier, about the potential of limited liability to promote dishonesty and fraud by lessening creditors' rights of redress. Others, who were influenced by the ideas of Thomas Jefferson, remained opposed because they believed that limited liability primarily benefited wealthy entrepreneurs and did little to improve the lot of yeoman farmers, who were considered to be the social backbone of the new American state. Proponents of the democratic ideals espoused by Andrew Jackson, however, eventually proved most influential in this legal debate. They favored limited liability, believing that it was a mechanism for placing the interests of impecunious businessmen on a

[31] See Michael Chatfield, *A History of Accounting Thought*, revised ed. (Hinsdale, Ill.: Dryden, 1974), pp. 113–19; P. L. Cottrell, *Industrial Finance, 1830–1914: The Finance and Organization of English Manufacturing Industry* (London: Methuen, 1979), chapt. 3 passim; Hunt, *Development of the Business Corporation in England*, chaps. 5–7 passim; and Kindleberger, *Financial History of Western Europe*, pp. 204–205. See also Edgar Jones, *Accountancy and the British Economy, 1840–1980: The Evolution of Ernst & Whinney* (London: Batsford, 1981), pp. 51–54; Harold Pollins, "Aspects of Railway Accounting before 1868," in Littleton and Yamey, eds., *Studies in the History of Accounting Thought*, pp. 332–55; and H. C. Edey and Prot Panitpakdi, "British Company Accounting and the Law, 1844–1900," in ibid., pp. 356–79 passim.

par with those of the wealthy. They reasoned that, with limited liability, two corporations having comparable financial standing could both have equal access to credit without regard to the economic circumstances of their principals.

A sensitivity to the need for greater information about limited liability corporations was evident in New York State's general incorporation statute of 1848, which served as a model for many other states. This law sought to protect creditors by requiring that companies prepare annual reports indicating the amount of paid-in capital and the total debt outstanding. In addition, shareholders would be held liable "to an amount equal to the amount of stock held by them respectively for all debts and contracts made by such company, until the whole amount of stock fixed and limited by such company shall be paid in." Moreover, heavy fines were assessable on corporate agents responsible for falsifying corporate records. This latter stricture sought to prevent "stock watering" through either the overstatement of assets or the understatement of liabilities.[32]

Although government in the United States, as in Britain, also became a major source of financial information, its dissemination in the nineteenth century was limited primarily to natural monopolies, especially the railroads. This process began on the state level, where financial data were gathered for two separate purposes: (1) to assist in determining the equity of railroad rates and (2) to promote managerial probity and competency in the stewardship of enterprise resources. Massachusetts, for example, had addressed these problems in the 1860s by promulgating "sunshine laws," which made the operating and financial activities of local railroads more transparent to public scrutiny. Other states, particularly in the South and West, began establishing commissions in the 1870s that collected financial data for local rate regulation. In 1887 the newly formed ICC incorporated both state objectives in its mandate. One of its major achievements was gradually standardizing the practice of financial reporting in the industry through its *Annual Financial Statistics of Railways of the United States*.[33]

---

[32] Herbert Hovenkamp, *Enterprise and American Law, 1836–1937* (Cambridge, Mass.: Harvard University Press, 1991), chapt. 5 passim.

[33] Thomas K. McCraw, *Prophets of Regulation: Charles Francis Adams, Louis D. Brandeis, James M. Landis, Alfred E. Kahn* (Cambridge, Mass.: Harvard

Unlike Great Britain, only regulated businesses in the United States were required to file financial statements regularly with the national government. It was not until the 1930s, when the U.S. securities market was reformed, that corporate reporting to the federal government's Securities and Exchange Commission (SEC) became required for a wider range of business enterprises. However, in the years before these reforms were implemented, many such U.S. firms that sought to raise capital in London began, often at the behest of their investment bankers, to follow the British practice of issuing these reports and engaging independent public accountants to certify their contents.[34]

Advances in communications technology, such as the telegraph (1837), the transoceanic cable (1866), the telephone (1876) and wireless (1896), made possible a rapid transmission of information about corporate financial affairs. These innovations greatly reduced the risk of loss due to delayed receipt of vital knowledge. These new capabilities led to greater financial market integration by allowing faster international transactions.[35]

The establishment of specialized business publications and journals provided information to railroad investors and thus assisted the emergence of broad, impersonal financial markets. In Britain a daily railway share list quoting security prices first appeared in 1844. By that date most of the London dailies sponsored financial departments. After 1844 the *Economist* (founded in 1843) absorbed the short-lived *Railway Monitor* and provided financial coverage for this industry. Railroad finance was also an important topic in three other business publications formed during this century: *Banker's Magazine* (1844), *Investors' Chronicle* (1860, later merged into the *Money Market Review*), and the *Statist* (1878). A wealth of annual statistical information was also provided in an annual compendium, *Burdett's Official Intelligence* (1882), a forerunner of the *Stock Exchange Yearbook*.[36]

University Press, 1984), pp. 17–25; George H. Miller, *Railroads and the Granger Laws* (Madison: University of Wisconsin Press, 1971); and Miranti, "Mind's Eye of Reform," pp. 469–75.

[34] Miranti, "Mind's Eye of Reform," pp. 478–82; and idem, *Accountancy Comes of Age: The Development of an American Profession, 1886–1940* (Chapel Hill: University of North Carolina Press, 1990), pp. 33–34.

[35] E. C. Kirkland, *History of American Economic Life,* 4th ed. (New York: Appleton-Century-Crofts, 1969), pp. 304–307.

[36] Morgan and Thomas, *London Stock Exchange,* p. 165.

Similar patterns were evident in the United States. Henry Varnum Poor began publishing the *American Railroad Journal* in the 1850s, primarily for investors; later he launched the highly successful analytical compendium *Poor's Manual of Railroad Securities*.[37] Technical and financial information was communicated by the *Railroad Gazette* and *Railway World*. General financial newspapers, including, early on, the *Commercial and Financial Chronicle* and later the *Wall Street Journal* and *Barron's*, provided extensive coverage of railroad affairs.

Besides reports of parliamentary committees and periodicals, British investors learned about railroads through thoughtful books that began to appear about midcentury. A classic that emphasized the unique economic relationships in the industry was Dionysius Lardner's *Railway Economy* (1850). Herbert Spencer raised questions about industry governance and financial probity in *Railway Morals and Public Policy* (1855). The thorny problems of capital cost measurement were addressed in Mark Huish's *On Deterioration of Railway Plant and Road* (1849) and Samuel Laing's *Report on the Question of Depreciation and on the Policy of Establishing a Reserve Fund* (1849).

Later, the railroads also became the subject of scholarly treatises in the United States. Many studies were concerned with the problem of regulation: *Cost of Railroad Transportation, Railroad Accounting and Government Regulation of Railroad Tariffs* (1875) by Albert Fink of the Louisville and Nashville Railroad; *Railroads: Their Origins and Problems* (1878) by Charles Francis Adams of the Massachusetts Board of Railroad Commissioners; and *Railroad Transportation: Its History and Its Laws* (1885) by Arthur T. Hadley of Yale University. Railroad finance was also a popular topic in such works as *Railroad Promotion and Capitalization in the United States* (1909) by Frederick A. Cleveland and Fred Wilbur Powell of Columbia University and *Railroads: Finance and Organization* (1915) by William Z. Ripley of Harvard University.[38]

---

[37] Alfred D. Chandler, Jr., *Henry Varnum Poor: Business Editor, Analyst and Reformer* (Cambridge, Mass.: Harvard University Press, 1956); and idem, *Visible Hand,* pp. 109 and 121.

[38] For references to British books, see Pollins, "Aspects of Railway Accounting," pp. 332–55 passim. For U.S. authors, see Albert H. Fink, *Cost of Railroad Transportation, Accounts, and Governmental Regulation of Railroad Tariffs* (Louisville, Ky.: Extract from Annual Report of Louisville and Nashville Railroad, J. P. Morgan & Co., 1875); Charles Francis Adams, *Railroads: Their*

Although the increased volume and speed of information transfer diminished uncertainties about railroad economics, it could not surmount the risks associated with the asymmetry of information between owners and managers. Unscrupulous managements were not above manipulating the financial press for their own ends. In some cases boards of directors were not diligent in protecting the interests of the investors they represented. Moreover, the financial statements certified by accountants or filed with regulatory bodies were not always reliable because of either inconsistency in terminology or limitations in accounting measurement techniques. Although by 1887 the formats of railroad financial statements had been standardized in the United States at the behest of the ICC, there was no standardization of accounting methodology for the industry until after the advent of the Hepburn Act of 1906. A common abuse was the inconsistent measurement of capital costs. Some railroads wrote off the entire cost of new fixed assets when acquired; others depreciated the value of assets over their estimated lives of varying duration; a few made no provision whatsoever for the diminution of the worth of these investments; and many companies shifted periodically among these alternatives. Nor did federal reporting requirements extend to ancillary services such as lighterage, express or leasing companies, which were suspected of serving as conduits for siphoning off the earnings of parent railroads.[39]

The potential for diminishing risk through improved information had definite limits. The chronic dilemmas of risk perceptions and informational asymmetry shaped both the type and the relative amounts of equity and debt securities marketable by nineteenth century railroads.

Origins and Problems (New York: Putnams, 1878); Arthur T. Hadley, *Railroad Transportation: Its History and Its Laws* (New York: Putnams, 1885); Cleveland and Powell, *Railroad Promotion*; and William Z. Ripley, *Railroads: Finance and Organization* (New York: Longmans, Green, 1915).

[39] Richard P. Brief, "The Evolution of Asset Accounting," *Business History Review* 40 (Spring 1966): 1–23; idem, "Nineteenth Century Accounting Error," *Journal of Accounting Research* 3 (Spring 1965): 12–31; and Miranti, "Mind's Eye of Reform," pp. 480–88.

IV. Financing through Debt

The limited knowledge possessed by outside investors about the economic prospects of railroads was a major problem that threatened to frustrate the development of finance. The key problem was to reduce the perception of risk associated with a new form of business enterprise whose operations were spread over distant locales.

One method for reducing perceived risk was to limit debt to a small proportion of capitalization, so that debt holders could be repaid (unless the venture was a complete failure). In England, railroad loans were limited to one-third of authorized capital in the corporate charter, and borrowing was entirely forbidden until one-half of share capital was paid up. This policy was formalized by a standing order of Parliament in 1836.[40]

Attempts to specify capital ratios in the United States were unsuccessful in spite of the advocacy of the ICC and its allies in Congress for such powers. In 1911, the regulatory agency did indirectly shape thinking about these matters by influencing the recommendations made by a presidential commission on railroad financing. It was not until passage of the National Transportation Act in 1920 that the ICC was granted limited power to review – but not to mandate – the details of railroad financial plans.[41]

In the United States the federal government's intervention to control rates curtailed disruptive market competition and thus bolstered the railroad industry's image of stability. The gradual extension of federal regulatory authority over the mandating of both maximum and minimum rates reduced opportunities for speculators such as Jay Gould, James Fisk and Daniel Drew to profit by threatening the vital interests of established railroad lines. During the period 1867–87, these opera-

---

[40] Reed, *Investment in Railways in Britain*, pp. 224–27. Some states such as Massachusetts limited borrowing; see Ripley, *Railroads: Finance and Organization*, p. 116. In the latter case, however, these statutes may not have been effective since much equity capital was thought to be "water," that is, sold below par.

[41] Miranti, "Mind's Eye of Reform," pp. 493–95. Ari Hoogenboom and Olive Hoogenboom, *A Short History of the ICC: From Panacea to Palliative* (New York: Norton, 1976), pp. 94–97; K. Austin Kerr, *American Railroad Politics, 1914–1920: Rates, Wages and Efficiency* (Pittsburgh, Pa.: University of Pittsburgh Press, 1968), pp. 211–12; William Norris Leonard, *Railroad Consolida-

tors had successfully manipulated the security prices of many railroads through sudden announcements of decisions to build lines to compete with established railways, to acquire important feeder systems or to begin rate wars to divert traffic away from rivals. Although these activities induced many companies to respond defensively by creating large, integrated regional rail networks, the threat posed by Gould and other speculators was not defused until the ICC extended its control over rate setting. Gradually over the period 1887–1911, the ICC's control increased to the point that individual railroads exercised little discretion in pricing decisions.[42]

Another method for reducing perceived risk was through liens. By 1913, in the United States, 90 percent of the huge $11.2 billion funded railroad debt was backed by some type of mortgage (if only against other securities in the case of the $1.2 billion of collateral trust bonds), and only 10 percent consisted of "debentures."[43] Most of the latter were convertible; apparently, the increase in risk due to the absence of liens was considered sufficiently likely that it required compensation by an equity option.[44] A widely read British book provides what seems to have been the conventional wisdom and warns that all debt offerings should include "a clause stating that the security on which they are based, and it is very important that they should be shown to carry a mortgage on property and assets which appear from the valuation given the prospectus to promise an ample margin." Outside in-

tion under the Transportation Act of 1920 (New York: Columbia University Press, 1946), chapt. 2 passim; and I. L. Sharfman, *The Interstate Commerce Commission: A Study in Administrative Law and Procedure,* 4 vols. (New York: Commonwealth Fund, 1931–37), vol. 1, pp. 177–244, and vol. 3A, pp. 51–55.

[42] See Chandler, *Visible Hand,* pp. 145–87 for a discussion of how competition between speculators and investors was resolved by the advent of federal regulation. See also the contrasting appraisals of the effects of federal regulation on industry economics in Paul MacAvoy, *The Economic Effects of Regulation: The Trunk Lines and the Interstate Commerce Commission before 1900* (Cambridge, Mass.: MIT Press, 1965); Gabriel Kolko, *Railroads and Regulation, 1877–1916* (Princeton, N.J.: Princeton University Press, 1965); Albro Martin, *Enterprise Denied: Origins of the Decline of American Railroads* (New York: Columbia University Press, 1971); and Davis and North, *Institutional Change and American Economic Growth,* pp. 157–62.

[43] Ripley, *Railroads: Finance and Organization,* p. 139.

[44] Cleveland and Powell, *Railroad Promotion,* pp. 156–64.

vestors were not only likely to perceive equity securities as unduly speculative, but also loath to put their savings at risk when there was any potential for fraud and malfeasance.[45]

Consistent with the theory that debt securities were used to obtain funds from poorly informed investors was the tendency of railroads to rely on loans only when attempting to procure capital from distant investors. In densely populated England and New England, sufficient local resources enabled the railroads to be primarily equity financed. Large populations ensured high density of traffic, which was a major determinant of line profitability. By contrast, railroads constructed through the virgin frontier relied more heavily on debt finance.[46] Investors were sensitive to the inherent risk in financing service in sparsely populated regions with low traffic densities. In this environment, distant investors minimized their risks by restricting their purchases to fixed obligations with either contingent claims on corporate assets in the event of bankruptcy or the guarantee of local governmental entities.

Federal and state governments helped to reduce the perception of risk by providing resources or privileges to emergent railroads. The federal government and several states made direct grants of public lands to facilitate line construction on the frontier, as was done in the formation of the Union Pacific during the 1860s.[47] State and local governments purchased the securities of local lines or in some cases exchanged them for municipal bonds. A few states subsidized emergent railroads by paying the costs of their land surveys or temporarily absolving them from taxation. Other governmental entities provided guarantees or endorsements of railroad debt obligations. The federal government in fact issued $130 million of its bonds to support the Union Pacific. Similar patterns were apparent in railroad funding in overseas locales remote from the main centers of finance capital. After 1857, the Indian imperial government raised over $50 million for its national railway system after it guaranteed a 5 percent annual return to bondholders. A turn-of-the-century text states the following:

[45] Hartley Withers, *Stocks and Shares* (New York: Dutton, 1910), pp. 95–96.
[46] Cleveland and Powell, *Railroad Promotion,* pp. 50–51; Dewing, *Financial Policy of Corporations,* p. 64; Reed, *Investment in Railways in Britain,* p. 35; and Ripley, *Railroads: Finance and Organization,* p. 105.
[47] Ripley, *Railroads: Rates and Regulation,* pp. 37–43.

The facility with which public subsidy bonds and the bonds of the railroads themselves were sold, suggested to promoters the possibility for building entirely out of the proceeds of the bonds, keeping the shares for themselves as a source of future profit. . . . The bonds were then sold at ruinous discounts, or exchanged at extravagant prices for construction work, services, and materials. Shares were often given as a bonus to facilitate the placing of bonds. In the end, the promoters had control of the property, which had cost them little or nothing, and the property was mortgaged far in excess of its value. . . . Such was the common course of railroad construction after 1850.

The same text claims that "the use of bonds as a means of providing for original capitalization almost invariably indicated the presence of outside capital," and it equates common shares with the "local supply of investment capital."[48]

Ripley, writing about the U.S. experience, states that before 1873 "all European capital for railroad purposes came in the form of mortgage loans."[49] In fact, many foreign investors embraced only government bonds and were reluctant to invest in railroad issues. Although later there was some equity investment, it remained largely confined to the well-established railroads with high traffic densities, such as the Illinois Central, the New York Central and the Pennsylvania Railroad. British overseas holdings in particular were characterized by "an aversion to risk-taking that generally prevented investment in government or corporation securities as long as there was any substantial degree of income uncertainty."[50] This aversion to speculation most likely arose from extensive experience with poorly conceived or fraudulent schemes. Besides the earlier example of the South Sea Company, English investors had witnessed by 1827 the collapse of three-quarters of the 624 new corporate entities floated during the 1824–25 boom.[51] In addition, public opinion was shocked by such machinations as the Erie Raid in 1869 and the failure of the Credit Mobilier in 1873.[52]

---

[48] Cleveland and Powell, *Railroad Promotion*, pp. 51–57.

[49] Ripley, *Railroads: Finance and Organization*, p. 106.

[50] John J. Madden, *British Investment in the United States, 1860–1880* (New York: Garland, 1985), p. 337.

[51] Hunt, *Development of the Business Corporation in England*, pp. 46–47.

[52] See Charles Francis Adams, Jr., "The Erie Row," *American Law Review* 3 (October 1868): 41–86; and idem, "A Chapter of Erie," *North American Review* 109 (July 1868): 30–106. For a more sympathetic, recent appraisal,

Investor receptivity to bonds issued by railroad corporations in the United States was augmented by the prevailing economic trends during this period. From the end of the Civil War until the outbreak of World War I, real living costs generally declined. The steady increase in agricultural and manufacturing output, the widespread adoption of gold-backed currencies and the maintenance of relatively peaceful international relations all contributed to the longer-term stability of prices.[53] These factors helped contribute to the attractiveness of holding low-risk, fixed-income obligations.

Besides providing the primary source of seed capital, debt was also the means by which most additional funds were solicited from the public. Nominal funded debt in 1913, for example, amounted to $11.2 billion, compared with $7.2 billion of par value common stock.[54] But these figures actually understate the heavy reliance on debt. About one-half of the common stock took the form of corporate cross holdings, versus about one-sixth of the outstanding bonds, and thus (because it was common then for railroads to have interlocking directorates and investments in other railroads) the par value of public holding of bonds dwarfed that of equity.[55] Common stock also appears much more likely to have been issued below par because promoters frequently obtained control gratuitously and because stock was given as a "free bonus" to sell bonds. Moreover, billions in short-term debt were not included in these figures.[56] This heavy reliance on debt

see Maury Klein, *The Life and Legend of Jay Gould* (Baltimore: Johns Hopkins University Press, 1986), chaps. 10–11 passim; and idem, *Union Pacific* (Garden City, N.Y.: Doubleday, 1987), chapt. 14 passim.

[53] Brownlee, *Dynamics of Ascent,* pp. 307–15; and Margaret G. Myers, *A Financial History of the United States* (New York: Columbia University Press, 1970), pp. 197–200.

[54] Ripley, *Railroads: Finance and Organization,* p. 109. Par value provides a better estimate of funds obtained by the sale of securities because retained earnings are generated internally.

[55] The ratios were derived from a 1908 ICC report noted in Ripley, *Railroads: Finance and Organization,* p. 63. The main reason for differing intercorporate holdings stems from regulation. Because state laws often required local incorporation, geographical expansion led to the holdings of securities of many operating subsidiaries in particular states.

[56] The textile industry experienced a similar pattern. Paul F. McGouldrick, *New England Textiles in the Nineteenth Century* (Cambridge, Mass.: Harvard University Press, 1968), p. 171, notes: "Net stock issues were an insignificant

leverage contributed to the high rate of railroad failures during the Depression of 1893, since it became increasingly difficult for railroads to service their debt. By 1897, the railroads forced into receivership represented more than 25 percent of the industry's total capitalization and more than 40 percent of its track mileage. This experience is consistent with the observation that debt issues were necessary in order to attract funds from distant investors with little knowledge of the business because asymmetric information impeded public markets in equity securities.[57]

The patterns apparent in corporate capital structure largely reflected imperfections in financial markets. Broad, anonymous markets first arose for debt securities because they faced fewer impediments than equity instruments and thus could be more readily sold to distant investors. Debt leverage enabled corporations to surmount the serious barriers to acquiring adequate financing that resulted from risks associated with economic risks, as well as the problems of agency and asymmetric information. Finally, the differential effects of taxation in this period seem to be negligible in explaining the strong preference for debt financing (whether based on income or some form of personalty).

V. Financing through Preferred Stock

Common stock and debt were not the sole sources of nineteenth century corporate finance. Preferred stock financing, which incorporated some of the contractual features of debt, was used extensively by the end of the century. From the inception of its usage in England in the 1840s, preferred stock began a metamorphosis from functioning as a true equity security to a fixed-income instrument that could effectively supplement bonds in a corporation's financing mix.

source of funds prior to the Civil War and minor or exceptional thereafter. . . . It is rather clear that stock financing was a last resort." Unlike railroads, internally generated cash flows seemed to have been more important. The small size of textile enterprises may have made it difficult to raise capital through bond issuance, and short-term lending from commercial banks may have provided the primary financial support for receivables and inventories.

[57] Chandler, *Visible Hand*, pp. 171–75; Ripley, *Railroads: Finance and Organization*, p. 108; Dewing, *Financial Policy of Corporations*, p. 750; and Jenks, *Migration of British Capital*, p. 292.

Preferred stock was developed as a financial innovation in Britain. It provided a means to raise additional capital to complete construction of financially troubled canals and railroads and was also an instrument that satisfied the government's debt–equity ratio requirements for these types of businesses. It was designed partially to overcome shareholder objections to the issuance of additional stock, which diluted the equity of the original owners. The new preference shares usually combined the features of both fixed-income and equity securities. It provided a guaranteed dividend rate and, if the shares were participating, could also receive dividends in excess of the guaranteed rate, thus in some ways resembling common stock. Moreover, a corporation could not be forced into receivership if dividends, unlike bond interest, fell in arrears. The significance of this development is reflected by the fact that, by 1849, 66 percent of the total share capital in British railroads took this form.[58]

The popularity of preferred stock financing in the United States was greatly enhanced when in 1871 the Pennsylvania Company used these securities to finance the formation of what was then the world's largest corporation (in terms of capitalization), the Pennsylvania Railroad. Preferred stock financing became a major source of funding, especially among the emergent industrial corporations that soon dominated the economy. Preferred stock was an attractive investment vehicle because it was a fixed-income instrument that could be more readily priced than common stock by investors with poor knowledge of the issuer's business. Moreover, it accustomed the public to a security whose payments were less certain than interest on debt and thereby appears to have been instrumental in the later acceptance of common stock as a legitimate vehicle for outside investors.[59]

---

[58] See Evans, *British Corporation Finance*, pp. 39–81; and idem, "Preferred Stock in the United States, 1850–1878," *American Economic Review* 21 (March 1931): 56–62. The offering of a guaranteed return was judged to be superior to selling discounted equity, possibly because it facilitated negotiating over values. See also Kindleberger, *Financial History of Western Europe*, pp. 200–202.

[59] The current eclipse of preferred stock is due primarily to the imposition of discriminatory corporate tax in the United States in 1909 and in the United Kingdom in 1947. However, utility corporations continue to make extensive use of preferred stock financing because they generally can shift its burden to consumers through the rate regulatory process.

From the perspective of corporate managers, preferred stock and debt financing were advantageous because they did not dilute control. Besides establishing claims against any future dividends declared, share ownership at that time often imparted rights to vote for directors. Voting rights generally had little value to small investors because of the inconsequential amounts of their holdings and their lack of motivation or sophistication for participating actively in corporate governance. But these voting rights exposed incumbent managers and directors to the danger of challenges to their leadership mounted by powerful rival syndicates. This was of great significance in the railroad industry, where the most efficient entities were large regional lines that had been built up in the 1880s by the merger of many small lines. Without the control of these vast consolidations, potential operating efficiencies could not have been achieved. Witness, for example, the bitter struggle between Vanderbilt and Gould for control of the Erie and the later struggle of the houses of J. P. Morgan and Kuhn–Loeb for the Northern Pacific.[60]

Control had other important implications for managerial discretion in directing corporate affairs. There were few regulatory barriers preventing officers and directors from exploiting the corporations they controlled for their own ends. Moreover, the poor quality of financial reporting made it difficult for shareholders to hold anyone accountable. The extremes of misrepresentation and misconduct observed in various scandals raised the question of whether corporate resources were managed in the best interests of shareholders.[61] These were the

---

[60] For competition over the Erie, see items cited in note 52, this chapter. For Morgan–Hill competition with Kuhn–Loeb–Harriman interests over the Northern Pacific, see Carosso, *The Morgans,* pp. 474–79 and 528–30.

[61] See, e.g., Arthur Stone Dewing, *Corporate Promotions and Reorganizations* (Cambridge, Mass.: Harvard University Press, 1914), pp. 112–64, for a discussion of the National Cordage failure in 1893. Although dominant in the domestic industry, the complex nature of the operations associated with rope manufacturing prevented its organizers from realizing any substantial economies of scale or scope. Consequently, the primary economic benefits accrued to the firm's promoters, who, like the earlier organizers of the South Sea Company, maintained the prices of its shares by disseminating misleading financial information and by using underwriting proceeds to pay large dividends. Some of the methods used early in the twentieth century to manipulate the prices of new securities issues are detailed in Thomas W. Lawson, *Frenzied Finance* (New York: Ridgeway–Thayer, 1905).

central themes underlying the Armstrong Committee's investigation of life insurance company investment policies in New York State in 1905 and the Pujo Congressional Committee's investigation in 1913 of the so-called Money Trust and the potential conflicts of interest arising from interlocking corporate directorates.[62] This concern was also echoed in Louis D. Brandeis's classic, *Other People's Money and How the Bankers Use It*.[63] Just as investors relished the safety of mortgage bonds, managers may have been loath to risk losing control of their companies and so were reluctant to encourage large public holdings of common stock.

The heavy reliance on debt financing during the nineteenth century created two problems. The first was associated with the belief that loans should be secured by liens on tangible property.[64] Financing expansion by issuing new mortgage bonds was frequently fraught with complex legal issues. Prior liens had to be reconciled with the collateral expected to provide security for new obligations. The intricate financial structures that developed from this process underlined the need for unsecured fixed-income securities. Although preferred stock helped to satisfy this requirement, these securities were partially displaced after World War I by the more widespread use of debentures.[65]

The other drawback was that debt finance increased the bankruptcy

[62] For the Armstrong Committee, see Carosso, *Investment Banking*, pp. 110–36; Morton Keller, *The Life Insurance Enterprise 1885–1910: A Study in the Limits of Corporate Power* (Cambridge, Mass.: Harvard University Press, 1963), pp. 200–15 and 254–59 passim; R. Carlyle Buley, *The Equitable Life Assurance Society of the United States, 1859–1964*, 2 vols. (New York: Appleton-Century-Crofts, 1967), pp. 609–95 passim; and Carosso, *The Morgans*, pp. 530–34. For Pujo, see Carosso, *Investment Banking*, pp. 137–55; idem, *The Morgans*, chapt. 18 passim; and George David Smith and Richard Sylla, *The Transformation of Finance Capitalism: An Essay on the History of American Capital Markets* (Cambridge, Mass.: Blackwell, 1993), pp. 23–27.

[63] Louis D. Brandeis, *Other People's Money and How the Bankers Use It*, reprint ed. (New York: A. M. Kelley, 1914, 1971).

[64] As noted earlier, ancient and medieval bankers had strong preferences for collateralizing their lending contracts with insured cargoes, tax receipts, land or exclusive state-granted privileges.

[65] The decline of interest in mortgage bonds began during the massive railroad reorganizations of the 1890s, when investors started to recognize the limited value of holding liens on assets that lacked liquidity. Creditors increasingly realized that repayment depended on the earnings of the borrowers. The value of past outlays was not relevant in assessing credit quality. Mortgages, in

risk of the enterprise. Bankruptcies were common during this period even among the largest corporations. Many of the new large industrial companies experienced tumultuous beginnings before they became securely established paragons of financial strength in the twentieth century.[66] In this environment there was need for a security that could be evaluated with reasonable accuracy by a poorly informed public and that also would allow managers to reduce cash payments to investors in the event of financial stringency. For this reason preferred stock was often substituted in corporate reorganizations for defaulted bonds. This practice was widespread among the major railroads that reemerged from bankruptcy after the great recession of the 1890s.[67]

Preferred stock had a lasting influence in the search for a method for raising funds while minimizing bankruptcy risk because it reinforced the idea that equity should provide a fixed dividend. However, other methods were tried. One stratagem was the issuance of deep-discount bonds that promised a capital gain at maturity. Another was to substitute an equity option in bonded debt contracts for the traditional lien on tangible property. This latter arrangement was a refinement of the earlier practice of giving bonus stock to purchasers of risky bonds. A rise in the share price above the conversion ratio could lead to the retirement of substantial long-term obligations without the need for cash payments. In fact, the debentures floated during the period 1901–14 mostly had convertible features.[68]

Income bonds, which were used at the turn of the century to recapitalize bankrupt firms, were another device having some similarities to preferred stock.[69] Although they had a higher preference on corporate assets in liquidation than preferred stock, their primary difference was

effect, occupied a position that inherently was not different from other investors. Dewing, *Financial Policy of Corporations,* p. 1428, indicates that, in early reorganizations "the fundamental legal distinction between the shareholder and the bondholder was usually forgotten, and it became the policy and practice of reorganization committees to look at the position of junior security holders as differing among themselves only in degree and not in kind." Dewing further notes that initially the practice was to make assessments rather than to secure new external financing. Thus, holders of senior obligations were in some cases charged more.

[66] Dewing, *Corporate Promotion.*
[67] Ripley, *Railroads: Finance and Organization,* pp. 98–99.
[68] Cleveland and Powell, *Railroad Promotion,* pp. 156–64.
[69] Ripley, *Railroads: Finance and Organization,* pp. 139–41.

the criterion that cash payments were contingent on the firm's achieving positive net earnings, while preferred dividends were contingent upon payment to common shareholders. However, income bonds fell into disfavor because of investors' suspicions that in a period of lax accounting standards, reported earnings could be manipulated to their disadvantage. By contrast, the continued reliance on preferred stock suggests that investors were better protected by the right of prior claim to dividends. Apparently, investors thought that common dividends were crucial for ordinary shares to be evaluated fairly in public markets. The lack of a cumulative feature in many early preferred issues evidences this belief as well as the importance of a continuous stream of common dividends.

As industrial financing established an important place in national public markets in the early years of the twentieth century, the popularity of preferred stock financing crested. A contemporary authority has noted:

In the promotion of many industrial and public utility enterprises, preferred stocks have been used for the purpose of enlisting capital from the public on what appears to have been liberal terms while the control of the enterprise was held by an issue of common stock which stood for the potential earnings power of the corporation but which represented no investment of capital.[70]

Heavy reliance on fixed-income securities was consistent with the view that it was the only means for soliciting funds on fair terms from a skeptical and poorly informed public. Nor was the high leverage implicit in these financing plans inconsistent with the prospective market power of the emergent economic enterprises. Many of the railroads and public utilities were natural monopolies whose propensities for extracting monopoly rents were constrained only by the intervention of regulatory agencies. An important motive for the industrial consolidations of this period was to reduce market competition. The drive to enhance market power through industrial concentration may have mitigated much of the perceived risk of high fixed-income burdens. In

---

[70] Dewing, *Financial Policy of Corporations*, p. 141. William H. Lough similarly noted in *Business Finance* (New York: Ronald Press, 1922), p. 75, "It has become customary to represent the tangible assets and current earnings power of corporations by bonds and preferred shares and to represent the intangible assets and expected income by common shares."

any event, common stocks were considered to be extremely volatile and were generally sold through informal channels. Preferred stocks, however, found a ready market and after 1900 were usually issued by established brokers and investment bankers.[71]

Why did industrial enterprises use preferred stock for raising capital more extensively than railroads did? Perhaps the pools of tangible assets that could serve as collateral were more limited than in the case of railroads. Perhaps the giant industrial firms were considered more risky; in this case, as it turned out, investors were wrong, as it was the railroads that suffered great losses in subsequent decades. In any case, anonymous public markets in industrial securities began with fixed-income instruments, which followed the pattern established earlier by the railroads and government debt.

VI. Conclusion

In what ways does the experience of this era complement the theoretical explanations advanced by contemporary scholars about the nature of corporate finance? How did changes in the institutional framework that affected finance contribute to the efficient functioning of the railroads?

The experience of early canal and railroad financing sheds light on the question of how corporate debt ratios were determined. At the beginning of the twentieth century, pioneering academic theorists broadly accepted the idea of "trading on equity." Central to this idea is the implicit recognition of the problem of asymmetric information and the effects it has on defining the relative shares of debt and equity in corporate finance. This theory is illustrated by the hypothetical case of investors who, although they control a business opportunity with expectations of favorable future returns, either are reluctant to risk personally or may be incapable of generating the investment capital necessary to achieve maximum economic output and efficiency. The original investors have to choose between two options. They may elect to share their potential profits (monopoly rents) in order to attract equity investment from less informed and more cautious outside ven-

---

[71] Thomas R. Navin and Marian V. Sears, "The Rise of a Market for Industrial Stocks, 1887–1902," *Business History Review* 29 (June 1955): 122.

turers who demand a premium rate of return for the greater risk they are running. Alternatively, they may decide to finance by issuing risk-free liabilities at market rates in order to maintain their monopoly of economic profits. In this case the original investors make up the capital deficiency exclusively through the issuance of debt. The debt ratio then is a function of the amount of original equity compared with the total investment.

These ideas became formalized by Gordon Donaldson in what has been called the "pecking order hypothesis." To illustrate: businesses initially seek to finance their operations by retaining earnings; when this source proves insufficient, managements turn to debt financing; the sale of additional equity will occur only under the most pressing of circumstances. Again this logic assumes that awareness of the asymmetry in information availability mitigates the willingness of various classes of potential investors to commit their wealth. The theory contends that firms desire to maintain steady dividend payments to avoid the loss of investor confidence associated with reduced payments. Consequently, firms are also reluctant to increase substantially the size of dividend payments to minimize the risk of future cuts. Faced with an inelastic supply of retained earnings, they are compelled to seek funding from external sources to finance any expansion of their activities. But equity sales are assumed to be constrained by the difficulties that managements face in pricing additional shares. Moreover, the decision of better-informed managements to sell equity to outsiders also signals that the shares are overpriced. Furthermore, investors' suspicions are aroused whenever managements seem uncertain enough about the future that they avoid incurring the fixed-interest charges resulting from new debt flotations. Consequently, the theory predicts that debt ratios are function-determined primarily by the level of retained earnings and the overall amount of investment. Debt becomes the residual or balancing factor in the balance sheet.

Although there is much empirical evidence supporting the pecking order hypothesis, it was eclipsed by the theories of Modigliani and Miller. In the 1963 (second) version of their a priori model, which assumed perfectly efficient capital markets, corporate debt ratios were explained as resulting from a trade-off between the risk of bankruptcy associated with increasing financial leverage and the tax benefits accruing from the deductibility of interest charges. Tax laws should encourage debt finance but the potentials for excessive leverage to the point of bankruptcy should encourage prudence. This theory, which claimed that corporations should and, in fact, do structure their capitalization according to a static trade-off between taxes and risk, soon permeated the pedagogical literature.

Although the two main elements providing the underpinning to Modigliani and Miller's work are logically correct, several questions have belatedly encouraged a search for supporting empirical evidence. It is impossible, for instance, to establish ex ante magnitudes for tax benefits and leverage risk; in addition, markets remain imperfect and information is never even remotely symmetrical.

As we have previously noted, the empirical literature does not seem to affirm Modigliani and Miller's revised explanation of the relationship between debt and taxes. One recent article reports no observable correlation between tax rates and the reduction of corporate costs of capital and only slight effects on enterprise risk; but this is not surprising considering the slow and complex adjustments that have shaped the policies in the Internal Revenue Code since its inception. These policies have, particularly in recent years, seemed to serve at cross-purposes. Similarly, recent British tax reforms are difficult to evaluate because they occurred at the same time as several other major economic changes. A long-term examination of how capital structures change over time may provide more useful insights into the role of corporate taxes and finance.

However, corporate practice reflected a strong preference for debt financing in both the United States and Britain during the nineteenth century, even in the absence of any substantial tax benefits. The evidence indicates that the primary determinant of debt leverage could not have been interest deductibility – it was simply too meager. Corporate taxes, in fact, were negligible both in the United States before 1909 and in Britain before 1947. In the United States a few states had unsuccessfully tried to establish income taxes before 1900, but this netted only small amounts of revenue. In Britain, on the other hand, with the exception of extraordinary wartime measures, corporate taxes during the period 1842–1947 were treated as withholdings applicable to the tax liabilities of an enterprise's investors. Moreover, the tax rate in Britain was modest during the nineteenth century, amounting to about 10 percent. It is doubtful whether assessments of such modest magnitude influenced corporate decision making in important ways. In addition, some governments imposed direct taxes on corporate equity capital. In New York and Massachusetts, franchise taxes were levied on railroads, utilities, banks and insurance companies, often by applying a low rate on total contributed capital and surplus. But again, the relative immateriality of these assessments as compared with the substantial revenue raised by the more onerous real estate taxes attests to the marginal role they no doubt played in corporate finance policy.

The heavy reliance on bonds during the nineteenth century, when income taxes were insignificant, suggests that the Modigliani–Miller thesis might be fruitfully extended by taking into consideration the influence that informational asymmetries had on investor preferences. The distribution of knowledge during this period was neither efficient nor frictionless. Initially investors were poorly informed about the underlying economics of a revolutionary transport modality; they also remained at a disadvantage in their knowledge of the firm when dealing with management. Prudence thus dictated a strong preference for bonds, which were endowed with provisions for preserving capital in the event of business failure and whose guarantees of fixed-income payments facilitated asset pricing. The attractiveness of this class of contracts was further enhanced by the monopoly power that many railroads exercised in particular markets during the formative years of the industry.

The penchant for debt financing was also reinforced by important managerial priorities. As noted earlier, many railroad promoters preferred debt because it avoided worrisome shifts in enterprise ownership and control. Moreover, debt was a less risky form of financing from the perspective of investors and thus represented a cheaper source of financing (whether or not interest charges were deductible for tax purposes). The position of creditors was insulated against the risks of bankruptcy by the cushion provided by common and preferred stock and retained earnings. This relative cost advantage no doubt made debt financing seem more attractive to managements in the capital-intensive railroad industry.

Besides the market imperfections that account for many of the variances between industry practice and the ideal world of theory, there was a fundamental difference in the priorities that conditioned the choices of nineteenth century railroad managers and a key behavioral assumption underlying the modern theory. In the latter case, finance was evaluated under the assumption that management's pri-

160

mary objective was to maximize the value of the firm. However important, that objective seems to have been secondary to the overriding concern of management to maintain control of the business entity. This circumstance created a strong bias in railroad financial planning in favor of debt over equity finance.

These tendencies toward heavy debt reliance gradually diminished as industry leaders and investors became more competent in assessing the risks inherent in this policy. A steady accretion of knowledge about the capacities and reliability of individual companies and their managements diminished uncertainty. Investor perceptions were constantly updated by reports of the courts and governmental authorities, financial statements, articles and books. They were also shaped by the industry's experience during great crises such as the crashes of 1871 and 1893; these dire events were acid tests of the viability of corporate financial plans. The relative performance of companies during these crises helped to set the boundaries of safety in debt finance. This experience also encouraged the promotion of preferred stock as a quasi-debt security that could neither trigger a bankruptcy nor disturb the allocation of enterprise ownership interests.

The history of the nineteenth century railroads also illustrated the changing role of the state in the monitoring of corporate affairs. This transition came about because of two factors. The first was the decline of the mercantilism that conceived of the corporation as an adjunct to the state. This was most apparent in Britain, where new beliefs emerged about the efficacy of free trade and about the benefits resulting from a laissez-faire attitude toward business. The second factor was the proliferation of corporations in the nineteenth century, which prevented government from maintaining the informal and intimate contacts with leading enterprises that had existed in the age of the great trading companies. A new order emerged that defined state–business relationships through impersonal laws and regulations.

British investors, however, had to rely primarily on the courts and private professional groups rather than state administrative agencies for protection against transgressions of corporate law. The Board of Trade and its subsidiary Registrar of Companies were essentially sunshine agencies monitoring the filing of periodic corporate financial reports, rather than enforcement agencies with significant powers. Corporate governance was thus highly dependent on the actions of many self-regulating expert groups – for example, those representing

161

lawyers, chartered accountants, underwriters, brokers and bankers. These private groups were crucial in ensuring the viability of the nation's financial markets.

Although the corporate form and its limited liability were also adopted into the commercial law of various states in the United States, government's role in corporate governance was initially most strongly felt in the regulation of natural monopolies such as railroads and utilities. Comprehensive national legislation comparable to the companies acts did not emerge in the United States until the passage of the securities acts in the 1930s.

Government monitoring of the railroad industry sought to satisfy a more complex set of stakeholder interests than has been contemplated in the explanations rendered thus far by agency theorists. A vast scholarly literature identifies a diversity of interests and objectives. Some railroad leaders welcomed federal regulation as a means of curtailing the destructive rate competition that eroded industry profitability and of containing the disruptive actions of speculators like Jay Gould. Shipping interests believed that government control over rates was necessary to prevent unfair and discriminatory pricing. Some government officials believed that rate regulation could assist in achieving a more equitable distribution of regional income; basing shipping rates on the value of service was a way of subsidizing southern and western farmers and eastern urban laborers by maintaining low charges for the transport of foods and fuels. These objectives were crucial to government leaders who had witnessed during the Civil War how disruptive it could be not to reconcile sectional economic differences. Others feared that the failure to regulate natural monopolies would corrupt politics and undermine democratic institutions. Finally, investors supported public governance because it promised to protect their interests by stabilizing competition and by assuring the distribution of vital financial information.

However, state intervention in the regulation of railroads also imposed heavy burdens on the U.S. economy, much as the monopoly powers of the seventeenth century trading companies had imposed burdens on the English economy. Federal regulation introduced distortions in the economy through the administrative pricing of rail services. The political support for such a structure was long lasting. During the Great Depression of the 1930s the problem was made worse by broadening the scope of the ICC's authority to include inland water transportation and interstate trucking. It was not until the 1980s that this costly form of market governance was finally abandoned.[72]

The experience of the railroads during the nineteenth century also revealed a relationship between owners and managers that was different from those that Meckling and Jensen had analyzed in their seminal study. These latter scholars stressed how agency costs and financing choices were influenced by the relative amount of enterprise equity held by managers. Owner-managers behaved differently than managers who owned insignificant amounts of enterprise equity. Their different outlooks were attributable to dissimilarities in the sources of their personal wealth and income. The potentials for managers to appropriate inordinate amounts of enterprise resources and so maximize their wealth and income provided the rationale for outside investors to protect their interests by incurring bonding and monitoring costs.

The nineteenth century experience of the railroads, however, indicated that it was a competition between two antagonistic classes of owners that served as the dynamic in decisions over investment and dividend policies. These groups – speculators and investors – were motivated by different financial objectives. As noted earlier, speculators were interested primarily in the railroads as vehicles for generating large profits in the stock market. Investors, on the other hand, desired stability in the securities markets and were more interested in steady dividend and interest payments than speculative capital gains. Typical of this latter group were the Boston capitalists led by John Murray Forbes and Peter Geddes who developed the Chicago, Burlington and Quincy Railroad (CBQ) after the Civil War. Initially, they had hoped to keep the railroad relatively small so as to be able to distribute a substantial fraction of the company's cash flow to stakeholders. This plan had to be abandoned with the threatened encroachment of Gould and others on their business. The investors, who through their roles as directors had exercised strong powers over the railroad, were compelled to undertake a costly, defensive strategy that required a major expansion of the line to ensure access to crucial terminals and to protect vital feeder lines. In creating an integrated regional system CBQ's trackage grew from 500 miles in 1870 to nearly 5,000 in 1887. Substantial capital had to be reinvested in the business

---

[72] Miranti, "Mind's Eye of Reform," pp. 499–509.

and thus limited the amount available to shareholders. The experience of the CBQ was not unique.[73] Contemporary parallels are found in the histories of the Pennsylvania, the New York Central, the Santa Fe and other leading railroads that created integrated, regional lines during this period.

The efficiency gains associated with railroad finance emanated from the formation of propitious linkages between several institutional developments. The rise of the modern corporation encouraged entrepreneurial activity by reducing the risks of equity ownership through limited liability. This new arrangement enabled business promoters to specify the maximum amount of loss they would incur for any particular venture. Equity owners were further protected because limited liability effectively shifted a greater portion of the risk of business failure to creditors, who in the event of business failure could seek to recover only the assets of the corporation. The diminishment of the creditor's position, however, was offset by increases in economic growth brought about by these corporate developments and the consequent broadened opportunities for profitable lending.

This change created new needs for knowledge of the financial and operational activities of the modern corporation. Information was critical to passive equity investors in large-scale enterprises with a substantial degree of separation of ownership from control because it helped to reduce risk perceptions and to ensure more effective monitoring of management activities. Information was also vital to lenders in assessing credit risk for businesses whose owners were protected by limited liability rules.

Although information was vital, the development of reliable channels for its distribution progressed slowly, which affected the preferences of investors for equity and debt securities. In an environment of imperfect information, the potential risks inherent in equity ownership were greater than those for debt. For risk-averse investors the primary advantage of debt was its stronger claims on enterprise property and income. Interest payments were guaranteed, while dividends payments were made at the discretion of the board of directors. Bondholders

[73] Alfred D. Chandler, Jr., and Richard S. Tedlow, *The Coming of Managerial Capitalism: A Casebook on the History of American Economic Institutions* (Homewood, Ill.: Irwin, 1985), pp. 227–45 passim.

were often better protected against the adverse consequences of bankruptcy by liens on property or by having a priority over shareholders in any recovery from liquidating assets. In reorganizations the stronger legal rights of bondholders translated into a better mix of securities in the reconstituted entity than that afforded equity owners. Moreover, bondholders could impose constraints on the freedom of action of corporate managements through the definition of restrictive covenants in bond indenture agreements. Finally, in the case of profitable businesses the pricing of bonds was simpler than that of equity. Valuation was determined essentially by reference to the current market price of issues with the same coupon and risk rating. In the case of equity, on the other hand, valuation was more problematic because it depended on projections of the trend of future earnings available to pay dividends.

Finance also served to promote railroad efficiency both directly and indirectly. Because of the great scale of railroad operating activities, one of the most direct economies involved the lowering of the cost of capital and the costs of financial transacting. In addition, railroad finance indirectly facilitated the achievement of other important economies. Stable financing made possible the realization of economies of scale from the exploitation of coal-based transportation technology. Financial stability also enabled the railroads to overcome severe market imperfections through the establishment of hierarchical administrative structures that made possible the coordination and control of rail transportation activities throughout their service regions.

In facilitating the enhancement of efficiency, the key objective of financial policy was to provide a stable environment that was conducive to extending corporate capabilities through a path-dependent process of firm-specific learning. Central to this effort was the need for sufficient time to learn what were the most efficacious ways for exploiting the economic potentials of technology and management. In this context it was finance's role to insulate these vital learning processes against external disruptions by structuring a flexible mix of debt and equity claims that balanced the cash flow requirements of the enterprise and outside stakeholders.

Many of the same factors that shaped railroad finance were also influential in the experience of the giant industrial and utility corporations of the twentieth century. As in the case of the railroads, government played a central role in their finance. In this latter case, however, the objective was not to control market competition. Instead, as the following chapter indicates, the regulatory structures that appeared in the 1930s sought to ensure probity and competency among the many professional groups on which the financial markets depended for efficient functioning.

CHAPTER FIVE

Common Stock Finance and the Rise of Managerial Capitalism, 1900–1940

I. Introduction

This chapter focuses on investors' growing interest in corporate common stock during the first four decades of the twentieth century. Although broad, anonymous markets for equity-share trading emerged in many centers worldwide, our discussion concentrates on developments in the foremost market for these securities of this period, the New York Stock Exchange (NYSE) on Wall Street, where a growing population of middle-class investors goaded by the prospects of capital gains and increasing dividends committed resources to industrial and utility shares. The increasing importance of equity is reflected in NYSE statistics: total annual share turnover rose from 159 million in 1900 to 1.1 billion at the height of the 1929 boom; the value of preferred and common stocks underwritten amounted to $405 million in 1910 and increased to $9.4 billion in 1929; and Standard and Poor's Composite Common Stock Index (1941– 43 = 10.0) zigzagged upward from 6.15 in 1900 to 26.02 in 1929.[1] The transition to broader common stock ownership in the United States was facilitated by the rise of what Alfred D. Chandler has termed "managerial capitalism." Large-scale, hierarchical business enterprises whose activities were controlled by professional managers became the source of great economic efficiency in both the manufacturing and utilities sectors.

---

[1] See U.S. Bureau of the Census, *Historical Statistics of the United States: Colonial Times to 1970*, 2 vols. (Washington, D.C.: Government Printing Office, 1975), p. 1006 for securities flotations and p. 1007 for sales volume. For a discussion of the rise of markets for industrial equities, see Baskin, "Development of Corporate Financial Markets," pp. 222–36.

Although first evident during the last quarter of the nineteenth century, firms of this caliber came to full flourish during the 1920s, many growing strongly because of their ability to exploit opportunities associated with the advent of the internal combustion engine or electrical power. The consequent increase in corporate wealth induced investors to seek to profit from these developments by purchasing corporate equity securities. This shift was encouraged by the rise of specialized intermediaries that insulated against some of the risks of equity ownership by offering financial management expertise and the chance to invest in diversified portfolios.

The rise of managerial capitalism, however, changed the position of investors in fundamental ways. Unlike the small, family-controlled firms characteristic of the preindustrial economy, there was a high degree of separation of ownership and control in the modern corporation. Professional managers, who usually owned only small portions of equity, became the primary decision makers within large corporations. The influence of founding families was generally eclipsed as successive generations frequently lacked either the ability or the interest to guide corporate affairs. Similarly, the influence of investment bankers on corporate boards declined with rising profits and the ability of the enterprise to finance its operational activities through retained earnings. Although the number of common stock investors increased greatly, they were generally relegated to the role of *rentiers* who exercised little power in corporate governance.

The new relationships brought about by managerial capitalism experienced a crisis with the stock market collapse in 1929, which led to a shift in the main focus of institution building in finance from the private to the public sector. Some idea of the severity of this dislocation, which motivated greater governmental activism, was communicated by changes in the level of the Standard and Poor's Composite Common Stock Index. It dropped precipitously to a record low of 6.93 in 1932, a level previously attained more than three decades earlier in 1900. Moreover, the index recovered only to 12.06 by 1939 and did not reach its 1929 highs again until 1954. The institutional changes that were mounted by the federal government in response to this great dislocation were of two types. The first and more successful were the efforts to use federal power to strengthen the functioning of the stock market. This was partially achieved by ensuring greater transparency of corporate affairs, which reduced risk aversion and also increased the range of opportunities for profitable transacting by market participants. It resulted also from the creation of new legal safeguards to protect investors against the dishonesty or incompetency of financial market agents. Such actions helped to restore confidence without diminishing the financial market's ability to provide investment liquidity or to price securities efficiently. The second and less satisfying direction of reform involved attempts to restore prosperity and stability by using federal power to place constraints on the free operation of market forces. This latter course, which was particularly notable in banking and in several public service industries, proved costly because it contributed to the inefficient distribution of scarce economic resources.[2]

This chapter analyzes this important transition in seven steps. It begins by assessing the fundamental business and economic changes underpinning the rise of managerial capitalism that enhanced the attractiveness of equity investment. This had two aspects. The first was technological, involving the exploitation of new sources of energy and the systematic application of scientific research, which created investment opportunities in the manufacturing and utilities sectors. The second was managerial, involving the establishment of new marketing strategies and administrative structures that bolstered efficiency and reduced risk. This promising coalescence of enhanced managerial and technological capacities induced many to accept the higher inherent risks of owning equity.

The chapter goes on to show how the public only gradually came to accept equity investing because it seemed to share common characteristics with better-established forms of finance. Thus, the third section explains how equity finance was initially perceived by investors as being similar to partnerships. The fourth section demonstrates how the problem of equity valuation was strongly influenced by patterns that had originally been established for rating bonds.

The next three sections consider the emerging role of financial accounting as a primary category of knowledge useful in the evaluation of equity shares. The fifth section explains the emergence of "book value" as an informal standard for judging the worth of securities, and the types of institutional and professional arrangements that

---

[2] U.S. Bureau of the Census, *Historical Statistics of the United States,* pp. 1004–1005.

made possible the dissemination of this information. The sixth section explains how problems associated with the standardization of financial accounting and a general lack of disclosure of corporate affairs encouraged some investors to rely on alternative indicators of corporate financial health such as the patterns evident in the payment of cash dividends. The seventh section analyzes the actions taken by the federal government to revive corporate finance by extending the scope of economic regulation during the Great Depression of the 1930s.

The conclusion considers how the experience of this period of strong equity growth amplifies the theoretical explanations rendered by contemporary scholars about the nature of corporate finance and how financial institutional innovation promoted firm efficiency. It also considers the factors that differentiated key patterns of institutional development in Britain and the United States. It concludes by comparing the economic trade-offs inherent in the type of institution building that changed U.S. corporate finance in the 1920s with that which followed in the 1930s.

II. The Economic Background of Corporate Financial Innovation

The rise of equity financing roughly coincided with a major economic transformation brought about by the extension of capacities for generating electrical power and by the exploitation of the potentials of the internal combustion engine. The establishment of large-scale electrical generating capabilities beginning in the 1880s contributed to growth in several ways: it reduced energy costs for consumers and industry; it made possible the formation of efficient rapid transit systems in large urban centers; it provided industry with a cheap and more flexible power source that facilitated cost-saving reconfigurations of plant design; and it induced demand for a wide range of manufactures including wire, cable, insulating material, electrical machinery, lighting equipment, radios, phonographs, home appliances, turbines and transformers. In the case of the internal combustion engine demand increased sharply, beginning during the first decade of the twentieth century for automobiles, trucks and, eventually, airplanes, new modalities that greatly enhanced the flexibility and the efficiency of transpor-

170

tation. Like electrical power, the automotive industry also exerted a multiplier effect on other manufactures, including petroleum, cement, steel, rubber, glass, paints and lacquers, fabrics and mechanical and electrical components.[3]

The development of new business strategies and organizational structures by leading enterprises in America's burgeoning industrial sector enhanced efficiency and reduced risk. Initially, this involved the achievement of economies of scale through horizontal and vertical integration. These strategies in turn depended on the buildup within the business enterprise of specialized managerial and technological knowledge. This process was exemplified in the history of the Standard Oil Company in asserting its leadership in the petroleum-refining industry. In the 1880s, John D. Rockefeller and his associates tried to overcome disruptions resulting from periodic oversupply in this market by experimenting with ways to concentrate the ownership of refining facilities. After first trying producer pools and then trusts, these managerial innovators achieved success by creating highly centralized corporate structures that acquired control over a large fraction of the nation's refinery capacity. This enabled management to reduce costs substantially by marshalling production activities in new, efficient plants and by closing redundant, marginal units. This strategy was soon imitated by forward-looking companies in chemical-processing industries, including brewing, chemicals, metal smelting and refining and vegetable oil processing. It was also utilized by machinery manufacturers that could schedule long production runs for the fabrication and assembly of products made from standardized components.

The realization of potential economies of scale also often depended on the ability of firms to integrate their operations vertically. Vertical

---

[3] Kirkland, *History of American Economic Life,* pp. 319–46; Brownlee, *Dynamics of Ascent,* pp. 384–94. For specific industry studies, see J. B. Rae, *The American Automobile Industry* (Boston: Twayne, 1984); idem, *American Automobile Manufacturers: The First Forty Years* (Philadelphia: Chilton, 1959); H. C. Passer, *The Electrical Manufacturers, 1875–1900: A Study in Competition, Entrepreneurship, Technical Change and Economic Growth* (Cambridge, Mass.: Harvard University Press, 1953); A. A. Bright, Jr., *The Electric-Lamp Industry: Technological Change and Economical Development from 1800 to 1947* (New York: Macmillan, 1949); and W. R. MacLaurin, *Invention and Innovation in the Radio Industry* (New York: Macmillan, 1949).

integration sought to lower transaction costs by establishing more efficient internal structures for coordination and control over the vital services and supplies than was possible through reliance on outside agencies. Because profitability in a high-fixed-cost manufacturing environment was strongly affected by plant utilization rates, many leading firms sought to maintain high levels of demand for their products by integrating forward to marketing. This required the mastery of new firm-specific skills for selling and distributing finished products in global markets. By the beginning of the twentieth century Standard Oil, for example, had created a marketing department whose functioning could be more closely controlled than the independent oil wholesalers that the firm had earlier relied on in selling its finished products. Backward integration, on the other hand, might be undertaken to secure reliable sources of raw materials in short supply. Standard Oil initiated its exploration and production efforts during a period of petroleum scarcity. This type of integration might also achieve savings by developing internal capabilities for coordinating the smooth flow of vital inputs to manufacturing processes. An example of this was the widespread establishment among leading industrial firms during this period of centralized purchasing departments that became highly efficient in setting up dependable supply channels.[4]

A second source of economies that resulted from a more intensive use of productive and distributive resources came about by widening the basic scope of an enterprise's business.[5] One aspect of this was the broadening of the geographic limits of the firm's markets. Besides increasing efficiency, it reduced risk by diversifying a company's markets internationally. Initially, this involved the formation of export departments to sell excess domestic output overseas. Later, this lead to substantial direct investment by U.S. firms in foreign markets. On the eve of World War I the value of these outlays was estimated to be $2.65 billion.[6] A British observer of this international expansion noted:

---

[4] Chandler, *Visible Hand*, chapts. 2 and 4 passim. See also the cogent discussion relating to the first wave of industrial mergers at the turn of the century in Naomi R. Lamoreaux, *The Great Merger Movement in American Business, 1895–1904* (Cambridge University Press, 1985).

[5] Chandler, *Scale and Scope*, pp. 38–44 and chapts. 5–6 passim.

[6] Mira Wilkins, *The Emergence of the Multinational Enterprise: American Business Abroad from the Colonial Era to 1914* (Cambridge, Mass.: Harvard University Press, 1970), pp. 201–202.

The most serious aspect of the American industrial invasion lies in the fact that these newcomers have acquired control of almost every new industry created during the past fifteen years. . . . What are the chief new features in London life? They are, I take it, the telephone, the portable camera, the phonograph, the electric street car, the automobile, the typewriter, passenger lifts in houses, and the multiplication of machine tools. In everyone of these, save the petroleum automobile, the American maker is supreme; in several he is the monopolist.

By 1914, a U.S. manufacturer, the Ford Motor Company, would also be supreme in the automobile market.[7]

Economies of scope also derived from corporate scientific research that sought to discover new products for ensuring the intensive utilization of manufacturing and distributive resources. The success experienced by some firms, such as the Du Pont Company, was facilitated by the inherent flexibility of their core technologies. Its management was eager to discover new markets for nitrocellulose chemicals used in explosives, whose production capacities had been built up enormously during World War I. Research eventually made it possible for the company to redeploy much of its manufacturing resources to a broader array of products. By 1940, its earlier dependence on explosives had been displaced by significant investments in markets for photographic film, pyroxylin plastics, rayon, dyes, paints and lacquers, industrial chemicals and solvents and nylon. Du Pont's success led subsequently to the adaptation of the strategy of diversification in other technologically flexible industries, including chemical, rubber, petroleum, electronics, electrical equipment and power machinery.[8]

The successful implementation of these strategic choices required

[7] Quoted and discussed in ibid., pp. 215–17.
[8] Chandler, *Scale and Scope*, pp. 38–44 and chapts. 5–6 passim. For detailed discussion of technological progress at Du Pont, see David A. Hounshell and John Kenly Smith, Jr., *Science and Corporate Strategy: Du Pont R & D, 1902–1980* (Cambridge University Press, 1988). For a more general discussion of scientific inquiry and business, see Louis Galambos, "The American Economy and the Reorganization of the Sources of Knowledge," in Alexandra Olesin and John Voss, eds., *The Organization of Knowledge in Modern America, 1860–1920* (Baltimore: Johns Hopkins University Press, 1979), pp. 269–82; John Rae, "Application of Science to Industry," in ibid., pp. 249–68; and David F. Noble, *America by Design: Science, Technology and the Rise of Corporate Capitalism* (New York: Knopf, 1979).

the formation of organizational structures and the adoption of managerial procedures that were effective in coordinating and controlling complex, interdependent operating activities. The centralized line and staff administrative structure inherited from the railroads proved to be appropriate in achieving the economies of scale for single-product companies. A more decentralized structure, however, was necessary to exploit economies of scope. This was especially true where there was a substantial diversification of product lines. In these cases, manufacturing and distribution were best centered in semiautonomous operating divisions that specialized in serving the requirements of particular product markets. What remained centralized in the corporate office at multimarket firms was performance monitoring, resource allocation and general staff functions.[9]

These developments in technology and management were dramatically reflected in national output statistics. During the period 1899–1929, the U.S. gross national product (GNP) jumped (in current prices) from $17.4 billion to $103.1 billion (+593 percent). During the same period the value added in manufacturing jumped from $4.7 billion to $30.6 billion (+651 percent).[10]

Leading electrical utilities, however, followed an approach that was different from those employed by industrial enterprises during this period. In this industry the interregional holding company became a predominant form of organization. The establishment of these entities came about for several different reasons. Some were formed by manufacturers of equipment or engineering consulting enterprises who wished to secure safe outlets for either their goods or their services. Such was the motivation in the General Electric Company's founding of the Electric Bond and Share Company in 1914 and in Stone and Webster's sponsorship of Engineers Public Utility Company and the General Public Service Corporation. Other holding companies such as Insull Utilities Investments, which was established in 1928 in Chicago and controlled Commonwealth Edison Company and Middle West Utilities Company, functioned primarily as operating entities. Finally, holding companies were also established by investment banking houses such as the United Corporation, capitalized at $300 million

---

[9] Chandler, *Scale and Scope*, pp. 221–33.

[10] U.S. Bureau of the Census, *Historical Statistics of the United States*, p. 224 for GNP and p. 666 for value added in manufacturing.

and launched by an alliance of J. P. Morgan & Company, Drexel & Company and Bonbright & Company in 1929.

Although a few integrated backward to safeguard sources of fuel supplies, the primary thrust among the holding companies was to integrate horizontally by acquiring generating units in different regional markets. This latter policy offered several potential advantages. First, the concentration of ownership provided negotiating leverage with both equipment and fuel suppliers and large consumers. Interstate holding companies were also effective in surmounting legal obstacles imposed by particular states to prevent foreign-chartered corporations from serving their markets. The creation of extensive electrical transmission grids, moreover, improved the feasibility of achieving economies of scale through the construction of large and efficient generating facilities. The larger holding companies, such as Electric Bond and Share, Stone and Webster, American Electric Power and Insull Utilities Investments, sought to maximize the capital raised from the public by allowing subsidiaries to float bonds and preferred stock issues. The parent companies, however, retained tight control over their affiliates by holding a majority interest in their common stocks. Finally, separate capital structures for holding company affiliates facilitated both the process of financial supervision by local regulatory authorities and future spin-offs of particular subsidiaries.[11]

These corporate financing policies contributed to a vast expansion of electric power production, which increased from 6.0 billion kilowatts in 1902 to 116.7 billion kilowatts in 1929, a jump of 1,945 percent. Demand for electrical equipment also grew in tandem with rising power consumption. The total value added in manufacturing for this category rose from a mere $80 million in 1904 to $1.4 billion in 1929, a more than seventeenfold increase.[12] Moreover, growth in

---

[11] Forrest McDonald, *Insull* (Chicago: University of Chicago Press, 1962), pp. 133–61 and 245–73 passim; Carosso, *Investment Banking*, pp. 295–99; Robert Sobel, *The Big Board: A History of the New York Stock Market* (New York: Free Press, 1965), pp. 242–46; George H. Soule, *Prosperity Decade: From War to Depression, 1917–1929* (New York: Holt, Rinehart & Winston, 1962), pp. 143–44 and 298–304; and Robert Chatov, *Corporate Financial Reporting: Public or Private Control?* (New York: Free Press, 1975), pp. 14–15.

[12] U.S. Bureau of the Census, *Historical Statistics of the United States,* p. 820 for power production and p. 679 for value added in manufacture.

equipment production took place largely in giant, technology-driven enterprises that were capable of diversifying into many product markets. It was during this epoch that firms such as General Electric, Westinghouse and American Telephone & Telegraph's Western Electric subsidiary became synonymous with economic progress in this sector.[13]

Yet in spite of these achievements, the underlying financial system was prone to periodic crisis, which contributed to demands for more effective protection of investor interests. A fundamental problem was the effect that the highly cyclic nature of the economy's most dynamic industrial sectors and the high earnings leverage of leading companies had on the financial markets. The consequent high degree of variability in corporate profits contributed directly to the volatility of stock prices. At the beginning of the century U.S. political leaders had tried to address these problems by focusing on the banking system. President Theodore Roosevelt, for example, had responded to the Panic of 1907 by enlisting the assistance of the house of Morgan in shoring up the liquidity of the banking system. The disruptiveness of these events eventually induced Congress to establish the Federal Reserve System in 1913, which was, in effect, a central banking mechanism that served as a lender of last resort in financial emergencies. Although this reform bolstered the stability of the system, the edifice of financial market governance remained incomplete as the Great Crash of 1929 painfully demonstrated.[14]

---

[13] Robert W. Garnet, *The Telephone Enterprise: The Evolution of the Bell System's Horizontal Structure, 1876–1909* (Baltimore: Johns Hopkins University Press, 1985); Kenneth Lipartito, *The Bell System and Regional Business: The Telephone in the South, 1877–1920* (Baltimore: Johns Hopkins University Press, 1989); George David Smith, *The Anatomy of a Business Strategy: Bell, Western Electric and the Origins of the American Telephone Industry* (Baltimore: Johns Hopkins University Press, 1985); Leonard S. Reich, *The Making of American Industrial Research: Science and Business at GE and Bell, 1876–1926* (Cambridge University Press, 1985); and George Wise, *Willis R. Whitney, General Electric, and the Origins of U.S. Industrial Research* (New York: Columbia University Press, 1985).

[14] For the Federal Reserve, see James Livingston, *Origins of the Federal Reserve System: Money, Class and Corporate Capitalism, 1890–1913* (Ithaca, N.Y.: Cornell University Press, 1986); Eugene Nelson White, *The Regulation and Reform of the American Banking System, 1900–1929* (Princeton, N.J.: Princeton University Press, 1983); and Henry P. Willis, *The Federal Reserve*

The following section begins with an explanation of the change in public attitudes toward equity finance. Traditional ideas carried over from partnership finance continued to influence the perceptions of early shareholders. What is new and unfamiliar is often clarified by reference to well-established forms.

III. Early Equity Finance and Partnerships

The rise of large-scale public markets for common stocks was very much a post–World War I phenomenon. Earlier, equity shares were a convenient way to transfer ownership between limited circles of business associates, rather than instruments to support broad public dealings. From this aspect ordinary shares were perceived as being akin to partnership interests, a view that persisted until the middle of the nineteenth century. As Bishop Carleton Hunt has noted:

Hoary ideas of partnership continued to confuse thinking with regard to corporate enterprise. Partnership law, hammered out of common experience by the courts and riveted to the legal mind by a long line of decisions, was a barrier to the essential change that had taken place in the position of the investor. The typical shareholder was no longer an entrepreneur in the full sense of the word.[15]

The principle of limited liability, which was essential for the establishment of public markets, had not been fully recognized in Britain as an inherent feature of ordinary shares, as noted in the preceding chapter, until the promulgation of the Corporation Act of 1856. Before that date this benefit had been extended by Parliament to a relatively limited number of corporations.[16]

Although equity shares in the early canal and railroad companies were usually sold for nominal amounts, it was common for promoters to require investors to make additional contributions of funds as needed. This emulated the practice, as we have seen, of the early trading companies, which would usually collect only a fraction of the

System: Legislation, Organization and Operation (New York: Ronald Press, 1923). See also Berle and Means, The Modern Corporation and Private Property.

[15] Hunt, Development of the Business Corporation, pp. 129–30.
[16] Ibid., p. 134.

total value of its equity from subscribers. In the case of the trading companies, subsequent calls were infrequent because of the high profitability of early ventures. This, however, was not true of the more capital-intensive investments in canals and railroads. To ensure available capital to finance the extension of service, it was essential that equity subscribers be wealthy and deeply committed to the success of the enterprise. Consequently, promoters usually took steps to screen out "dummies," that is, speculative subscribers who could not be relied upon to meet any future calls for additional capital contributions. These contingent claims, expected during periods of financial stringency, impeded the formation of broad, impersonal markets for common shares.[17]

At many corporations, "rights issues" were frequently used to raise additional funds even after shares were fully paid for. Evans, for example, notes how this practice was linked to new offerings of preferred stock in Britain during the nineteenth century:

Almost invariably the new shares were first offered pro rata to the proprietors, though sometimes only to those who paid all calls on their shares. . . . When, and if, the shareholders failed to take up the full amount on a pro rata basis, anyone who wanted more than his share was allowed to purchase some of the remainder, and then, in case the issue was still not taken, an appeal was made to the public. How often companies had to appeal to the public for newly created preferred stocks cannot be stated. There are, however, a number of reasons for believing that such occasions were not numerous prior to 1850.[18]

The primary evidence of the limited use of this practice was the infrequency of newspaper advertisements for these public offerings. This is not surprising in light of the general patterns of corporate financing; for example, shares were offered to the public only after they had been rejected by the well informed, either because they did not think the opportunity represented a good risk or because the investment exceeded the resources of the initial organizers. Although common shares were occasionally sold in this manner, some form of preferred issue predominated because these rights issues were floated during difficult financial times. Occasionally, it was actually necessary

[17] Reed, *Investments in Railways in Britain,* pp. 76–98; and Johnson and Supple, *Boston Capitalists,* pp. 35–36.
[18] Evans, *British Corporation Finance,* pp. 104–105.

to revise corporate charters to make additional calls obligatory.[19] In the United States, similarly, "when a railroad decides to increase its capital . . . preference is usually given to the shareholders in the matter of subscribing to new shares or bonds."[20]

Like partnerships, nineteenth century corporations were generally self-sufficient in equity finance. The practices they followed suggest that corporate financial officers thought that the public markets were inefficient except possibly for the fixed-income obligations of larger enterprises. The presumption developed that priority in raising additional risk capital was given to existing shareholders, who were already familiar with the business. Suspicions, however, were aroused when shares were initially offered to less well informed outsiders; the question in the minds of prospective external investors was why those with the best knowledge about the issuing entities' future prospects were unwilling to venture their own capital. Moreover, the problem of public reluctance to subscribe to secondary stock issues could become acute if the flotation involved a type of security that was inherently difficult to evaluate.

IV. Par Value as a Valuation Benchmark for Common Stock

Effective means to assess the value of business enterprises were a prerequisite for establishing broad, impersonal markets for equity shares. One early attempt involved the use of par values as a rudimentary standard for evaluation, which had, as we have seen, also been applied informally by investors in the early modern trading companies. This logical but insufficient basis represented one of the few sources of information about business enterprises. As we have noted in the preceding chapter, concerted efforts to formalize financial reporting slowly built up momentum only late in the nineteenth century.

Although the connection between par and market value was tenuous, it seems to have been influential in shaping the perceptions of investors during the nineteenth century. Par value was initially intended to represent the amount fully paid in from the sale of securities.

[19] Ibid., pp. 42–43.
[20] Cleveland and Powell, *Railroad Promotion,* p. 46.

In perfectly efficient markets the value of a business should be equivalent to the amount of capital invested in its operations. Although retained earnings would have been expected to augment the worth of the enterprise, it was frequently impossible for outsiders to acquire information about their magnitude. Moreover, the assumption of perfect competitive equilibrium – wherein all marginal risk-adjusted returns are equal – was basically unrealistic because of the dearth of reliable information. Consequently, investors resorted to heuristic processes based on the evaluation of a limited range of operating variables. In addition to careful analysis of particular ventures, investors were guided by such relationships as the ratio between their market and par values or by a comparison of market value of securities against those of more seasoned companies.[21]

Although par value theoretically should have represented an objective measure of contributed capital, initially the credibility of these balances for the securities of some leading companies was marred by several practices that diluted shareholders' equity. This was particularly true for railroads in the western United States, where promoters of these lines often compensated themselves by retaining a controlling stock interest. In addition, shares were often issued at a discount or simply distributed as bonuses to encourage bond sales. In other cases construction companies affiliated with railroad promoters received securities valued at grossly inflated prices in payment for their services. Despite these obstacles to determining reliable share valuations, the notion of par value was not abandoned. Instead, investors made strenuous efforts to uncover "water" in nominal capitalizations. Some early finance texts devoted whole chapters to this subject. Even federal and state government regulatory agencies became involved. These bodies worried that "watered stock" would inflate railroad rate bases and thereby lead to the imposition of unfairly high transportation charges on the public. The ICC eventually attacked this problem in 1913 by beginning a nationwide valuation of all railroad tangible assets. This mission, which was completed in the 1920s, although reflective of the

---

[21] The practice of assigning arbitrarily low par values emerged after 1918, and thus the use of this measure as a signal of value waned. Benjamin Graham and David L. Dodd, *Security Analysis,* 2nd ed. (New York: McGraw-Hill, 1940), p. 379, note the issuance of no-par stock as early as 1918. New York state law was the first to recognize no-par securities in 1912. Carl B. Robbins, *No-Par Stock* (New York: Ronald Press, 1927).

application of greatly improved accounting practices, failed to discover any substantial systemic patterns of overstatement, a conclusion
that failed to satisfy many contemporary critics. But given the generally parlous state of financial accounting through the early years of the
twentieth century for railroads and other industries, there were few
substitutes for par value as a crude starting point for share valuation.[22]

This was also reflected by the ways that investor perceptions of
common stock had been shaped by criteria developed initially to appraise bonds. For example, dividend payments were usually expressed
in the United States and Britain before World War II as a percentage
of the par value of the security, much as with a bond. Thus, a $100
par value share paying an annual dividend of $5 was said to yield 5
percent.[23] This commonplace convention is noteworthy because it
reflects a presumption that par value returns were relevant bases for
evaluating equity securities. The crucial factors differentiating debt
from equity remained blurred (possibly encouraged by the practices
employed in marketing preferred stock) as the public attempted to
confront the problem of determining the proper value of the new
common issues by applying the traditional standards developed earlier
for debt securities. Financial promoters certainly had a strong incentive to perpetuate this analogy in light of the easier marketability of
debt and preferred stock issues. Consider an excerpt from the 1910
report of the U.S. Federal Securities Commission:

The principal of a bond is a fixed sum, its interest a fixed charge. The
value of a share of stock is essentially variable, its profit essentially
indeterminate.

There is a persistent tendency to ignore this distinction; to emphasize
unduly the face value of the stock; to treat the shares in a railroad or
other public service corporation as claims against the community for the
number of dollars they represent, rather than as fractional interests in a
more or less hazardous enterprise in which the investors took risk of loss
and chance of profit; to allow corporations to claim immunity from

[22] Miranti, "Mind's Eye of Reform," pp. 490 and 494–95; Hoogenbooms, *ICC*,
p. 81; and Sharfman, *Interstate Commerce Commission*, vol. 1, pp. 117–32,
and vol. 3A, pp. 33–42 and 95–319 passim.
[23] For example, see the summary of dividends reported in George H. Burgess and
Miles C. Kennedy, *Centennial History of the Pennsylvania Railroad Company,
1846–1946* (Philadelphia: Pennsylvania Railroad Company, 1949), pp. 799–
805.

public regulation when the dividend rate on the face value of shares is below the prevailing rate of interest; and to subject them to vexatious attack when this dividend is above the prevailing rate of interest, even when such profit may be a fair compensation for risks actually incurred.[24]

This suggests that many investors clung to the idea that a corporate security should yield a relatively fixed annuity, just as did the government and railroad bonds with which they were already familiar.

The belief that equity shares, like debt, should promise a yield expressible as a fraction of the nominal value of capital balances was deeply ingrained. It was a view reinforced by the nineteenth century prohibition in British corporate law against issuing equity shares below their par value (although all capital subscriptions did not have to be immediately paid in full), which was intended to protect creditors against fraudulent company promotions. It was also reflected by the fact that the Internal Revenue Service (IRS) considered stock dividends to represent taxable income. It was not until the U.S. Supreme Court ruled in *Eisner v. Macomber* (1920) that it was recognized officially that increasing par value of equity is purely symbolic, as distinguished from an increase in the face value of debt.[25]

The distinction between debt and equity securities has not always been sharply differentiated. This was doubtless encouraged by the general belief, evident from the inception of public trading in corporate securities, that the marketability of equity issues would be bolstered if they were given a debtlike appearance. The development of preferred stock was largely based on this recognition. So too does the current high priority given to maintaining long, uninterrupted records of common stock dividend payments.

---

[24] Quoted in Ripley, *Railroads: Finance and Organization,* p. 93. The tenacity of the belief that nominal capitalization was significant was reflected in the following 1940 rationalization for stock dividend issuance: "By adding the reinvested profits to stated capital (instead of to surplus), the management is placed under a direct obligation to earn money and to pay dividends on these added resources. No such accountability exists with respect to the profit and loss surplus. The stock dividend procedure will serve not only as a challenge to the efficiency of management but also as a proper test of the wisdom of reinvesting the sums involved," Graham and Dodd, *Security Analysis,* p. 394.
[25] 252 U.S. 189 (1920).

V. Public Accounting and Book Value

The emergence of financial reporting formed the foundation of more modern equity markets. A key transition was the shift in focus away from par value to book value as a guide for making investment judgments about common stocks. The emphasis on book value had a strong logical basis. From an accounting standpoint common equity has two components: nominal paid in capital, representing the original investment in the enterprise, and any surplus resulting from the retention of earnings. Thus, economic earnings are defined by accretion in the value of the enterprise that can be paid out to shareholders without diminishing its core capital. The reinvestment of profits has the same effect on the enterprise's ability to pay future dividends as does the issuance of additional shares for cash. Retained earnings, when properly measured, thus increase capital.

But financial reporting during the nineteenth century was in disarray and failed to provide the needed measurements. In the United States, where the railroads had been compelled by the ICC since 1887 to report regularly using uniform statements, there was a considerable degree of variation in the methodologies applied to measure particular classes of transactions. The pressure for more reliable and informative reporting in this industry increased because of the decision rendered in *Smyth v. Ames* (1898), which mandated that investors in regulated industries were entitled to receive a "fair return" on the fair value of their investments. The problem, however, of how to measure "fairness" proved difficult to resolve. It was not until the passage of the Hepburn Act in 1906 that Congress ultimately granted the ICC the basic power of prescribing uniform accounting methodologies.[26] Moreover, the quality of financial reporting for unregulated manufacturing and commercial enterprises was poorer than that of the railroads. Indeed, the primary focus for accounting among many leading manufacturing firms, whose ownership interests were often concentrated narrowly within relatively few hands, was not on external reporting for investors but rather on providing detailed internal infor-

---

[26] Cleveland and Powell, *Railroad Promotion,* p. 121; Miranti, "Mind's Eye of Reform," pp. 480–88; Ripley, *Finance and Organization,* p. 38; Sharfman, *Interstate Commerce Commission,* vol. 1, pp. 16 and 74–77; and 169 U.S. 466 (1898).

mation for management about such matters as the relative costs and profitability of segments of the enterprise.[27]

The quality of financial disclosure was somewhat higher in England. Although commercial bookkeeping had been a creation of the Italian Renaissance, modern financial reporting was pioneered by the British. In England and Scotland public accountancy had arisen during the early decades of the nineteenth century as an adjunct to the legal profession. Some of its most important early functions included the preparation of financial statements and schedules to assist the courts in winding up partnerships and estates, as well as in liquidating insolvent businesses. These roles were further formalized in 1831 with the passage of legislation that allowed the courts to appoint independent accountants as official assignees in bankruptcy cases.[28] Moreover, many of the analytical approaches first employed for serving proprietorships and partnerships were subsequently modified to accommodate the rising corporate form. The Companies Act of 1844 mandated corporate publicity of its operating activities, requiring directors to issue periodically "a full and fair balance sheet" certified by auditors, at least one of whom was elected by shareholders.[29]

As we have seen in the preceding chapter, later legislation repre-

[27] For the status of industrial reporting, see David F. Hawkins, "The Development of Modern Financial Reporting Practices among American Manufacturing Companies," *Business History Review* 37 (Winter 1963): 135–68; Richard Brief, ed., *Corporate Financial Reporting and Analysis in the Early 1900s* (New York: Garland, 1986); and Richard E. Vangermeersch, *Financial Reporting Techniques in 20 Industrial Companies since 1861* (Gainesville: University Press of Florida, 1979). For developments in cost accounting, see S. Paul Garner, *Evolution of Cost Accounting to 1925* (University: University of Alabama Press, 1954); H. Thomas Johnson and Robert S. Kaplan, *Relevance Lost: The Rise and Fall of Management Accounting* (Boston: Harvard Business School Press, 1987), especially chapts. 2–4 passim; and Chatfield, *History of Accounting Thought*, chapt. 12 passim.

[28] For a discussion of the early functions of independent public accountants, see James Don Edwards, *History of Public Accounting in the United States* (East Lansing: Michigan State University, Bureau of Business and Economic Research, 1960), pp. 5–9; Jones, *Accountancy and the British Economy*, chapt. 2 passim; A. C. Littleton, *Accounting Evolution to 1900* (New York: American Institute Publishing, 1933), chapts. 16–18 passim; and Stephen P. Walker, *The Society of Accountants in Edinburgh, 1854–1914: A Study of Recruitment to a New Profession* (New York: Garland, 1988).

[29] Hunt, *Development of the Business Corporation*, p. 97.

sented a compromise over differing views concerning patterns that should be followed in extending corporate governance. Many, impressed by laissez-faire doctrines, believed that government's role should be reduced and that boards of directors and independent experts like members of the rising profession of chartered accountants should bear the primary responsibility for verifying the competency and probity of corporate financial reporting. Moreover, the Companies Act of 1862 explicitly sought to protect creditors against any diminishment of contributed capital by mandating that dividends could be paid only from accumulated earnings. But debacles like the sudden collapse of the City of Glasgow Bank in 1878 provided strong support to those who favored the reimposition of compulsory audits for banks. The demand for higher-quality financial information for capital-hungry public service enterprises led to the establishment of formal reporting requirements for railroads (1868) and gas (1871) and electrical utility (1882) companies. The Companies Act of 1900 furthered this trend by requiring that all registered companies have their financial statements certified by independent auditors, and the 1908 revision of this legislation required that such statements be filed with the Board of Trade. These latter acts were not completely effective, because they failed to require timely reporting or to mandate much in the way of specific disclosure. These shortcomings were remedied only by the 1928 Companies Act, which introduced new requirements for the form and content of financial statements and for their distribution to shareholders prior to general corporate meetings.[30]

Practice could not be created entirely by legislative fiat, however, and the progress of the accounting profession in Great Britain was important in building public confidence in external reporting. Although the number of practitioners and their institutions expanded rapidly, no attempt was made to establish standardized reporting formats or accounting methodologies, as was done for U.S. railroads. Instead, in England accounting practice was viewed as an art that depended on the judgment of seasoned practitioners whose personal

[30] Ibid., pp. 140–42; Chatfield, *History of Accounting Thought,* chapt. 11; Miranti, *Accountancy Comes of Age;* Cleveland and Powell, *Railroad Promotion,* pp. 113–15; and J. R. Edwards, "Company Legislation and Changing Patterns of Disclosure in British Company Accounts, 1900–1940," in idem, ed., *Studies of Company Records, 1830–1970* (New York: Garland, 1984), pp. 71–155 passim.

fitness for these important tasks were vouched for by a highly respected qualifying association, such as the regional chartered accountancy institutes that emerged in England, Wales, Ireland and Scotland
during the nineteenth century. The accumulation of experience with a
growing range of corporate clients engendered improvements in practice and the quality of service rendered to the investment community.[31]

After 1900, U.S. investors were aided by efforts of government and
private groups to provide more information about economic conditions that would be helpful in assessing market risk. The Tariff Commission provided statistics about the composition and direction of
foreign trade; the Treasury Department reported the details of national
public finance; the controller of the currency analyzed the deposit and
loan experience of nationally chartered banks. Beginning with the
administration of President Theodore Roosevelt there was a growing
interest in extending statistical reporting for the nation's expanding
industrial and commercial sectors. Initially the focus of these efforts
was within the Bureau of Corporations of the Department of Commerce and Labor, which was formed in 1903 and compiled massive
quantities of data on the growing concentration of ownership in leading industries. After World War I, its successor agency, the Department
of Commerce, under the direction of Secretary Herbert Hoover and
assisted by experts like Professor Wesley C. Mitchell of Columbia
University, established statistical series providing information about
sales, inventories and investments in particular industries to assist
businessmen in their planning. Many private groups such as the Babson Statistical Organization headed by Roger W. Babson, Moody's
Investors Services founded by John Moody and Harvard University's
Committee on Economic Research led by Professor Warren M. Persons, established forecasting services useful for both businesses and
investors. In addition, rating services, such as those provided by *Financial World,* Brookmire Economic Service, Fitch Publishing Company,
Poor's Publishing Company, the Standard Statistical Corporation and
Moody's Investors Services, estimated the relative risk of particular
securities.[32]

---

[31] Miranti, *Accountancy Comes of Age,* pp. 29–30.
[32] Guy Alchon, *The Invisible Hand of Planning;* Ellis W. Hawley, "Herbert
Hoover, the Commerce Secretariat and the Vision of an 'Associative State,'
1921–1928," *Journal of American History* 51 (June 1974): 116–40; and

As in Britain, however, efforts to extend financial reporting requirements to unregulated industries experienced substantial opposition. The attempt in 1914 by the administration of President Woodrow Wilson to vest the Federal Trade Commission (FTC) with the power to require industrial and commercial firms to file uniform financial statements was defeated politically on the eve of America's entry into World War I. At the same time the Federal Reserve Board (FRB) sought to assist bank credit officers by circulating a standard balance sheet form that industrial and commercial entities might use when requesting bank loans. The reluctance to mandate strict rules of financial disclosure was also evident at the NYSE. Although this mart had adopted an official policy of requiring some financial reporting as early as 1869, the rule was largely ignored – to the extent that in 1885 the Exchange's Unlisted Department was created for firms providing no information. That department was abolished in 1910, and by 1926 nearly all listed companies issued audited reports. But even then the dominant floor-trader faction among the Exchange's membership was reluctant to see the costs of corporate financial monitoring rise by mandating more informative disclosure requirements, fearing a loss of listings to competing regional exchanges.[33]

Two other factors slowed the development of financial accounting, the first conceptual and the second institutional. From a conceptual standpoint, the pace of accounting progress was deliberate because this form of knowledge attempts to apply fixed measures to things that can by their nature be variously defined. Cost and valuation are not necessarily absolutes but are generally meaningful only relative to a specific application. Expensive specialized equipment may be worthless in the context of a forced liquidation; nor does the measurement

Miranti, *Accountancy Comes of Age,* pp. 94–99. For a discussion of Mitchell, see Morgan, *The History of Econometric Ideas,* pp. 44–56, and for a discussion of Persons, see pp. 56–63. For forecasting and rating services, see Charles Amos Dice, *The Stock Market* (Chicago: A. W. Shaw, 1926), chapts. 26–27 passim.

[33] Paul J. Miranti, Jr., "Associationalism, Statism and Professional Regulation: Public Accountants and the Reform of the Financial Markets, 1896–1940," *Business History Review* 60 (Autumn 1986): 448–53; idem, *Accountancy Comes of Age,* pp. 106–10; and Hawkins, "Development of Modern Financial Reporting," pp. 149–50. For the unlisted department at the New York Stock Exchange, see Dice, *The Stock Market,* p. 156.

of long-term assets at their original costs of acquisition provide much useful insight during a period of strong inflation. Efforts to promulgate invariant rules inevitably exposed the conflict between relevancy and objectivity latent in managers' and investors' differing informational requirements. Moreover, because the implications of new knowledge are often conjectural – becoming clear and then changing over time – the criteria for standardized accounting methods and the contents of public disclosure statements were not intuitively apparent.

Modern accounting methods were derived from the practice of recording receipts and expenditures, and the prevailing accrual basis of accounting still seeks to approximate the longer-term patterns apparent in the flow of funds from an enterprise. The underlying notion of profit was grounded in the idea of completed transactions, wherein revenue is matched with associated expenses. This straightforward practice would have been natural among the early trading companies. However, the application of this simple concept became more problematic as economic life became dominated by the complex operations of giant transportation and manufacturing firms. For example, ingenious rules were set down for allocating fixed costs, which had only a tenuous connection with the actual revenue generated during specific periods. Moreover, a primary attraction of the completed transaction basis was that profits thus derived were relatively impervious to manipulation. Income was also recognized near the time when money became available for either reinvestment or distribution. Dividends could thereby be paid concurrently with reported income without the necessity of resorting to borrowing in the financial markets. Furthermore, book value was increased through retained earnings when funds were freed from previous investments and could be profitably employed elsewhere. Consequently, it was logical to demand that management distribute some return from the enterprises' earned surplus.

But managements had broad discretion to choose among many modes for measuring complex and long-term business phenomena. Consider the wide latitude allowed in the timing of fixed-charge allocations such as depreciation or of the estimated magnitude of probable future losses. This flexibility limited the ability of investors to make inferences from accounting earnings and shifted their attention to the observed dividend stream. In fact, it appears that the public viewed undistributed profits dubiously, the general presumption being that reported earnings should be paid out. Managers' reaction to these expectations was to try to maintain a steady dividend stream by manipulating other discretionary accounts. Cleveland and Powell reported that, during the nineteenth century,

many railroad managers have made it a practice to pay regular dividends, and to keep to themselves the essential facts concerning the corporation. When revenues are large they expended large amounts in rehabilitating the property, and charged them to expenses. When revenues were small, they reduced such expenses to a minimum.[34]

Even in 1940, after the beginning of broader standardization of financial reporting under the auspices of the SEC, Graham and Dodd in their influential *Security Analysis* would report:

We are thus led to the question: "To what extent is common-stock analysis a truly valid exercise, and to what extent is it an empty but indispensable ceremony attending the wagering of money on the future of business and the stock market?" We shall ultimately find the answer to run somewhat as follows: "As far as the typical common-stock is concerned – an issue picked at random from the list – an analysis, however elaborate, is unlikely to yield a dependable conclusion as to its attractiveness or real value. But in individual cases the exhibit may be such as to permit reasonably confident conclusions to be drawn from the process of analysis."[35]

The perverse effect of lax standards was to force profit accounting along lines that basically validated a desired dividend policy, and thus it was crucial that earnings be reported when funds were available for distribution.

VI. Common Stock Valuation and the Coming of Industrial Securities

During the early twentieth century, public skepticism of common stock remained high because of the difficulties encountered in gathering reliable information useful in assessing future corporate earnings trends. The conventional wisdom at that time was for investors to

[34] Cleveland and Powell, *Railroad Promotion,* pp. 142–43.
[35] Graham and Dodd, *Security Analysis,* pp. 344–45.

confine themselves to debt securities with clear liens. Moreover, the dearth of information heightened suspicions about the honesty of corporate promoters, as implied by the warning of a contemporary authority: "All prospectuses should be scanned in a spirit of jaundiced criticism, and with the most pessimistic readiness to believe that they are speciously alluring traps laid by some designing financier to relieve the reader of some of his money." [36] Misgivings about the safety of equity securities even continued after the advent of mandatory audits of financial statements. But these attitudes gradually changed with the steady accretion of knowledge about finance and the general improvement in the quality of information about corporate operations. This shift in opinion was reflected in the dramatic increases in the number of individuals owning common shares. Estimates increased from a mere half million in 1900 to two million in 1920 and to ten million in 1930. [37]

In valuing common stocks during this transition investors were hesitant to place much credence in the new reported financial information. Instead, dividend patterns served as the primary indicators of investment quality in the minds of many contemporaries. This was certainly clear in the writings of two leaders of the rising profession of securities analysts, Benjamin Graham and David L. Dodd, who, writing in 1940 about conditions in the United States, noted:

Until recent years the dividend return was the overshadowing factor in common stock investment. This point of view was based on simple logic. The prime purpose of a business is to pay dividends to its owners. A successful company is one that can pay dividends regularly and presumably increase the rate as time goes on. Since the idea of investment is closely bound up with that of dependable income, it follows that investment in common stocks would ordinarily be confined to those with a well established dividend. It would follow also that the price paid for an investment in common stock would be determined chiefly by the amount of the dividend. [38]

---

[36] Withers, *Stocks and Shares,* p. 92.

[37] Hawkins, "Modern Financial Reporting," p. 145.

[38] Graham and Dodd, *Security Analysis,* p. 372. Withers, *Stocks and Shares,* p. 158, describes the British experience: "Unfortunately, the amount of dividend paid by a company is too often taken as the only test of its welfare, and since dividends and depreciation are the two chief competitors for the balance of net profits, the temptation to pamper dividends at the expense of depreciation is a powerful influence on the side of bad finance."

Because of the lack of reliable information, it was rational for investors to value common stock based on dividends. Although the precise details of the underlying economic processes leading to the creation of corporate income that could finance dividend payments remained obscure to most outsiders, investors could base their estimates of security values on the extrapolation of predicted future distributions. Corporate financial executives, on the other hand, had a strong incentive either to sustain or to increase the level of dividends. These circumstances also constrained managers from taking any actions that would radically alter investors' expectations. Managers did not wish to undermine the confidence of investors in their ability to forecast dividend payments. Therefore, an important objective of corporate financial policy was the establishment of a smooth, rising trend of dividends. The view that a steady dividend record exerted a salutary effect on the perception of poorly informed investors was clearly espoused in Lough's leading finance text in 1917:

The principle of greatest practical importance is that regularity in the dividend rate is highly desirable. This principle must be regarded as almost a discovery of the last generation or two. Formerly, the unquestioned practice was to regard shareholders as standing in substantially the same relation as partners. They were supposed to be familiar with the status and fluctuations in the business and were expected to share in its ups and downs. . . . As a matter of fact this is the practice of a great number – perhaps the majority – of corporations. In so far as it is followed by close corporations, all the stock of which is held by men who are themselves active in the business and familiar with its every phase, it is probably unobjectionable. . . . But the corporation which has shareholders who are not active in business or familiar with it is in a different situation. This remark applies with especial force to the great corporations that number their shareholders in the thousands or tens of thousands. The great majority of the shareholders of such corporations have only the barest information as to the manner in which the business is handled and as to the results that are being achieved, and are not sufficiently familiar with the business or sufficiently interested in it to absorb more detailed information if it were given to them. They regard their ownership of a company's stock purely as an investment of capital that will bring them an income. They buy a railroad or industrial stock with much the same purpose as they would have in buying a real estate mortgage – the only purpose being that of securing a dependable income with a chance of profits. The object that is actually in their minds in making the purpose is not a partnership interest in a going enterprise, but certain pieces of paper called "certificates of stock" which at regular intervals will bring dividend checks.[39]

But it was not the importance of regular dividends that was unique during this epoch. Rather it was the growth in the number of large corporations issuing common stock and the willingness of investors to include these securities in their portfolios.

The importance of dividends was well established in British finance. The liquidation of ships and cargoes for the early British trading companies was in effect the ultimate dividend payout. As we have seen, the East India Company provided generous distributions after it adopted a more permanent capital structure. Moreover, expectations of high and immediate dividends were strong among investors in British mining projects in South America during the 1850s.[40] By 1854, after an initial decade of marginal profitability due to cost overruns, British railways began to exhibit stability in dividend payments. Consequently, the aggregate nominal dividend rate amounted to 3.39 percent that year, while the average return earned by loan capital was 4.27 percent. But the British penchant for relatively large dividend payments was still very evident on the eve of World War I. In 1914, corporations paid out common and preferred dividends amounting to 76.4 percent of total profits.[41]

---

[39] Lough, *Business Finance*, pp. 440–41.

[40] Jenks, *Migration of British Capital*, p. 187.

[41] Evans, *British Corporation Finance*, p. 108. Cost overruns resulted partly from poor supervision and control in innovative businesses, which Ellis T. Powell notes in *The Evolution of the Money Market, 1385–1915*, reprint ed. (New York: A. M. Kelley, 1915, 1966), p. 360; Lough, *Business Finance*, p. 438. Payout ratios did not fluctuate much until World War II, when they began to shrink, being about one-third of earnings by 1956. P. E. Hart, *Studies in Profits, Business Savings and Investment in the United Kingdom, 1920–1962* (London: Allen & Unwin, 1965), provides estimates of post-1920 earnings retention rates. S. J. Pais, "Dividend Policy and Income Appropriation," in Brian Tew and R. F. Henderson, eds., *Studies in Company Finance: A Symposium on the Economic Analysis and Interpretation of British Company Accounts* (Cambridge University Press, 1959), pp. 26–49, also notes a shrinkage in British payments after 1945. W. A. Thomas, *The Finance of British Industry, 1918–1978* (New York: Methuen, 1978), p. 221, notes a slight increase in British payments early in the 1960s but with a reversion to decline after 1966.

In the United States, on the other hand, some companies during the late nineteenth century dedicated a portion of their earnings to finance either new internal investment opportunities or the replacement of obsolete capital equipment. This practice of retaining earnings became known as the "American theory."[42] The incipiency of this practice was described by railroad economist William Z. Ripley:

A generation ago it was the common practice to divide all profits in sight and finance all new construction by the issue of securities. Such policies were fully sanctioned by the public opinion of the day. But a few roads, undoubtedly well in advance of their time, during the '80's began to devote a good part of their earnings to new construction and betterment.[43]

This differs from the view of many British shareholders in the Pennsylvania Railroad, who in 1881 sent a representative to the United States to demand that "all earnings should be distributed."[44] The reasons for these differences in national attitudes at the time are not clear. Their receptivity to the reinvestment of earnings probably developed in part because U.S. investors were less accepting of the idea that corporations were akin to partnerships. In addition, the pressures of highly leveraged capital structures may have served as a strong motive for infusing more equity capital.

But the ownership of industrial common stock was not widespread in the United States during most of the nineteenth century. Before 1890, the Pullman Company was the only manufacturing enterprise whose common stock was regularly traded on the NYSE. This seeming anomaly was explained by the company's large size and its ability to overcome the public's skepticism about industrial stock because of its intimate connections with the predominant railroad industry. Other large-scale industrial enterprises such as Du Pont, Singer and McCormick were controlled during this period by their founding families. Moreover, the Boston-based market for the relatively small New England textile companies remained highly localized and attained only modest levels of share trading volume.[45]

---

[42] Graham and Dodd, *Security Analysis,* p. 379.
[43] Ripley, *Railroads: Finance and Organization,* p. 244.
[44] Burgess and Kennedy, *Centennial History,* p. 441.
[45] Navin and Sears, "Rise of a Market for Industrial Securities," pp. 109–110; Carosso, *Investment Banking,* pp. 42–50; and idem, *The Morgans,* pp. 486–98 passim.

This pattern began to change with the industrial merger boom of 1897–1904. Many investors became more positive about the potentialities of industrial common stock. The formation of giant enterprises – such as the United States Steel Company, the nation's first billion dollar manufacturing corporation – held out the prospects for high profits by stabilizing markets and by achieving economies of scale and scope. This enthusiasm for common stocks was further reinforced as many of the recently consolidated companies began to pay substantial dividends.

But the initially sanguine outlook about the prospects of common stocks gave way to a more sober view after the spectacular failure of some of these enterprises. Eighteen major enterprises that had been consolidated became insolvent and had eventually to be reorganized, including such important companies as National Cordage, United States Leather, Corn Products and Westinghouse. In the cases of National Cordage and United States Leather, failure came about because of the inherent inability to structure the underlying business so as to achieve any substantial economies from consolidation. These two companies manufactured too many types of dissimilar products to reduce their costs significantly through scale production.[46] Moreover, in most of the failures there was strong evidence that dividend payments were far too liberal in light of the risks associated with unseasoned ventures. Dewing, who evaluated the financial performance of these mergers, concluded:

The haste with which these early dividends were declared was at a variance with the principles of sound finance. In the majority of cases dividends were begun almost immediately after the organization of the corporation, before an opportunity had been given for the new enterprise to manifest its independent earning power. . . . Why was such lack of conservation shown by these corporations? Able financiers were on the directorates of nearly every case. . . . One motive that often prompted declaration of dividends was a desire to make a market for the stock.[47]

Although rich payout ratios were also evident in the financial histories of successful U.S. firms, they generally were lower than the

---

[46] See Chandler, *Visible Hand*, pp. 331–44 for an analysis of factors contributing to the success or failures of contemporary consolidations.
[47] Dewing, *Corporate Promotions*, p. 550.

British averages noted earlier. During 1902, its initial year of operation, the conservatively financed U.S. Steel Company paid $56 million of preferred and common dividends, which represented 62 percent of its net earnings.[48] Another industrial company, the International Harvester Company, recognized the importance of dividends in building a following among investors after going public in 1902. Initially capitalized with $120 million of par value common stock, its directors voted to retire half of that in 1907, replacing it with an equivalent amount of 7 percent preferred stock. In 1909, the payout ratio for the former McCormick Reaper Company amounted to $4.2 million, or 28 percent of net earnings.[49] Sensitive to the need to assuage common stockholders with some sort of return, directors resorted to the expedient of paying periodic stock dividends. This bolstered the illusion that some sort of economic return was being earned while reclassifying earned surplus, from which dividends might legally be declared, to capital surplus, which could not make distributions to shareholders except in liquidation. Dividend sensitivity was also apparent at a leading utility, the American Telephone and Telegraph Company. As a natural monopoly its payments could be expected to be higher than those of strong industrials. In fact, in 1909 it paid its shareholders $21 million, or 78 percent of that period's net earnings.[50]

Although these ratios may have been distorted by the conservative policies of expensing rather than capitalizing certain plant and financing balances (when compared with current practice), the high payout ratios are reflective of the importance of dividends to the thinking of contemporary investors. These patterns coupled with the dire warnings against high distributions strongly suggest that many investors would be induced to hold shares only if a high proportion of earnings were returned as a dividend.[51]

---

[48] See the analysis of income state for U.S. Steel in Brief, ed., *Corporate Financial Reporting and Analysis,* pp. 17–18.

[49] McCormick Reaper Annual Report, partially reproduced in ibid., p. 58.

[50] AT&T 1910 Annual Report, partially reproduced in ibid., p. 145.

[51] Withers, *Stocks and Shares,* p. 99. For later evidence of high dividend payments as a way to bolster shareholder confidence, especially among larger firms, see Daniel M. Holland *Dividends under the Income Tax* (Princeton, N.J.: Princeton University Press, 1962), p. 49; and for the 1960s and 1970s, see Baskin, "On the Financial Policy of Large Mature Corporations," Ph.D. diss., Harvard University, 1985.

During the 1920s, the broadening of public ownership of common equity was further facilitated by the growth of several types of financial market intermediaries that had hitherto played only minor roles in American finance. First, there was the aforementioned public utility holding company, a device dating back to the 1890s, which mobilized substantial amounts of capital after World War I by selling common and preferred stocks and bonds of their subsidiary companies. Second, there were investment trusts that sold shares to the public and used the proceeds to finance stock portfolios. Investment trusts had originated in Britain in the 1860s, where they offered investors the safety of diversified portfolios and expert financial management. Although only 41 such trusts had been founded in the United States by 1921, this number increased to 770 by 1929. The total value of unit trust portfolios jumped from $1 billion in 1926 to $7 billion in 1929. This massive reallocation of funds was partially induced by the potential for speculative gains in a rising market that could be accentuated by the high debt leverage characteristic of many investment trusts.[52] The third category of intermediary was the security subsidiaries of commercial banks, which primarily served as underwriters and financial advisers. Some indication of the importance of this class of enterprise was reflected by the fact that the National City Company, a subsidiary of the National City Bank in New York, ranked fifth among the country's underwriters in 1926 with its floatation of $310 million in new issues. The final category of intermediary was the retail brokerage firm, including Charles E. Merrill & Co., Bache & Company, Francis I. Du Pont and E. F. Hutton, which depended on the commission it earned selling shares directly to middle-class investors.[53]

The strong growth in interest in common stocks, however, was not

---

[52] An estimate of the degree of speculation at the height of the 1929 bull market, based on an analysis of the trend in prices for closed-end mutual funds, may be found in J. Bradford De Long and Andrie Shleifer, "The Stock Market Bubble of 1929: Evidence from Closed-end Mutual Funds," *Journal of Economic History* 51 (September 1991): 675–700. See also the study by Peter Rappoport and Eugene N. White, "Was There a Bubble in the 1929 Stock Market?" *Journal of Economic History* 53 (September 1993): 549–74.

[53] Carosso, *History of Investment Banking,* chapt. 17 passim; and Sobel, *The Big Board,* chapt. 11 passim.

without its critics, as we shall see in the following section. Several thoughtful and respected accountants, attorneys and economists raised worrisome concerns about serious shortcomings in contemporary corporate finance and governance. But their calls for reform initially went unheeded until after the Crash of 1929 and the onset of a severe and prolonged depression. It was only then that the public's demand for relief motivated vigorous federal intervention.

VII. A New Framework for Corporate Financial Governance

Some of the most critical economic reforms introduced by the New Deal administration of President Franklin D. Roosevelt helped to place corporate finance on a firmer footing by reducing the perceptions of the riskiness of holding financial assets. Federal securities legislation of this period bolstered investor confidence by ensuring the greater transparency of corporate affairs. These laws also extended and defined more precisely the responsibilities of financial market agents to the public. Moreover, banking reforms gave government new powers to counter disruptive volatility in the financial markets and provided insurance protection for depositor accounts.

With respect to corporate transparency and market governance, a major focus of criticism during the 1920s had been on the shortcomings of contemporary financial reporting. One such problem which made it difficult for investors to assess the likelihood of future dividend payments that was crucial in common share valuation, was the inconsistency of procedures followed in adjusting earned surplus accounts. This measure was critical because it represented the legally distributable portion of shareholders equity. In his widely read polemic, *Main Street and Wall Street* (1927), Harvard University Professor William Z. Ripley railed against what he believed to be the abusive accounting innovations that affected these balances. Accountant Arthur Andersen echoed this concern when he pointed out that no state laws defined how earned surplus should be measured – even though the payment of dividends greater than these balances represented an ultra-vires action. Working in conjunction with the American Institute of Accountants (later to become the American Institute of Certified

197

Public Accountants), Andersen vainly sought to discover by a survey of hundreds of practitioners a consistent pattern of accounting for these vital adjustments.[54]

Another barrier to establishing useful projections of future dividends was the heavy emphasis placed on the balance sheet in contemporary accounting practice. The so-called proprietary theory of accounting, which concentrated on the measurement of assets, liabilities and equity, was most useful to creditors in forming assessments of enterprise liquidity and solvency.[55] An alternative, the entity theory of accounting, which placed greater emphasis on the income statement, was more useful in forming estimates of the likelihood of future dividend payments because of the wealth of information it provided about the revenue and cost elements that determined a company's annual profit. Although this latter approach better satisfied the changing information needs of the expanding equity markets of the 1920s, it had a limited influence on accounting practice.[56] Thus, standard references such as *Standard and Poor's Industrials* usually presented balance sheets prior to 1933 and in only a few cases provided details about operating results. Many companies refused to report net sales or other operating accounts, because of purported fears that this information would benefit competitors. Other firms provided this data, though averaged out over a single three-year period, thus mitigating any meaningful trend analysis. In some cases operating data were simply egregiously misleading, as in the case of Bethlehem Steel's disclosure

[54] William Z. Ripley, *Main Street and Wall Street* (Boston: Little, Brown, 1927), pp. 194–207, 222–28 and 229–55 passim. See also John L. Carey, *The Rise of the Accounting Profession*, 2 vols. (New York: American Institute of Certified Public Accountants, 1969–70), vol. 1, pp. 158–59; and Miranti, *Accountancy Comes of Age*, pp. 132–37.

[55] Charles B. Couchman, *The Balance-Sheet: Its Preparation, Content and Interpretation* (New York: Journal of Accountancy Press, 1924). For a discussion of the theory, see Chatfield, *History of Accounting Thought*, pp. 220–23; and Gary John Previts and Barbara Dubis Merino, *A History of Accounting in America: An Historical Interpretation of the Cultural Significance of Accounting* (New York: Wiley, 1979), pp. 169–77.

[56] William A. Paton, *Accounting Theory* (New York: Ronald Press, 1922). For a discussion of this theory, see Chatfield, *History of Accounting Thought*, pp. 223–25; and Previts and Merino, *Accounting in America*, pp. 176–80 and 220–23.

in its statement about the salaries and bonuses paid to senior executives.[57]

The lack of a clear body of accounting standards encouraged manipulative financial reporting, and this enhanced the perception of the riskiness of equity investment. The formation of holding companies in the electric power and railroad industries led to the misleading pyramiding of earnings between the many corporate tiers within these groups. The shortcoming of these practices was revealed by the collapse of Samuel Insull's Insull Utility Investments and the Van Sweringen Brothers' Allegheny Corporation. Moreover, gains achieved by some corporations by dealing in their own shares (treasury stock) were reported as income available for dividend payments rather than as adjustment to stockholders equity.[58]

Many financiers who were concerned about the insufficiency of financial information were unable to establish a consensus for reform within the NYSE during the 1920s. Leaders of the growing commission brokerage sector, such as Paul Shields of Shields & Co. and E. A. Pierce of E. A. Pierce & Company, had argued for fuller financial disclosure rules for listed companies. They believed that this reform would strengthen the type of shareholder capitalism they had been promoting among America's middle class.

The lack of mandatory standards for financial disclosure in the 1920s had also undermined the position of the public accountants who certified financial statements; it was difficult for them to constrain overly aggressive clients who sought to incorporate false or misleading accounting in their financial statements. The strongest action that they could take was the economically damaging step of withdrawing from an engagement. More frequently, accountants faced with this problem tried to insulate themselves from responsibility for deficient financial reporting by the use of ambiguous "qualified" auditors' reports.[59]

---

[57] Robert Hessen, *Steel Titan: The Life of Charles M. Schwab* (New York: Oxford University Press, 1975), pp. 271–75.

[58] Carosso, *Investment Banking,* pp. 294–98 and 340–42; Chatov, *Corporate Financial Reporting,* pp. 14–15; and Soule, *Prosperity Decade,* pp. 298–304.

[59] Miranti, *Accountancy Comes of Age,* pp. 137–40; Carey, *Rise of the Accounting Profession,* vol. 1, pp. 298–301; and Michael E. Parrish, *Securities Regulation and the New Deal* (New Haven, Conn.: Yale University Press, 1970), pp. 36–41. See also John Brooks, *Once in Golconda: A True Drama of Wall*

Nor was the position of purchasers of common stock well protected under the law against losses due to agent malfeasance during this period. Lacking the privity of contract, shareholders could not sue auditors for losses resulting from incompetent financial statement examinations. The only available option was to sue for fraud under either the common law or some state "blue skies" laws that prohibited fraudulent dealing in securities. But fraud was difficult to prove without a body of well-defined rules, especially when regulatory agencies were starved for resources, as in the laissez-faire 1920s.[60]

After the 1929 Crash, however, reform accelerated to address the shortcomings that threatened the viability of financial institutions. A first step in New York State was the extension under the civil law of the rights of shareholders to sue in cases where financial reports had been negligently prepared. Although they had little recourse then for "ordinary negligence" because of the lack of contractual privity, under the doctrine propounded by Justice Benjamin N. Cardozo in the *Ultramares* decision (1932) shareholders could sue if financial statements had been prepared in a "grossly negligent" manner.[61]

A second step was the decision taken by the NYSE to embrace several key recommendations put forth by Adolf A. Berle and Gardiner C. Means in their classic work, *The Modern Corporation and Private Property* (1932). This research, which had been supported by the Social Science Research Council, documented how important financial assets had become as repositories of personal wealth in the U.S. economy by the 1920s. In addition, the authors persuasively argued that the separation of ownership and control that was so characteristic of the modern corporation made it imperative that new channels of communication be established to protect investor interests. Specifically, there was a strong need for more reliable information to enable investors to judge both operating performance and the effectiveness of managerial stewardship of enterprise resources. From Berle

Street, 1920–1938 (New York: Harper & Row, 1969), for a highly readable account of the reform of the NYSE during the New Deal era.

[60] Carosso, *Investment Banking*; Parrish, *Securities Regulation and the New Deal*, pp. 5, 7, 13 and 28–29; and Miranti, *Accountancy Comes of Age*, pp. 139–40.

[61] Miranti, *Accountancy Comes of Age*, pp. 139–40; Carey, *Rise of the Accounting Profession*, vol. 1, pp. 254–58; Edwards, *History of Public Accounting*, pp. 141–46; and Previts and Merino, *Accounting in America*, p. 204.

and Means's perspective the logical focus for mandating such monitoring was the NYSE, which could be assisted in this task by the public accounting profession. Thus, in 1933, the NYSE in conjunction with the American Institute of Accountants began to promulgate accounting rules for listed companies. But by that time it was already too late for these actions to lessen the great public pressure for governmental intervention.[62]

The reforms subsequently implemented at the federal level by the New Deal administration were much more sweeping. A key initiative was the establishment of a comprehensive structure of governance for the securities markets. A coterie of former students of Harvard Law School Professor Felix Frankfurter crafted the far-reaching Securities Acts of 1933 and 1934. This legislation addressed the problem of information and risk by defining legal responsibilities for three broad sets of agency relationships. The first of these nexuses was between corporations and their shareholders. For this the framers of the securities acts took guidance from trust law, which vested oversight authority for corporate affairs to boards of directors who served as fiduciaries for outside investors. Under this system managerial stewardship of enterprise resources was evaluated through periodic accounting reports that informed investors about financial condition and the results of operations. Similar requirements were included in the New Deal's legislation. The Securities Act of 1933 stipulated the financial information that had to be disclosed in registration statements for floatations of new securities issues; the Securities Act of 1934 mandated continuous disclosure for corporations whose securities were publicly traded.[63]

Second, the architects of the new legislation extended the definition

---

[62] Carey, *Rise of the Accounting Profession,* vol. 1, pp. 163–66; Previts and Merino, *Accounting in America,* p. 238; and Joel Seligman, *The Transformation of Wall Street: A History of the Securities and Exchange Commission and Modern Corporate Finance,* revised ed. (Boston: Northeastern University Press, 1982, 1995), pp. 35–41. For a discussion of the ineffectiveness of policies of the administration of President Herbert Hoover in confronting the dislocations that emerged after the crash, see Albert U. Romasco, *The Poverty of Abundance: Hoover, the Nation, the Depression* (New York: Oxford University Press, 1965), chapts. 3–5 passim.

[63] For the extension of banking regulation, see Myers, *A Financial History of the United States,* pp. 319–22 and 334. For securities market regulation, see

of agency responsibilities to a broad array of professional specialists that the financial markets depended on for effective functioning. Market efficiency and equity were perceived as deriving from the joint efforts of many experts, including brokers, financial analysts, underwriters, accountants, engineers and appraisers. To protect investors the securities acts imposed civil or criminal sanctions against professional agents that were found guilty of either dishonest or incompetent practice. The Securities Act of 1933 was particularly stringent, requiring that plaintiffs had to prove only that they had experienced a loss on the purchase of a new issue whose registration statement contained materially false information or omitted a material disclosure of fact. In these cases the burden of proof was essentially shifted to defendants. One possible defense required proving that a plaintiff's loss resulted from reliance on information other than that contained in the registration statement. Alternatively, defendants might prove that they had acted in "good faith"; that is, they had performed their professional responsibilities with "due diligence."

The third aspect of the New Deal's financial market reforms involved the placement of corporate financial governance within a broader political context. What emerged was a tripartite structure involving Congress, the SEC and professional groups.[64] The New Deal administration was eager to encourage the participation of business and professional groups in the process of regulation for several reasons. A high degree of self-regulation by financial market participants reduced the need to increase the size and costs of government. This style of monitoring also promised to win the political support of professionals like attorneys and public accountants who had experienced a sharp falloff in the demand for their services during the depression. Moreover, this approach was appealing because it seemed

---

Parrish, *Securities Regulation and the New Deal,* pp. 44 and 48–51; Carey, *Rise of the Accounting Profession,* vol. 1, pp. 183–84; Seligman, *Transformation of Wall Street,* pp. 51–57; Carosso, *Investment Banking,* pp. 352–81 passim; and Smith and Sylla, *Transformation of Finance Capitalism,* pp. 32–38.

[64] This pattern, which involves the division of economic regulatory power between private and public groups, is common in the United States and is discussed in Louis Galambos's perceptive book *America at Middle Age: A New History of the United States in the Twentieth Century* (New York: McGraw-Hill, 1982).

consistent with the traditional U.S. political ideal of "government by the governed." Business interests also favored this form of governance because it lessened the likelihood that corporate financial reporting would be commandeered by advocates for stronger government regulation of market competition, as had earlier been done at the ICC.

Ultimately, the continuance of this system of regulation depended on public opinion. If private groups were perceived as being derelict in their regulatory duties, the public would pressure Congress for relief. Such a development raised the prospect of SEC encroachment on the regulatory prerogatives of business and professional groups. Political pressure would compel the federal agency to play a more active role in restoring order to the financial markets. Thus, the fear of losing autonomy to government and the potential for costly sanctions for malpractice served as strong incentives for private groups to establish monitoring arrangements that were effective in protecting the public interest.[65]

The basic structure of financial governance was extended by later New Deal legislation. The Public Utility Holding Company Act of 1935 empowered the federal government to promote the physical integration of the public utility industry. This act led to the simplification of corporate holding company structures and the end of abusive accounting practices such as the pyramiding of earnings. The Trust Indenture Act of 1939 required that publicly offered debt securities had to conform to a standard trust indenture approved by the SEC. The Investment Company Act of 1940 established a regulatory framework for companies primarily engaged in securities investing and trading activities. Finally, the Investment Advisers Act of 1940 defined responsibilities similar to the ones imposed on brokers and dealers for individuals engaged in counseling investors.[66]

In addition to extending the scope of securities market regulation, the administration of Franklin D. Roosevelt helped to diminish the perceived risks of financial assets during this crisis era by introducing

[65] Miranti, *Accountancy Comes of Age,* pp. 179–89; and idem, "Associationalism, Statism and Self-Regulation," pp. 460–68. See also McCraw, *Prophets of Regulation,* pp. 181–203, and idem, "With the Consent of the Governed: The SEC's Formative Years," *Journal of Policy Analysis and Management* 1 (1982): 346–70.

[66] K. Fred Skousen, *An Introduction to the SEC,* 5th ed. (Cincinnati, Ohio: South-Western, 1991), pp. 31–36; and Carosso, *Investment Banking,* pp. 381–407 passim.

reforms to the nation's banking industry. The Banking Act of 1933 (Glass–Steagall) helped to restore confidence by authorizing the formation of the Federal Deposit Insurance Corporation (FDIC) to provide deposit insurance for small savers. To reduce the danger of insurance losses the law also restricted the speculative activities of insured banks and mandated the separation of commercial and investment banking. In addition, the Securities Act of 1934 empowered the Federal Reserve to control brokers' margin requirements, which it did under Regulation T; in 1936 margin governance was further extended under Regulation U to cover securities purchases financed by banks. The Banking Act of 1935 further extended the authority of the Federal Reserve. In addition to strengthening its powers to set the discount rate, this legislation allowed the central bank to establish reserve requirements for member banks, to place interest ceilings on time deposits, and to restrict market entry and expansion.[67]

VIII. Conclusion

How did new institutions associated with the rise of managerial capitalism help solve the corporate financing puzzle? What factors explain the differences in financial institutional development in Britain and in the United States after the stock market collapse of 1929?

The rise of broad, impersonal markets for common stock represented an important turning point. Before the twentieth century the ability to raise capital by issuing common stock had been severely constrained. This reflected a recognition by investors of the insufficiency of available information to assess adequately the risks and returns of new forms of business and technologies that were at the forefront of industrialization. The complex dynamics that determined the profitability of large-scale, capital-intensive enterprises were poorly understood. The small, atomistic firms that were the focus of classical microeconomics provide few insights into the functioning of oligopolistic corporations. Thus, it proved difficult to develop reliable measures to assist investors in evaluating the performance of compa-

---

[67] S. Kerry Cooper and Donald R. Fraser, *Banking Deregulation and the New Competition in Financial Services* (Cambridge, Mass.: Ballinger, 1984), pp. 50–56.

nies of great scale and scope. In addition, there was a persistent concern about the possibility of losses resulting from the dishonesty or incompetency of agents. In this latter case barriers of time and space were difficult to overcome; passive investors were at a disadvantage with respect to knowledge relevant for assessing their investments. This combination of problems created a strong predilection among investors for financial instruments with credible guarantees of fixed payments and with the security of clear liens on valuable property.

Investors historically came to accept the risks of common and pre-ferred stock ownership only after the early issues were designed to exhibit debtlike features. Basic attributes such as par values, stated dividend returns and a consistent record of cash payouts were highly prized by prospective investors in the early 1900s. Investors ap-proached an uncertain future by relying on guides that had proved useful in achieving success in the past. During this epoch markets were not very efficient, and information about corporate cash flows in the form of either dividend or interest payments were crucial in judging investment quality. Contrary to the conclusions of the efficient market hypothesis, cash flows were useful valuative standards for investors whose sources of information were sporadic and unreliable.

By the 1920s the public's aversion to equity investing began to diminish because of a growing recognition that this class of security represented an ideal vehicle for capturing the substantial economic gains generated by the thriving institutions of managerial capitalism. This was especially true within the industrial sector, where the most successful enterprises, after their initial capitalization, relied heavily on retained earnings to finance their operations. In addition, the at-tractiveness of equity was enhanced because the supply of shares for successful companies did not grow significantly due to the understand-able concerns of professional managements about the possible loss of control resulting from shifts in enterprise ownership. The primacy of management derived from its domination of boards of directors, the ultimate focus of corporate governing authority. To ensure their ten-ure, managements of successful, leading firms usually followed financ-ing agendas consistent with those predicted by the pecking order hypothesis. They sought to preserve their autonomy and keep financ-ing costs low by retaining earnings and avoiding the issuance of com-mon shares except in the most dire emergencies. Incremental financing requirements were usually met by incurring debt or issuing debtlike equity such as nonvoting preferred stock. Although debt contracts generally seemed more favorable than preferred stock because they provided greater flexibility with respect to term and rates, this latter choice could also be sensitive to other variables such as managerial risk preferences and capital market conditions.

The stabilization of managerial authority was a source of financial strength because it facilitated the implementation of long-term planning objectives. This was especially true among companies that were involved in advancing innovative technologies or forms of management. Lengthy commitments were necessary in order for corporate bureaucracies to learn the full economic potentials of their new ventures. Such advanced knowledge often provided competitive advantages that enabled particular companies to dominate major markets. For example, it took Standard Oil Company about two decades to learn how to achieve the great efficiencies in refining and marketing that ensured its leadership in the production of petroleum products.

But the insulation of management had a potential financial downside. Shareholders generally could do little during this period to oust mediocre or self-serving corporate leaders. Moreover, in some industries the potential benefits from either technological or organizational innovation were severely limited. Thus, when a company's performance was poor, dissatisfied investors had little recourse other than to sell their shares and redeploy their capital elsewhere.

Although the financial organizations that helped to promote common stock investment in the 1920s proved highly effective in mobilizing capital and assuaging perceptions of risk, they also greatly increased the susceptibility of the financial markets to disruptive shocks. Although public utility holding companies, bank investment subsidiaries and brokerage companies all made their individual contributions, the best example of this pattern was the investment trusts. This class of intermediary was able to diminish concerns about the limited information available for evaluating equity securities by promising to protect investors through the application of their money management expertise and through the diversification of their portfolios. But the problem remained that the most attractive sectors for investing, such as the businesses making up the automotive complex, were highly cyclical. In addition, leading industrial firms were usually capital intensive and exhibited a high degree of earnings leverage. Thus, the amplitude of swings in equity values became accentuated as professional

206

managers in the new institutions of finance rapidly redeployed their capital on a massive scale to profit from inflections in the business cycle. There were few ways to guard against this inherent systemic volatility other than, perhaps, maintaining balanced portfolios of stocks and bonds. Moreover, the potentials for instability were further increased by highly accommodative credit arrangements that allowed security purchases with as little as 10 percent margin.

The growth of governmental regulatory institutions during the 1930s, on the other hand, traded off higher monitoring costs and in some cases lower market efficiency for reductions in risk aversion. In the case of securities market reform, public confidence was enhanced by the increased transparency of corporate affairs and by the extension of the legal responsibilities of financial market agents. Although the overall budget of the SEC remained modest, relatively heavy monitoring costs were incurred by public companies for such matters as annual audits, federal reporting compliance and corporate oversight by boards of directors. But this new structure of governance did not interfere significantly with the stock market's basic functions of providing investment liquidity or in serving as an efficient mechanism for security pricing. Over the longer term the investment in a higher-quality information infrastructure actually contributed to financial market efficiency. More reliable information made possible more precise analyses of corporate financial prospects and also helped to bolster trading volume by increasing the range of opportunities for profitable transacting by market participants.

The reduction of risk aversion through banking reform was more disruptive to market efficiency. A key element in restoring confidence was the introduction of deposit insurance, which was financed by imposing assessments on participating banks. However, companion measures to this reform lessened the efficiency of the credit markets by placing restrictions on banks with respect to scope of service, pricing of deposits, market entry and expansion and financial leverage. Such actions later placed U.S. banks at a competitive disadvantage in terms of the range of services they offered, as compared with foreign banks or domestic nonbanking financial organizations.

The concomitant extension of federal regulatory authority to restore prosperity and stability to the markets for goods and nonfinancial services led to costly reductions in allocational efficiency. Most egregious was the National Recovery Act of 1933, which, prior to being struck down as unconstitutional by the Supreme Court two years later, sought to control prices and competition through a complex and unwieldy structure based on industry codes of fair competition. More lasting, however, was the extension of federal authority over public service industries such as interstate transportation and power generation. Although tight regulation represented a politically viable policy during a prolonged period of severe recession, it imposed heavy burdens on the economy over the longer term through the inefficient distribution of resources that resulted from administered pricing.

Several factors answer the second question relating to the differences in the nature of institutional developments in finance between Britain and the United States. Before the onset of the Great Depression of the 1930s, the British had moved through extensions of the companies acts to define a system for the regular dissemination of financial information. The British system incorporated legal and professional agents but did not involve either the executive or legislative branches of government to the same extent as in the United States. In a more tradition-bound and homogeneous society, greater deference was accorded to the judgment of seasoned practitioners to ensure probity and competency in financial dealing. The performance of these groups was monitored by peers operating through qualifying associations or business groups. Aggrieved shareholders could also sue in court to recover losses, but they lacked the strong rights accorded to U.S. investors in the securities acts. Moreover, the recourse to litigation in Britain was fraught with danger for unsuccessful plaintiffs. Failed suits brought against corporate managements or financial market professionals could lead to counteractions for character defamation, a remedy unavailable in American law.

Nor was the British market hit as hard by the collapse of a speculative bubble in common share values as was the U.S. market in 1929. In the United States the fires of speculation had been fanned by economic prosperity, accommodative credit policies and a maldistribution of national income. The latter factor led to overinvestment and insufficient consumption. In addition, many investors were attracted to common stocks as outlets for their capital after the U.S. Treasury under the leadership of Secretary Andrew W. Mellon succeeded in reducing the national debt, which had peaked at $23 billion in 1919, to $16 billion in 1927. These transfers were facilitated by the expansion of several types of financial market intermediaries, including investment trusts, retail brokerage chains, public utility holding companies and bank investment subsidiaries, which proved to be highly efficient mobilizers of capital for stock market investment.

Unlike the same period in the United States, the 1920s in Britain was not a decade of great prosperity but rather a time of economic trial. Growth was kept in check by an overvalued currency, a burdensome war debt, wartime manpower losses, labor strife and depressed Continental export markets. Moreover, the deflationary effects of the postwar reversion to the gold standard diminished the appeal of equity shares and enhanced the appeal of holding fixed-income securities. London thus avoided the overvaluation of share prices that eventually created such havoc in New York during October 1929. In addition, the British economy did not experience the great degree of expansion of giant industrial enterprises that had provided the basis for the investment boom in the United States. Instead, the United Kingdom remained a bastion of what Alfred D. Chandler has termed "personal capitalism," rather than the managerial capitalism that transformed U.S. industry.[68] There, family-controlled businesses whose principals sought to maximize current dividend income predominated in many industries. Consequently, there was less of a drive to enhance operational efficiency in the corporate sector by making costly investments in state-of-the-art facilities or in developing managerial capabilities.

The following chapter carries forward this analysis of financial institutional development in America's system of managerial capitalism to the post–World War II period. Its focus is on the patterns evident in the largest and most dynamic enterprises that provided leadership as U.S. business became more deeply integrated in a global economic order.

[68] Chandler, *Scale and Scope*, chapts. 3 and 7.

PART III

THE TRANSITION TO THE CONTEMPORARY ERA

CHAPTER SIX

The Financing of Center Firms, 1940–1973

I. Introduction

This chapter focuses on the financing of what economist Robert T. Averitt, in his book *The Dual Economy* (1968), has termed "center firms," which represent one of three leading classes of enterprises that figured prominently in the development of contemporary corporate finance. (The other two – the conglomerate and the leveraged-buyout partnership – are discussed in Chapter 7.) The importance of center firms from the standpoint of financial history derives from their robust industrial capacities, which have contributed strongly to national economic vitality. In evaluating center firm finance, this chapter lays greatest stress on the role of management in devising financial policies that sought to satisfy two sets of interdependent priorities. The first was functional, involving the integration of finance both in the basic procedures designed to ensure effective coordination and control of operational activities and in the strategic planning processes that are dedicated to ensuring the future profitable employment of enterprise resources. The second set of priorities was contractual, involving the definition of financial relationships to reconcile the often dissimilar interests of managers and other constituencies, such as shareholders and creditors, whose actions might impinge in important ways on the firm.

The dynamism of center firms was partly attributable to their leadership in three types of investment that were critical for industrial growth: research and development, product innovation and capital goods production. The center firms that Averitt studied were in a limited range of activities (Table 6.1). For instance, all but three of the forty-one industrial categories studied by Averitt were classified under

Table 6.1. *Key Industries, Percentage of Shipments by Largest Producers, 1963*

	Four Largest	Eight Largest
1. Machinery		
A. Machine tools		
1. Metal-cutting machine tools	20	32
2. Metal-forming machine tools	22	39
B. Electrical machinery, excluding electronics		
1. Motors and generators	50	59
2. Engine electrical equipment	69	79
3. Electrical products, not elsewhere classified	38	48
C. Farm machinery		
1. Farm machinery and equipment	43	55
D. Miscellaneous machinery		
1. Construction machinery	42	53
2. Internal combustion engines	49	65
3. Computing and related equipment	67	80
4. Industrial trucks and tractors	54	61
2. Iron and steel		
1. Blast furnaces and steel mills	50	69
2. Electrometallurgical products	79	95
3. Steel pipe and tube	27	42
4. Steel foundries	23	36
3. Nonferrous metals		
A. Aluminum		
1. Primary aluminum	n.a.	100
2. Aluminum rolling and drawing	68	79
B. Copper		
1. Primary copper	78	98
2. Copper rolling and drawing	45	67
4. Transportation equipment, other than aircraft and automobiles		
1. Shipbuilding and repairing	48	63
2. Locomotives and parts	97	99
3. Railroad and street cars	53	73
5. Aircraft		
1. Aircraft	59	83
2. Aircraft engines and parts	56	77

Table 6.1. *(cont.)*

	Four Largest	Eight Largest
6. Chemicals, especially industrial		
1. Alkalies and chlorine	62	88
2. Industrial gases	72	86
3. Intermediate coal tar products	54	70
4. Inorganic pigments	68	84
5. Organic chemicals, not elsewhere classified	51	63
6. Inorganic chemicals, not elsewhere classified	31	49
7. Cellulosic man-made fibers	82	100
7. Rubber products		
1. Tire and inner tubes	70	89
2. Reclaimed rubber	93	100
8. Petroleum		
1. Petroleum refining	34	56
2. Lubricating oils and greases	36	48
9. Electronics		
1. Radio, TV communication equipment	29	45
2. Semiconductors	46	65
3. Electronic components, not elsewhere classified	13	21
10. Automotive		
1. Motor vehicles and parts	79	83
2. Truck trailers	59	69
11. Instruments		
1. Scientific instruments	29	40
2. Mechanical measuring devices	22	36
3. Photographic equipment	63	76

Source: U.S. Bureau of the Census, *Concentration Ratios in Manufacturing Industry,* *1963,* cited in Robert Averitt, *Dual Economy,* pp. 43–44.

five two-digit Standard Industrial Classification (SIC) classes: oil, rubber, chemicals, machinery and metals. In addition to investment patterns, center firms shared other similarities: they exhibited a high degree of organizational complexity involving at least vertical integration forward from manufacturing to marketing and distribution; they were oligopolists, with the top eight firms in thirty-five of Averitt's categories accounting for about half their industries' total shipments and those in the remaining six categories accounting for from 32 to 42 percent of shipments; they were based in leading growth sectors; they exerted a strong effect on the level of prices, costs and wages in other industries in the "peripheral economy"; and they were situated in industries that were likely to experience production bottlenecks soonest as the economy approached full employment.[1]

The analysis in this chapter, however, broadens the definition of "center firms" to include entities that did not satisfy all of Averitt's original criteria but nevertheless were crucial to national economic vibrancy because of their size and leadership in specialized investment. Added to Averitt's list are those companies that ranked among the largest 100 manufacturing enterprises in the food and beverages and tobacco industries (Table 6.2). They conformed most closely to Averitt's sample in terms of their organizational complexity and oligopolistic status, while investing heavily in developing strong marketing and distribution capabilities.[2]

The capacity of center firms to realize their inherent financial potentials was contingent on the definition of effective business strategies and organizational structures. As previously noted, two patterns of development predominated among the nation's largest and most dynamic manufacturing enterprises. The first was the drive to achieve efficiency gains through economies of scale. This involved the establishment of centralized staff and line administrative structures to manage large, integrated, capital-intensive units that manufactured a nar-

---

[1] Robert T. Averitt, *The Dual Economy: The Dynamics of American Industry Structure* (New York: Norton, 1968), chaps. 2–4 passim. See also Chandler, *Visible Hand*, p. 371. The three industries noted by Averitt that did not fall within the five SIC categories were scientific instruments, measuring devices and steel pipe and tube manufacture. In addition, Averitt also defines a second category of peripheral firms that lacked the capacities for growth through the exploitation of managerial and technological capacities. Because of these limitations this latter category of firms were large in number, generally remained small in size and maintained narrow lines of relatively uncomplicated products. See Averitt, *The Dual Economy*, pp. 86–94 passim.

[2] Averitt, *The Dual Economy*, pp. 38–58 and chapt. 11.

Table 6.2. *Location of the Largest Manufacturing Enterprises, 1929, 1948 and 1960*

SIC Group[a]	1929	1948	1960
20 Food	8	9	6
21 Tobacco	4	3	2
22 Textiles	1	2	1
23 Apparel	0	0	0
24 Lumber	1	1	0
25 Furniture	0	0	0
26 Paper	2	1	3
27 Printing/publishing	0	0	0
28 Chemicals	5	10	9
29 Petroleum	19	17	18
30 Rubber	4	4	4
31 Leather	1	0	0
32 Stone/glass/clay	1	2	2
33 Primary metals	16	15	15
34 Fabricated metal	1	2	2
35 Machinery	4	6	6
36 Electrical machinery	3	3	4
37 Transportation equipment	8	5	7
38 Instruments	1	1	1
39 Miscellaneous manufactures	1	0	1
Total	81	81	81

Source: Chandler, *Visible Hand*, p. 370.
[a] The two-digit groups used by the U.S. Bureau of the Census in its Standard Industrial Classification.

row range of homogeneous products. High-volume throughput in high-fixed-cost plants led to dramatic reductions in unit costs of manufacture. In this context scientific research was primarily directed toward sharpening competitive capabilities by bolstering the efficiency of manufacturing processes or by improving product quality. The second pattern was the drive to achieve efficiency gains through economies of scope. This involved the enhancement of returns by the more intensive utilization of marketing and distribution facilities brought about by the opening of new geographic markets or by the establishment of positions in new product markets through either scientific research or corporate acquisition. Besides the potentials for improving

217

the profitability of resources threatened with redundancy or low returns, this strategy also helped to reduce the risk associated with a dependency on a single market. Ultimately, diversification led to organizational transformation. By the mid-twentieth century, these companies found that they could serve their multiple markets most effectively through decentralized operating divisions that were monitored by small central offices.[3]

The process of financial planning had to take cognizance of the need for center firms to preserve their leadership by continually perfecting managerial and technological capabilities. The changes that led to the emergence of the modern center firm came about through a slow accretion of knowledge about how an enterprise's productive resources could be ordered to satisfy the requirements of the market. Most fundamental was the perfection of routines and skills necessary to conduct basic operating activities such as manufacturing and marketing. More challenging was the level of understanding that had to be mastered before complex, interdependent functions could be effectively coordinated and controlled. Also, a strategic dimension needed to be developed that was primarily concerned with monitoring operations and making decisions about the allocation of corporate resources in light of changing market circumstances.

In this context the finance function was a service activity whose objective was to structure cash flows and liabilities in ways that insulated the process of knowledge building from disruptive external shocks. Thus, the fundamental priority of the corporate treasury function was to establish financial arrangements that provided sufficient time for these path-dependent processes to generate long-term resources. The concern of corporate managements for maintaining enterprise stability strongly influenced, as we shall see, the choices they made in resolving the capital structure puzzle.[4]

In this chapter the financial history of U.S. center firms in the contemporary era is evaluated from six perspectives. The second sec-

---

[3] Chandler, *Scale and Scope*, Parts 1 and 2; and idem, *Visible Hand*, chapt. 14.

[4] Alfred D. Chandler, Jr., "Winning and Losing in Post-War American Industry," unpublished working paper, pp. 27–31 and Part 1, pp. 61–65; and idem, "Organizational Capabilities and the Economic History of the Industrial Enterprise," *Journal of Economic Perspectives* 6 (Summer 1992): 79–100.

tion analyzes the changes in the domestic and international political economy after World War II that impinged on the financing of these enterprises. The third section evaluates the effects on corporate finance of a growing cognitive base about center firm economics deriving from the further standardization of accounting, the maturation of business journalism, the emergence of electronic media allowing the rapid transmission of business information and the revitalization of business education and scholarly research. The fourth section focuses on the performance of center firms in the financial markets and the factors that influenced investor preferences for holding debt or equity securities during this period. The fifth section identifies a set of interrelated operating and financing imperatives that have historically impinged on the strategic planning processes of mature center firms. The sixth section analyzes the patterns followed by such enterprises in satisfying their strategic objectives and in resolving the corporate financing puzzle. The penultimate section provides a brief case study of how the General Motors Corporation (GM) confronted these problems in the 1980s and the 1990s, when it sought to restructure extensively both its operations and its financing. The conclusion contrasts the financial practices evident in the experience of center firms with the theoretical explanations put forth by some scholars.

II. The Post–World War II Economic Revival

Several convergent factors provided the impetus for strong growth of U.S. center firms in the three decades following World War II. One was the liberalization of international agreements on trade and finance, which improved the access of American companies to foreign markets. These prospects were brightened by the steps taken to restore demand in the war-shattered economies of Europe and Japan by governmental grants and loans and the direct foreign investment of U.S. companies. Besides these international initiatives, domestic economic policies proved beneficial to center firms. For example, the federal government became involved with the formulation of fiscal policies to promote consumption and investment. Domestic demand for consumer durables, especially automobiles and appliances, surged when the purchasing power pent up after four years of forced saving was finally released. In addition, many corporations began to invest in new technologies perfected during the war that had applications in a peacetime economy.[5]

With respect to international trade and finance, the Bretton Woods Agreement of 1944 created three institutions that were critical in reviving the global economy. The first was the International Monetary Fund (IMF), whose function was to provide short-term loans to member states whose international reserves had become seriously depleted. IMF members were pledged to a system of fixed exchange rates pegged to the U.S. dollar, a gold-equivalent asset. Under this system the U.S. dollar, which was backed by a large proportion of the total world gold stock, became the numeraire for settling international transactions. This decision was logical in light of the strong international reserve position held by the United States after World War II. In 1952, U.S. reserves were valued at 24.7 billion special drawing rights, or about half of the world total. The second institution, the World Bank (known originally as the International Bank for Reconstruction and Development), supplied members with long-term loans, usually for infrastructure investments such as highways, power plants and dams. Finally, the General Agreement on Tariffs and Trade sought to achieve gains from international specialization envisioned in the law of comparative advantage. It fostered this goal through negotiating rounds that sought to elicit agreements from member states to eliminate tariffs and similar impediments to the free flow of goods and services.[6]

---

[5] Harold G. Vatter, *The U.S. Economy in the 1950s: An Economic History*, revised ed. (Chicago: University of Chicago Press, 1963, 1985), pp. 1–26 and 258–81.

[6] Gray, *International Trade, Investment and Payments*, pp. 594–611; Michael D. Bordo, "The Bretton Woods International Monetary System: A Historical Overview," in Michael D. Bordo and Barry Eichengreen, eds., *A Retrospective on the Bretton Woods System: Lessons for International Monetary Reform* (Chicago: University of Chicago Press, 1993), pp. 3–98; and Sir Roy Harrod, "Problems Perceived in the International Financial System," in A. L. K. Acheson, J. F. Chant and M. F. J. Prachowny, eds., *Bretton Woods Revisited: Evaluations of the International Monetary Fund and the International Bank for Reconstruction and Development* (Toronto: University of Toronto Press, 1972), pp. 5–19. See also Kindleberger, *Manias, Panics and Crashes*, pp. 221–29, for a discussion of how the Bretton Woods system helped to restore confidence by providing a "lender of last resort" capability to the postwar international financial system. See also *The Economic Report of the President:*

Center firms were both beneficiaries and participants in the drive to restore international economic vibrancy. Most dramatic was the infusion of $30 billion in investment capital in Europe by the Marshall Plan in 1947. This was followed by stepped up investment in Europe and Asia by American private enterprise. By the early 1960s the value of U.S. direct foreign investment had grown to $54.6 billion. Much of this total was concentrated in the center industries of transportation equipment, chemicals and allied products, electrical machinery and electronics and machinery other than electrical.[7] This strong showing motivated French economist Jean-Jacques Servan-Schreiber to note in 1967:

Fifteen years from now it is quite possible that the world's third greatest industrial power, just after the United States and Russia, will not be Europe, but *American industry in Europe*. Already, in the ninth year of the Common Market, this European market is basically American in organization.[8]

Center firms benefited from new domestic economic policies embraced by the federal government to avoid any repetition of the long depression of the 1930s. Most influential in this transition from the laissez-faire attitudes that had prevailed during the 1920s to the new beliefs about the need for state activism in economic affairs were the writings of John Maynard Keynes. His analytical framework as interpreted by U.S. economists envisioned a pivotal role for national

Transmitted to the Congress February 1995 (Washington, D.C.: Government Printing Office, 1995), Table B 109, p. 399.

[7] For the Marshall Plan, see Kindleberger, *Financial History of Western Europe*, pp. 433–46. See also Wilkins, *The Emergence of the Multinational Enterprise*, pp. 215–17; William H. Branson, "Trends in United States International Trade and Investment since World War II," in Martin Feldstein, ed., *The American Economy in Transition* (Chicago: University of Chicago Press, 1980), pp. 183–257 passim; and John M. Stopford and John H. Dunning, *Multinationals: Company Performance and Global Trends*, reprint ed. (London: Macmillan, 1983, 1984), chapt. 4. For a cogent discussion of the theoretical implications of these historical patterns of international trade and investment, see John H. Dunning, *Explaining International Production* (Boston: Unwin Hyman, 1988), especially chapts. 3–4; and idem, *Multinational Corporations and the Global Economy* (Wokingham: Addison-Wesley, 1993), pp. 96–136 passim.

[8] J.-J. Servan-Schreiber, *The American Challenge* (New York: Atheneum, 1968), p. 3.

governments in ensuring full utilization of resources. Moreover, the experience of World War II seemed to support the Keynesian contention that massive levels of public spending could ensure high levels of output and employment. The acceptance of this view was evidenced by the passage of the Employment Act of 1946, which among other provisions authorized the establishment of a Council of Economic Advisers to assist the president in formulating macroeconomic policy. In addition, the appropriations for defense, scientific research, agriculture, education and infrastructure improvements served as a powerful engine for growth. Tax policy augmented aggregate demand by allowing individuals to deduct sales taxes, real estate taxes and most types of interest on their personal tax returns. Private fixed investment, on the other hand, was encouraged through liberal allowances for the depreciation of capital assets and for the depletion of mineral assets, as well as the preferential treatment accorded to capital gains.[9]

Although center firms prospered at home and abroad after the war, their primary domestic markets were beset by regulatory policies that contributed to a misallocation of national economic resources. The New Deal's regulatory policies helped to ensure stability and employment at the cost of curtailed market competition. Such a trade-off was inherent in the programs of the former National Recovery Administration and the Agricultural Assistance Administration; it was also central to the missions of a host of specialized boards continued through the postwar period to control industries as diverse as railroads, trucking, barges, airlines, electrical power, pipeline, television, radio and banking.[10]

[9] Robert Lekachman, *The Age of Keynes* (New York: Random House, 1966), pp. 176–202; Hyman P. Minsky, *John Maynard Keynes* (New York: Columbia University Press, 1975), chaps. 8–9; Herbert Stein, *The Fiscal Revolution in America,* revised ed. (Washington, D.C.: American Enterprise Institute, 1969, 1990), chaps. 7–10 passim; Robert M. Collins, *The Business Response to Keynes, 1929–1964* (New York: Columbia University Press, 1981), chaps. 1, 6 and 7; S. K. Bailey, *Congress Makes a Law: The Story behind the Employment Act of 1946* (New York: Columbia University Press, 1950); Louis Galambos and Joseph Pratt, *Rise of the Corporate Commonwealth: U.S. Business and Public Policy in the Twentieth Century* (New York: Basic, 1988), chapt. 6; Vatter, *The U.S. Economy,* pp. 282–94; and Beardsley Ruml, "Tax Policies for Prosperity," *Journal of Finance* 1 (1946): 81–90.
[10] Galambos and Pratt, *Rise of the Corporate Commonwealth,* pp. 142–53; Otis L. Graham, *Toward a Planned Society: From Roosevelt to Nixon* (New York:

In addition, antitrust legislation inherited from the Progressive Era sought to combat concentrations of economic power. Some believed that the FTC's enforcement activities were necessary to preserve competitive markets and democratic values. They equated the rise of fascism with the cartelization of industry in Germany, Italy and Japan. These concerns about economic concentration often had a strong regional component. Agricultural interests in the South and West frequently supported federal regulatory initiatives because of misgivings that voters in these regions had about the predominance of financial and industrial power in the Northeast. But as Alfred Chandler has shown, the prohibitions against monopoly had only a tangential effect on the organization and operation of giant industrial enterprises. Moreover, as Louis Galambos has persuasively argued, by checking the rise of monopoly the antitrust laws only accelerated the formation of oligopolistic market structures in center industries.[11]

Federal regulation, however, did adversely affect corporate finance indirectly because of the implementation of policies that weakened the competitiveness of U.S. banking. The fear of the rise of a financial plutocracy engendered regulation that limited the scale and scope of U.S. banking institutions. The failure of the Second Bank of the United States to be rechartered during the presidency of Andrew Jackson (1832) and the later adoption of a federal structure for the Federal

Oxford University Press, 1976); Michael A. Bernstein, *The Great Depression: Delayed Recovery and Economic Change in America, 1929–1939* (Cambridge University Press, 1987); Ellis W. Hawley, *The New Deal and the Problem of Monopoly: A Study in Economic Ambivalence* (Princeton, N.J.: Princeton University Press, 1966); Richard H. K. Vietor, *Contrived Competition: Regulation and Deregulation in America* (Cambridge, Mass.: Harvard University Press, 1994), pp. 10–22; and Murray L. Weidenbaum, *Business, Government and the Public*, 5th ed. (Englewood Cliffs, N.J.: Prentice-Hall, 1995), chapt. 2. See also the introduction by Louis Galambos in Louis Galambos, ed., *The New American State: Bureaucracies and Policies since World War II* (Baltimore: Johns Hopkins University Press, 1987), pp. 1–20.

[11] Hawley, *The New Deal and the Problem of Monopoly*, pp. 404–19 and 456–71; Kenneth M. Davidson, *Mega-Mergers: Corporate America's Billion-Dollar Takeovers* (Cambridge, Mass.: Ballinger, 1985), pp. 109–12; Chandler, *Scale and Scope*, pp. 78–79 and 89; and idem, *Visible Hand*, pp. 365–68; Louis Galambos, "The Triumph of Oligopoly," in Thomas Joseph Weiss and Donald Schaefer, eds., *American Economic Development in Historical Perspective* (Stanford, Calif.: Stanford University Press, 1994), pp. 241–53.

Reserve Board during the presidency of Woodrow Wilson (1913) were manifestations of deep-seated and abiding fears about the concentration of financial power. The New Deal's Banking Act of 1933 (Glass–Steagall) contributed to the trend of disaggregation by mandating the separation of commercial and investment banking. In addition, prohibitions imposed by both federal and state authorities restricting the scope of branch networks limited the ability of banks to build deposit bases as great as those of overseas competitors. The desire to maximize the number of credit-granting institutions had induced the government to charter over 13,000 commercial banks by 1970. This fragmentation, not found in the highly integrated foreign national banking systems, was a major reason why U.S. banks were not counted among the world's largest depositary institutions. Moreover, ceilings imposed under the Federal Reserve's Regulation Q on the amount of interest payable for deposits made the banking system more prone to periodic credit stringencies. The unreliability of commercial banks during crises persuaded corporate treasurers, as we shall see, to turn to other sources of short-term credit.[12]

The exploitation of the technological advances achieved in national defense research programs, on the other hand, strengthened the competitiveness of many center firms. The expansion of the petrochemical and polymer industries was spurred by discoveries made through wartime efforts to refine high-octane gasoline and to synthesize rubber. Electronics benefited from improvements in radar and telecommunication technologies. Data processing flourished by extending advances first achieved in defense cryptography. The pharmaceutical industry established a strong base for new products by its successful manufacture of penicillin, Atabrine and sulfa drugs. The development of atomic weaponry made possible the harnessing of nuclear power for commercial purposes. Besides the advances from scientific inquiry, the wartime expansion of productive capabilities in basic industries such

---

[12] Myers, *A Financial History of the United States,* chapt. 4; Carosso, *Investment Banking in America,* chapts. 17–18; Smith and Sylla, *Transformation of Finance Capitalism,* pp. 32–38; Richard H. K. Vietor, "Regulation-Defined Financial Markets: Fragmentation and Integration of Financial Services," in Samuel L. Hayes, III, ed., *Wall Street and Regulation* (Boston: Harvard Business School Press, 1987), pp. 7–62; and Benjamin M. Friedman, "Postwar Changes in the American Financial Markets," in Feldstein, ed., *The American Economy in Transition,* pp. 9–78.

as steel, aluminum and copper created a platform to support a takeoff in the production of both consumer and producer durables.[13]

Four years of forced savings and rationing had created an enormous pent-up demand for peacetime goods. Although the war had eradicated the high unemployment of the Depression years, opportunities for increasing personal consumption were limited; thus, the labor force was compelled to channel much of its income into savings. The personal consumption expenditure rate, which amounted to 94.8 percent of disposable income in 1940, dropped dramatically due to the exigencies of war production to 74.6 percent in 1944; the consumer savings rate stayed above 20 percent between 1942 and 1945. Much of the increase in savings was channeled into government bonds, which increased in volume from $2.0 billion in 1940 to $51 billion in 1945.[14]

The high wartime savings rate helped to spark the initial stages of a long period of national economic prosperity. Real GNP grew at about an average annual rate of almost 3.5 percent rising, from $487.7 billion (in 1972 dollars) in 1948 to $1,233.4 billion in 1973. The economy also registered moderate average annual increases in productivity of 2.5 percent from 1948 to 1966, a rate that fell off to 2 percent per annum for the seven years through 1973.[15]

[13] Sumner H. Slichter, "Technological Research as Related to the Growth and Stability of the Economy," in National Science Foundation, *Proceedings of a Conference on Research and Development and Its Impact on the Economy* (Washington, D.C.: National Science Foundation, 1958), pp. 107–14 and 117; and Leonard S. Silk, *The Research Revolution* (New York: McGraw-Hill, 1963), chapt. 4 passim. See also Vannevar Bush, *Science the Endless Frontier: A Report to the President* (Washington, D.C.: Government Printing Office, 1945); idem, *Modern Arms and Free Men: A Discussion of the Role of Science in Preserving Democracy,* reprint ed. (Cambridge, Mass.: MIT Press, 1949, 1968); U.S. Civilian Production Administration, *Industrial Mobilization for War: History of the War Production Board and Predecessor Agencies, 1940–1945,* reprint ed. (New York: Greenwood, 1947, 1969), pp. 50–88, 160–63, 395–409 and 941–59; and Brian Balogh, *Chain Reaction: Expert Debate and Public Participation in American Commercial Nuclear Power, 1945–1975* (Cambridge University Press, 1991).

[14] Paul B. Trescott, *Financing American Enterprise* (New York: Harper & Row, 1963), pp. 213–17; and Emma S. Woytinsky, *Profile of the U.S. Economy: A Survey of Growth and Change* (New York: Praeger, 1967), pp. 147–51.

[15] For the GNP, see *Economic Report of the President* (Washington, D.C.: Government Printing Office, 1976); and for productivity, see Edwin Mansfield,

Besides the improving economic trends, the revival of the securities markets was also assisted by the emergence of new ideas and sources of information about finance.The expansion of knowledge was propitious because it helped to overcome the uncertainties that had worried investors since the great stock market debacle of 1929.

III. Finance's Widening Cognitive Base

The quality and volume of information about corporate financial conditions continued to improve after the war. Investor decision processes were enriched by the clearer perspectives made available by the expanding cognitive base for business and financial matters. Four aspects of these developments were most salient. First, corporate financial communication was improved by the refinement of generally accepted accounting principles and by a clearer definition of the professional responsibilities of independent accountants who audited corporate financial statements. Second, a proliferation of specialized periodicals and journals heightened investors' knowledge about current business affairs. Third, new electronic media that instantaneously broadcast a wealth of current transactional data greatly facilitated the market's price-searching function. Fourth, finance was invigorated by its further professionalization through the strengthening of education and the flourishing of scholarly research.

A major problem confronting financial reporting was the development of a comprehensive measurement model that satisfied the information requirements of equity owners. This particular emphasis was uniquely American and was associated with the general rise of investment in common stocks since the 1920s. European precedents were not helpful because accounting there had been geared to inform other types of financial statement users. In England, for example, accounting had been structured more toward meeting the needs of that nation's predominant investor constituency, bondholders; in France, measurement practices had been ordered since the mercantilist regime of Colbert to facilitate tax reporting; and in Germany, greatest stress had been placed on managerial and cost accounting. In the United States,

"Technology and Productivity in the United States," in Feldstein, ed., *The American Economy in Transition*, p. 565.

226

on the other hand, financial reporting sought to provide precise measures of the many elements that affected the calculation of net income, a crucial variable in the evaluation of common stocks.[16]

The standardization of financial accounting, however, proved to be a challenging undertaking. To be useful to investors, accounting standards had to reflect accurately the complexities of underlying economic processes that drove the modern corporation. An example of this was the difficulties encountered in promulgating rules for the measurement of pensions, contingent losses, income taxes and other corporate liabilities. Another problem involved the broad time horizons of many business transactions, which required accounting estimates about likely future outcomes. Consider, for example, the problem of profit recognition in long-term construction projects and in installment sales or the problem of valuing current, future-directed outlays such as research and development and product promotion. Moreover, because modern business was dynamic there was a continuing pressure to develop new accounting methods to measure the economic effects of innovative technologies or forms of business management.

Many critics, however, had been concerned about the pace and adequacy of the standardization process established during the Depression. Responsibility for this function had initially been vested in two successive committees of the American Institute of Certified Public Accountants (AICPA, which was known as the American Institute of Accountants until 1959): the Committee on Accounting Procedure (1936–59) and the Accounting Principles Board (1959–72). Although research support was recognized as vital in promulgating standards, insufficient resources had been committed for this purpose. Moreover, the coordination between the performance of research that was supposed to inform the standards-setting process and the actual issuance of authoritative guidance had often broken down. New standards were sometimes promulgated before completion of the preliminary

---

[16] See Paul H. Aron, "International Accounting and Financial Reporting," in Lee J. Seidler and D. R. Carmichael, eds., *Accountants' Handbook*, 6th ed., 2 vols. (New York: Wiley, 1981), vol. 2, pp. 40/1–40/35. See also International Practice Executive Committee, *Professional Accounting in 30 Countries* (New York: American Institute of Certified Public Accountants, 1975), pp. 193–230, 597–696; and Stephen Zeff, *Forging Accounting Principles in Five Countries: A History and an Analysis of Trends* (Champaign, Ill.: Stipes, 1972).

research undertaken to evaluate the theoretical issues that impinged on particular accounting practices. Critics also suspected that an overly solicitous attitude toward major clients had motivated the practitioners who served on these committees to define standards that allowed too much measurement flexibility. In addition, the pressing demands of practice distracted the CPA firm partners who served on these standards-setting committees and thus prevented them from devoting their full energies to these tasks. Nor were these activities supported by any comprehensive theoretical framework for the emerging edifice of financial accounting rules. Finally, not enough was done to integrate the perspectives of either the users or issuers of financial statements in the standardization process.[17]

The result was a body of standards that pleased few groups. Statement issuers, generally represented by the Financial Executives Institute (formerly the Controllers Institute), often believed that proposed accounting changes were too restrictive and rigid. On the other hand, many academic accountants disagreed with the controllers, believing that the rules were too flexible and lacked a sufficient theoretical grounding.

These sources of dissatisfaction, combined with concerns about the growing incidence of professional liability lawsuits in the 1960s, gave a new urgency to the drive for standards-setting reform. The AICPA formed two special committees in 1971 whose deliberations shaped the future direction of financial reporting. The first was chaired by Frank Wheat, a former SEC commissioner. It was given the responsibility to review the standards-setting process with an eye toward recommending changes that would better satisfy the requirements of the investing public. The next year a second committee, chaired by Robert Trueblood, a partner in the firm of Touche Ross & Co. (now Deloitte & Touche LLP), had the mission to define the fundamental objectives of financial accounting. In 1973, this latter committee also issued a special report, entitled *Objectives of Financial Reporting*.[18]

---

[17] Chatfield, *A History of Accounting Thought*, pp. 290–99; Chatov, *Corporate Financial Reporting*, chaps. 9–14; and Previts and Merino, *Accounting in America*, pp. 286–92.

[18] Previts and Merino, *Accounting in America*, pp. 307–308 and 314–15; Wallace E. Olson, *The Accounting Profession: Years of Trial, 1969–1980* (New York: American Institute of Certified Public Accounting, 1982), pp. 65–68.

These developments paralleled the formation in 1972 of the Financial Accounting Foundation (FAF), whose principal subsidiary, the Financial Accounting Standards Board (FASB), became the new focal point for standardization. Unlike predecessor bodies, which had been exclusively controlled by the accounting profession, the FAF was supported by a host of statement user and issuer groups. In addition, the seven-member FASB included three voting members drawn from outside the public accounting profession. The FASB was served by a large professional staff, which did research in support of prospective practice standards; it also undertook an ambitious project to define the basic conceptual framework for financial accounting.[19]

Another problem in accounting was the need for a clearer delineation of practitioner responsibilities to the public in their role as attestors to the reliability of corporate financial statements. The failure of accountants to discover material inaccuracies that existed in the statements of some of the major companies that failed during the period, such as Penn Central, Continental Vending, National Student Marketing and Equity Funding, was damaging to their profession's public image. During the 1970s, separate congressional committees headed by Senator Lee Metcalf and Representative John Moss conducted searching probes into what they characterized as the "accounting establishment." These politicians believed that professional regulation would be materially strengthened by greater governmental intervention.[20]

The SEC also responded to this new crisis. The steps it took centered on strengthening the image of practicing accountants as independent and objective agents protecting the public interest. For example, the federal agency encouraged the formation of audit committees composed of outside directors to deal with all matters relating to the services provided by their independent accountants. It also required

---

[19] Chatov, *Corporate Financial Reporting*, chapt. 6; Olson, *The Accounting Profession*, chapt. 4; and Previts and Merino, *Accounting in America*, pp. 323–24.

[20] "The Accounting Establishment," Staff Study prepared by the Senate Government Operations Subcommittee on Reports, Accounting and Management, Senate Doc. No. 95-34, 95th Cong., 1st Sess. (1977); and Olson, *The Accounting Profession*, chapts. 2 and 5.

that registrants disclose the fees paid to public accountants for audits and other types of professional services.[21]

The AICPA also took steps to restore public confidence. New auditing standards were issued to address shortcomings in practice that had been revealed in malpractice litigation. During the 1970s, the national organization began to require peer reviews of practice quality in order for professional firms to maintain membership in its prestigious Division of Firms. It also supported the organization of the Public Oversight Board, which was composed of five respected public figures who had the responsibility for reviewing annually the effectiveness of the practice quality assessment program.[22]

In addition to the formal disclosures communicated through the financial statements of center firms, periodicals and journals increased the amount of business information available to investors. Foremost among the business magazines of this era was Time Inc.'s *Fortune*, McGraw-Hill's *Business Week* and privately owned *Forbes*. A host of more specialized publications provided regular coverage of particular industries. The statistical compendia and the research reports published by Standard and Poor's and Moody's services also found wide acceptance.

Brokerage companies specializing in serving the requirements of both institutional and retail clients also became important sources of information about center firms and their investment securities. These companies began to procure cathode-ray tube display equipment, which transmitted price and volume data from the stock exchanges with minimal delay. The larger brokerage firms also supported research staffs that published analyses of particular stocks. Securities analysis became more professional with the formation of a representative association, the Financial Analysts' Federation, which sponsored a challenging examination for those who wished to certify their competency in this field.

The professionalization of finance progressed because of educational reforms. The aforementioned criticisms of business education leveled by the Ford and Carnegie Foundations during the 1950s led to

---

[21] Olson, *The Accounting Profession*, pp. 100–102, 207–209 and 213–22; and Seligman, *Transformation of Wall Street*, pp. 551–68.

[22] Olson, *The Accounting Profession*, chaps. 7–8.

an extensive restructuring of curriculums. The desire to make education more challenging intellectually was partly fulfilled by raising the requisite competency in quantitative disciplines. Pedagogy in finance became influenced by the same style of neoclassical analysis that was transforming contemporary economics.[23]

In addition to their role in professional education, scholars began to formulate theories to explain aspects of the finance phenomenon. One pioneering milestone was the work in 1959 of H. M. Markowitz relating to greater investment efficiency and the diminishment of risk through diversified portfolios. This was extended by the capital asset pricing model studies initiated by W. F. Sharpe in 1963 and J. Lintner in 1965. Their work differentiated between systematic and unsystematic risk and provided a framework for assessing the trade-off between risk and return inherent in investing. The theoretical work of E. Fama, M. Modigliani and M. M. Miller during the 1970s explored the connections between information and market efficiency. In 1973, F. Black and M. Scholes formulated their options pricing model. Later that decade W. H. Meckling and M. C. Jensen raised serious questions about market efficiency in comprehending corporate financing decisions. They suggested as an alternative that more attention be focused on the problem of agency relationships.[24]

The strong performance in the real economy and the expansion of the cognitive base of finance contributed to the restoration of investor confidence in the securities market. As we shall see in the following section, one important consequence of these changing circumstances related to the relative attractiveness of bond and equity investing.

---

[23] Leontiades, *Mythmanagement*, chapt. 1; Pierson, *The Education of American Businessmen*; and Gordon and Howell, *Higher Education for Business*.

[24] Markowitz, "Portfolio Selection"; W. F. Sharpe, "A Simplified Model for Portfolio Analysis," *Management Science* 10 (January 1963): 277–93; and idem, "Capital Asset Prices: A Theory of Market Equilibrium under Conditions of Risk," *Journal of Finance* 19 (1964): 425–42; Lintner, "Valuation of Risky Assets"; Modigliani and Miller, "Cost of Capital"; Fama, "Efficient Capital Markets"; F. Black and M. Scholes, "The Pricing of Options and Corporate Liabilities," *Journal of Political Economy* 31 (May–June 1973): 637–59; and Jensen and Meckling, "Theory of the Firm."

IV. Recovery in the Financial Markets

Growing confidence in the continuance of prosperity and a growing cognitive base about business affairs helped to revive the financial markets. The number of shareholders in the United States, after declining from 10 million in 1930 to 6 million in 1952, rebounded to 20 million in 1965. By 1975, there were over 25 million investors on the NYSE alone. Also notable was the increase in the number of institutional investors, whose holdings grew from 6 percent of aggregate equity in 1950 to 40 percent in 1990.[25] There was also a great increase in share trading volume. On "Black Tuesday" of 1929, a total of 16.4 million shares changed hands on the NYSE, and the record volume of that year totaled 1.1 billion shares. After the Crash, however, the exchanges became somnolent, and in 1934 only 324 million shares were sold on the NYSE. Activity began to revive during the 1950s, and in 1956 annual volume reached above 500 million shares. By 1968, the pace had quickened and over 2.9 billion shares were traded in that year.[26]

Growing confidence was reflected in the decline of dividend yields on common stock relative to cash yields on debt instruments. In the past the dividend yield had been expected to compare favorably with interest rates; investors looked to the dividend stream to provide the preponderance of risk-adjusted return. For example, in England during 1926 (an unexceptional year) the average stock yield was about 7 percent and the current yield on consols was 4.5 percent. In the United States during the twentieth century, average dividend yields exceeded the interest rate on government bonds until 1959. A brief exception occurred during the 1929 summer rally, when interest rates on treasury bonds rose to about 4 percent and the average dividend yields fell to about 3 percent. As late as 1950, the aggregate U.S. dividend–price ratio for industrial common stock was over 6.5 per-

[25] New York Stock Exchange, *Shareownership, 1990* (New York: New York Stock Exchange, undated), p. 10; and Federal Reserve Board, *Flow of Funds, Seasonally Adjusted and Unadjusted* (Washington, D.C.: Government Printing Office, 1993).

[26] U.S. Department of Commerce, *Historical Statistics of the United States*, pp. 1006–1007 for data on share volume; and Carosso, *Investment Banking in America*, pp. 300–302 for volumes during the Great Crash of 1929.

cent, while the yield on high-grade corporate debt was about 2.6 percent.[27]

This change in relative yields also reflected the impact of greater inflation as well as the boom in stock prices. Theoretically, the dividend yield should have kept pace with the rate of inflation, and the current cash yield on stocks should have corresponded to a real measure of return. Because bond payments were fixed, an inflation premium was needed to compensate for changing price levels. Thus, the difference between bond and stock yields should in theory have varied directly with the rate of inflation that escalated during the 1960s and the 1970s.

Another factor depressing dividend yields was the boom in stock prices. This was clearly reflected in the aggregate Standard and Poor's price–earnings ratio, which rose from about 7 in 1950 to 18 in 1968.[28] A fall in the dividend payout ratio did not seem to have had any material effect, as aggregate distribution ratios appear to have been stable since World War I.

The fall in yields and the rise in trading volume also reflected an emerging view of common stock as a source not merely of dividend streams but also of capital gains. Before World War II, dividend yield was considered the primary basis of common stock valuation in public markets. But in the boom conditions of the 1950s and the 1960s, the dividend yield was increasingly overshadowed by the prospects of capital gains. As markets became more liquid, investors sought short-term capital gains, which served to increase trading volume. The expectation of capital gain diminished the requirement that dividends provide an adequate holding period return. Although the underlying basis for market valuation of common stock had already long been abstracted away from the original idea of a proportional active interest in a business, in the modern era it appeared to even be divorced from

[27] See U.S. Department of Commerce, *Historical Statistics of the United States,* p. 1003 for U.S. bond and stock yields; see also Sydney Homer and Richard Sylla, *A History of Interest Rates,* 3rd ed. (New Brunswick, NJ: Rutgers University Press, 1991), chapts. 17 and 18 passim for data on U.S. interest rates and chapt. 19 passim for data on rates in Britain.

[28] Standard and Poor's Corporation, *S & P Statistical Services: Current Bulletin-Security Price Index Record* (New York: Standard and Poor's Corporation, Division of McGraw-Hill, 1995).

the dividend stream. The new strategy became more to forecast future price returns than to gain possession of the eventual distribution of dividends.

Income tax policy contributed to the relative decline of dividends, especially to high-income investors. In a regime where the highest marginal tax rates reached 92 percent and the maximum long-term (i.e., six months or longer) capital gain tax rate was 50 percent, it was understandable that high-bracket investors would prefer the expectation of stock price appreciation rather than current dividend payments. These investors favored corporations that retained their earnings to finance internal investment opportunities, which would enhance the prospects for significant market value appreciation of their shares. Moreover, the retention of earnings and the consequent rise in share values allowed purchasers to defer income recognition until the moment most propitious to sell their shares, which thus facilitated the efficient management of portfolios.

Although these patterns were indicative of the factors that conditioned the choices taken by outside investors, they shed little light on finance from the perspective of corporate planners. In the following section, however, we focus more directly on the question of how the corporate financing puzzle was resolved by the managements of center firms.

V. Strategic Planning and the Integration of Financial and Operating Imperatives among Mature Center Firms

Much of the contemporary research that has addressed the corporate financing problem did not distinguish between practices employed by center firms and practices employed by those on the periphery. This was partly due to the use of research methods that were not suited for considering the significance of the unique company characteristics that figured prominently in the work of institutional scholars. Thus, little cognizance was taken of the implications of heterogeneity in such qualities as size, industry, organizational structure, technology or products. Instead, many scholars assumed that corporations were a homogeneous class of economic institutions and selected analytical techniques that would have been most effective for assessing the characteristics of populations with uniform attributes. Moreover, the need

234

to define precise relationships led to hypotheses for testing large data sets, which encouraged researchers to simplify assumptions to a degree that at times bordered on reductionism.

In this section we follow a different approach, relying on the in-depth studies of corporate behavior conducted by such institutional scholars as Alfred D. Chandler, Jr., Gordon Donaldson and Jay Lorsch. Their studies provide a rich and detailed explanation of the interplay between financing and operating patterns among center firms. Their findings have a high degree of validity because they concentrated on leading center firms in oligopolistic industries. This approach enabled these researchers to analyze comprehensively the practices of firms that accounted for major portions both of output and of finance capital in the most dynamic sectors of the economy.

These institutional scholars addressed the problems of agency, information and finance in the context of organizational structures and strategic and operational decision making. As Alfred Chandler's work has indicated, the efficiencies deriving from the great scale and scope of operations of the modern center firm were closely associated with their hierarchical managerial structures. Center firms were able to achieve dramatic cost savings by establishing organizations that made possible more effective coordination and control of many interdependent operational elements. The need to maintain high levels of utilization in capital-intensive factories to achieve high returns served as a strong incentive for the integration of manufacturing, distribution and marketing. Many center firms sought to maintain high returns on invested capital and to reduce risk by diversification. The profitability of particular products often declined as demand leveled off during their life cycle and competitive pressures were felt from new entrants to these markets. Many center firms relied on their research and development departments to discover new opportunities for utilizing their pools of technological and managerial skills. Both trends contributed to the emergence of the unique, highly integrated and diversified business institutions that provided much of the modern world's economic abundance.[29]

---

[29] Chandler, *Scale and Scope*, chaps. 1–2; idem, *Visible Hand*, pp. 473–83; Donaldson and Lorsch, *Decision Making at the Top*; Donaldson, *Managing Corporate Wealth*; and idem, *Corporate Debt Capacity*. See also Baskin, "Financial Policy of Large Mature Corporations."

In multiproduct center firms, finance was located within the central office along with other specialized staff activities concerning such functions as law, real estate and purchasing. Besides its responsibility for monitoring segment performance, the central office was the focus of strategic planning and the allocation of corporate resources. Operational activities such as manufacturing, marketing and distribution were relegated to decentralized divisions that focused on satisfying the requirements of particular product markets.

Four broad objectives were critical in arranging the financing of center firms.[30] First, financial planning was basically concerned with the survival of the enterprise. In financial terms this meant that the corporation had to command sufficient purchasing power to continue to fund its basic operations. Second, financial planning sought to ensure the continuity of managerial independence and to preserve its autonomy in corporate decision making against encroachments by outside elements. A third objective was to plan for the acquisition of vital resources to ensure the highest degree of corporate self-sufficiency. Finally, planning was integral to managements' quest to maintain congruence between the goals of individual achievement and of organizational success. The advancement of the enterprise's interests was crucial to management because it provided the greatest opportunity for realizing personal career goals.[31]

Financial planning also had to take into account the goals of key stakeholder constituencies. One such group was represented by the capital markets, which reflected the interests of creditors and equity owners. Their objectives were varied: some were concerned about dividends, some were eager for capital gains, while others favored

[30] The samples on which most of the following generalizations about financing practices are based derive from two separate studies involving a total of 220 firm-years of experience. The first was the sample used by Gordon Donaldson in his book *Corporate Debt Capacity*, which surveyed in depth the experience of five companies during the period 1939–58. This first sample was centered in five industries: rubber, machine tools, chemicals, ethical drugs and baking and biscuits. The second sample was used in Donaldson's *Managing Corporate Wealth* and Donaldson and Lorsch's *Decision Making at the Top*. In this latter case, twelve firms were studied for the period 1968–78. Their industrial distribution was three capital-intensive manufacturers of commodity products, four consumer-goods manufacturers, three high-tech firms and two conglomerates.

[31] Donaldson, *Managing Corporate Wealth*, pp. 11–15 and 20–22.

policies that provided stronger guarantees of interest and principal payments. Moreover, their relative importance increased greatly during periods of financial crisis, when a firm's survival was often contingent on its ability to secure new funding. Another constituency was the product market, which encompassed both customers and suppliers. This aspect of a center firm's business defined the basic economic activities that were the source of its operating cash flows. Consequently, it exerted strong influence on the planning process, especially with regard to ongoing funding requirements. Yet another constituency was the business organization's own managerial cadre. Ideally, the relationship between the group and the individual was mutually reinforcing. The corporation was the vehicle that enabled the individual professionals to "self-actualize," to use Maslow's term, by acquiring scarce social resources such as income, wealth and status. The collective managerial and technical skills of the professional staff, on the other hand, defined the enterprise's competitive capabilities and the range of market opportunities that it was competent to pursue. Finally, corporations operated in a broader and interdependent societal context, which impinged on the process of establishing goals in finance and other functional and operating activities. Antitrust legislation, for example, influenced decisions at large industrial corporations about how particular strategies such as diversification were to be achieved. The fear of adverse litigation motivated some companies to develop internally the capabilities for serving new markets rather than trying to establish footholds by acquiring existing enterprises.[32]

The most pressing priorities driving financial planning were associated with the product market where there was considerable variation between companies in the specific details of their planning. One aspect of this was the definition of a fundamental business strategy that involved decisions as to what product markets the enterprise would continue to commit resources. For example, after World War II chemical companies were especially successful in defining growth strategies. Some companies followed the "low road" to growth by emphasizing process innovation for the efficient production of commodity chemicals. This was the pattern at Dow Chemical and Allied Chemical. Others took the "high road" to growth involving product innovation to bolster profits by concentrating on high-value-added manufactur-

[32] Ibid., pp. 25–32.

ing. This was the pattern followed by such leaders as Du Pont, Monsanto, Rohm & Haas and American Cyanamid. The latter strategy was especially challenging because it required the establishment of new markets and the formation of capacities to serve them. The companies that were successful in these ventures demonstrated a consistent ability to build on acquired skills in technology and management to satisfy new market requirements. Witness, for example, the Du Pont achievement of this period. As we have noted, after World War I this company first diversified to find new outlets for its nitrocellulose-processing capabilities. This led to the penetration of markets for lacquers and paints, cellophane, pyroxylin plastics and rayon. During the 1920s, Du Pont sponsored polymer research designed to provide a better understanding of the formation of complex carbon molecules, which eventually resulted in the discovery of nylon, which came to market in 1939. Subsequent synthetic fiber research yielded a host of valuable new products including Dacron, Orlon, spandex and Teflon. A parallel line of polymer research led to the development of new plastics and synthetic rubber. During World War II, neoprene rubber was created by the Wilmington-based firm; after the war, nylon plastics, Mylar and Kevlar became major products.[33]

A second element was the definition of a competitive strategy which equated the scale of operations for particular markets to overall enterprise performance goals. Market objectives were generally expressed in rates of growth and/or rates of return on net assets. These operating standards were amplified in the degree of market share penetration that was essential to ensure a high level of plant utilization. High market penetration promised favorable cost–profit relationships as well as the possibility of disciplining the market through price leadership. A viable competitive strategy required an accurate estimate of the resources necessary to support planned levels of operations.[34]

The importance of the nexus between market share, capacity utilization and rates of return had been recognized by industrial market leaders since the beginning of the twentieth century. For example, Arthur Moxham, a senior executive at Du Pont, had argued that it was better

[33] Ibid., chapt. 3; and Chandler, *Scale and Scope*, pp. 170–81; idem, *Visible Hand*, pp. 438–54; and idem, "Chemicals and Electronics," Part 1, pp. 3–19.
[34] Donaldson, *Managing Corporate Wealth*, chapt. 7; and Chandler, *Scale and Scope*, chapt. 2.

for the firm to concentrate on dominating only 60 percent of the domestic powder market rather than try to secure a monopoly position. Such an objective, coupled with the company's traditional commitment of remaining the industry's most efficient producer, Moxham reasoned, would guarantee a high level of utilization of corporate resources and profitability even in weak markets. In the latter case the brunt of economic contractions would be borne by marginal competitors.[35]

However, although the Du Pont emphasis on maintaining market share to ensure full utilization of corporate resources was implemented by other leading industrial enterprises such as Alcoa, American Tobacco and Standard Oil, it was not a universal pattern. One notable exception was the U.S. Steel Company during the long tenure of Elbert H. Gary as president. Gary, an attorney, was highly sensitive to the potentials of adverse antitrust litigation, given the size of his company. To avoid this worrisome outcome U.S. Steel consciously sacrificed efficiency and market dominance. Although U.S. Steel, unlike other leading industrial companies, was not subject to disruptive dissolutions, it was a success achieved only at the cost of longer-term economic decline.[36]

The definition of a competitive strategy also required the financing of a lengthy, preliminary learning period during which management determined how best to integrate the new product into the corporation's operational activities. This was particularly evident in manufacturing, where learning derived from a gradual increase in the scale of plant output. Initially, production was conducted in a small pilot plant. Later it was increased to the semi-plant scale and then, ultimately, to full-scale production. These steps yielded valuable information about how production could be most efficiently achieved and how high product quality could be ensured. Paralleling these steps in manufacturing were initiatives taken to modify administrative practices in marketing and other support activities to accommodate the new product line.[37]

---

[35] Chandler and Tedlow, *The Coming of Managerial Capitalism*, pp. 374–78.

[36] See Thomas K. McCraw and Forest Reinhardt, "Losing to Win: U.S. Steel's Pricing, Investment Decisions, and Market Share, 1901–1938," *Journal of Economic History* 49 (September 1989): 593–619.

[37] Hounshell and Smith, *Science and Corporate Strategy*, chaps. 12–13 passim; and Robert A. Burgelman and Leonard R. Sayles, *Inside Corporate Innovation: Strategy, Structure and Managerial Skills* (New York: Free Press, 1986).

However, the accuracy of projections of financial returns that were developed as part of the strategic planning process was often beset by the difficulties encountered in forming basic estimates. This was especially true in developing discounted cash flows for prospective projects. A key difficulty was the specification of the hurdle rate, or minimum acceptable rate of return in rationing scarce capital between competing investment alternatives. The common tendency to choose a high discount rate inevitably introduced a bias that favored short-term benefits. The discount factor and the payoff period were inversely related; the higher the hurdle rate, the shorter the payment period. In addition, the discounting that was central to this sort of cash flow projecting was not intended as an estimate of "option value" of a prospective investment. This form of analysis was not well suited for determining the value of unexpected opportunities that might materialize if an investment is made in a new technology.[38]

The financial results achievable from a particular strategic plan might not be optimal from the perspective of efficient resource allocation if the transfer prices used to value inputs received from other corporate components were unreliable, as the work of such scholars as Robert Solomons, H. Thomas Johnson and Robert Kaplan makes clear. Difficulties may be encountered in developing a method for allocating joint costs of production that is not arbitrary and that yields useful insights into underlying economic processes. Transfer prices could also be distorted by managerial opportunism. In the latter case prices might not be established at levels commensurate with the economic value of the resources expended; rather, they are set in ways that reflect most favorably on the performance of particular managers. Moreover, as the work of Carliss Baldwin and Kim Clark illustrates, capital budgeting techniques often failed to provide useful guidance in planning because they failed to take into consideration the value of an entity's investment in its organizational capabilities. This shortcoming was also a source of suboptimal allocations of corporate investment capital.[39]

Between 70 and 76 percent of total research and development expenditures were accounted for by developmental activities during the 1945–69 period; see the schedules presented in Silk, *Research Revolution*, pp. 236–37.

[38] Donaldson, *Managing Corporate Wealth*, pp. 120–24; and Stewart C. Myers, "Finance Theory and Financial Strategies," *Interfaces* 14 (1984): 126–37.

[39] Johnson and Kaplan, *Relevance Lost*, chaps. 5–7; and David Solomons,

The problem of strategic financial planning became more intricate when corporations had to form projections for a broad array of product lines. Consider the experience of the General Electric Company (GE) in the 1960s, when its central office was faced with the problem of evaluating the annual budgets of 190 separate departments and 43 strategic business units. Planning in this case was merely a functional review rather than an assessment of comprehensive business plans. It was a system that did not identify broad strategic directions for the operating entities or establish any criteria for establishing investment priorities. The result was a decade of sales increases without any commensurate profit growth. Financial resources were simply spread too thin to achieve the types of returns that planners had sought.

It was not until the 1970s that GE began to overcome the frustrations of diversity in its strategic planning. For planning purposes, the company's basic businesses were arrayed into six broad market sectors. The central office began to play a more active role in identifying broad goals by introducing annual challenges that the operating units were to incorporate into their plans. For example, the central office might specify a percentage increase in sales or some reduction in energy consumption as the overall corporate target for a particular year. Finally, a system of resource planning was introduced to estimate the needs for nonfinancial resources, such as managerial or technical competencies, that had significant effects on the performance of operating segments.[40]

Another strategic issue involved the allocation of discretionary capital to achieve competitive objectives. Although the actual combination of priorities varied among firms, the choice of funding sources was influenced by several factors. Foremost was the need to identify sources of funding that provided great certainty with respect to the timing, amount and duration of capital commitments. It was crucial that these sources be able to provide funds on a scale consistent with

Divisional Performance: Measurement and Control (Homewood, Ill.: Irwin, 1965). The problem of insensitive capital budgeting is addressed in Carliss Y. Baldwin and Kim B. Clark, "Capital-Budgeting Systems and Capabilities Investments in U.S. Companies after the Second World War," *Business History Review* 68 (Spring 1994): 73–109.

[40] Robert Slater, *The New GE: How Jack Welch Revived an American Institution* (Homewood, Ill.: Business One Irwin, 1993).

corporate purposes. Moreover, the cost of funds had to be reasonable and free of restrictive covenants that would overly constrain managerial prerogatives.[41]

VI. Patterns of Finance among Mature Center Firms

How, then, did these various criteria associated with planning influence the resolution of the corporate financing puzzle among mature center firms? Concerns about the implications of relying on inherently variable capital markets in ensuring corporate survival conditioned managements of center firms to prefer the funding of their operations through retained earnings, where possible. This source was generally thought to be the least expensive alternative and was most readily controlled by management. For example, the *FTC–SEC Quarterly Surveys of Manufacturing* indicate that, between 1952 and 1968, 64 percent of the funds raised by reporting manufacturing enterprises came from earnings retention and capital consumption allowances. Mature industrial enterprises tended to view public capital markets as sources of reserve financing to be tapped when internal cash flows were insufficient. This finding is also affirmed in Federal Reserve data, which indicate that about 65 percent of the total $292.9 billion in funds acquired by nonfinancial corporate businesses between 1946 and 1970 was generated internally.

Managements were far more likely to turn to the debt markets to finance cash flow deficits. This attitude emanated from a belief that funds could be borrowed even during the most dire economic circumstances. Debt, if adequately serviced, did not raise the disturbing specter of ownership changes. Thus, mature center corporations structured their financing plans so as to operate comfortably within the limits imposed by borrowing covenants. For many years, interest paid on debt was deductible without restriction in calculating taxable income.[42]

---

[41] Donaldson, *Managing Corporate Wealth*, pp. 97–102.

[42] Ibid., pp. 42–48 and 72–73. Average earnings retention rates were calculated from data reported on industrial firms in the *FTC–SEC Survey of Manufacturing*, summarized in John J. McGowan, "The Supply of Equity Securities, 1952–1968," in Raymond W. Goldsmith, ed., *Institutional Investors and Corporate Stock – A Background Study* (New York: National Bureau of

This preference for the issuance of debt was supported by two sets of statistics detailing practices among larger firms. First, the total net dollar value of common and preferred equity issued during the period 1950–70 increased by $41 billion. The corresponding increase in the net value of bonds and notes outstanding amounted to $151 billion, nearly three times the value of the equity growth. Second, comparisons of long-term debt versus capital stock and retained earnings for companies with asset values in excess of $100 million exhibited a similar pattern. In 1950, the aggregate debt of these companies amounted to $33 billion, or about one-third of the $98 billion in combined capital stock and retained earnings. Note, however, that by 1970 long-term debt had climbed to $240 billion and was almost one-half of the $499 billion combined values of capital stock and retained earnings.[43]

Innovative ways to tap the short-term debt markets were also developed by center companies during this period. Growing public confidence in the financial viability of these enterprises supported a rapid expansion of the commercial paper market. Center companies could borrow with notes having maturities of up to 270 days with no guarantees other than their reputation for solvency. This source offered rates significantly below that of commercial banks which were burdened with costly reserve requirements; nor did this form of borrowing require costly registration with the SEC. Total outstanding commercial paper (including that issued by finance companies) rose from $921 million in 1950 to over $31 billion in 1970. By 1984, these totals far exceeded $200 billion.[44]

The development of the Eurodollar market opened a second avenue of cheap and reliable short-term financing for center companies. These facilities began to flourish during the 1960s when the USSR decided to maintain credit balances generated by its international trade in dollar deposits in Western European banks. Eurodollar deposits mounted as

Economic Research, 1973), p. 179. The Federal Reserve data were calculated from schedules developed by Benjamin M. Friedman in "Postwar Changes in the American Financial Markets," in Feldstein, ed., *The American Economy in Transition*, p. 23. See also Donaldson, *Corporate Debt Policy*, chapt. 4 passim.

[43] Vatter, *The U.S. Economy*, pp. 190–94.

[44] Eduard Ballarin, *Commercial Banks amid the Financial Revolution: Developing a Competitive Strategy* (Cambridge, Mass.: Ballinger, 1985), pp. 120–23.

U.S. entities transferred dollar balances to Europe to escape the ceiling on domestic deposits imposed under the Federal Reserve's Regulation Q. The Eurodollar market grew even more strongly after the 1973 oil crisis by the recycling of receipts taken by Middle Eastern producers from consumer nations. The estimated size of this market increased from a relatively low $9 billion in 1964 to $247 billion in 1976. In the latter year about $180 billion of the total were for contracts denominated in U.S. dollars.

Center firms were attracted to the Eurodollar market for the same reasons that had induced them to sell commercial paper. The Eurodollar market was free from restrictive interest rate ceilings that U.S. central bankers periodically imposed in their drives to curtail inflation. European central bankers, on the other hand, did not impose any reserve requirements on these balances other than what prudence would normally require. The cost of this financing remained relatively low because it was a wholesale market with a minimum transaction size of $1 million. The growth of this market was accelerated by the acumen of Eurodollar bankers, who successfully crafted flexible lending arrangements that could accommodate the needs of a broad spectrum of borrowers.[45]

The managements of center firms were generally loath to finance their activities by issuing equity. Data from firms whose financing activities were analyzed in the *FTC–SEC Quarterly Surveys of Manufacturing* indicate that equity represented only 3.6 percent of the funds raised from 1952 to 1968. This is also affirmed by Federal Reserve data, which indicate that, on average, equity represented only 3.5 percent of all sources of funds generated by nonfinancial corporate entities from 1946 to 1970. This was partly due to a belief among corporate managers that the markets did a poor job in accurately evaluating their equity. The issuance of large amounts of new equity was unpopular because it might have led to ownership changes that could have adversely affected managerial independence and autonomy. Moreover, the vicissitudes of the capital markets diminished the perception of equity as a reliable, continuous and predictable source of

---

[45] Gray, *International Trade Investments and Payments*, pp. 621–39; and Paul Einzig and Brian Scott Quinn, *The Euro-Dollar System: Practice and Theory of International Interest Rates*, 6th ed. (New York: St. Martin's, 1977).

funding. Managements were also reluctant to issue equity; they believed that it sent a signal to the market of miscalculation in corporate planning. Thus, many managers thought that equity functioned as the ultimate source of reserve financing, to be drawn upon only during periods of extreme stringency. Even the issuance of preferred stock could be problematic, because these securities often possessed contingent voting right provisions that became effective in the event of any dividend payment arrearage. In a comprehensive study conducted by Donaldson and Lorsch that covered 120 firm years, there was only one year when an entity in their sample resorted to equity finance and that involved the issuance of preferred stock. The reluctance to increase significantly the amounts of outstanding voting equity is certainly reflected in the capital structures during this period of such leading center firms as Du Pont, GE, Eastman Kodak and International Business Machines.[46]

VII. Financial Restructuring at GM: An Illustrative Case

The experience of GM in two major refinancings illustrates how, as the pecking order hypothesis contends, the issuance of substantial amounts of equity can prove problematic for the continuity of managerial tenure. In the first case GM's management was able to diversify through acquisitions financed in part by the issuance of substantial amounts of equity in the 1980s. By structuring these transactions in ways that did not dilute either the voting power or dividend income of GM's shareholders, management was able to avoid jeopardizing its position of primacy in corporate governance. The second episode involved the issuance of substantial amounts of common stock in the 1990s to replenish a depleted corporate equity and to stabilize a deteriorating leverage position. This, however, led to the displacement of senior management because of dissatisfaction on the part of institu-

---

[46] Donaldson, *Managing Corporate Wealth*, pp. 43–46. Equity issuance rates for industrial companies were derived from data in the *FTC–SEC Quarterly Survey of Manufacturing*, summarized in McGowan, "The Supply of Equity Securities," p. 179. The Federal Reserve data was derived from Table 1.5 in Friedman, "Postwar Changes in American Financial Markets," p. 23. See also Donaldson, *Corporate Debt Policy*, chapt. 3 passim.

tional investors and their allies on the board of directors with the adverse effects that the latter financing had on the position of common shareholders.

The diversification drive that enabled GM to enter two high-tech businesses outside of the automotive industry was partially financed by issuing two new classes of common stock. In October 1984, GM acquired Electronic Data Systems Corp. (EDS) for $2.5 billion, and in December 1985 it acquired Hughes Aircraft Company for $5.3 billion.[47] The EDS acquisition was financed by offering investors a choice for their shares of either $44 in cash or a combination consisting of $32.50 in cash, a seven-year promissory note and one-fifth of a share of a special Class E common stock. Shareholders of Hughes Aircraft, on the other hand, received half of their payment in cash and the other half in shares of a new Class H common stock. Although dividends were paid from the earnings of each subsidiary, ownership of the E or H shares did not convey any direct rights either to the underlying corporate equities or to assets. But both the E and H shares could be converted to one full share of GM common in the event that the GM board chose to exercise this option or the subsidiaries were subsequently spun off.[48]

Steps were also taken by GM to minimize the impact of these acquisitions on the distribution of its own voting power. The holders of the E and H common were granted less than full voting rights in any matters presented to GM shareholders for resolution: in 1994, for example, one E share was equivalent in voting matters to one-eighth of a share of GM common, and each H share exercised a one-half vote. The position of GM shareholders was further reinforced by granting them 5 percent stock dividends payable in E shares in 1984

---

[47] Except for where otherwise noted, the information about GM's finances that supports the following discussion is derived from the company's *1994 Annual Report* and from *Moody's Industrial Manual* for the period 1990–94.

[48] Subsequent to the writing of this section, GM elected to "split off" its EDS subsidiary and granted one share of the newly independent entity for each GM Class E common share outstanding. This was done after GM's board of directors received approval from GM's shareholders to amend its incentive plan for EDS; see *New York Times*, April 2, 1996, D, 11:4; and press release from GM entitled, "EDS Split-off from GM Completed Today" (New York, June 7, 1988). The shares of the split-off EDS began trading on the NYSE on June 8, 1996.

and in H shares in 1985. The 30 million shares issued to GM share-holders in these latter transactions accounted, respectively, for about 20 percent of the total E shares outstanding in 1984 and about 24 percent of the total H shares outstanding in 1986. In 1988 and 1989, GM also created new classes of E and H preference shares with a mandatory provision requiring their conversion into E and H common shares in stages over a four-year period.

These arrangements also provided other advantages to GM. First, the acquisition of two well-established industry leaders lowered the risks that the diversification into two highly complex technical markets might prove unsuccessful. Second, the financing plan supporting these acquisitions helped to conserve cash, minimized the dilution of GM shareholders' voting power and reduced risk perceptions by strengthening the firm's debt–equity ratio. Third, the creation of the E and H shares provided GM with a means to finance future growth by either selling or distributing shares in these subsidiaries without actually giving up any control over their equity or assets. Fourth, the seemingly friendly merger with EDS and Hughes was thought to place a substantial amount of the new equity classes in the hands of groups favorably disposed to GM management. Fifth, the tax-free status of share swap at the time of acquisition provided a strong inducement for the original holders of the EDS and Hughes shares to hold the E and H common stock in order to defer recognition of any taxable gains. This same attribute also functioned as an incentive for executives of the acquired enterprises to continue their employment after the merger by providing a means for them to defer recognition for tax purposes of any future enhancement in the value of these businesses. Sixth, GM was also indirectly able to offset the dilution of its own shareholders' voting power by granting them stock dividends payable in E and H shares.

Nevertheless, a subsequent negative development from the merger with EDS illustrated how major shifts in equity ownership can lead to potent challenges to managerial leadership. H. Ross Perot, the founder of EDS and the largest individual shareholder in GM, was elevated to the board of directors in 1985, where he soon made public his fundamental disagreements with the business plans and policies formulated by the company's management. Although Perot lacked sufficient equity to force any change in control, his criticisms were nevertheless damaging to the public image of the company and the administration

247

of its president, Roger B. Smith. In 1986, this embarrassing conflict was finally resolved when the GM board agreed to buy out Perot's investment in the firm for $700 million, an amount approximately double his original cost.[49]

The experience with the H shares was less contentious because the major holder of this security, the Howard Hughes Medical Institute, was not to participate actively in management but rather to preserve its investment capital and maximize its dividend income. A central feature of this latter relationship was the step taken by GM to assuage concerns about the riskiness of the class H common stock. To guard against any loss of principal GM entered into an option agreement with the Institute to hedge against any adverse fluctuations in the market value of the H shares. In 1994, for example, GM held call options on 15 million H shares exercisable at $37.50 through February 28, 1995, while the Institute held the corresponding put options exercisable at $30 per share.

The second episode in GM's recent history that also sheds light on how a substantial increase in equity shares can weaken the position of top management occurred between 1990 and 1993, when the company was compelled to write down material amounts of obsolete plant and equipment and to recognize the cumulative costs of previously unrecorded postretirement benefits other than pensions, as was required under Financial Accounting Standard Number 106 (effective date January 1, 1992). The write-downs fluctuated between $1.0 and $3.0 billion annually during this period: the postretirement benefit accrual that was recorded in 1992 amounted to $20.6 billion. The financial impact of these developments was heavy (Table 6.3). GM's net loss rose from $2.0 billion in 1990 to $23.5 billion in 1992. During that same period the company's retained earnings account changed from a positive $27.1 billion to a deficit of $3.4 billion while overall stockholders' equity dropped from $30.0 billion to $6.2 billion.

This deterioration created conditions that were potentially threatening to the status of corporate leadership. First, the losses raised risk perceptions about the basic viability of thecompany which at a mini-

[49] See articles in the *New York Times:* "Perot Is Removed from GM Board but Has Big Profit," December 2, 1986, I, 1:1; and "GM's Brief Fling with Perot," December 3, 1986, IV, 1:3.

Table 6.3. *Select Statistics for General Motors, 1990–1993*
($ Billions)

Year	Plant Closing Adjustment	Net Income	Retained Earnings	Shareholder's Equity
1990	3.3	−2.0	27.1	30.0
1991	2.8	−4.5	21.5	27.3
1992	1.2	−23.5	−3.4	6.2
1993	1.0	2.5	−2.0	5.6

Source: Moody's Industrial Manual, 1994 (with GMAC on the equity basis).

mum could lead to burdensome increases in the cost of acquiring additional capital. The attendant decline in share prices also had the potential for inducing disgruntled institutional investors or even corporate raiders to demand representation on the board of directors and a greater voice in enterprise governance. Finally, the depletion of retained earnings and equity threatened to shift control of one-quarter of the board's membership to representatives of those who held the $5 cumulative preferred stock (first issued in 1930) and the $3.75 cumulative preferred stock (first issued in 1946). This latter outcome could result from the activation of contingent voting rights in the event of arrearage on the payment of dividends that lasted for more than six months.

The restructuring of GM's equity under these conditions of duress had four main elements. The most significant was the floatation of several new classes of preference stock and the sale of additional common stock between 1991 and 1992, which raised in aggregate $8.1 billion of new cash. The most novel of these initiatives involved raising $727 million through the issuance in 1991 of 17.8 million Series A Preferred Equity Redemption Cumulative Stock (PERCS). This security had a mandatory three-year redemption feature requiring its conversion, generally on a one-for-one basis, into GM common shares. To minimize the potential dilution of such a conversion, the maximum appreciation allowable on the PERCS was set at 35 percent above their par value. If the market value of the common exceeded the 35 percent threshold, PERCS holders could expect to receive less than a full share of common at conversion. But unlike ordinary convertible preferred stock, if the common equity were to fall subsequently, the

249

redemption value of the PERCS would be reduced proportionally. The second element of restructuring was the issuance beginning in 1991 of four classes of depository preference shares that, while callable, had no specific redemption dates. These were straight preference securities except for the C issue, which was convertible into E common shares. The third element involved the floating of the largest dollar value of common shares thus far recorded. In 1992, GM sold 57 million shares, which generated proceeds amounting to $2.1 billion, and also issued an additional $500 million of shares to finance a portion of its unfunded pension liability.[50] In 1994, an additional 17.8 million common shares were issued through the redemption of the PERCS shares. The final element was the 1993 retirement of the $5 and $3.75 cumulative preferred issues, which were both endowed with the threatening contingent voting provisions. Some idea of the importance accorded to this latter transaction by GM's management was its willingness to pay the call price of $120 for each $5 preferred share whose market value had not exceeded $64 in 1992.

Even giving effect to these additions to equity, the percentage of long-term capitalization represented by long-term liabilities jumped from 13.2 percent in 1990 to 51.6 percent in 1992, primarily because of the enormous accrual made during the latter year for the postretirement benefits. As a consequence of these developments the average number of outstanding common shares had increased from 601.5 million in 1990 to 710.2 million in 1993, a growth of 18 percent, which was mostly accounted for by the public offering in 1992. Total aggregate common dividend payments also declined from $1.9 billion in 1990 to $727 million in 1993: during this same period these payments decreased on a per share basis from $3.00 to $.80.

The use of redeemable shares such as PERCS and depository preference shares during these years of turmoil alleviated to some degree these adverse trends. These issues served as substitutes for medium-term debt obligations whose interest charges would have increased the company's heavy losses and contributed to a further deterioration to its liability–equity ratio, a basic index of solvency risk. Instead, the PERCS and preference shares bolstered corporate equity, and their

[50] See "General Motors Shifts Operations and Plans Huge Stock Offering," *New York Times*, April 25, 1992, I, 1:1; and "GM Adds More Stock to Offering," ibid., May 20, 1992, D, 1:3.

dividend payments were not recorded as expenses. The PERCS's mandatory redemption feature also enabled GM to allocate the distribution of additional common shares over a wider time horizon: it reduced the number of common shares GM had to float under the adverse conditions existing in 1992 by scheduling the recall for 1994, a year when the firm had been restored to profitability. In addition, the PERCS and other preference shares introduced since 1990 all had the arrearage period for contingent voting rights extended to six dividend payments (roughly eighteen months), rather than the six months characteristic of the older preferred issues.

Consistent with one of the central insights of the pecking order hypothesis, the disruption of ownership interests, which was brought about by the impending issuance of common shares, triggered a major shake-up of GM's management on April 6, 1992. The impetus for change came from among the eleven outside directors who served on the company's fifteen-member board of directors. The leading activist was John G. Smale, chairman of Proctor and Gamble Company. He was strongly supported by two investment bankers, Dennis Weatherstone, Chairman of J. P. Morgan & Co, Inc., and Thomas H. Wyman, chairman of S. G. Warburg & Co., Inc., whose institutional investment clients, major holders of GM common stock, had become restive because of the impending dilution of their shares and the poor recent operating performance of the company. To restore investor confidence, John Smale replaced Robert C. Stempel as GM's chairman and also headed a special committee to monitor management performance. In addition, the board also appointed John F. Smith, Jr., who had previously been in charge of the company's European operations, as president and chief operating officer. There then ensued an extensive reorganization of top management, culminating in the resignation from the board of its former chairman, Roger B. Smith, on January 27, 1993.[51]

In 1993, GM's operational results began to reflect some of the benefits brought about by the extensive financial reordering of recent years. Cash flows generated from operations increased from $4.7 billion in 1991 to $11.4 billion in 1993. In 1993, the firm also recorded

---

[51] See "President Is Demoted at GM," *New York Times,* April 7, 1992, D, 1:6; "Rubber Stamp Is Tossed Aside by GM Board," ibid., April 8, 1992, A, 1:1; "Message from GM's Board: Cut Losses Fast," ibid., April 8, 1992, D, 19:1; and "Ex-Chief Denies Report He Plans to Quit GM Board," ibid., January 28, 1993, D, 4:1.

its first profit in three years, which amounted to $2.0 billion. The strengthening of operating performance due to the closure of obsolete facilities was also reflected in the reduction of the cost of sales margin from 89.5 percent in 1991 to 85.03 percent in 1993. The total return on shareholder's equity shot up to 104.2 percent in 1993, as compared with the negative 169.3 percent of the preceding year. The recovery was well under way.[52]

VIII. Conclusion

How did center firms use financial institutional arrangements to foster growth? How did the expansion of such entities amplify theories that have been set forth to explain the corporate financing puzzle?

With respect to the first question, the development of financial institutions augmented center firm growth in two ways. First, the finance function was a source of transactional efficiencies that were associated with both the scale and scope of center firm activities. The scale of financing for these businesses was generally sufficiently large to qualify for the most attractive terms in negotiating for services with leading creditor or underwriting organizations. Economies of scope in finance, on the other hand, derived from the accessibility of center firms to the full range of contractual arrangements available in international capital markets. But unlike advantages derived from investment in science and technology, these sources of financial efficiency could not be made proprietary by the acquisition of exclusive legal rights such as patents. Although the attainment of more efficient financing arrangements was a goal that all firms shared, it was especially vital to those entities that were constrained by adverse market conditions, inflexible technologies and other barriers that prevented them from achieving significant operational efficiencies. The following chapter focuses in detail on how some in this latter group of firms sought to overcome such limitations through financial innovation.

Second, the corporate finance function could reduce risk perceptions by maintaining a stable economic environment for the conduct of operational activities and by facilitating the enhancement of enterprise

---

[52] Taken from *Moody's Industrial Manual, 1994*, p. 1128, with GMAC reported on the equity basis.

competitiveness. Exploitation of the efficiency potential of investing in capital assets and in improved managerial and technological capabilities could be achieved only if enterprise liabilities were adequately serviced. Equally vital was the role of finance in providing sufficient time for center firms to learn how best to integrate newly acquired capacities in both their strategic plans and their administrative routines.

The reduction of risk through diversification, however, was a far more costly and time-consuming process in the management of a center firm than in the management of a portfolio of financial assets. For the industrial firm, the transition to new markets, which entailed the application of technical knowledge to create new products and the revision of established procedures for coordinating and controlling operations, often took years to effectuate. In financial portfolios, on the other hand, highly liquid financial assets were much more easily reallocated to new investment outlets.

Another difference between industrial and portfolio diversification relates to the degree of negative correlation that may be achieved in the variability coefficients of component investments. It is easier to achieve a high degree of diversification in a financial portfolio than it is in an industrial firm that relies on research and development to identify new investment opportunities. The problem in the industrial case is that new products discovered by extending knowledge of a core technology will usually have demand characteristics that are similar to those of existing product lines. Consider, for example, Du Pont's experience in the synthetic fiber business. During the 1920s Du Pont had taken out licenses to manufacture rayon as one means to keep its capacities for processing cellulose (an important component in explosives manufacture) profitably employed. The company also begin to sponsor research in the polymerization of carbon molecules, which eventually led to the discovery of nylon. The further extension of Du Pont's skills and knowledge in polymer chemistry led to additional product innovations in both fibers and plastics. During World War II it patented neoprene, a synthetic rubber; after the war it went on to develop Mylar and Kevlar plastics. In fibers, its research led to the discovery of Orlon, Dacron, Qiana, spandex and Teflon. Although Du Pont had succeeded in adding many new products, they all tended to respond to changes in the business cycle in similar ways. Thus, diversification through research in a core technology did not lead to the types of countercyclical effects that would be possible to achieve in an investment portfolio.

However, scholars remained divided over the merits of corporate investment policies directed toward diversifying product lines. For example, business historians, whose analyses have focused on managers of center firms operating in oligopolistic markets, argue that diversification through scientific inquiry is essential both for minimizing risk and for achieving high returns on enterprise resources. In this context diversification is seen as a key element in a Schumpeterian process of creative destruction that seeks to avoid the adverse economic consequences resulting from the inevitable decay in product life cycles. It involves the continuous search for more profitable outlets for a company's specific pool of skills and knowledge. Success in these endeavors is seen as being critical to the economic health of the firm and the competitiveness of the national economy.

Modern market and agency theorists who have evaluated this process from the perspective of shareholders have questioned the wisdom of financing corporate diversification. Some of their misgivings about this process derive from the neoclassical conception of the firm that is incorporated in their studies. This model does not stress the potentialities for augmenting corporate competitiveness and market power by making investments to strengthen managerial capabilities. Instead, the firm is viewed as a price taker that is incapable of controlling market conditions in any significant way. In addition, some scholars do not discern any significant advantages accruing to shareholders through the purchase of shares of diversified businesses. Instead, they argue that investors may diversify more efficiently by holding portfolios of securities. Some agency theorists further hold that the risk reductions inherent in industrial diversifications are far more beneficial to the interests of professional managers than to those of shareholders: diversification reduces the likelihood of career-disrupting bankruptcies; it also creates a larger corporate entity, offering greater opportunities for career advancement.

With respect to the second question, the experience of center firms represents the principal scholarly support of the pecking order hypothesis's explanation of how corporations resolve the capital structure puzzle. These histories indicate that comprehending corporate financing choices involves more than the simple weighing of probable levels of risk and return. These decisions are also shaped by complex social

254

processes involving the reconciliation of the differing objectives of professional managers and investors. A key insight of the pecking order hypothesis is the strong influence that management's concerns about status and about the preservation of their leadership exert on the definition of corporate financial policy. This induced risk-averse behavior designed to ensure firm survival and to avoid any adverse circumstances that might lead to shifts in ownership and thereby threaten managerial tenure.

Shareholders, on the other hand, are depicted by the hypothesis as passive wealth maximizers whose understanding of a particular corporation's financial prospects is fundamentally impeded by informational asymmetries. These investors are at a basic disadvantage in financial contracting because they are less well informed about the business than management. Although this problem can never be fully overcome, its degree may be diminished by a wide array of institutional arrangements. Many of these are formal, such as the endowment of financing contracts with special provisions to protect investors, the establishment of formal mechanisms for corporate monitoring and the creation of regular channels of information about corporate affairs. Others are informal, such as management's proclivity for maintaining stable dividend payment patterns to garner shareholder support. What, however, remains poorly specified in this model is how these relationships are modified by the intervention of financial market intermediaries such as mutual funds and pension funds, which represent the interest of large blocks of investors.

The pecking order patterns evinced by the experience of center firms has several corollary implications. The hypothesis, for example, tends to affirm the contention of Professor Stewart Myers and others that dividend payments represent critical signals of corporate financial health. In the short run the actions of center firm managements generally did not significantly affect shareholder wealth. Instead, the more pressing demands of the market or other constituencies that might influence the chances of firm survival take precedence. Center firm managements try to maintain steady levels of dividend payments to assuage shareholders and thus avoid shifts in the distribution of ownership that could imperil their own ability to maintain control of the enterprise. Moreover, because they are funded from corporate cash flows, dividends may be more reliable indicators of financial health than are earnings, an accounting construct that is subject to many types of estimates and adjustments that often have no immediate effects on cash levels. For these reasons it is logical to assume that unexpected interruptions of dividend payment trends are reflective of a significant decline in the sufficiency of current and future cash flows to fund corporate operations.

Similarly, the experience of center firms also suggests that changes in the sources of incremental financing may serve as a signal of financial condition. Again, managerial aversion to loss of enterprise control because of shifts in equity ownership implies that common stock financing is an alternative contemplated only in times of dire emergency. The expected pattern involves relying on either retained earnings, debt or nonvoting equity securities such as preferred stock. The relative amounts of these financing alternatives would presumably vary with the operational performance of the firm, the risk preferences of management and general financial market conditions. Stock dividends or stock splits, however, do not represent negative signals about firm solvency because they merely increase the total number of shares outstanding without changing the relative distribution of ownership interests.

The importance of dividends to center firm finance also created a strong, abiding demand for more extensive and accurate information about corporate profitability. Equity was inherently a more difficult class of security to evaluate than debt. Estimating the fluctuations in the size of the net income residual available to fund dividend payments was a challenging task in the case of business enterprises of great scale and scope. It required the precise measurement of a host of revenue and expense categories. Frequently, this process depended on making estimates about the probable outcomes of long-term transactions. The growing sensitivity to this problem in the United States was reflected in the persistent drive to broaden the scope and improve the quality of financial accounting standards.

As we shall see in Chapter 7, the pecking order patterns evident in the experience of center firms in resolving the capital structure puzzle were not universally embraced by all public companies. Other theories about finance and about the nature of the business firm provided intellectual support for the formation of new types of corporate entities beginning during the 1960s. The first innovation was the conglomerate, which superficially seemed to employ strategies much akin to those that guided the traditional center firm. The second was the leveraged-buyout partnership, which represented a far more radical departure from the center firm model. In both cases the goal of efficiency enhancement was pursued primarily by placing greater reliance on financial rather than managerial and technological innovations.

CHAPTER SEVEN

Conglomerates and Leveraged-Buyout Partnerships

I. Introduction

During the latter half of the twentieth century, two new types of business organization emerged for attracting investment capital: the conglomerate and the leveraged-buyout (LBO) partnership. Unlike center firms, these enterprises sought efficiency in financial innovation rather than in managerial or in technological innovation. And while both conglomerates and LBOs shared broadly similar objectives, the circumstances and rationales that supported their formation differed sharply.

As to conglomerates, their promotion during the 1960s and 1970s was initially predicated on the assumption that economic synergism could be achieved by applying modern management techniques to the combining of heterogeneous businesses. Although the diversification drives of conglomerates seemed superficially similar to the creation of center firms, the theoretical underpinnings lending support to these activities were not comparable to those that explain the policies of center firms and thus require a different understanding of the financial system.

Conglomerate acquisition was more sensitive to portfolio theory than to more effective coordination and control of complementary businesses. Nor did conglomerates usually penetrate industries in which operating economies of scale and scope could be realized. In fact, there was little evidence that conglomerate growth resulted from superior management. Instead, the growing size of these companies made possible the achievement of economies in financial transacting. In addition, their success in the financial markets stemmed from manipulating the looseness both in financial accounting standards relating to the measurement of consolidated net income and in tax rules relating to the allocation of unapplied credits and loss items.

On the other hand, the formation of LBOs in the 1970s and 1980s responded to criticisms leveled at corporate governance practices that were intended to protect investor interests. This was apparent in the ambiguous relationship between shareholders, corporate managers and boards of directors. Under trust law, directors served as fiduciaries for shareholders and had supervisory responsibility for the stewardship of corporate resources. Thus, a board's monitoring activities represented a major safeguard against managerial opportunism or incompetence. Moreover, shareholders were supposed to be able to influence policy formulation indirectly through their proxies and the agency of the board. Skeptics, however, retorted that equity investors had been effectively disenfranchised by professional managers and their nominees who dominated corporate boards. This co-optation was possible because of the fragmentation of shareholders and the reluctance of institutional investors to challenge managerial authority.

By the 1970s, scholars of economics and law began to propose new ways of thinking about the relationship between investors and managers. One school of thought, that of agency theory, held that the corporation was essentially a "nexus of contracts," the purpose of which was to allocate residual cash flows among various stakeholder groups: managers, creditors and shareholders. By this line of reasoning financial relationships were malleable and capable of redefining the rights and obligations of stakeholders. Thus, the belief emerged that firm efficiency could be enhanced by innovative contracts that better blended the interests of disparate stakeholder groups than traditional arrangements did.

One product of the new thinking was the LBO partnership. The nexus of contracts supporting these enterprises made the economic interests of owners and managers more concentric. A carrot-and-stick approach also motivated managers. The stick was the pressure imposed by the need to service substantial amounts of debentures issued by the LBO in the acquisition of businesses. The carrot was that managers could increase the value of their substantial equity holdings by reducing the debt burden. The strong incentive for efficient debt servicing in turn aligned the interests of management with those of bondholders, the primary class of external investors.

The image of LBOs and conglomerates, however, eventually became tarnished because their economic performance was uneven and far-reaching reforms were imposed on some of their business practices. A collapse in the prices of conglomerate shares resulted from the combination of stricter tax and accounting rules and more negative, albeit accurate, projections of profit growth. LBO formation, on the other hand, slowed because of increased bond default rates and the lack of liquidity of secondary markets for such securities. These factors came about as a result of the high prices paid for these businesses and of major banking reforms in the 1980s.

This chapter discusses these changes in business organization and finance in four sections: the first describes a changing economic context, which was conducive to institutional innovation; the next two, the strategies and structures employed by organizers of conglomerates and LBO partnerships; and the last, how this experience amplifies theoretical constructs in corporate finance and also how institutional innovation promoted economic efficiency. In addition, Appendix B (p. 322) compares and contrasts the different patterns employed in corporate governance in Germany, Japan and the United Kingdom with that of the United States.

II. The American Economy in Transition, 1964–93

The development of conglomerates and LBO partnerships occurred during the course of a three-decade period that witnessed a substantial degree of economic institutional innovation. This broad pattern of institutional change was partially induced by challenges to U.S. economic leadership that had surfaced during the late 1960s and much of the 1970s. A major aspect of this transition was the dismantling of the old, tightly regulated economic order that had been created during the Depression and World War II. By the last decade of the twentieth century a new regime had emerged that allowed for greater market competition and was more open to international influences.

At the beginning of this epoch, however, the outlook for the continuation of strong U.S. economic performance did not seem propitious. By the 1970s, evidence of slippage from the levels achieved in the two decades immediately after World War II were legion. First, there was a sharp reduction in the rate of growth in productivity and real wages.

During the period 1947–66, private business sector output and compensation per man-hour both grew at an annual rate of 3.3 percent. However, during the period 1966–78, the annual average growth rate of private business sector output declined to 1.83 percent while that of compensation per man-hour fell to 0.83 percent. Although these declines were endemic to the industrialized world, only the Canadian economy reported lower growth rates.[1] Second, a falloff in productivity contributed to rising domestic inflation. One gauge, the GNP deflator, climbed from 5.4 percent in 1970 to 9.6 percent in 1975 and ultimately peaked at 10.0 percent in 1981. Third, higher inflation led to higher interest rates. Fourth, there were highly negative trends in U.S. international trade. For instance, in 1968 the current account balance turned negative and remained in deficit for much of the 1970s.[2] By 1973 this situation had become so untenable that President Richard M. Nixon was compelled to abandon the dollar-based, fixed-exchange-rate system put in place by the Bretton Woods Agreement.[3] The problem of maintaining external balance was further aggravated by sharply increased oil prices, which rose from $3 to over $30 a barrel in 1974.[4] Later, the trade position continued to deteriorate

[1] See Richard B. Freeman, "The Evolution of the American Labor Market," in Feldstein, ed., *American Economy in Transition*, pp. 349–56; Bruce R. Scott, "U.S. Competitiveness: Concepts, Performance and Implications," in Bruce R. Scott and George C. Lodge, eds., *U.S. Competitiveness in the World Economy* (Boston: Harvard Business School Press, 1985), pp. 16–19 and 30–34; Michael L. Dertouzos, Richard K. Lester and Robert M. Solow, *Made in America: Regaining the Productive Edge* (New York: Harper Perennial, 1990), pp. 23–39; Martin N. Baily and Alok K. Chakrabarti, *Innovation and the Productivity Crisis* (Washington, D.C.: Brookings Institution, 1988); George N. Hatsopoulos, Paul R. Krugman and Lawrence H. Summers, "U.S. Competitiveness: Beyond the Trade Deficit," *Science* 241 (1988): 299–307; and Lawrence R. Klein, "International Productivity Comparisons (A Review)," *Proceedings of the National Academy of Sciences, USA* (July 1983): 4561–68.

[2] Branson, "Trends in United States International Trade," p. 183.

[3] Gray, *International Trade, Investment and Payments*, pp. 604–18; Peter M. Garber, "The Collapse of the Bretton Woods Fixed Exchange Rate System," in Bordo and Eichengreen, eds., *A Retrospective on the Bretton Woods System*, pp. 461–93; and Galambos and Pratt, *The Rise of the Corporate Commonwealth*, pp. 211–13; Scott, "U.S. Competitiveness," pp. 13–70; and Brownlee, *Dynamics of Ascent*, pp. 470–73.

[4] Brownlee, *Dynamics of Ascent*, pp. 472–73; and Galambos and Pratt, *Rise of the Corporate Commonwealth*, pp. 221–26.

because of an influx of manufacturing imports from East Asia.[5] The combination of these negative economic trends was reflected in a lackluster stock market performance. In 1970, the average annual value of the Dow–Jones Industrial Average (DJIA) amounted to 753; by 1980, this average had risen to only 891.

The economic deterioration of the 1970s was conditioned by several factors. One was the restoration of the vitality of the Japanese and European economies. Between 1950 and 1975, Japan's gross domestic product (GDP) increased more than sevenfold, while Germany's increased nearly fourfold. Unburdened by heavy defense expenditures, which usually consumed from 5 to 7 percent of America's GDP, these trading partners had concentrated on rebuilding their industrial capabilities.[6] Second, policies in force during the long and costly Vietnam War contributed to America's economic attenuation. The failure of government to cut consumption and the decision to expand domestic social spending led to a dangerous overheating of the economy and a growing dependence on foreign sources of supply. Moreover, reducing tax allowances for capital consumption in order to contain wartime deficits weakened the manufacturing sector.[7] Third, U.S. competitiveness waned because of the high cost of capital brought on by a low domestic savings rate. By the mid-1970s, one estimate placed the average cost of capital in the United States at 20.8 percent versus 7.8 percent in Japan.[8] Fourth, the curtailment of market competition by

[5] Scott, "U.S. Competitiveness," pp. 49–63.

[6] John Cavanagh and Frederick Clairmonte, "The Transnational Economy," *Trade and Development: A United Nations Conference on Trade and Development Review* (Winter 1982): 8–13; Bruce R. Scott, "National Strategies: Key to International Competition," in Scott and Lodge, eds., *U.S. Competitiveness in the World Economy*, pp. 71–143; and Branson, "Trends in United States International Trade," pp. 183–203.

[7] Cathie J. Martin, *Shifting the Burden: The Struggle over Growth and Corporate Taxation* (Chicago: University of Chicago Press, 1991), chaps. 3–4 passim; Robert J. Gordon, "Postwar Macroeconomics: The Evolution of Events and Ideas," in Feldstein, *The American Economy in Transition*, pp. 107 and 121; Benjamin M. Friedman, "Postwar Changes in American Financial Markets," in ibid., p. 68; and James R. Schlesinger, "Wither American Industry?" in ibid., pp. 551–52. For a contemporary view of the problem, see Murray L. Weidenbaum, *Economic Impact of the Vietnam War* (New York: Renaissance Editions, 1967).

[8] Otto Eckstein, Christopher Caton, Roger Brinner and Peter Duprey, *U.S. Manufacturing Industries* (Cambridge, Mass.: Data Resources, 1984), pp. 33–

the regulatory structures (inherited from the New Deal) contributed to an inefficient allocation of national economic resources.[9] Fifth, the depletion of natural resource endowments, most notably petroleum and iron ore, exacerbated inflation and aggravated the international trade problem.[10] Sixth, tax policy continued to encourage consumption and to provide few incentives for saving and investment. Consumption was subsidized, for example, by generous personal income tax deductions allowed for interest and for real estate and state sales taxes.[11] Finally, some scholars have argued persuasively that these dilemmas were compounded by a loss of venturesomeness on the part of U.S. business leaders. Concerns about disturbing patterns of economic flux made managements more risk-averse and attuned to seeking short-term payoffs. This defensiveness was reflected in the reluctance of corporate leaders to authorize major investment projects without first securing guarantees of generous subsidies or tax benefits.[12]

However, efforts were mounted in many sectors of the economy to reverse the decline. For example, government and industry both tried to restore economic vibrancy by supporting the development of new technologies. The invention of the semiconductor by AT&T's Bell Laboratories in the 1960s led to the displacement of vacuum tubes and allowed the miniaturization of circuitry in electronics. Semiconductors provided the technical core for the perfection of electronic chip tech-

42; Scott, "U.S. Competitiveness," p. 64; and Dertouzos et al., *Made in America,* pp. 59–61.

[9] Galambos and Pratt, *Rise of the Corporate Commonwealth,* pp. 241–42; Paul W. MacAvoy, *The Regulated Industries and the Economy* (New York: Norton, 1979), pp. 31–52 and 121–24; McCraw, *Prophets of Regulation,* pp. 216–21; and Vietor, *Contrived Competition,* pp. 9–22 and 310–30. For origins of regulatory commissions, see Marver Bernstein, *Regulating Business by Independent Commission* (Princeton, N.J.: Princeton University Press, 1955).

[10] Galambos and Pratt, *Rise of the Corporate Commonwealth,* pp. 220–26; and Peter R. Odell, *Oil and World Power* (New York: Penguin, 1983).

[11] Martin, *Shifting the Burden,* pp. 107–14. For a discussion of the effects of governmental deficits on savings and investment, see Benjamin M. Friedman, "Savings, Investment, and Government Deficits in the 1980s," in Scott and Lodge, eds., *U.S. Competitiveness in the World Economy,* pp. 395–428.

[12] Robert H. Hayes and William J. Abernathy, "Managing Our Way to Economic Decline," *Harvard Business Review* (July–August 1980): 67–77; and Scott, "U.S. Competitiveness, pp. 46–47.

nology, which made possible the manufacture of cheap, powerful computers. Enhancements in chip design increased computational power and dramatically reduced the costs of data processing. These changes in turn induced a strong demand for the specialized skills of programmers and systems designers.[13]

Federally sponsored research continued to create economic opportunities. The space program, launched during the administration of President John F. Kennedy, drew on the expertise of the aircraft, electronics, computer and chemical industries. Eventually, the program made possible the successful formation of a commercial satellite industry that improved communications and weather monitoring. Federal support of the biological sciences, on the other hand, fostered the rise of the biotechnology and genetic engineering businesses, which supplied the nation's pharmaceutical industry with a host of commercially viable drugs and therapies. National defense programs also provided indirect financial and technological support for commercial aircraft manufacturing.[14]

There was also strong growth in specialized services that improved the quality of life of a growing middle class. Health care expenditures, for example, accounted for about 12 percent of GNP in 1989. Rising disposable income created demand for the skills of attorneys, accountants and many types of financial experts. Increasing affluence and the desire for enrichment created employment and investment opportunities in education, entertainment and tourism. And the growth in medical specialties improved care in areas where previously there were few cures. Due to new surgical techniques, Americans who encountered such maladies as clogged arteries and broken hips could enjoy a qual-

---

[13] Ernest Braun and Stuart MacDonald, *Revolution in Miniature: The History and Impact of Semiconductor Electronics* (Cambridge University Press, 1978).

[14] For an assessment of the government's research commitment and efforts to support commercial development, see Bruce L. R. Smith, *American Science Policy since World War II* (Washington, D.C.: Brookings Institution, 1990), pp. 52–65. For space program policy formulation, see Bruce L. R. Smith, *The Advisers: Scientists in the Policy Process* (Washington, D.C.: Brookings Institution, 1992), pp. 122–36 passim. See also U.S. Congress, Office of Technology Assessment, *Commercial Biotechnology: An International Analysis* Report OTA-BA-218, January (Washington, D.C.: Government Printing Office, 1984); and John Newhouse, *The Sporty Game: The High Risk Competitive Business of Making and Selling Commercial Airliners* (New York: Knopf, 1982).

ity of life that was better than what they would have expected in earlier periods.[15]

The economic system was buoyed by financial innovations that expanded the scope of service, reduced risk, enhanced transactional efficiency and better utilized professional knowledge. For example, the abandonment of fixed currency exchange rates and interest rate ceilings allowed hedging mechanisms to protect against losses from financial volatility. A proliferation of futures and options contracts soon appeared to satisfy this need. The first to debut were futures contracts on foreign currencies (British pound, German mark, Italian lire and Japanese yen) which were traded beginning in 1972 on the International Money Market of the Chicago Mercantile Exchange (CME). Contracts were soon established for debt instruments: by 1977 the Chicago Board of Trade (CBOT) had successfully introduced futures contracts for Ginnie Maes, long-term Treasury bonds and commercial paper, while the CME began trading for Treasury bills and notes. Contracts based on stock indices found sponsorship at three exchanges: the Value Line Index at the Kansas City Board of Trade, the Standard & Poor's 500 Index at the CME and the NYSE Composite Index at the New York Futures Exchange. The first exchange-traded options contracts, on the other hand, were launched on the Chicago Board of Options Exchange of the CBOT in 1973. Soon, security options were also being traded on the NYSE and the American, the Philadelphia and the Pacific Exchanges. By 1982, there were listed options for over 300 corporate stocks being traded on these exchanges.[16]

---

[15] Karl Albrecht and Ron Zemke, *Service America!: Doing Business in the New Economy* (Homewood, Ill.: Dow–Jones Irwin, 1985); Alan S. Blinder, "The Level and Distribution of Economic Well-Being," in Feldstein, ed., *The American Economy in Transition,* pp. 415–79 passim; and Victor R. Fuchs, "Some Implications of the Growing Importance of the Service Industries," National Bureau of Economic Research, *Forty-Fifth Annual Report* (New York: NBER, 1965), pp. 5–16. Data on health care expenditures and GNP in 1989 are taken from U.S. Census Bureau, *Statistical Abstract of the United States, 1993* (Washington, D.C.: Government Printing Office, 1993), pp. 108 and 442, respectively.

[16] J. Duncan LaPlante, "Growth and Organization of Commodity Markets," in Perry J. Kaufman, ed., *The Concise Handbook of Futures Markets: Money Management, Forecasting and the Markets* (New York: Wiley, 1986), pp. 1/3–1/54.

The financial markets benefited from innovations that reduced transaction costs. Fearing the loss of business to the NASDAQ over-the-counter system or to offshore markets such as London, the NYSE began to abandon its fixed commission rates in favor of a more flexible arrangement that allowed brokers to grant volume discounts. New discount brokerage firms such as Charles Schwab & Company of San Francisco cut transaction costs by concentrating on order execution services and by avoiding research and investment advice.

Governmental reforms sought to reverse the economic decline by dismantling the regulatory structures that had curtailed market competition. Two industries foremost in this drive were transportation and communications. The Airline Deregulation Act of 1978 disbanded the Civil Aeronautics Board and phased in greater market competition. The ICC also relinquished its role as the regulator of interstate transportation rates by the provisions of the Motor Carrier Act of 1980 and the Staggers' Rail Transportation Act of 1980. In 1981, AT&T complied with a federal court mandate to divest its regional operating companies but retained control over long-distance phone service, Bell Laboratories and the Western Electric manufacturing subsidiary. Competition in long-distance providers soon increased with the entry of MCI and General Telephone's Sprint service.[17]

[17] For the airlines, see Elizabeth E. Bailey, David R. Graham and David P. Kaplan, *Deregulating the Airlines* (Cambridge, Mass.: MIT Press, 1985); Stephen G. Breyer, *Regulation and Its Reform* (Cambridge, Mass.: Harvard University Press, 1982), chapt. 11; Anthony E. Brown, *The Politics of Airline Deregulation* (Knoxville: University of Tennessee Press, 1987); McCraw, *Prophets of Regulation*, pp. 259–99; Steven A. Morrison and Clifford Winston, *The Economic Effects of Airline Deregulation* (Washington, D.C.: Brookings Institution, 1986). For other transportation industries, see Marcus Alexis, "The Political Economy of Federal Regulation of Surface Transportation," in Roger G. Noll and Bruce M. Owen, *The Political Economy of Deregulation: Interest Groups in the Regulatory Process* (Washington, D.C.: American Enterprise Institute, 1983), pp. 115–31; and Miranti, "Mind's Eye of Reform," pp. 503–509. With respect to competition in telecommunications, see Peter Temin with Louis Galambos, *The Fall of the Bell System: A Study in Prices and Politics* (Cambridge University Press, 1987). See Vietor, *Contrived Competition*, chapts. 3–5 passim for an analysis of the impacts of regulation and deregulation on leading companies in the airline, natural gas, telephone and banking industries.

New legislation promoted banking competitiveness by ending restrictions on interest rates and on the scope of service. The Depository Institutions Deregulation Act of 1980 and the Garn–St. Germain Depository Institutions Act of 1982 eliminated interest rate ceilings on deposits, increased the geographic range for branch banking and eliminated some of the barriers that had prohibited diversification into nonbanking services. Such reforms allowed savings and loan associations to purchase the low-grade bonds issued by LBOs. In addition, the Federal Home Loan Bank Board (FHLBB) made successive cuts in the minimum capital requirements for saving and loan associations and so bolstered industry profitability; in 1980, the minimum capital requirement was reduced from 5 to 4 percent, and in 1982 it was reduced to 3 percent.[18]

Two quite different tax reforms launched in the 1980s spurred economic expansion. In the Economic Recovery Tax Act of 1981, strong incentives for investment were provided by more liberal capital consumption allowances in the form of shorter depreciable lives for qualifying assets and more generous investment tax credits. These preferences benefited capital-intensive businesses by reducing their implicit rates of taxation. The shorter depreciation periods allowed under the new Accelerated Cost Recovery System (ACRS) introduced by this legislation for real property also helped to spark a real estate boom that was partly financed by the formation of large limited-partnership syndicates that drew capital from individual investors. These syndicates were popular because they enabled individuals to reduce their personal tax liabilities by their allocable shares of partnership losses. (Such passive activity losses were often high early in a real estate project because of substantial depreciation and interest deductions.) Moreover, individual savings were encouraged by the establishment

---

[18] Cooper and Fraser, *Banking Deregulation and the New Competition in Financial Services*; Galambos and Pratt, *Rise of the Corporate Commonwealth*, pp. 244–45; Martin E. Lowy, *High Rollers: Inside the Savings and Loan Debacle* (New York: Praeger, 1991), pp. 17–20 and 49–52; Vietor, "Regulation-Defined Financial Markets," pp. 46–47; and idem, *Contrived Competition*, pp. 280–309 for discussions of the effects of deregulation on BankAmerica; and Lawrence J. White, *The S&L Debacle: Public Policy Lessons for Bank and Thrift Regulation* (New York: Oxford University Press, 1991), chaps. 2 and 4.

of Individual Retirement Accounts, which allowed contributions of up to $2,000 per year to be taken as a deduction on individual tax returns.[19]

The radical changes introduced by the Tax Reform Act of 1986 kept expansion alive. The new law eliminated key elements of tax preference. It curtailed accelerated depreciation permitted under ACRS by extending cost recovery periods, ended the investment tax credit and lowered tax rates on capital gains. In addition, the deductibility of passive activity losses from limited partnerships for individuals was severely cut back. Nor were individuals allowed any longer to deduct state sales taxes or most nonmortgage interest charges. The discontinuance of these items, which previously had enabled corporations and individuals to reduce their implicit tax rates, was traded off for a lowering of the explicit rates for all taxpayer classes.[20]

The 1986 tax reforms altered investment patterns in the United States. First, the elimination of the subsidies inherent in the earlier capital consumption allowances placed service industries and light manufacturing on a more even playing field with heavy industry with respect to taxation. Second, the elimination of capital gains, combined with the long-standing failure of the U.S. tax code to reimburse investors for the double taxation of dividends, undermined the relative attractiveness of corporate equity ownership. Instead, the provisions of the 1986 regime enhanced the appeal of fixed-income investment and of partnerships over corporations as vehicles for conducting business. Third, the reduction of explicit U.S. tax rates made U.S. investments more attractive to foreigners, who could receive credits in their home countries for any income taxes paid overseas. This step improved the expected returns that investors in Japan and the United Kingdom – countries with higher explicit corporate income tax rates – could earn in the United States. This latter benefit in conjunction with a lowering in value of the U.S. dollar led to an influx of foreign investment in the last quarter of 1986. The value of foreign acquisitions of U.S. businesses jumped to $15.5 billion that quarter. This was more than four times the quarterly value of such acquisitions during

[19] Martin, *Shifting the Burden*, chapt. 5.
[20] Ibid., chapt. 7.

the preceding year and 39 percent of the average annual volume of acquisitions during the 1981–85 period.[21]

Finally, the Federal Reserve sought to strengthen the economy, combating inflation with a tight money policy. Under the leadership of Paul Volcker, who had been appointed chairman by President James E. Carter in 1979, a tight credit policy was pursued until 1982, when the rate on the U.S. thirty-year Treasury bond exceeded 12.5 percent.[22] A relaxation of credit stringency did not occur until Friday, 13 August 1982, when the long bond rate began a gradual decline that lasted for most of the following decade. This change in credit policy also signaled the beginning of a boom on the stock market, which in the next fourteen years ascended to over the 6,000 level on the DJIA.

The evolving economic system proved its durability and resiliency in two serious financial crises. The first resulted from the combination of long-standing problems that came to a head and threatened to undermine U.S. banking liquidity. The second was the sudden, massive downturn in stock prices that affected stock markets worldwide in October 1987. In both cases, however, the economic system withstood these shocks and avoided becoming a full-blown disturbance that involved a substantial and lasting decline in real output.

With respect to banking, the reforms of the 1980s had not satisfactorily confronted all of the industry's difficulties. The first of its unresolved quandaries was the decreasing liquidity of leading U.S. banking institutions because of defaults on the substantial loans extended to governments and nationalized industries in the Third World, particularly in Latin America. Lending to developing countries was one of several new markets that attracted leading commercial banks. Beginning in the 1970s, money center banks played an important role in recycling petrodollars among energy-importing nations in the Third World, especially in Latin America.[23] Besides foreign lending, the banks tried to grow by developing consumer lending and credit cards, real estate finance, trust services and securities trad-

---

[21] Myron S. Scholes and Mark A. Wolfson, *Taxes and Business Strategy: A Planning Approach* (Englewood Cliffs, N.J.: Prentice-Hall, 1992), pp. 83–99 and 510–20.

[22] Ballarin, *Commercial Banks Amid the Financial Revolution*, pp. 72–76.

[23] Ibid., pp. 76–80.

ing.[24] Second, many regional mortgage lenders were imperiled by developments that adversely affected the real estate markets. One was the precipitous drop in the price of oil from $28 to $10 per barrel that undermined the southwestern economy beginning in December 1985. Also negatively affecting banks was the repeal of liberal depreciation and interest deduction provisions of the Tax Reform Act of 1986, which undermined the economic viability of many real estate tax shelter syndications and was estimated to have been responsible for about a 20 percent contraction in the value of northeastern commercial properties. The consequent extensive failures of savings and loan institutions became so massive that it wiped out the capital of the Federal Savings and Loan Insurance Corporation (FSLIC) in 1987, forcing Congress to recapitalize the deposit guarantee agency. Finally, the elimination of restrictions on the types of assets that specialized lenders like savings and loan associations could hold under the Garn–St. Germain legislation encouraged many institutions to engage in financing activities for which they often lacked competency or experience. Nor did the legislation provide any mechanisms for preventing the general decline in bank asset quality that eventually did occur because of an increasing exposure to securities of marginal quality, especially junk bonds.[25]

The resolution of these banking problems was pursued in two ways. The response to the foreign debt problem took the form of an elaborate plan named for U.S. Secretary of the Treasury Nicholas F. Brady for restoring the liquidity of Latin American obligations and for creating capital markets in this region. Although the details were often worked out in country-specific ways, the Brady plan's basic objective was to induce foreign borrowers to pay down their external indebtedness with the proceeds generated by the privatization of state-owned businesses. By the early 1990s, Chile, Mexico, Brazil and Argentina had made substantial progress in restoring their national finances by this means.[26]

---

[24] For the effects of these patterns of change on one typical money center bank, see John Donald Wilson, *The Chase: The Chase Manhattan Bank, N.A., 1945–1985* (Boston: Harvard Business School Press, 1986), chaps. 8–12.

[25] Lowy, *High Rollers*, pp. 131–35 and 188–89; and White, *The S&L Debacle*, pp. 106–11.

[26] Nicholas F. Brady, "Dealing with the International Debt Crisis," *Department of State Bulletin* 89 (May 1989): 53–56; Howard P. Lehman, "International

The second reform was the promulgation of the Financial Institutions Reform, Recovery and Enforcement Act of 1989 (FIRREA), which strengthened the banking system by mandating higher capital requirements and by providing incentives for enhancing the quality of portfolio assets. FIRREA represented the American response to the Bank of International Settlements (BIS) resolution of the preceding year that called for raising minimum capital ratios to 8 percent of risk-adjusted assets within the banking system of member states. In addition, the new law required that capital adequacy evaluations be made by taking into consideration the relative riskiness of a bank's assets. This latter provision was a safeguard against imprudent investing that had been overlooked in the Garn–St. Germain legislation, which had ended restrictions on the types of assets that banks might hold.[27]

FIRREA also reordered the framework for regulating the savings and loan industry. Supervisory authority was transferred to the newly organized Office of Thrift Supervision, which ended the tenure of its predecessor agency, the Federal Home Loan Bank Board. The FDIC, which had previously had responsibility for insuring deposits at commercial banks, displaced the bankrupt FSLIC as the guarantor of depositor balances at savings and loans. Another new agency, the Resolution Trust Corporation (RTC), was established to liquidate the assets of savings institutions forced into federal conservatorship because of inadequate capital. By the close of the 1980s about half of the nearly 4,000 institutions existing at the beginning of the decade had disappeared because of bankruptcy or forced mergers.[28]

Besides banking, crises in important linkages connecting the international financial markets contributed to a dramatic crash in equity

Creditors and the Third World: Policies from Baker to Brady," *Journal of Developing Areas* 28 (January 1994): 191–217; and Jeffrey Sachs, "Making the Brady Plan Work," *Foreign Affairs* 68 (Summer 1989): 87–104. See also *The International Debt Crisis: A Review of the Brady Plan: Hearings before the Subcommittee on Foreign Affairs,* House of Representatives, 101st Cong., 1st Sess., April 19 (Washington, D.C.: Government Printing Office, 1989).

[27] William Keeton, "The New Risk-Based Capital Plan for Commercial Banks," in Anthony Saunders, George F. Udell and Lawrence J. White, eds., *Bank Management and Regulation: A Book of Readings* (Mountain View, Calif.: Mayfield, 1992), pp. 20–41; Lowy, *High Rollers,* chapt. 17; and White, *S&L Debacle,* chapt. 9.

[28] Lowy, *High Rollers,* pp. 223 and 225–28; and White, *S&L Debacle,* 180–93.

prices on the world's major bourses on October 19–20, 1987. The total magnitude of the decline of U.S. markets that month amounted to 21.5 percent. Similar losses were also registered in October for securities markets in the United Kingdom (-26.1 percent), West Germany (-22.9 percent) and Japan (-12.6 percent).[29]

The downturn had been set off by a deterioration in the U.S. long-term bond market during the preceding week, which was brought on by a growing apprehension about the size of the recently announced U.S. trade deficit. Japanese institutional investors began to liquidate their positions in the U.S. long bond, fearing a currency loss from an anticipated decline in the dollar's exchange rate. The Japanese had been eager purchasers of U.S. bonds early in the decade because of a strong dollar and the high real rates of interest. The sell-off translated into the current yield on the long bond exceeding 10 percent. This adjustment raised questions about the valuation of the stock market, which had risen strongly during the course of the preceding summer and in early October had a dividend yield of only about 2.5 percent as measured by the DJIA.[30]

The severity of the decline in New York had been exacerbated by several factors that greatly increased trading volume and volatility. First, there was, on October 17, the pressure of the "triple witching hour," which involved the simultaneous expiration of contracts on individual stock and index options and on index futures. In addition, trading velocity had increased because many institutional investors used computer-driven index arbitrage programs. The resultant avalanche of transactions threatened to overwhelm the resources of the floor traders, whose responsibility it was to maintain orderly markets at the NYSE. The market began to show some stability by the end of

[29] Paul Bennett and Jeanette Kelleher, "The International Transmission of Stock Price Disruption, October 1987," *Federal Reserve Bank of New York Quarterly Review* (Summer 1988): 17–27; Gikas A. Hardouvelis, "Evidence on Stock Market Speculative Bubbles: Japan, the United States and Great Britain," *Federal Reserve Bank of New York Quarterly Review* (Summer 1988): 4–16; and U.S. Securities Exchange Commission, *The October 1987 Market Break* (Washington, D.C.: Government Printing Office, 1988), chaps. 1–3.

[30] R. Taggart Murphy, "Power without Purpose: The Crisis of Japanese Global Financial Dominance," *Harvard Business Review* (March–April 1989), pp. 73–74; and Marumi Ichiki, "Japanese Overseas Investment," in Fair Facts Series II, *Japan's Financial Markets* (Tokyo: Foundation for Advanced Information and Research, 1991), pp. 303–16.

the day because the SEC temporarily banned program trading and the Federal Reserve began to inject additional liquidity into the credit markets. The worldwide panic began to dissipate, however, on October 20, when the Japanese Ministry of Finance took decisive action by instructing that country's four major brokerage houses to support the Tokyo market.[31]

Although by the close of this era much progress had been made in rectifying the weaknesses in the U.S. economy evident since the 1960s, not all of the problems had been resolved. Serious deficits persisted both in the federal budget and in the nation's external accounts; the public debt rose enormously, as did the value of claims held by foreigners on U.S. entities both private and public. However, what was most important was that the evolving economic system was sufficiently durable to withstand serious shocks.

III. The Rise of Conglomerates

Conglomerates, which first emerged in the 1960s, sought to reduce risk and to maximize returns by uniting many heterogeneous businesses into one corporation. What differentiated them from center firms was the general lack of common market or technological characteristics to unify the activities of their operating subsidiaries. The product lines of two leading conglomerates illustrate this pattern. Gulf and Western (later Paramount Communications) had operated at various times in sugar refining, railroading, film production and distribution, publishing and zinc mining. And LTV Corporation had diversified into aircraft manufacture, electronics, meat packing, coal mining, steel and ocean shipping.[32]

Although the management of conglomerates was fraught with serious difficulties, this business form did have a lasting impact. By 1973,

[31] Murphy, "Power without Purpose," pp. 73–74.

[32] For LTV, see John F. Winslow, *Conglomerates Unlimited: The Failure of Regulation* (Bloomington: Indiana University Press, 1973), chapt. 8; for Paramount's early days, see by the editors of *Fortune*, "Gulf and Western's Rambunctious Conservatism," in *The Conglomerate Commotion* (New York: Viking, 1970), pp. 44–60; for Time-Warner, see Connie Bruck, *Master of the Game: Steve Ross and the Creation of Time Warner* (New York: Simon & Schuster, 1994).

Table 7.1. *Conglomerates Ranking among the Fortune 200 Largest Firms, 1979*

Rank	Company	Number of Industries	
		Mfg.	Nonmfg.
8	International Telephone & Telegraph	14	24
15	Tenneco	13	15
42	Gulf & Western Industries	19	22
51	Litton Industries	11	8
66	LTV	8	10
73	Illinois Central Industries	11	15
103	Textron	14	2
104	Greyhound	7	12
128	Martin Marietta	8	6
131	Dart Industries	12	6
132	U.S. Industries	17	7
143	Northwest Industries	11	7
173	Walter Kidde	12	10
180	Ogden Industries	5	8
188	Colt Industries	6	3

Source: Adopted from table in Chandler and Tedlow, eds., *The Coming of Managerial Capitalism*, p. 772.

15 of the top 200 U.S. manufacturing companies were in this category (Table 7.1).[33] The patterns of their formation were conditioned by differing financing modes and by the type of firms targeted in merger drives. Until 1965 most of the conglomerate acquisitions were of relatively small and closely held businesses financed by the exchange of equity. In 1961, for example, 60 percent of the nearly $1 billion in tender offers were for stock. In these cases the successor generation of a founding family usually had little interest in continuing the venture. Bids by large corporations were welcomed because they afforded founders the opportunity to liquidate their holdings at acceptable exit prices. After 1965, however, cash tender offers became the norm in conglomerate acquisitions. That year, for example, 70 percent ($450 million) of all tender bids were for cash. The target firms were also

---

[33] Norman A. Berg, "Corporate Role in Diversified Companies," in Chandler and Tedlow, eds., *The Coming of Managerial Capitalism*, p. 772.

different in this second stage of development. Some conglomerates grew by acquiring firms spun-off by other companies that had decided to abandon their efforts to diversify into particular markets. Other conglomerates mounted hostile takeovers of poorly performing entities that nevertheless remained attractive because of potentially valuable assets. This became more common late in the cycle of conglomerate building as the number of willing merger candidates began to dwindle.[34]

The elaboration of portfolio theory in the 1950s and 1960s provided one of the chief intellectual foundations for conglomerate formation. The studies of Harry Markowitz, John Lintner and William F. Sharpe structured efficient portfolios that equated risk and returns, useful considerations in evaluating a broad spectrum of capital allocation alternatives. Moreover, portfolio theory provided a rationale for acquiring subsidiaries in highly dissimilar lines of business: it held that diversification was most effective in reducing risk when the elements in a portfolio had highly negative activity correlation coefficients.[35]

A second rationale was the claim that conglomerates could achieve "synergy," that is, efficiency derived from the application of advanced management techniques in spite of the extreme diversity of product lines. Five factors promised the realization of this goal. First, advances in management science and computer technology were supposed to provide the means to manage backward companies more efficiently. Second, the stronger financial position of conglomerates supposedly allowed subsidiaries to maximize the returns from research and development rather than the licensing or sale of these rights. Third, the central office staffs assisted by establishing data-processing capabilities, which presumably strengthened the management of service enterprises. Fourth, high corporate tax rates provided strong incentives for the merger of companies with substantial net operating loss carryforwards or unused investment tax credits. These tax attributes could be used to offset the taxes incurred from the more profitable elements of

---

[34] Allen Kaufman and Lawrence Zacharias, "From Trust to Contract: The Legal Language of Managerial Ideology, 1920–1980," *Business History Review* 66 (Autumn 1992): 547–59. See also Allen Kaufman, Lawrence Zacharias and Marvin Karson, *Managers vs. Owners: The Struggle for Corporate Control in American Democracy* (New York: Oxford University Press, 1995), pp. 66–67 and 70.

[35] See note 24, Chapter 6.

the conglomerate group. Finally, the rising cost of capital also made it advantageous to acquire subsidiaries with substantial liquid or liquefiable assets.[36]

Loose financial accounting practice facilitated conglomerate formation financed by the issuance of stock that created the illusion of rising earnings and higher returns on capital. Such subtleties in measurement were poorly understood by many investors. The core of the problem was the pooling of interests method, which was used to account for the consolidated net income of conglomerate groups. It introduced several distortions in accounting valuations not encountered in the more conservative alternative, known as the purchase method. Pooling failed to require adjustments to reflect the fair market value of the assets acquired by conglomerates. Instead, these assets were recorded at their historical costs when originally acquired by the merged subsidiary. In inflationary periods, this often led to a substantial understatement of both assets and equity when compared with current market values. Under this latter criterion it also meant that profits and rates of return might be inflated because of the low values attached to the cost of inventory sold or to the depreciation of fixed assets. Similarly, the failure to use current market values inflated the gains resulting from the sale of redundant assets. Finally, the earnings illusion was further exaggerated because merged entities consolidated their income from the beginning of the fiscal year rather than from the date of merger. Thus, some conglomerates may have been encouraged to acquire subsidiaries at the end of the year if they had high earnings and, by merging them with other entities within the group, to report greater overall profitability.[37]

Internal Revenue Service (IRS) rules allowing for nontaxable stock swaps in mergers facilitated the financing of acquisitions by share issuance. These arrangements could be structured in ways that pro-

[36] Neil H. Jacoby, "The Conglomerate Corporation," in Chandler and Tedlow, eds., *The Coming of Managerial Capitalism*, pp. 740–55.

[37] Chatov, *Corporate Financial Reporting*, pp. 207–209 and chapt. 14; Seligman, *Transformation of Wall Street*, pp. 419–30; and Patrick A. Gaughan, *Mergers and Acquisitions* (New York: HarperCollins, 1991), pp. 23–25. For a detailed discussion of the financial analytical issues, see Leopold A. Bernstein, *Financial Statement Analysis: Theory, Application and Interpretation*, 3rd ed. (Homewood, Ill.: Irwin, 1983), pp. 242–61.

vided substantial benefits to the former owners of closely held companies. First, these deals enhanced the liquidity and reduced the risk of the wealth that a subsidiary's original proprietors had built up during their careers. What they received for their equity in small, obscure enterprises was the stock of highly visible, diversified growing companies that were usually listed on major securities exchanges. The acceptance of stock payment enabled the former owners to defer the taxation of any capital gains inherent in their old businesses by allowing them to have the same tax basis in their new shares as they had in their old. Moreover, their heirs benefited because they would eventually own common stock of great conglomerates, for which there was a ready market. Heirs also enjoyed important tax advantages. They were provided a step up in tax basis to the fair market value of the property at the decedent's death, thus avoiding upon sale of the new shares any income tax that had been deferred earlier. In addition to the potential for wealth enhancement through dividend income and capital gains from the ownership of conglomerate shares, the acquisition arrangements were often coupled with employment contracts for former owners.[38]

Advantages accrued to conglomerates that financed acquisitions by share issuance. Although this contradicted the pattern noted among center firms, it was tolerable among conglomerates as long as share issuances remained relatively small and thus did not lead to significant shifts in the allocation of ownership interests. This approach helped to preserve liquid assets and keep borrowing costs low. The issuance of stock and the subsequent engagement of former owners as managers of a merged entity helped to satisfy two key tests of the IRS rules that determined whether acquired tax attributes such as net operating losses from an acquired entity could be carried forward to offset the taxable income of the acquiring company. Moreover, the engagement of former owners as managers provided personnel who were experienced in the industry of the acquired subsidiary and often lacking in

---

[38] For a general discussion of the personal and corporate tax advantages accruing to mergers, consider Alan J. Auerbach and David Reishus, "The Impact of Taxation on Mergers and Acquisitions," in Alan J. Auerbach, ed., *Mergers and Acquisitions* (Chicago: University of Chicago Press, 1988), pp. 69–85. For a more detailed explanation of current law, see Scholes and Wolfson, *Taxes and Business Strategy*, pp. 531–43.

the parent company. Finally, stock buyouts served to make the interests of the new managers more concentric with that of the consolidated company.[39]

After 1965, the tax advantages associated with the issuance of common stock became less important in financial planning among aggressive conglomerates that had fixed their sights on large, established companies in banking, insurance, oil and steel.[40] The advantages of share exchanges were less clear when the ownership of a target firm was widely diffused among shareholders with dissimilar tax circumstances. Moreover, it was impossible to reinforce any contemplated share swap schemes with postmerger employment opportunities, as was possible when dealing with the owners of closely held companies. Instead, in these cases the predictions of the pecking order hypothesis were operative. When confronted with uncertainty about the prospects of a revolutionary business like the conglomerate, poorly informed investors seemed to prefer the certainties associated with cash or debt securities over equity shares, which were inherently difficult to appraise. This concern was assuaged by the greater reliance placed on convertible debenture financing, which during most of the 1960s could be structured as tax-free transactions. In 1968, for example, an estimated 20 percent of the 173 acquisitions valued over $10 million were funded by the issuance of debentures.[41]

The primary benefit to those making the acquisition was that the interest on the debt incurred to finance these transactions was deductible and thus helpful in reducing the overall cost of capital. Although the achievement of high earnings might lead to a dilution of equity because of debenture conversion and to changes in the composition of ownership, a successful management would be in a strong position to initiate new expansion plans to obviate these potential problems.

The drive to form conglomerates, however, proved to be transitory. Although the movement had gained momentum during the early 1960s, it peaked dramatically in 1968, and subsequently the popularity of this form of business organization began to wane.[42] Disillusion-

---

[39] Ibid., pp. 549–70.

[40] Kaufman and Zacharias, "From Trust to Contract," pp. 547–49.

[41] Chatov, *Corporate Financial Reporting*, pp. 209–10.

[42] See Norman A. Berg, *General Management: An Analytical Approach* (Homewood, Ill.: Irwin, 1984), pp. 124–25; Chatov, *Corporate Financial Reporting*, pp. 200–202; Kenneth M. Davidson, *Mega-Mergers: Corporate America's*

ment about the prospects for conglomerate growth set in because of the recognition that some of the managerial advantages were not achievable. A tightening of regulatory, accounting and tax rules also placed serious constraints on some of the techniques used to expand these businesses.

Prominent among the reasons for the leveling off of interest in conglomerate building was a rising skepticism conditioned by the findings of business scholars about the ability to achieve operating efficiencies from synergistic management. Foremost among critics was Professor Norman A. Berg, who compared the managerial capabilities of central offices in conglomerate and center firms. His research discovered that in virtually all cases the corporate staffs of conglomerates were much thinner than those of multidivisional center firms. Conglomerate central offices provided little support to subsidiaries in research and development, production or marketing. Given this laissez-faire attitude toward subsidiary operations, the claims of synergy resulting from superior management or more intense development of research capacities seemed doubtful. Thin corporate staffs instead focused more narrowly on financial monitoring, leaving the operational decisions almost exclusively to subsidiary management. Thinness at the top was partially conditioned by the heavy personnel investment that would have been necessary to build a knowledgeable and experienced staff capable of servicing subsidiaries in disparate markets. These conclusions found support in the studies of Alfred Chandler and of Richard P. Rumelt.[43]

Also, Professor Milton Leontiades makes the point that the most readily exploitable synergies available to conglomerates relate to finance rather than management. Leontiades identifies the advantages accruing from "complementary cash flows" in "nonspecialized" diversification. One example of this is the ability to finance capital-hungry ventures that promise future rapid growth and increases in profits by

Billion-Dollar Takeovers (Cambridge, Mass.: Ballinger, 1985), pp. 140–43; and Gaughan, *Mergers and Acquisitions*, pp. 18–20.

[43] Berg, *Management*, pp. 151–55; and idem, "Corporate Role in Diversified Companies," in *The Coming of Managerial Capitalism*, pp. 756–75. See also Chandler, *Visible Hand*, pp. 480–82; and Richard P. Rumelt, "Diversification Strategy and Profitability," *Strategic Management Journal* 3 (1982): 361; and idem, *Strategy, Structure and Economic Performance*, revised ed. (Boston: Harvard Business School Press, 1974, 1986).

using the excess cash flows generated by mature entities within the conglomerate group. In addition, the size advantage when coupled with strong financial performance enhances the conglomerate's negotiating position with banks and other credit providers.[44]

The reluctance of many conglomerate corporate offices to exercise stronger control over subsidiary activities was also conditioned in part by the desire to avoid violating the tax code in ways that could have affected the deductibility of acquired net operating losses (NOLS). As already noted, the code required business and management continuity within the merged entity as a prerequisite for carrying tax attributes forward in the consolidated tax return of the acquiring conglomerate. Evidence of having satisfied this requirement included the maintenance of substantial investment by former owners in the conglomerate and the continuance of the corporate status of the merged subsidiary. The fear of failing these tests deterred central offices from intruding on the managerial autonomy of subsidiaries.

Tax reforms made it more difficult for conglomerates to utilize acquired tax attributes such as NOLs or unused investment tax credits. Although the Internal Revenue Code specifically prohibited the offset of income, losses and credits among subsidiaries in dissimilar lines of business in a conglomerate's consolidated tax return, these rules were subjective and avoidable in subtle ways. For example, profitable elements within a conglomerate group might structure intercorporate transactions to subsidize loss subsidiaries, thus enabling them to take advantage of unused tax attributes. Such practices, however, were increasingly challenged by the IRS. These loopholes were eventually closed by the promulgation of more objective tests in the Tax Reform Act of 1976.[45]

In addition to tax reform, conglomerate building encountered new roadblocks in the form of more stringent financial accounting standards. Criticism leveled by respected commentators at the deficiencies of the pooling method raised public awareness for the need for reform.

---

[44] Milton Leontiades, *Managing the Unmanageable: Strategies for Success within the Conglomerate* (Reading, Mass.: Addison-Wesley, 1986), chapt. 3 passim.

[45] Scholes and Wolfson, *Taxes and Business Strategy,* chapt. 26; and Joint Congressional Committee on Taxation, *Staff Report on General Explanation of the Tax Reform Act of 1986,* 100th Cong., 1st Sess. (Washington, D.C.: Government Printing Office, 1987), pp. 288–327, provides a discussion of the evolution of these tax rules.

Professor Abraham Briloff of Baruch College, for example, attacked what he termed "dirty pooling" in many articles in *Barron's*, in scholarly journals and in his book *Unaccountable Accounting* (1972).[46] Arthur R. Wyatt, a partner in the accounting firm of Arthur Andersen & Company, also questioned the fairness of many contemporary pooling practices in articles and in the Accounting Research Study entitled *Accounting for Business Combinations*.[47] This latter document provided the basis for Accounting Principles Board (APB) Opinion No. 16 issued in 1971, which severely restricted the use of the pooling method. The new financial accounting standard required that only business combinations that met twelve preconditions could be treated as a pooling. All other business combinations had to be accounted for under the more restrictive purchase method.[48]

The purchase method was a far less attractive alternative for conglomerate builders. Unlike pooling, the purchase method required the market valuation of acquired assets and the recording of goodwill for any premium paid over their fair market value. Although goodwill reduced financial statement net income because it was required under APB Opinion No. 17 to be amortized over a period of not less than forty years, IRS rules prohibited the deductibility of these charges for tax purposes. By adversely affecting earnings and cash flow in this way, the purchase method tended to raise the cost of capital in financing mergers over what they might have otherwise been under the pooling method. These features made the purchase method unpopular

[46] Some of the more important contributions of Abraham J. Briloff on this topic include "Dirty Pooling," *Accounting Review* 42 (July 1967): 489–96; "Pooling-of-Interests Accounting," *Financial Analyst Journal* 24 (March–April 1968): 71–81; "Much-Abused Goodwill," *Barron's* (April 28, 1969): 3, 14, 16, 18, 20 and 24; "The 'Funny-Money' Game," *Financial Analyst Journal* 25 (May–June 1969): 73–79; and *Unaccountable Accounting* (New York: Harper & Row, 1972).

[47] Arthur R. Wyatt's contribution to this debate included *Accounting for Business Combinations*, Accounting Research Study No. 5 (New York: American Institute of Certified Public Accountants, 1963); and "Accounting for Business Combinations: What Next?" *Accounting Review* 40 (July 1965): 527–35.

[48] See also Chatov, *Corporate Financial Reporting*, pp. 211–22; and Seligman, *Transformation of Wall Street*, pp. 418–30. The rules that formerly prohibited the tax deductibility of goodwill have been relaxed somewhat under the Omnibus Budget Reconciliation Act of 1993, which allows purchased goodwill to be amortized in certain circumstances over a period of fifteen years.

among conglomerate organizers whose firms needed to exhibit strong earnings trends.[49]

Political opposition engendered by the hostile takeovers launched by some of the more aggressive conglomerates led to more restrictive regulation. The backlash took the form of critical investigations by legislative and executive committees and the promulgation of more restrictive rules for effectuating mergers. By the end of the 1960s, there were as many as eight separate federal investigations of mergers, economic concentration and the transfer of corporate control.[50] The requirements of the Williams Act in 1968, for example, were helpful to managements of targeted companies in developing strategic responses to defend against unwanted takeovers. One such provision that served as an early warning of a potential impending bid was the mandatory disclosure of any corporate acquisition of 5 percent or more of the equity of another enterprise. This law also required that a cash offer be maintained for at least twenty business days, thus allowing an embattled management time to develop a counteroffer.[51] But even more damaging to the interests of conglomerates was a modification to the Internal Revenue Code by the Tax Reform Act of 1969. The key feature of this change was the imposition of a $5 million ceiling on the total amount of interest that could be deducted annually on debt incurred to finance acquisitions.[52]

Another dilemma was that conglomerate growth required a geometrically expanding pace of mergers, which was ultimately unsustainable. Firms such as Litton, Synerdyne and Gulf and Western entered into an accelerating spree that culminated in late 1968. The conglomerates were forced to spread a wider net and pay higher prices for target companies in the ensuing heated competition. The principle of adverse selection began to operate; many acquisitions proved ulti-

[49] Bernstein, *Financial Statement Analysis*, pp. 245–55; Chatov, *Corporate Financial Reporting*, pp. 212–14; and Gaughan, *Mergers and Acquisitions*, pp. 488–90.

[50] Kaufman and Zacharias, "From Trust to Contract," pp. 548–49.

[51] Ibid., pp. 548–53; Davidson, *Mega-Mergers*, pp. 49–53; and Seligman, *Transformation of Wall Street*, pp. 431–34 and 443. See also Kaufman et al., *Managers vs. Owners*, pp. 68–75 for a discussion of the origins of this legislation.

[52] Chatov, *Corporate Financial Reporting*, p. 209; Davidson, *Mega-Mergers*, p. 142; and Gaughan, *Mergers and Acquisitions*, p. 25.

mately to be unsuccessful. In January 1969, Litton Industries announced that quarterly profits fell by two-thirds, and investors began to pay more attention to the skeptics who claimed that there could be no magic in combining steel, meat packing and the manufacturing of tennis balls.[53] The following months saw the catastrophic collapse of National Student Marketing, which had sustained a price–earnings ratio of about 100 on the basis of bald accounting manipulation and a wild string of acquisitions. National Student Marketing was notable because its victims included such sophisticated investors as Morgan Guaranty, Bankers Trust, Harvard and Cornell.[54]

The performance of firms that engaged in many acquisitions was disappointing. Numerous event studies have been published on the share-price behavior of takeovers.[55] The typical finding is that the acquired firm's shareholders obtain a statistically supranormal return of 20 to 30 percent on the days leading up to the public announcement. The effect on the bidder's stock is more difficult to discern (the concern's other businesses usually dwarf the recent acquisition), but no one has found large gains proximate to the merger event. Some studies, especially those employing a longer time period, have found a significant reduction in the acquirer's share price.[56] A study (using new FTC data on internal corporate operations) found an apparent decline in the rate of return of acquired businesses.[57] The findings are consis-

---

[53] John N. Brooks, *The Go-Go Years* (New York: Weybright & Talley, 1973), p. 181.

[54] John Brooks, *The Takeover Game* (New York: Dutton, 1987), p. 68.

[55] See, e.g., the summarizations of this literature provided by Michael C. Jensen and Richard S. Ruback, "The Market for Corporate Control," *Journal of Financial Economics* 11 (1983): 5–50; and Richard Roll, "Empirical Evidence on Takeover Activity and Shareholder Wealth," in John C. Coffee, Jr., Louis Lowenstein and Susan Rose-Ackerman, eds., *Knights, Raiders, and Targets: The Impact of the Hostile Takeover* (New York: Oxford University Press, 1988), pp. 241–52.

[56] Paul H. Malatesta, "The Wealth Effect of Merger Activity and the Objective Functions of Merging Firms," *Journal of Financial Economics* 11 (1983): 155–81; and Ellen B. Magenheim and Dennis C. Mueller, "Are Acquiring-Firm Shareholders Better Off after an Acquisition?" in Coffee et al., eds., *Knights, Raiders, and Targets*, pp. 171–93.

[57] David J. Ravenscraft and F. M. Scherer, *Mergers, Sell-Offs and Economic Efficiency* (Washington, D.C.: Brookings Institution, 1987). See also David J. Ravenscraft and F. M. Scherer, "Mergers and Managerial Performance," in Coffee et al., eds., *Knights, Raiders, and Targets*, pp. 194–210.

tent with administrative diseconomies usually associated with the lack of a core of related businesses to achieve economies of scale or scope. The uniting of dissimilar businesses, each requiring a specific set of skills and knowledge, overwhelms managerial capabilities and thus undermines operational efficiency.[58]

Like many of the unsuccessful industrial mergers of the early twentieth century, the drive to form conglomerates originated from an incomplete understanding of the economics of giant business enterprises. In the earlier merger wave, many corporate promotions failed because their architects did not realize that the concentration of industrial asset ownership per se was insufficient to enhance operating efficiency. The potential for realizing economies of scale depended on the existence of standardized products whose unit costs could be dramatically reduced by long manufacturing runs. In the case of conglomerates, on the other hand, the elements that were necessary for the achievement of economies of scope were usually lacking. Conglomerate organizers conceived the problem of industrial organization in terms of financial portfolio theory, a risk-sensitive rationale for blending heterogeneous business units. What was underestimated was the efficiency potential resulting from the closer coordination and control over subsidiaries operating in complementary markets or technologies. In the latter case, progress stemmed not from merely holding diversified portfolios of productive assets. Instead, it came about through a steady process of firm-specific learning about how resources could be more effectively integrated to enhance efficient functioning.[59]

By 1970, the conglomerate boom had run its course. Premiums commanded by the securities of these companies had evaporated because of changes adversely affecting their economic performance. The market prices of one such sample of firms analyzed by Norman Berg

---

[58] Berg, *Management,* pp. 129–31; Chandler, *Scale and Scope,* pp. 14–46; Leontiades, *Managing the Unmanageable,* pp. 59–61; Harry H. Lynch, *Financial Performance of Conglomerates* (Boston: Graduate School of Business Administration, Harvard University, 1971), pp. 284–87; and Richard P. Rumelt, "Diversification Strategy and Profitability," *Strategic Management Journal* 3 (1982): 361.

[59] Chandler, "Chemicals and Electronics," Part 1, pp. 27–30 and 61–65; and Leontiades, *Managing the Unmanageable,* pp. 61–69.

fell on average by 86 percent from the highs reached in 1968, while their price–earnings ratios fell from 35 to the single digits.[60]

Eventually some of the conglomerates, presented with the opportunity to restructure their activities, abandoned the eclecticism that had formerly guided them. During a subsequent merger boom during the mid-1970s, about half the total merger transactions represented divestitures of subsidiaries whose performance failed to satisfy earlier expectations.[61] Two of the more successful entities that began to reinvent their businesses during the period were Warner Communication and Paramount Communications. Both concentrated on establishing a strong presence in mass media markets such as cinema, publishing, recording and cable television operation. A less successful effort involved LTV Corporation's plan to further consolidate the steel industry through its acquisition of Jones & Laughlin Industries, Republic Steel and Youngstown Sheet and Tube.

With the passing of the conglomerate era, the spirit of financial innovation passed to yet another business form, the LBO partnership. This new type of organization was inspired by shortcomings in agency relationships within the traditional corporation. Consequently, organizers of LBOs sought to bolster efficiency by reunifying the interests of owners and managers. Besides new ideas about the connections between organization and finance, the development of the LBOs was impelled by felicitous changes in the tax laws and in financial regulation.

IV. Leveraged-Buyout Partnerships

Criticisms that emerged in the 1960s of the prevailing fiduciary model of corporate governance led to the formulation of new frameworks for evaluating financial institutions. The nub of the problem was that although many rights had been defined to protect shareholders against the grosser forms of fraud and incompetence, there was little recourse available to combat the type of managerial opportunism that resulted in poor corporate performance and the suboptimal allocation of re-

---

[60] Berg, *Management*, pp. 123–28; and Leontiades, *Managing the Unmanageable*, pp. 14–17. See also Gaughan, *Mergers and Acquisitions*, pp. 22–23.
[61] Gaughan, *Mergers and Acquisitions*, pp. 461–64.

sources. Control remained largely in the hands of professional managers. Concerns about this problem, however, eventually led to the establishment of a new paradigm that emphasized the role of contractual relationships in reconciling the differing interests of corporate stakeholders. Although these ideas initially emanated from academic theoreticians, they found practical expression in the initiatives taken by financial entrepreneurs in the development of LBO partnerships beginning in the 1970s.

The impressive array of powers for protecting shareholders against dishonesty and negligence in the fiduciary firm stemmed from two sources, the common law and federal securities regulations. Under the common law the crucial nexus between the corporation and shareholders was the board of directors, who had the responsibility of monitoring management's performance. In this regime shareholders were also entitled to periodic accountings that documented how well management maintained their stewardship over enterprise resources. Moreover, shareholders could protect their interests by exercising their voting rights over such important matters as the election of board members and auditors, the ratification of bylaws and the approval of management compensation schemes. The second body of regulations, the federal securities laws, strengthened the position of shareholders by explicitly defining the form, content and timing of corporate disclosures. These regulations also imposed penalties on agents who, through either dishonesty or incompetence, provided false or misleading information to investors. These regulations imposed sanctions on shareholder agents who took unfair advantage of their privileged information about corporate affairs.

However, these rights were ineffective in protecting shareholders against self-serving, opportunistic behavior on the part of management that could lead to inferior operating performance and decreases in the firm's value. Managers' dominance of the membership of boards of directors ensured their primacy in guiding corporate affairs. The exception to this general rule was in the rare cases of financial crisis, when external directors with standing in the financial community often assumed a prominent role in order to bolster public confidence.[62] Managements effectively controlled the process of proxy solicitation. Shareholders' legal challenges to particular policies often failed be-

[62] Chandler, *Visible Hand*, pp. 490–97.

cause the courts tended to abide by the business judgment rule, generally deferring to management.[63]

These shortcomings of fiduciary regulation induced legal scholar Henry G. Manne to propound in the 1960s an alternative model that was based on contractual relationships between stakeholders in the corporate enterprise. In his view the market was potentially much more effective than regulatory structures for curing the problems of managerial incompetence or opportunism. The key lay in allowing shareholders to seek redress from inferior management performance through transfers of corporate control. Dissatisfied shareholders could protect their interests against poor management by tendering their shares to external buyers. In unfettered markets, corporate managers would be disciplined by a simple rule: a decline in market value below the replacement cost of the firm would induce outsiders to bid for control with the intention of enhancing their wealth by the liquidation or reorganization of the acquired business.[64]

One drawback to Manne's model was that it was underspecified. He was arguing in essence that a perfectly fluid system would allow discipline to be imposed on inefficient managers and firms: a perfectly competitive environment with recontracting for all managerial talent with short-term contracts. This, however, introduces a second set of factors not directly addressed in his analysis. It was not only regulation that inhibited Manne's theory, but also the need for managers to have some tenure in order to perform their professional functions. Management skills are, to some degree, industry specific, and good management does not generate instant success. Financial markets alone could not cure shortcomings and trade-offs in an arena that includes imperfect substitution of goods as well as financial variables.

---

[63] William A. Klein and John C. Coffee, Jr., *Business Organization and Finance: Legal and Economic Principles*, 3rd ed. (Mineola, N.Y.: Foundation Press, 1986), pp. 140–44; and Mark J. Roe, "Political and Legal Restraints on Ownership and Control of Public Companies," *Journal of Financial Economics* 27 (1990): 7–41; and idem, *Strong Managers, Weak Owners: The Political Roots of American Corporate Finance* (Princeton, N.J.: Princeton University Press, 1994).

[64] Henry G. Manne, "The 'Higher Criticism' of the Modern Corporation," *Columbia Law Review* 62 (1962): 399–432; and idem, "Mergers and the Market for Corporate Control," *Journal of Political Economy* 73 (1965): 110–20.

However, as Manne and others noted, the effectiveness of the market as a tool for monitoring management had been enervated by a host of governmental regulations. The combined effect of antitrust laws, federal rules concerning stock tenders and state anti-takeover legislation made it difficult to oust entrenched managements. In addition, regulations applicable to leading classes of financial institutions limited the roles they could play in corporate takeovers. Banks and trust companies, for example, were prohibited from maintaining a controlling interest in nonfinancial businesses. Fiduciary responsibilities also compelled trust and insurance companies, mutual funds and pension funds to avoid the risks associated with a concentration of ownership in a few firms. Moreover, the Employment Retirement Safety Act of 1974 (ERISA) prohibited pension fund representatives from serving on the corporate boards unless they possessed competence in the underlying business.[65] Finally, besieged managements were permitted to mount "poison pill" defenses, such as the payment of a large semiliquidating dividend, and to employ other practices that would make any successful takeover a Pyrrhic victory.[66]

Nevertheless, Manne's ideas influenced paradigms that were emerging in two related fields of scholarship that described the problem of corporate governance in terms quite different from that of the traditional fiduciary model. The first was managerial economics, where Oliver E. Williamson and Masahiko Aoki established new frameworks for evaluating how corporations achieved efficiency by reducing transaction costs and how the organizational rents generated in this process were distributed by the bargaining between various stakeholder groups.[67] The second line of inquiry was that of financial agency theory, which was unified in the view that the firm was best under-

---

[65] Henry G. Manne, "Tender Offers and the Firm Market," *Mergers & Acquisitions* 2 (1966): 91–95. For a discussion of the Williams Act and its effects on tender offers, see Kaufman and Zacharias, "From Trust to Contract," pp. 547–60; and Davidson, *Mega-Mergers,* pp. 49–53.

[66] Anti-takeover defenses are outlined in Gaughan, *Mergers and Acquisitions,* chapt. 5 passim; and Richard S. Ruback, "An Overview of Takeover Defenses," in Auerbach, ed., *Mergers and Acquisitions,* pp. 49–67.

[67] Oliver E. Williamson, *Markets and Hierarchies, Analysis and Antitrust Implications: A Study of the Economics of Internal Organization* (New York: Free Press, 1975); and Masahiko Aoki, *The Co-operative Game Theory of the Firm* (New York: Oxford University Press, 1984).

288

stood as a nexus of contracts whose purpose was to allocate its residual income among stakeholders.[68] What these schools of research shared was the belief that the economic interests of shareholders and professional managers were poorly aligned. Although shareholders were generally presumed to be risk-averse, they preferred corporate management to pursue risky growth strategies that promised higher dividends or capital gains. This was explained by the fact that shareholders could accommodate to the high risk of particular firms by the simple expedient of maintaining diversified personal portfolios. The investment of managers in their firms, on the other hand, primarily took the form of untransferable intangibles such as perquisites and status based on firm-specific knowledge. Unlike shareholders, managers were unable to diversify their risks outside the firm and thus had a strong incentive to reduce the overall risk of the firm. This led to the deferring of dividend increases in favor of earning retention as a safety buffer against any unforeseen adversity. It encouraged the building of diversified enterprises that reduced risk and provided expanded career opportunities for management. It also induced some managements to negotiate "golden parachute" contracts, which guaranteed substantial economic benefits in the event of loss of employment because of an unfriendly takeover.[69]

By the late 1970s, a new generation of financial entrepreneurs who were knowledgeable about these ideas concerning corporate governance sought to overcome stakeholder conflicts and to promote efficiency by means of an innovative organization, the LBO. Two stages were discernible in this development. The first was the acquisition of relatively small companies. In 1980, for example, 75 percent of the mergers initiated had valuations of less than $25 million. Two catego-

---

[68] Alchian and Demsetz, "Production, Information Costs and Economic Organization"; Stephen A. Ross, "The Economic Theory of Agency: The Principal's Problem," *American Economic Review* 63 (May 1973): 134–39; Jensen and Meckling, "Theory of the Firm: Managerial Behavior, Agency Costs and Ownership Structure"; Fama, "Agency Problems and the Theory of the Firm"; Fama and Jensen, "Agency Problems and Residual Claims"; and idem, "Separation of Ownership and Control."

[69] For a review of the effects of these lines of analysis, see Kaufman and Zacharias, "From Trust to Contract," pp. 553–56; and John C. Coffee, Jr., "Shareholders versus Managers: The Strain in the Corporate Web," in Coffee et al., eds., *Knights, Raiders, and Targets,* pp. 77–134.

Table 7.2. *Ten Largest Leveraged Buyouts of the 1980s*

Acquirer	Target	Year	Price ($ Billion)
KKR	RJR Nabisco	1989	24.72
KKR	Beatrice	1986	6.25
KKR	Safeway	1986	4.24
Thompson Co.	Southland (7–11)	1987	4.00
AV Holdings	Borg–Warner	1987	3.76
Wings Holdings	NWA, Inc.	1989	3.69
KKR	Owens–Illinois	1987	3.69
TF Investments	Hospital Corp of America	1989	3.69
FH Acquisitions	Fort Howard Corp.	1988	3.59
Macy Acq. Corp.	R. H. Macy & Co.	1986	3.50

Source: A. Kaufman and E. J. Englander, "Kohlberg Kravis Roberts & Co. and the Restructuring of American Capitalism," *Business History Review* 67 (Spring 1993): 78.

ries of firms were predominant in this drive: owner-managed firms whose principals were approaching retirement and wished to liquidate their equities; and subsidiaries spun-off from larger corporations because of their disappointing performance.[70]

The second stage, that of so-called megamergers, began in the mid-1980s with the acquisition of much larger enterprises. The top twenty buyouts of the decade all occurred after 1984, the largest being the acquisition by the Kohlberg Kravis Roberts & Co. partnership of RJR Nabisco and Co. for $24.7 billion in 1989. Moreover, 4 percent of the mergers initiated in 1988 exceeded $1 billion, while the aggregate value of the smaller transactions contracted to 38 percent of the total bids tendered that year (Table 7.2).[71]

Such transactions focused on two types of merger targets. The

[70] Allen Kaufman and Ernest J. Englander, "Kohlberg Kravis Roberts & Co. and the Restructuring of American Capitalism," *Business History Review* 67 (Spring 1993): 66 and 78–79; and Scott C. Linn and Michael S. Rozeff, "The Corporate Sell-Off," in Joel M. Stern and David H. Chew, Jr., eds., *The Revolution in Corporate Finance* (New York: Basil Blackwell, 1986), pp. 428–36.
[71] Kaufman and Englander, "Kohlberg Kravis Roberts," pp. 77–79.

first was companies in industries that were adjusting to governmental deregulation or changing market conditions. Many of these mergers were friendly and provided important advantages to buyers. Enlisting the support of existing managements ensured access to the best information about the prospects of the target firm; it also helped to avoid the high costs of contested mergers. The second type was unfriendly takeovers. Although they were not numerous, they were generally takeovers of large businesses. Although only 35 of the more than 3,000 mergers launched in 1985 were hostile, their aggregate value amounted to 22 percent of the total bids for that year.[72]

One important method applied by LBO organizers to achieve superior performance was to change ownership structures. This strategy concentrated the ownership of equity in the hands of general partners and operating management, while limiting the participation of outside investors to that of creditors. Such an arrangement provided an incentive for management to increase the value of their shares by quickly paying down the substantial amounts of high coupon debt incurred to finance these mergers. General partners could augment their incomes from the fees they earned for promoting the association and for serving as monitors for external investors. Although equity was primarily an insider security, it was also acquired by some institutional investors, especially state-employee pension funds and commercial banks. Retirement funds for employees of Oregon and Washington became major holders of LBO equity in the expectation that high returns earned by these investments would close anticipated deficits. These state retirement funds were able to invest in this class of security because of their exemption from ERISA restrictions and the accommodative legislation passed by their state assemblies.[73] Leading commercial banks such as Chase Manhattan, Citicorp and Bankers Trust, who had initially been involved in LBO financing as secured creditors, became more venturesome after some of the early partnerships yielded high profits.[74]

Ownership of the large quantities of debt issued to finance the LBOs was distributed among institutional investors. Senior debt secured by liens on all corporate tangible assets was usually held by commercial

[72] Ibid., pp. 79–81.
[73] Ibid., pp. 69–73.
[74] Gaughan, *Mergers and Acquisitions*, pp. 318–20.

banks, while subordinated debentures were held by insurance companies, specialized mutual funds, and state-employee pension funds. In addition, savings and loan associations were allowed to purchase these obligations after the Garn–St. Germain legislation lifted the restrictions on the types of assets they might hold in their portfolios. In spite of its low rating, subordinated debt was attractive to many investors. Debenture holders benefited from the diligent amortization of these obligations that derived from management's holding of LBO equity. Moreover, high coupons became more attractive in the 1980s with the decline in tax and inflation rates. Some LBO organizers sought to diminish bankruptcy risk by acquiring mature companies with a strong cash flow. But in the event of failure, debenture holders could expect to receive stock for their dishonored paper and possibly a "prepackaged" reorganization that would facilitate rapid recapitalization.[75]

Besides modifying ownership structures, some LBO partnerships introduced organizational innovations intended to reduce agency costs. The experience of Kohlberg Kravis Roberts & Co. in the 1980s illustrates how this objective was achieved. The partnership controlled subsidiaries in three industries: lumber and wood products, machinery and equipment, as well as publishing and printing. Unlike the modern center firm, the partnership made no effort to integrate close operation of the component businesses. Instead, managers were encouraged to exercise a high degree of autonomy. This policy was reinforced by a general ban prohibiting the subsidization of other entities within the group by cash transfers. Monitoring costs were kept low because investors and managers jointly owned the equity of each company. The accessibility of partners to the component entities and their management obviated the need for elaborate supervisory structures. Moreover, the lack of extensive operational integration reduced the need for costly accounting services; the high degree of subsidiary autonomy avoided vexing accounting problems that had often contributed to resource misallocation in multiproduct corporations such as the development of transfer prices and the allocation of joint costs. In addition,

---

[75] Robert A. Taggart, Jr., "'Junk' Bond Market's Role in Financing Takeovers," in Auerbach, ed., *Mergers and Acquisitions*, pp. 5–24; and Gaughan, *Mergers and Acquisitions*, pp. 338–39.

informal communication channels within the group facilitated internal contracting that might be less costly than relying on external markets.[76]

The heavy issuance of junk bonds to support LBO growth had an adverse affect on the overall quality of business credit. In 1977, when the process of LBO formation was just getting under way, the total number of high-yield (read: high-risk) bond issues amounted to 26, with a total value of $908 million. In 1984, the number of issues jumped to 102, with a value of $11.6 billion. By 1986, 200 such issues were floated, with an aggregate value of $30.9 billion. For the entire period 1977–86, $71.5 billion had been raised by the sale of 741 separate high-yield bond issues having an average yield to maturity of 13.65 percent. These trends led to a worsening in corporate debt–service ratios. During the 1980s this ratio increased in stable industries from 0.15 to 0.20, while in cyclical industries the deterioration was reflected in a rise in the ratio from 0.10 to 0.15. The effects of increasing leverage is even more pronounced in the evaluation of individual firms. RJR Nabisco, the largest LBO, was financed by the issuance of $23.3 billion in debt and a mere $1.5 billion in equity securities. Similar patterns were also evident in the financing of the next twenty largest LBOs, which ranged in value from a low of $1.7 billion to a high of $6.25 billion.[77]

Market liquidity was maintained by the investment banking houses who had originally floated these securities. The leader was Drexel Burham Lambert, whose junk bond financing operations were led by Michael Milken. The growth in junk bond sales at this firm was of

---

[76] Kaufman and Englander, "Kohlberg Kravis Roberts," pp. 68–71 and 89–97; and Kaufman et al., *Managers vs. Owners,* pp. 145–52. For a more general discussion of this firm, also see George Anders, *Merchants of Debt: KKR and the Mortgaging of America* (New York: Basic, 1992); and Sarah Bartlett, *Money Machine: How KKR Manufactured Power and Profits* (New York: Warner Books, 1991).

[77] Paul Asquith, David W. Mullins, Jr., and Eric D. Wolff, "Original Issue High Yield Bonds: Aging Analysis of Defaults, Exchanges and Calls," *Journal of Finance* 44 (1989): 926–28; Kaufman and Englander, "Kohlberg Kravis Roberts," pp. 82–84. For a discussion of RJR Nabisco, see Bryan Burrough and John Helyar, *Barbarians at the Gate: The Fall of RJR Nabisco* (New York: Harper & Row, 1990).

heroic proportions: in 1981, it sold $5 billion of these securities; in 1986, this figure had increased to $40 billion.[78]

Although the 1980s was an expansive period for LBOs, several factors conjoined to slow the rise of this business form. The first was the increasing shortage of willing merger candidates, leading to a rising incidence of hostile takeovers. By the 1980s, the financing available for these ventures had grown far more than the number of potentially amicable transactions available. This scarcity of opportunities compelled many LBO specialists to adopt a more aggressive posture toward potential takeover targets; witness, for example, the unsuccessful drives of T. Boone Pickens for Gulf Oil, Sir James Goldsmith for Goodyear Tire and Carl Icahn for U.S. Steel. Although many deals aborted, they often yielded high profits for their sponsors. This might take the form of either "greenmail," wherein the target management agreed to purchase its shares from a corporate raider, or the acquisition of shares by the higher bid of a rival company.[79]

A second problem was that superior returns diminished with new entrants into these markets. Prices for potential targets were bid up by a proliferation of groups eager to undertake LBOs. In addition, hostile takeovers increased transaction costs by lengthening the acquisition period and increasing the fees spent for attorneys and other specialists. Moreover, transaction costs increased when potential targets began to mount defenses that imposed costly requirements in the event of a successful takeover.[80]

A third problem was the opposition of business and labor, whose interests were threatened by LBO growth. The Business Roundtable, for example, began in 1984 to criticize hostile takeovers. From their perspective, LBOs represented a game played by investment banking houses to extort speculative profits and high professional fees. They also argued that these actions destroyed the cooperative relationships that had previously unified stakeholders. They further contended that these contests drew management's attention away from long-term stra-

---

[78] Kaufman and Englander, "Kohlberg Kravis Roberts," p. 76; and Gaughan, *Mergers and Acquisitions,* pp. 338–39.

[79] Ibid., pp. 34–35; and idem, "The New J. P. Morgans," *Fortune* 29 (February 1988): 44.

[80] Kaufman and Englander, "Kohlberg Kravis Roberts," pp. 80–83.

tegic planning, forcing it instead to focus on short-term financial exigencies. The AFL/CIO also voiced its concerns. The labor group believed that the heavy financial burdens associated with LBOs would eventually force the layoff of workers and the reduction of employee compensation.[81]

A fourth problem was the high default rates experienced on the type of high-yield bonds that financed LBOs. Asquith, Mullins and Wolff reported a cumulative default rate of 34 percent by December 31, 1988, on high-yield bonds issued in 1977–78. The default rate on bonds issued between 1978 and 1983 amounted to 19 to 27 percent by 1988.[82] This pattern of long-term decay in asset quality was confirmed the following year by Barrie Wigmore's study.[83] These findings indicated a far more serious pattern of deterioration than that discovered in the risk and returns associated with junk bond portfolios.[84] Equally disconcerting was the implication that a lowering of credit quality held for financial market viability in the event of a prolonged economic downturn.

The drive to improve bank asset quality, brought about by the aforementioned FIRREA legislation, had a severe impact on LBO financing. A key linkage between the LBOs and banking was through the savings and loan industry's ownership of an estimated 7 percent of outstanding high-yield bonds. Moreover, this ownership was concentrated in a few institutions: only 6 of the over 2,000 savings and loans had portfolios of high-yield bonds amounting to more than 10 percent of their total assets. The problem that FIRREA posed for the savings and loans was that it required the full liquidation of these assets by

[81] Ibid., pp. 85–88; and Business Roundtable Ad Hoc Taskforce, *Analysis of the Issues in the National Industrial Policy Debate: Working Papers,* Business Roundtable, revised 15 May 1984.

[82] Asquith et al., "Original Issue High Yield Bonds," pp. 923–52.

[83] Barrie Wigmore, "The Decline in Credit Quality of Junk Bond Issues, 1980–1988" (New York: Goldman Sachs, 1989), quoted in Gaughan, *Mergers and Acquisitions,* pp. 353–55.

[84] See, e.g., Edward I. Altman and Scott A. Namacher, "The Default Rate Experience on High Yield Corporate Debt," quoted in Gaughan, *Mergers and Aquisitions,* pp. 348–51. For a more recent work that casts a more favorable light on this type of financing, see Glenn Yago, *Junk Bonds: How High Yield Securities Restructured Corporate America* (New York: Oxford University Press, 1991).

1994. This led to rapid liquidation in the attempt to avoid equity-threatening write-downs as portfolios were marked to market.[85]

The forced sale of high-yield bonds by the savings and loans had a domino effect on other financial institutions holding these assets. Soon both insurance companies and mutual funds, each of which held about 30 percent of the value of outstanding junk bonds, also began to disgorge, creating a panic that forced the savings and loans with high junk bond exposure out of business. It also overwhelmed the ability of the premier junk bond issuer, Drexel Burham Lambert, to maintain an orderly secondary market for these securities and ultimately forced this firm into receivership.[86]

Although junk bonds and LBOs had been discredited in the wake of the collapse of Drexel Burham, neither had been completely banished from the U.S. financial scene. The high-water mark was reached in 1989, when there were more than 300 LBO transactions valued at $75.8 billion. But like the conglomerates before them, in the panic they demonstrated their limitations as financial vehicles. The promise of revolutionary change brought about by this institutional innovation would henceforth evoke a more skeptical reaction by investors who experienced the sobering debacle of the junk bond market. By 1993, the number of LBO deals still exceeded 150, but their total valuation amounted only to $9.8 billion.[87]

V. Conclusion

The two questions that permeate this study of financial history must again be addressed. What light does the experience of the conglomerates and LBOs shed on theoretical constructs put forth to explain corporate finance and how did the institutional innovations of this era help to promote economic efficiency?

With respect to the first question, although the financial planning of conglomerates and LBOs was influenced by insights from several theoretical models, their heavy reliance on debt was consistent with

---

[85] Lowy, *High Rollers*, pp. 155–58.
[86] Ibid., p. 159; and Gaughan, *Mergers and Acquisitions*, pp. 390–94.
[87] See "A Kinder, Gentler Barbarian," *Economist*, 17–23 September 1994, pp. 83–84.

the predictions of the pecking order hypothesis. In untested and poorly understood ventures, the strong property rights, liquidity and ease in pricing of debt securities were features that made them more attractive to investors than equity. Debt also provided important advantages for management: the tax deductibility of interest reduced the overall cost of capital to the firm; debt markets were constantly accessible, and borrowing contracts were for fixed terms; and liability finance did not lead to changes in ownership and control.

One seeming exception to this pattern was the acquisition of small, closely held companies, acquisitions that were financed with equity in the first wave of conglomerate building. This choice of financing was largely conditioned by the IRS's business continuity rules. These regulations required the continued participation of former owners in order for conglomerates to take advantage of any acquired tax attributes such as NOLs or unused investment tax credits. Nevertheless, the exchange of lower-quality equity shares in small, closely held businesses for that of large, publicly traded conglomerates was consistent with the spirit of the pecking order hypothesis. From the perspective of former owners the key benefit was that these deals reduced the risk and increased the liquidity of equity built up over a lifetime.

Although the pecking order hypothesis predicts the progression of corporate financial preferences, it does not provide guidance with respect to either the relative weight placed on these alternative sources or the rates at which this process progressed. For example, it does not provide an answer to the question of why LBOs favored debt finance to a far greater degree than did conglomerates. Nor does it give any indication of the mechanisms that companies apply in weighing the three different sources – debt, preferred stock and common equity – in their financing mix. Moreover, since the hypothesis is diachronic it provides little insight into the factors that influence the speed with which this process advances. As we have seen in this study of conglomerates and LBO partnerships, questions of weight and rate were most responsive to the obtrusion of edge conditions that were diverse and transient. These included such matters as taxes, measurement conventions and contracting. It is these aspects of the corporate financing puzzle that seem most susceptible to traditional historical research methods stressing the uniqueness of particular events and showing how circumstances change over time. The financial system is susceptible to short-run fevers and fads that are sensitive to institutional conditions, to use Douglass North's term. Only history can cope with this. But history cannot forecast any better than financial theory can. Thus, the key question, as Charles Kindleberger and Hyman Minsky have argued, is, Does the financial system have the resilience to ride out the waves of miscalculation brought about by excessive animal spirits?

The experience of conglomerates and LBOs suggests that the scope of Modigliani and Miller's model might be fruitfully extended by analyzing the effects of a wider range of tax variables. One such revision might involve relaxing the assumption that corporate financing decisions are reached in static and closed economic environments. Instead, it could be respecified to assume that these choices were responsive to conditions in an open global economic system with a multiplicity of tax regimes. This latter approach holds promise for evaluating the differential effects on corporate finance of tax systems based on explicit rates versus those that contain substantial items of tax preference. Similarly, the model might also be modified to determine the effects that specific tax rules have on the implementation of managerial policies for enhancing efficiency. As this chapter has reported, particular requirements such as the business continuity rules may operate in ways that may hinder the achievement of higher efficiency levels through intensive coordination and control over acquired subsidiaries.

Historically, however, the recognition of the potential benefits deriving from intensive management induced some conglomerates to pursue economies of scope by restructuring around complementary businesses. This enabled them to exploit efficiencies resulting from the transference of specialized knowledge, as well as those deriving from a broader and stronger financial base. Both Paramount Communications (formerly Gulf and Western Industries) and Time Warner began to follow this pattern during the late 1980s. They tried to increase efficiency by integrating film production and distribution, publishing and cable television. The acquisition of publishing companies, for example, provided film studios with access to more literary properties, as well as the creative services of seasoned writers. The need to find profitable outlets for film productions encouraged forward integration into cable television and the video rental business. Moreover, the desire to control a broad gamut of artistic assets also induced Time Warner to maintain a leading position in the recording industry.

298

Diversification strategies among LBOs and conglomerates derived more from an understanding of the theory of portfolios than from an understanding of the growth of the firm. From the perspective of finance, the primary purpose of diversification was to reduce risk by creating portfolios whose components had negatively correlated activity coefficients. This differed from the findings of business historians who, while accepting risk reduction, stressed a high utilization of corporate resources. In this latter view, diversification was a path-directed process that sought investment opportunities by a systematic increase in firm-specific knowledge of technology or management.

Theoretical claims impinged on the second question relating to the connections between efficiency, finance and institutional innovation. Although "efficiency enhancement" had been claimed by those wishing to promote financial innovation, the definition of this term often remains obscure. In this study we consider two efficiency standards. First, efficiency could be measured by focusing on the residual earnings of the enterprise that enhance the wealth of shareholders. Alternatively, a more holistic view would include the totality of returns shared by all stakeholder groups who had claims on an enterprise's cash flow. This would include management, employees and creditors.

The conglomerates, as we have seen, were unable to exploit many of the sources of efficiency enhancement that were available to center firms. A long list of impediments to effective management explains why aggregate returns were not greatly augmented. First, the penchant for acquiring subsidiaries whose activity was negatively correlated had a leveling effect on consolidated profits: at any phase of the business cycle, income increases recorded by some members were often offset by declines registered by others. Second, conglomerates frequently controlled subsidiaries that operated in industries that had limited potential for realizing significant economies of scale. Third, economies of scope eluded many conglomerates because their subsidiaries usually did not share common technological or market bases. Moreover, tax rules deterred intensive management control over subsidiary operations. Nor were many component enterprises based in advanced technology and thereby immune from the discovery of useful products by scientific inquiry. Although some conglomerates had acquired "high-tech" companies specializing in military electronics and aircraft, the prospects of these entities were frequently poor because of declining federal defense expenditures.

Yet in spite of these problems, efficiencies were achievable through conglomerate organization. This process most benefited those companies operating in the peripheral economy that were unable because of the nature of their operations to realize economies of scale or scope. The inclusion of these units within a profitable conglomerate array generally enhanced the efficiency of finance above the level that would have prevailed had they remained independent, stand-alone operations.

Although LBO partnerships pursued efficiency by applying some of the insights deriving from scholarship in agency theory and by exploiting tax reforms, their aggregate performance was marred by a high incidence of bankruptcy. The primary beneficiaries of the restructuring of contractual relationships were share- and bondholders. The claim made by agency theory was that operating efficiency might be increased by a redefinition of contractual relationships to eliminate debilitating conflicts between stakeholders in a business enterprise. Management was motivated by holding a high proportion of equity whose value was contingent on the successful pay-down of onerous debt burdens imposed on the enterprise. The elimination of many tax preferences favoring share ownership and the reduction in tax rates in 1986 also suggested that debt might be substituted for equity as the primary source of long-term capital. This had been implied in Modigliani and Miller's first rendition of the modern theory of finance.

Many of the same factors that frustrated conglomerate growth also undermined LBO efficiency. First, high fixed-interest charges drained these entities of cash that might have financed internal investment. Second, IRS business continuity rules restricted managerial discretion in directing merged entities with substantial tax attributes. Third, many LBOs acquired subsidiaries lacking the potential for significant economies of either scale or scope.

Highly diverse product lines and extensive decentralization created barriers to effective management for both LBO partnerships and conglomerates. These circumstances increased the difficulties of allocating resources, monitoring performance and providing consulting assistance to line units. The problem was essentially one of incompetence at the center: senior managers lacked the training and experience necessary to perform these functions for disparate businesses. Although they were capable of comprehending financial activities, central office management had only a superficial understanding of the technology or marketing that shaped the long-term viability of the subsidiaries. Moreover, it would have been very costly for these enterprises to recruit the wide array of specialists necessary to provide managerial support for many dissimilar businesses.

The tendency of LBO and conglomerate managers to view their subsidiaries as portfolio investments rather than as integral components of an organic business conditioned attitudes about investment duration. This was because knowledge of subsidiary activities was best understood at the center in narrow financial terms rather than in either technological or managerial terms. Operating results, rather than technical or managerial innovations, most affected the thinking of the generalists who ran these companies. Short-term financial results were more influential in shaping decisions than were long-term advantages accruing from what often were costly and poorly understood development projects. There was a predilection for resolving poor short-term financial performance by spinning off disappointing subsidiaries. Leading investment banking houses eagerly assisted this process by the specialized services of their merger and acquisition departments.

Like conglomerates, LBOs held out the promise of financial efficiency for businesses that were incapable of achieving significant operating economies of scale or scope. But in spite of the superior returns realized by some individual ventures, their higher bankruptcy rates suggest that, overall, LBOs were less effective than conglomerate firms in exploiting these potentials.

The rhetoric about agency and efficiency also influenced the outlooks of professional money managers. Some of the larger funds, such as the California Public Employees Retirement Fund (CALPERS), abandoned their traditional policy of liquidating positions in poorly performing companies. Instead, they sought to play a more active role in their governance. The sale of poorly performing securities had become an unattractive alternative for fund managers because it implied capital losses and transaction costs. Greater activism in corporate governance, on the other hand, held out the promise of retrieving losses by the elimination of incompetent or self-serving management. By 1993, there was a crescendo of senior management replacements due partly to pressures exerted by large institutional investors. Senior executives from American Express, Eastman Kodak, IBM, General Motors and Westinghouse became casualties in the new war on corporate inefficiency. By 1994, Secretary of Labor Robert Reich exhorted managers of private pension funds to play a more direct and active role in the governance of the companies in which they invested.[88]

In addition, some corporations sensitive to the criticism of managerial opportunism in agency theory sought to make the interests of their employees much more concentric with those of shareholders by requiring them to hold substantial amounts of its stock. Such was the case beginning in 1993 when executives at both Eastman Kodak and Campbell Soup were required to hold a substantial portion of their personal wealth in the form of their company's common shares.

Although the insights derived from agency theory have shaped business organization and finance, the issues emphasized in this body of scholarship promote a view inimical to the processes that center firms have depended on for survival. The priority given to the analysis of the conflicts that divided principals and agents fosters a perception that long-term, future-directed expenditures are forms of managerial opportunism. Such activities as product innovation and research and development are characterized as being more beneficial to professional managers than to shareholders. This has led to the conclusion that there is no advantage to corporate diversification from the perspective of shareholders and that financial risk can better be reduced by diversifying personal portfolios.

But this overlooks the costly investments that center firms must continually make to improve the quality of their stocks of human capital that are crucial for maintaining competitive capacities. The danger is that the benefits that derive from this long-term process will be sacrificed by the decision to enhance in the short-run returns to finance capital. This approach places in jeopardy the ability of the business entity to exploit potential economies of scale or scope that may be realized through the internal perfection of firm-specific knowledge of management and technology. Such a policy becomes, in effect, a prescription for enterprise decay and the longer-term erosion of all stakeholder interests.

---

[88] This trend continues in spite of CALPERS's decision to take a less adversarial position with respect to poorly performing companies in its portfolio; see "Calpers Chooses a Less Adversarial Voice," *New York Times,* September 17, 1994, D, 37.

Epilogue

Two questions remain for this epilogue. First, how can the long-term environmental factors that have invigorated institutional innovation be integrated in a general statement with the traditional firm-specific financial parameters that usually inform decisions about corporate capital structure? Second, what specific patterns of environmental–institutional interaction were evident historically?

I. The Integration of Environmental and Firm-Specific Factors

Concerning the first question, it is appropriate to use the example of the capital structure problem, which has, through time, been sensitive to two sets of variables. Long-term factors have, as we have seen in this study, influenced the capital structure of firms through four dimensions of evolution: social governance structures (including bodies of law and political arrangements); communication modalities; knowledge of science and technology; and knowledge of management. These are important because they facilitate the establishment of financial institutions that enhance the capacity of corporations to concentrate capital and realize gains by reducing risk perceptions, achieving economies of scale and/or scope, overcoming market imperfections, and enabling the entity to accommodate unexpected externalities. Although the influence of these environmental elements is omnipresent, their effects are generally not central in short-run analysis and decision making because they change only over the long term, and these changes are irregular in both rate and scope. Thus, because they generally exhibit in the short run a stable rather than a dynamic character, they are rarely seen as exerting much direct or identifiable influence over financial planning decisions.

The interplay of the two sets of factors can be depicted symbolically as determinants of a firm's debt–equity ratio,

$$D/E = f(S_k; L_k) \tag{1}$$

where the S_k comprises expected growth rate (s_g), expected before tax earnings (s_p), the interest rate (s_i), the tax rate (s_t), the earnings retention rate (s_r) and management's risk preference (s_{mrp}); and the L_k comprises the previously noted social governance structures (l_{sgs}), communication modalities (l_{cm}), knowledge of science and technology (l_{kst}) and knowledge of management (l_{km}). There are two levels of interaction. The roles of S_k are determined by the regnant static values of the L_k, and these remain constant in the absence of any change in the L_k. The role of institutions is passive. When the values or functional forms of the L_k are different, as in international comparisons, or change, as in intertemporal or dynamic analysis, the values of the S_k cannot be given their historical values or functional forms. During a period of change, a new set of institutions will evolve, and with it, a new form of financial organization will provide the firm with a competitive advantage.

If the values and/or functional forms of the set of L_k variables remain stable over time (or move so imperceptibly that the S_k can adapt gradually), the firm-specific financial variables are the only ones that are relevant:

$$D/E = g(s_g, s_p, s_i, s_t, s_r, s_{mrp}) \tag{2}$$

This is the perspective from which financial planning problems are usually analyzed. It provides an adequate specification of the problem, provided that the longer-term environmental factors do not change in ways that significantly alter corporate economic circumstances.

However, if environmental factors prove to be dynamic in the short run, the solution provided in equation (2) will prove inadequate on two counts. First, the range of variables included in the function will be incomplete, and second, the arguments run the risk of being improperly specified. This latter point can be illustrated by reference to two hypothetical examples. Consider, for example, the effect on a multinational corporation that the takeover of a foreign host government by an extreme, xenophobic socialist party would have on expected before-tax profits and on management's preferences for risk. Since political risk conditions may be expected to change more rapidly than the financial environment, these variables are important concerns. Or, alternatively, consider how the same firm-specific variables would shift if the multinational's research department discovered an effective cure for cancer. In this case, security pricing becomes highly problematic because of the uncertainty that permeates attempts to form accurate estimates of future income streams.

II. Patterns of Environmental–Institutional Interaction

Although the range of possible responses for each environmental category was diverse, there was, nevertheless, a fundamental core of unifying elements. In virtually all cases the changes in environmental circumstances represented a disruption of a system of economic relationships that had previously been at equilibrium. The introduction of such a shock often created multiple opportunities for business organizations to capture gains and to stabilize their finances by reordering their institutional arrangements in ways that facilitated adjustment to changes in long-term environmental factors.

Social governance structures were, for example, important because they could be effective in surmounting perceptions of risk by ensuring a more stable environment for conducting business affairs and in providing a system for the protection of property rights. Historically, this has had three aspects. The first element was the establishment of a political order that was effective in maintaining the social tranquility essential for fostering economic growth. Wars and civil disturbances were dangerous from an economic perspective because they led to the wasting of scarce resources, which limited society's ability to increase its surplus. On the firm level these developments were often deleterious because they could disrupt the stable environment that is necessary for complex business enterprises to develop and implement their managerial capacities. The failure of the Medici Bank, for example, coincided with the collapse of the Florentine republic. On the other hand, the centuries-old position of both London and New York as a safe haven for flight capital was largely due to the long-term political and social stability of Britain and the United States in modern history.

Another dimension of social governance involved the definition of property rights and commercial law conventions that provided security for parties to business contracts. Many of these were crucial to the development of markets that provided liquidity for portfolios and served as a pricing mechanism for investment securities. Such was the effect of the legal and political reforms of the Glorious Revolution of 1688 in England, which contributed to the rise of the London Stock Exchange. A more recent example was the establishment of the regulatory regimes brought into being by the securities acts in the United States during the 1930s, which protected investors against inadequate corporate disclosure and the incompetence or malfeasance of corporate managers and financial market professionals.

A third aspect of social governance structures that was significant in this study of corporate finance related to the contractual arrangements between investors and the business entity. Financial contracts were crucial in defining the rights of investors to corporate cash flows and also in overcoming the risks associated with the asymmetric distribution of information about the firm. Investor preferences for debt contracts was strongest when access to information about the enterprise was limited and unreliable. Consequently, debt predominated as the primary source of external capital through the nineteenth century. Investors could adapt to the uncertainties during these early, poorly informed periods only if their financing contracts granted them creditor status, thus guaranteeing fixed terms and interest payments. Such features also facilitated valuation and enhanced liquidity.

Equity contracts, on the other hand, were more suitable for insiders with better knowledge of the firm, such as managers and promoters, who were yet often reluctant to finance by this means because it could lead to unfavorable shifts in control. This was the general pattern throughout the preindustrial era, as manifested by such dissimilar enterprises as the Medici Bank, the East India Company and the early railroads. Moreover, with the evolution of business law, other advantages accrued to corporations issuing equity, including easy transfer of ownership without disruptive liquidation and limited investor liability in bankruptcy.

When there was a dearth of business knowledge, the scope of equity broadened slightly because of its potential for both speculation and superior contracting. Equity served those wishing to bet on impending changes, such as trading fleet arrivals in the seventeenth century or the conclusion of railroad rate wars in the nineteenth century. Equity was also used by the Medici Bank and the East India Company for forging alliances with political leaders, creditors and customers. It even became a substitute for bonds when it took on debtlike characteristics: witness, for example, the rise of preferred stock to reduce leverage in the railroad reorganizations of the 1890s.

Another long-term innovation that had far-reaching effects on corporate finance was the improvement of communication modalities. Although the advancement of communication capacities was a logical subcomponent of scientific and technological knowledge, its overall impact has been so great on finance that it is treated as a separate environmental category in this analysis. In the case of financial markets, greater accessibility to current and reliable information about economic events bolstered efficiency and reduced risk perceptions. A greater abundance of useful business intelligence and market data increased the confidence of market participants for estimating risk and for pricing securities. In addition, stronger information flows increased both the number of opportunities for profitable transacting and the volume of trading activity, a combination that often led to a reduction in transaction costs.

The emergence of a vastly improved cognitive base for the modern corporation made possible the wider public holding of equity securities in the twentieth century. The proliferation of channels for transmitting information about corporate affairs helped to diminish the asymmetries that had long undermined the attractiveness of equity investment. Moreover, this class of security was inherently more difficult to evaluate than bonds because it required more abundant and precise financial data. The determination of what income accrued to shareholders was a daunting task for giant organizations with complex and widely dispersed operations. Analytical capacities improved when governmental, professional and business groups gradually established new channels for communicating higher-quality corporate information. The consequent problem of interpretation also provided an opportunity for new professions, such as financial analysts, to apply specialized skills to assist investors.

The enhancement of managerial capacities through improved communications also made possible the concentration of great amounts of financial capital in business enterprises of great scale and scope. Witness, for example, how vital effective communication was to the growth of center firms; consider also the competitive advantages that derived from the rudimentary information networks that supported the activities of the Medici Bank and the English East India Company. Moreover, improved communications could often overcome serious market imperfections. The realization of the efficiency potentials of the nineteenth century railroads was dependent on the telegraph, which made possible the effective coordination of line traffic flows. Finally, strong communications also strengthened firm responsiveness to sudden external developments. One such example was the legendary advantage gained by Baron Rothschild when he profitably adjusted his portfolio on receiving advance knowledge via carrier pigeon of Wellington's victory at Waterloo.

The third environmental factor affecting the development of corporate financial institutions was the increase in the stock of scientific knowledge. Many of these advances were exogenous and thus provided potential opportunities for all firms to capitalize on change. One such development was the improvement in navigation techniques and geographic knowledge, which, by opening a new Atlantic trade route to Asia during the fifteenth century, overcame a serious market impediment for European consumers of spices. Another example was the perfection of new fuel sources – coal, petroleum, nuclear – which made possible the achievement of economies of scale in industry and the surmounting of transportation market imperfections.

The economies of scale and scope deriving from increases in scientific knowledge have also often been firm specific. Knowledge developed through internal research activities could be made proprietary by means of patent law. Improvements in process technology were an important source of economies of scale. The achievement of John D. Rockefeller derived in important measure from the recognition of the dramatic cost savings that could be realized by increasing the size and throughput of the Standard Oil Company's refineries. Economies of scope, on the other hand, were also made possible by the development of new products from a firm's basic technological expertise. This was especially important for firms based in flexible technologies, because it provided the opportunity to continually develop new markets through the invention of new products. Such a strategy has been fundamental during the twentieth century in high-tech industries.

The fourth factor affecting the corporate financial environment was knowledge of management. Superior management could contribute to the augmentation of corporate wealth by strengthening enterprise competitiveness. For example, managerial acumen enabled some companies to reduce transaction costs by internalizing functions that were poorly performed by market structures. This knowledge was also instrumental in devising strategies to reduce risk perceptions, strategies such as diversifying product lines or building market power through horizontal integration. Moreover, management knowledge was central to the formulation of strategies and structures for achieving economies of scale or scope.

Management capacities, however, were not evenly distributed among corporate entities. During the contemporary era there were four major classes of business organizations with different potentials for enhancing their competitiveness through the application of managerial knowledge. These differences also influenced the range of financing options open to them.

The first category was that of the center firm, which sought economies of scale and scope by exploiting specialized knowledge of management or technology. Because of their strong market position, these firms tended to finance their activities primarily through retained earnings and debt. Equity was generally abjured because it raised uncertainties about management's status by changing the patterns of corporate ownership. Thus, when equity was utilized it was often interpreted as a signal of poor financial planning.

Historically, firms of this caliber have often successfully confronted the imperatives implicit in both short- and long-term variables through a path-dependent process of institutional development. In these cases the adjustment of firm activities generally derived from the assessment of factors that in the past had been effective in achieving stability and in promoting competitiveness and growth. This learning guided the advance of financial and managerial practices at progressive firms in two ways. Shorter-term goals were pursued partly by defining administrative procedures for the execution of routine, recurring transactions; they were also served by establishing managerial hierarchies for coordinating and controlling the integration of finance with other staff and operating functions. Longer-term priorities, on the other hand, derived from strategic thinking about how the firm's investment in financial, real and human resources could be best allocated to accommodate future changes in the business environment.

The second class, the conglomerate, was a hybrid of the traditional center firm. Conglomerates were usually formed by drawing together dissimilar peripheral firms incapable of achieving significant economies of scale or scope on their own. The primary advantages accruing to the conglomerates was risk reduction through diversification and greater efficiency in finance. Although failure rates were low, their ability to achieve superior earnings without resort to flexible accounting was limited.

The third class, LBOs of the 1980s, on the other hand, represented a radical departure from the theory of corporate governance that supported center and conglomerate firms. Efficiency was pursued by eliminating costly conflicts between stakeholders through modification of the partnership and by providing incentives for effective management through leveraged financing. The primary shortcoming of these entities, however, was their relatively high level of deteriorating credit quality and default risk.

The fourth type of entity, which was not central to this analysis because of the limited scale and scope of its operations, was the "representative firm" described by Alfred Marshall. This was the small company that contracted according to events and its efficiency. It was not an important phenomenon in the capital markets, and intermediation did not work well for it. This type of enterprise raised capital by borrowing through bank loans and mortgages on its equipment and by plowing back profits. The closest that this study came to evaluating the practices of such a class of businesses was in the discussion of the medieval firm.

In these and other ways, institutions have influenced the development of corporate finance. Their role has been critical in understanding how business enterprises have responded to flux in the longer-term factors that shape the environment of business. Their significance to economic analysis will grow as the pace of future social change continues to accelerate and as variables that have traditionally been considered relevant in the long term begin to assume a shorter-term character. Moreover, such a broad-based approach holds promise for achieving the profitable blending of statistics and history that John N. Keynes and Joseph Schumpeter had thought was the essence of sound economic inquiry.

Finance and Informational Asymmetries
in the Ancient World

This appendix describes how businesses in ancient civilizations adjusted to the problems of financial risk. As in the medieval period, the greatest accumulations of wealth derived primarily from agriculture and trade. But the organizational innovations that bolstered the scale and scope of leading Italian business enterprises in the Middle Ages were lacking during antiquity. Instead, the largest and most important organizations during these early times were those of government. The following three sections identify several important institutions that were developed to reduce risk and increase the efficiency of financial transacting in the Babylonian, Greek and Roman periods.

I. Babylonian Beginnings

Babylonian civilization contributed three fundamental notions to the advancement of finance: (1) control of usury by interest-rate ceilings, (2) fixed-income obligations and defining the rights of creditors and (3) mortgage lending secured by liens on a wide array of chattels.

Economic surpluses created by irrigation agriculture provided a florescence of banking and commerce. By about 1800 B.C. the Code of Hammurabi began to formalize business and financial relationships regulating landownership and rental, agricultural employment, commercial transactions and loan contracts. In farming regions, grain, particularly barley, served as a medium of exchange. In urban centers, however, merchants both transacted and maintained their accounts using silver weights. Liquidity was enhanced through the maintenance

313

of silver deposits at temples. Exchanges were evidenced at these locations through symbolic transfers of ownership.[1]

The Code also standardized lending arrangements. For example, to be enforceable, all debt contracts had to be drawn up in the presence of an official witness. The law was also sensitive to the problem of usury. It stipulated a rate maximum of 20 percent on silver-based loans and 33.3 percent on grain loans. The differential was partly explainable by the lower grain prices that often prevailed at harvesttime when these loans matured. The higher grain-based rate was also due to the moratorium on interest and principle payments mandated in the event of crop failure.[2]

Debt financing seems to have flourished because it was more effective in protecting investors against risk than partnerships were. A fixed-income obligation insulates an external investor from the underlying risks of the firm more effectively than does an equity in a partnership. The decision to lend generally depends on the merchant's assessment of whether the likely yield is sufficient to pay interest and principle. In a partnership, on the other hand, the merchant must ascertain the farmer's proficiency, the land's fertility and likely future weather patterns. The merchant also requires an effective means for guaranteeing honesty in measuring the true crop yield. There is, moreover, the problem of motivating the farmer, who recognizes that a portion of his output accrues to an inactive coventurer.

The riskiness of lending was further reduced by the extensive use of mortgage clauses in debt contracts.[3] For example, a lender had fewer concerns about the farming or business competence of a borrower when the loan was secured by a lien on more valuable property. Even questions about borrower integrity became less worrisome if loans were secured by real estate or by valuables deposited with the creditor. The Code allowed farmland, houses, slaves, concubines, wives and children to be hypothecated as security. Thus, these arrangements encouraged lending beyond closely knit kinship groups as well as the growth of impersonal markets for credit.[4]

---

[1] C. H. W. Johns, *Babylonian and Assyrian Laws and Letters* (New York: Scribners, 1904), pp. 15–21 and 211.
[2] Homer and Sylla, *A History of Interest Rates,* pp. 25–31 passim.
[3] L. Delaporte, *Mesopotamia* (New York: Knopf, 1925), p. 129.
[4] Ibid., p. 133.

In addition to debt, Babylonian business was financed by equity investments in partnerships. This form was useful in managing complex business affairs requiring travel for coordinating activities in distant lands. In these situations a single partner had the power of attorney to contract for his firm. A primitive postal system provided a vital communications link in ordering these affairs. Concerns about partner probity were handled by maintaining arrangements under tight control. Thus, partnerships were often liquidated annually and profits were usually distributed under legal supervision.[5]

These ideas and practices had an important impact on commercial life in ancient Greece. As we shall see in the following section, the experience of Athens and the other Aegean city-states can best be characterized as an extension of, rather than a departure from, the patterns of finance pioneered in adjacent regions in the Eastern Mediterranean and Near East.

II. Finance in Athens and Ancient Greece

Three developments distinguished the unique contributions of the ancient Greeks to the advancement of finance: (1) coinage as a medium of exchange and a store of value, (2) asset-based banking and the perfection of bills of exchange to finance foreign commerce and (3) new forms of public finance to underwrite the costs of protecting vital interests such as overseas trade and colonies.

Coinage originated between Greece and Assyria around 700 B.C.[6] According to Herodotus, the Lydians "were the first nation to introduce the use of gold and silver coin, and the first who sold goods by retail."[7] Modern archaeological findings confirm this claim. Gradually, this innovation spread to Greece and Mediterranean colonies.

Coinage in turn facilitated the rise of deposit banking and commercial lending. Three factors were influential: (1) a need to serve a highly decentralized and far-flung maritime trading economy, partially accommodated by money changers who accepted coin deposits to

[5] Johns, *Babylonia and Assyrian Laws and Letters,* pp. 287–94.
[6] A. R. Burns, *Money and Monetary Policy in Early Times,* reprint ed. (New York: Kelley, 1927, 1965), pp. 39–47.
[7] Herodotus, *The History of Herodotus,* 2 vols., reprint ed. (London: Dent, 1945), vol. 1, p. 50.

fund bills of exchange drawn on correspondents in distant cities (a safer and more convenient manner of transferring wealth than the cumbersome alternative of shipping bags of coins), (2) the need for secure places to deposit cash and other valuables and (3) large agglomerations of capital held in trust for extended periods, which also provided money changers with the opportunity to increase their profits by making loans.

After successfully resisting subjugation by the Persian Empire during the fifth century B.C., Athens emerged as the financial center of the Aegean. Athenian banks were organized either as proprietorships or as partnerships. Because bankers risked their own capital, they employed conservative lending policies. Loans were, for example, usually collateralized by liens on valuable property:

We hear of loans on various kinds of security. To take one or two instances that come to hand, money is loaned by a bank on a merchant vessel and the slaves who constitute her crew, on a mining plant and slaves, on the endorsement of another patron of the bank, in pledge; and finally, we have instances of unsecured loans, protected by the personal credit of the borrower. The great bulk of the money, however, seems to have been secured by first mortgages on real property, for example, farms, dwellings, and apartment houses.[8]

The structuring of sea loans, or "bottomry," provides an example of how the problems of information and agency relationships were addressed in Greek finance.[9] These arrangements were set up to minimize investors' information requirements. A boat's hull and/or its cargo secured these loans. Because creditor claims were extinguishable in the event of shipwreck, lenders were also implicit insurers of these ventures. Consequently, these arrangements were unlikely to influence merchant behavior materially.

But if the loans had lacked the cancellation provision, the lenders'

---

[8] George M. Calhoun, *The Business Life of Ancient Athens* (Chicago: University of Chicago Press, 1926), pp. 102–103. See also the discussion in Paul Millet, *Lending and Borrowing in Ancient Athens* (Cambridge University Press, 1991), pp. 197–217 passim.

[9] Calhoun, *Business Life of Ancient Athens,* p. 103, argues against the traditional view that these were common types of contracts.

316

information requirements would have changed significantly. In this latter hypothetical situation, the risk of shipwreck default would have been shifted to the merchant, and voyage financiers would have confronted the daunting and probably impossible task of gathering accurate information about the financial viability of participating merchants.

Nor could additional information ensure greater security to investors in other agency relationships in these ventures. The fear of violent death, for example, served as a strong incentive for ship captains to operate in a cautious manner. Moreover, the randomness of losses to piracy or storms was independent of the unique characteristics of particular ships or crews.

Concerns about both political risk and the role of agents also limited the development of public finance.[10] In this primitive economy the ability to float loans to fund risky ventures such as wars was limited. Many cities provided for these contests by laying away in advance treasure troves of jewels and precious metals. In fact, the "borrowing" that several city-states engaged in during the second and third centuries B.C. was not based on free contract. Rather it constituted either compulsory assessments imposed on local citizens or accommodations made to friendly powers. Loans in these cases, however, were secured by claims on state-owned property.

But even in less tumultuous times, investor concerns about the riskiness of all types of governmental enterprises compelled civic leaders to raise funds through either the sale or the leasing of valuable assets. Thus, it was common for particular states to resort to such expedients as selling the rights to farm particular taxes, monopolizing particular trades or controlling foreign commerce. In some instances governments resorted to dealing in real estate and even in honorific titles.

As we shall see in the following section, the Greek refinements of Near Eastern financial innovations had a lasting impact on Western economic development. Greek traditions continued to be influential

---

[10] A. M. Andreades, *A History of Greek Public Finance* (Cambridge, Mass.: Harvard University Press, 1933), pp. 168–75; and Millet, *Lending and Borrowing in Ancient Athens*, pp. 188–96.

primarily because of their incorporation by the Romans into their institutional and legal frameworks for ordering commercial life.

III. Finance in the Roman Empire

The political unification of Western Europe and the eastern Mediterranean within the Roman Empire exerted a positive influence on commerce and finance. Regional and local barriers to trade were obliterated. Trade and travel grew, while piracy was reduced and the seas became safer. The construction of vast road networks connecting the Empire's burgeoning commercial centers also accentuated these trends. Moreover, the standardization of law and the creation of viable state administrative capacities strengthened Roman finance. Law became more formalized and predictable, and its sanctions could be effectively enforced by a well-organized government bureaucracy. In this environment more complex contractual relationships could be developed than had hitherto been possible.[11]

A comparison of Roman interest rates with those of other epochs evidences the favorable financial effects of these conditions. Rates in Italy were about 4 percent at the beginning of the Empire. They were somewhat higher (about 8 to 12 percent) in the provinces that were far from the imperial financial centers, comparing favorably, however, to loans in primitive societies, where rates often exceeded 100 percent.[12] In Babylonia rates from Hammurabi to the Assyrians were only occasionally as low as 10 percent. In Athens after the initial defeat of the Persians, rates fell to about 8 percent, and remained near that level through the ascendancy of Alexander. After the decline of Rome, on the other hand, interest rates in Western Europe remained somewhat higher until the sixteenth century and the advent of the modern world.

Although Roman law was developed by the time of the Republic to the point where corporations could be formed, they were largely limited in function to assisting the state to raise revenue. These organizations specialized either in farming taxes or in operating public property

[11] Calhoun, *Business Life of Ancient Athens*, pp. 130–31.
[12] Homer and Sylla, *History of Interest Rates*, p. 61.

such as mines or saltworks. They also existed for limited terms, generally being formed at the time of each census. Although viewed as more speculative than investments in either land or mortgages, a ready market emerged near the Temple of Castor in Rome to trade *particulae,* or shares in these enterprises.[13]

The sale of equity in revenue-gathering activities enabled Roman officials to overcome limitations inherent in their system of administrative control. Reliance on public officials earning fixed incomes would have led to serious problems in tax collection. Such a system would have required more rigid regulatory controls including more reliable accounting and economic information than was available during this period. Moreover, success depended on how effectively the collector exercised his discretion in dealing with taxpayers. In these circumstances dependence on salaried officials for administration encouraged indifference or fraud. But by entrusting this function, instead, to profit-seeking entrepreneurs, the Roman government at least provided a strong incentive for efficiency and diligence.[14]

The favorable motivational effects of selling equity in state revenue collection activities, however, had limitations. Although it worked well during prosperous periods, this system's narrow emphasis on collection created social stress during economic downturns. This became apparent during the Empire's declining years. A long-lasting depression and relentlessly heavy taxation to finance the defense of the beleaguered Empire encouraged many citizens to abandon farms and trades. Frustrated by the consequent inability to raise sufficient revenues, Diocletian responded by freezing most Romans in their particular vocational categories. Although this drastic measure failed to cure Rome's economic ills, it contributed to the rise of the static social hierarchy characteristic of the subsequent medieval period.[15]

---

[13] Tenney Frank, *An Economic History of Rome,* 2nd ed. (Baltimore: Johns Hopkins University Press, 1927), p. 194; and M. I. Rostovtsev, *The Social and Economic History of the Roman Empire* (Oxford: Oxford University Press, 1926), p. 31.

[14] Frank, *Economic History of Rome,* pp. 286–87; and Rostovtsev, *Social and Economic History of the Roman Empire,* p. 145.

[15] Previté-Orton, *Shorter Cambridge Medieval History,* pp. 15–20 and 21–24; Luzzatto, *Economic History of Italy,* pp. 9–10; and LaMonte, *World of the Middle Ages,* pp. 8–10 and 14–19.

The Roman state, however, eschewed loan finance until the declining years of the Empire, probably because future tax revenues were routinely sold to tax farmers. Any borrowing would necessarily have been unsecured and thus difficult to float on a voluntary basis. In fact, subscriptions to public loans were eventually made compulsory during the crises of the later Empire.

Private finance, on the other hand, was more primitive. Business was usually conducted through partnerships, which enjoyed few special privileges under Roman law. With the exception of the previously noted quasi-public enterprises for revenue collection, there were no markets for private securities. Individual businesses depended heavily on the equity investments of their principals. For most firms, debt was the only source of external funds. This was, however, often limited by the personal credit of the owners and their mortgageable assets. The cumbersomeness of borrowing procedures also evidenced the immaturity of Roman commercial credit markets. These were highly ritualized affairs dependent on oral contracts verified by official witnesses.[16]

But these developments failed to fuel the sort of economic takeoff that might conceivably have afforded the resources necessary to save the Empire from its ultimate collapse at the hands of barbarian invaders. The Romans' achievements had been primarily military and administrative. They had failed to innovate in either technology or management and thus did not produce large economic surpluses. Consequently, agriculture usually operated near the subsistence level and provided only a narrow margin of protection from dislocations brought about by war or inclement weather. Industry and the crafts were also inefficient, having benefited neither from mechanization nor from any broadening of scale and scope of operations. Finally, an underdeveloped financial and credit system did little to stimulate output.[17]

The lack of resilience of the imperial economy ultimately proved fatal during the fourth and fifth centuries. The military requirements of defending against barbarian encroachment placed a heavy tax burden for money and labor on the citizenry. War casualties depleted the population. So too did famines from lost agricultural output brought

[16] Usher, *History of Deposit Banking,* pp. 33–49 passim.
[17] Luzzatto, *Economic History of Europe,* pp. 1–13; and Lopez, *Commercial Revolution of the Middle Ages,* pp. 1–26 passim.

about by the ravages of war. Finally, sudden and unexpected weather "pulses" or shifts also compounded the problems of lost agricultural productivity and declining population.

The demise of imperial Rome impeded the immediate future development of Western Europe's economy. Rampant political and social chaos accelerated economic decay. It was not until the tenth century that conditions were again ripe for recovery. But the medieval revival contained the seeds for a millennium of gradual progress that radically transformed human history.

APPENDIX B

International Patterns of Corporate Governance

Corporate finance has been influenced by two distinct patterns of governance in the world's leading securities markets. At one end of the spectrum are the similar systems that have emerged in the United States and the United Kingdom and are characterized by freely competitive markets, transparency in corporate affairs and regulatory structure to protect investors from the incompetency or dishonesty of agents. These are quite different from the uninformative, opaque regimes of Japan and Germany, where powerful private and/or governmental institutions dominate local markets through informal, cooperative relationships.[1]

Reliable information strengthens the Anglo-American financial markets, facilitating the pricing of securities and thereby enabling the market to allocate capital efficiently. In addition, it augments economic growth by increasing opportunities for profitable transacting by investors.

Complementary monitoring patterns – one professional and the other governmental – provide assurances in the Anglo-American markets of the reliability and currency of corporate information. The agencies were originally limited to boards of directors, public accountants, attorneys, investment bankers and other professionals whose scope of fiduciary responsibility derived largely from a path-dependent process involving legal precedents. The state later provided a second level of monitoring, which also reinforced the position of professional groups.

[1] For an excellent discussion of these issues, see Ingo Walter, *The Battle of the Systems: Control of Enterprises and the Global Economy* (Kiel: Institut für Weltwirtschaft, 1993).

In Britain the connection to government was initially defined in various companies acts that mandated filing corporate financial statements with the Board of Trade (now the Department of Industry and Trade). Before 1986, regulation of the share market remained largely in the hands of the Stock Exchange, attorneys, accountants and other professional groups. In a highly homogeneous society like Britain, such an informal system worked relatively well because of a more general willingness of the public to defer to the judgments of respected professionals. Moreover, the authority of practitioners was further reinforced by strong laws prohibiting libel. For example, shareholders who lost suits brought against professionals could in turn be sued for defamation.

In response to the "big bang" that made British financial markets more open to international competition, the Financial Services Act of 1987 established the Securities Investment Board (SIB) to support the traditional self-regulatory system of governance. The SIB monitored the activities of a host of self-regulatory organizations such as the Institute of Chartered Accountants of England and Wales, whose activities were vital for the efficient functioning of the financial markets. The SIB basically required professional groups to enforce meaningful codes of professional conduct, as well as qualifying standards to certify practitioner competency. Although the SIB had the power to intervene in special cases, the individual self-regulatory organizations remained the primary focal point for professional governance. In addition, the Financial Services Act delegates authority for banking and public debt markets to the Bank of England and mergers to the Takeover Panel.[2]

Although similar to British practices in many respects, corporate regulation in the United States differs to the extent that government's role is far more pervasive and direct. Federal securities law enables investors to sue for damages in cases of agent malfeasance. Federal sanctions also provide professionals with leverage to countervail the improper intentions of aggressive clients. Finally, public perceptions that investors have not been protected might induce Congress to au-

[2] Michael J. Mumford, *Corporate Governance and the Cadbury Report* (Lancaster: University of Lancaster); William Kay, *The Big Bang: An Investor's Guide to the Changing City* (London: Weidenfeld & Nicolson, 1986); Ian M. Kerr, *Big Bang* (London: Euromoney Publications, 1986); and W. A. Thomas, *The Big Bang* (Deddington: Philip Allan, 1986).

thorize more active intervention by federal agencies. The threat of such governmental encroachment on professional prerogatives provides a strong incentive for due diligence in practice.[3]

In both Germany and Japan, post–World War II prosperity came initially from the expansion of the industrial rather than the financial sector. Consequently, their financial institutions remain less developed than those in Britain or the United States. The information systems that support corporate governance are calculated to satisfy a few dominant banking institutions rather than a broad, anonymous universe of investors.

At the center of the German governance system are the leading banks (*Hausbanks*). The state's role is peripheral, being confined to the limited securities legislation passed by regional assemblies (*Lander*). The banks' dominance in finance derives in part from their ownership of substantial blocks of equity in both large and medium-sized public companies. In addition, trust departments of banks serve as intermediaries for investors who wish to maintain share portfolios. Moreover, because of the sparsity of information about corporate affairs and the thinness of equity market volume, few Germans own shares directly, preferring instead the less risky debt of public entities.

The governance process is informed by two channels of corporate information. The more important one, from the perspective of the leading banks, is informal and privileged: information is transferred through interlocking directorates and reports rendered by specialized trustees or agents (*Treuhander*), who are engaged by the banks to monitor client business activities.[4] The second channel is public, but less useful because of the underdeveloped state of German financial reporting. Financial statements issued by public companies are certified by a second category of professional agents, the *Wirtschaftsprüfer*, roughly equivalent to Anglo-American public accountants.[5]

---

[3] Miranti, *Accountancy Comes of Age*, chaps. 8–9 passim.

[4] For origins of *Treuhand* companies, see David F. Lindenfeld, "The Professionalization of Applied Economics: German Counterparts to Business Administration," in Geoffrey Cocks and Konrad H. Jaurausch, eds., *German Professions, 1800–1950* (New York: Oxford University Press, 1990), pp. 222–23; and Robert R. Locke, *The End of the Practical Man: Entrepreneurship and Higher Education in Germany, France and Great Britain, 1880–1940* (Greenwich, Conn.: JAI Press, 1984), pp. 260–67.

[5] Walter, *Battle of the Systems*, pp. 17–23.

Although the leading banks also play a key role in Japanese finance, the relationship between these organizations and corporations and government differs from that of Germany. Japanese banks are the central elements in *keiretsu,* consortia of firms drawn together by cross-ownership of equity and by supplier relationships. Japanese banks not only maintain investment positions; they play a key role in the financial planning of the affiliated companies. The primary informational linkages are informal and private. They include communication through interlocking directorates and through the coordination of business plans of the group. As in Germany, relatively few investors are direct owners of equity because of the thin share float and the sparsity of reliable information about corporate affairs.

However, government plays a much more active role in guiding corporate policies in Japan than in Germany. The Ministry of Finance (MOF) is the primary contact point between the government and the leading banks. Although information channels are often informal, they can also be highly effective. Recall the MOF's achievement in mobilizing Japanese financial institutions in stanching the October 1987 stock market decline.[6]

The open Anglo-American markets are more conducive to innovation in finance. It is unlikely that either LBOs or conglomerates could have arisen in the German or Japanese markets because banks, the nucleus of economic interest, are held together by shareholding and by interlocking directorates. It is difficult for outsiders to acquire control of companies that are part of these broad groups. Witness, for example, the frustration encountered by U.S. investor T. Boone Pickens in his unsuccessful attempt at a hostile takeover of one of Toyota's main suppliers.[7]

---

[6] Ibid., pp. 11–16. For a fuller discussion of Japanese administrative practices in international trade, see M. Y. Yoshino and Thomas B. Lifson, *The Invisible Link: Japan's Sogo Shosha and the Organization of Trade* (Cambridge, Mass.: MIT Press, 1986). For Japanese finance, see Eisake Sakakibara and Robert Alan Feldman, "The Japanese Financial System in Comparative Perspective," in Edwin J. Elton and Martin J. Gruber, eds., *Japanese Capital Markets: Analysis and Characteristics of Equity, Debt and Financial Futures Markets* (New York: Harper & Row, 1990), pp. 27–54; and James E. Holder and Adrian E. Tschoegl, "Some Aspects of Japanese Corporate Financing," in ibid., pp. 57–80.

[7] W. Carl Kester, *Japanese Takeovers: The Global Contest for Corporate Con-*

Ironically, Anglo-American receptivity to financial innovation creates an unfavorable environment for long-term internal investment.
The emphasis on maximizing investor returns by conglomerates and
LBOs reflects the prevailing climate. Strong pressure for the growth of
earnings induces managers to prefer projects that promise short-term
payoffs. Long-term developments are inherently unattractive because
delayed payoffs often seem like evidence of managerial opportunism
or incompetence. Although this perspective has been perceived as an
impediment to long-term investing, a recent study by the McKinsey
Global Institute argues that it is one important factor explaining the
much higher level of capital productivity (defined as the value of
output produced by a dollar's worth of capital input) in the United
States as compared with either Germany or Japan. According to this
study American corporate managers are more discriminating in their
selection of capital investment projects because of the stronger pressures exerted by investors for superior financial performance.[8]

On the other hand, governance practices in Germany and Japan do
not produce a bias in favor of short-term investment since corporations there are not under intense shareholder pressure to maximize
returns. The Germans and Japanese are more willing to tolerate long-
term investment horizons because of the close integration of the interests of management, debt holders and equity investors. The most
important investors are the leading banking institutions, which, besides being well informed about affiliates, function effectively as coventurers. Such circumstances enable managements to consider the
merits of long-term development projects with little worry about losing control over the entity.

In addition, the greater tolerance for the concentration of political
and economic power that exists in Germany and Japan influences the
costs of financial governance.[9] These national systems that are closely

trol (Boston: Harvard Business School Press, 1991), pp. 254–60; and Walter,
Battle of the Systems, pp. 15–16.

[8] The findings of the McKinsey Global Institute study, "Capital Productivity"
(Washington, D.C., 1996), are reported in "America's Fantastic Factories,"
Economist, June 8, 1996, pp. 19-20; and "America's Power Plants," ibid., p.
82.

[9] H. Peter Gray, "The Influence of Financial Intermediaries and International
Competitiveness," *Weltwirtschaftliches Archiv* 130 (December 1994): 828–
40.

controlled by insiders have tended to devote fewer resources to the governance process than the outsider system that prevails in the Anglo-American economies. This seeming advantage, however, can be a drawback when trying to attract substantial amounts of foreign capital to domestic financial markets.

The lack of transparency and prevailing patterns of governance weaken the attempts in Germany and Japan to transform their local markets into major centers of international capital. For example, it is difficult for outsiders to gather sufficient data to analyze corporate performance. This makes the accurate valuation of securities more difficult, which in turn encourages speculation based on rumors and inaccurate projections. Foreigners are reluctant to risk their capital, fearing insider trading on privileged information. There is also evidence of discrimination in favor of the larger clients of local brokerage houses. This was most prevalent in Japan, where important customers were reimbursed for trading losses on the Tokyo exchange in the 1980s. Finally, rules inhibiting corporate control by foreigners are a barrier to the free international flow of capital. These restrictions invite retaliatory actions by trading partners who follow more liberal policies.

Patterns of governance and communication raise the question, Is there a likelihood of an international convergence of structures for financial ordering? In the United States the size of the portfolios of financial intermediaries enable them to exercise strong countervailing power in dealing with corporate management. Had pension and mutual funds not grown so large, the contractual view of the firm emanating from agency theory would probably have remained an inert academic artifact. What transformed finance was the leverage of these institutions to advance client interests.

Yet in spite of institutional transformation, it is doubtful that U.S. practice will follow in the path of either the German *Hausbank* or the Japanese *keiretsu*. A major barrier is the deeply ingrained belief that great concentration of political or economic power is evil. Jefferson and Jackson, who shared a vision of an egalitarian society, expressed this prejudice in the early years of the republic. Such notions reconcile differences in a polity divided along regional, ethnic, national, political, religious, functional and other lines. Consistent with this perspective is the need for vigilance against the threat of a tyrannical plutocracy. Such an outlook partly motivated the federal intervention to control the great shifts of power and wealth in the rise of nineteenth century railroads and twentieth century conglomerates and LBOs.[10]

The strong vested interest in the status quo of the investing public and the professional groups serving the financial markets is another deterrent to broad change. The public has no incentive to abandon institutional arrangements that ensure transparency of corporate financial affairs and afford protection against incompetency and fraud in financial dealing. In addition, a vast array of attorneys, accountants and other specialists depend on these governance structures to apply their professional skills.

The most compelling issue in the recent history of U.S. financial governance is not whether there should be regulatory regimes; it is whether these regimes come within the purview of professional or governmental agencies and what the boundaries of supervisory authority are. Thus, in the mid-1990s, issues on the SEC policy agenda include the evaluation of regulatory practices for the vastly expanded mutual fund industry and the sufficiency of corporate disclosure for innovative financial derivative contracts.[11] Other critics warn of the limitations of contemporary accounting models and call for changes that would provide more useful insights into the nature of corporate affairs.[12]

Although emphasis on the advancement of earnings in the U.S. corporate governance system has inhibited long-term investment, several factors promise a corrective to this problem. One is an exposition by scholars of the trade-off inherent in two competing views of the firm: the first stresses the importance of contracting for the division of

[10] For the strong, abiding influence of these views in U.S. history, see, e.g., Davidson, *Mega-Mergers*, pp. 109–12; Galambos and Pratt, *The Rise of the Corporate Commonwealth*, chapt. 3; Hawley, *The New Deal and the Problem of Monopoly*, pp. 404–19 and 456–71; Kirkland, *A History of American Economic Life*, pp. 319–46; and Arthur M. Schlesinger, *The Age of Jackson* (Boston: Houghton Mifflin, 1945). See also Roe, *Strong Managers, Weak Owners*, chapt. 4.

[11] See, e.g., "SEC Wants Mutual Fund Risk Disclosed," *New York Times*, September 27, 1994, D, 1.

[12] See, e.g., Robert K. Elliott and Peter D. Jacobson, "U.S. Accounting: A National Emergency," *Journal of Accountancy* 172 (November 1991): 54–58; and Robert K. Elliott, "The Third Wave Breaks on the Shores of Accounting," *Accounting Horizons* 6 (June 1992): 61–85.

cash flow between stakeholders; the second emphasizes the critical role of corporations as centers of industrial learning and progress. Heightened investor sensitivity to these issues might be achieved by widening the scope of corporate communications and increasing the detailed disclosure of the prospective costs, benefits and special issues associated with internal investment activities. Although more costly than current reporting practices, this would establish a clearer understanding of the enterprise's economic potential. It would also provide investors with a future-directed framework for evaluating managerial performance based on well-documented objectives.

Alternatively, corporations could implement strategies for shifting developmental costs. One option is to contract with outside entities specializing in the development of a particular type of product. IBM, for example, has contracted with Cyrix Technologies for the design of a new line of computer chips and with Microsoft, Inc., for the development of its DOS operating system for small computers; both Pfizer and Becton–Dickinson have engaged specialized research enterprises like Oncogene Science Corporation to develop specialized diagnostic products. In addition, corporations might form joint ventures to defray developmental expenses and to share firm-specific skills. This was done by Dow Chemical and Corning Glass in producing fiber-optic cable. Another alternative would be joint business–government promotion of promising technologies. A highly successful precedent was the World War II programs that developed synthetic rubber, high-octane gasoline, penicillin, electronic computers and atomic energy.

British governance began to incorporate some American practices during the 1970s and 1980s in response to malpractice litigation resulting from a number of corporate failures, for example, those of Guiness Peat, Polly Peck Stores, the Bank of Commerce and Credit International and Maxwell Publications. One response was the further extension by British chartered accountants of formal professional standards beginning in the 1970s. In 1992, the Cadbury Commission recommended that boards of directors include more external members who saw their role as monitors rather than as advocates of management.[13]

In Germany and Japan, on the other hand, two different reforms helped to create more vibrant financial markets with a capacity like

[13] "The Invisible Band," *Economist*, October 8, 1994, 81.

that of London and New York for raising capital worldwide. In Germany the initiative bolstered the protection afforded shareholders. One aspect of this was the 1994 passage of a ban on insider trading. Another was improvement in the transparency of corporate affairs by standardization of accounting and disclosure practices.[14] But progress is likely to come slowly in this case because of the difficulties of the European Union in resolving national differences in accounting professionalism.[15] Japan has emphasized increasing the direct access of foreign investment organizations to trading on the giant Tokyo exchange. This is a high priority because it defuses criticism of the closed nature of the Japanese economy and the persistence of enormous trade surpluses. Ultimately, however, Tokyo's position as an international center for raising capital will compel the Japanese to establish a reputation for financial transparency and probity.[16]

[14] "Insider Law for Germany," *New York Times,* November 4, 1994, D, 15; and "Bridging the GAAP," *Economist,* September 17, 1994, 89.

[15] Louis H. Orzack, *International Authority and Professions: The State Beyond the Nation-State* (San Domenico: The European Policy Unit at the European University Institute, 1992), pp. 23–27.

[16] Sensitivity to the need for reform is reflected in Jun Ikeda and Noriyasu Osawa, "A Summary of Reports by the Fundamental Research Committee of the Securities and Exchange Council," in Foundation for Advanced Information and Research, ed., *Japan's Financial Markets,* pp. 553–61.

Index

Abbé Prevost d'exiles, 111
Abbott, Morris (Sir), 65
Accelerated Cost Recovery System (ACRS), 267, 268
accommanda, 44; *see also* Medici Bank
accommandita, see *accommanda*
accounting and bookkeeping: standardization of financial accounting, 10; in medieval commerce, 33; in Florentine merchant banks, 41; and Venetian commission agencies, 49–50; profit measurement in Venetian *colleganzia,* 50; in medieval finance, 53; in English East India Company, 67, 69, 77; in Dutch East India Company, 97; in nineteenth century railroads and corporations, 140–43; limitations in corporate monitoring, 145; evolution of British corporate accounting, 184–86; impediments to U.S. standardization, 187–89; retained earnings measurement, 197–98; proprietary theory, 198; entity theory, 198; pyramiding of earnings, 199; standardization and retail brokers, 199; accounting emphasis in England, France, Germany and U.S. contrasted, 226–27; U.S. post–World War II standardization, 226–31; income measurement and center firms, 256; pooling of interests and conglomerates, 276; merger accounting reform, 280–82; LBO and joint costing and transfer pricing, 292–93
Accounting for Business Combinations, 281
Accounting Principles Board, *see* American Institute of Certified Public Accountants
Adams, Charles Francis, Jr., 144
Adams, Henry Carter, 133–34
Adriatic Sea, 35

adverse selection, 6–7
AFL/CIO, 295
Africa, 55
agency problems: and contracting, 6; and informational asymmetries, 6, 20–25; and monitoring, 6; and moral hazard, 6; work of Alchian and Demsetz, 13; work of Meckling and Jensen, 20, 231; and the Medici Bank, 40–41, 43, 44–45; and Venetian trading partnerships, 48–51; medieval partnerships and, 52; reduction of, by accounting and internal information, 53; joint-stock companies and reduction of, 62; monitoring overseas agents at East India Company, 65–66; safeguards at East India Company, 68; global information and East India Company, 69; Dutch East India Company and shareholders, 97; London financial markets and reduction of, 102–103; and advantages of debt, 122–23; and disadvantages of equity, 123; quasi-public appearance of rail and canal companies and, 132–34; preference for railroad debt securities, 134–35, 146–58; financial disclosure and nineteenth century industry, 140–43; limitations of accounting, 145; conflicts between speculators and investors, 163–64; investors and agent negligence during 1920s, 200; Securities Acts and responsibilities of agents, 201–203; scholarship and the problem of agency, 235–36; and the rise of LBO partnerships, 259; LBOs as mechanisms for surmounting, 285–89, 300; influence on perspectives of money managers, 301; agency and center firm efficiency, 301–302; public finance and agency in ancient Greece, 317–18

331

engraftment of public debt, 103–104; as
market regulator, 118, 119
Bank for International Settlements (BIS),
271
bank investment subsidiaries, 196, 206,
209
Bank of Saint George (Genoa), 94; *see also*
Casa di San Giorgio
Bank of Stockholm, 94
Banker's Magazine, 143
Bankers Trust Company, 283, 291
banking, 278
Banking Act of 1933 (Glass-Steagall, U.S.),
204, 223
Banking Act of 1935 (U.S.), 204
banking regulation (U.S.): establishment of
Federal Reserve, 176,
187; extension during New Deal, 204;
post–World War II trends, 223–24
banks: of deposit and exchange in medi-
eval era, 35; of pawn, 35; *see also* gold-
smith-bankers
Banque de France, 116
Banque Generale, 106, 135
Banque Royale, 107, 108, 113
Bantam, 66
Barbarian invasions, 30
Barcelona, 37, 41
Bardi Company, 42, 52, 59; centralization
of decision making, 42; problem of royal
loans, 42–43; financial failure, 43
Baring Brothers Bank, 135
barley, 313
Barron's, 144
Baruch College, 281
Beatrice Foods Company, 290
Becton–Dickinson Corporation, 329
Bell Laboratories, AT&T, 263, 266
Bengal, 80
Berg, Norman A., 279, 284, 285
Berle, Adolf A., 13, 200–201
Bermuda, 60
Bernard, Samuel, 106
Bethlehem Steel Corporation, 198–99
"big bang, the," 323
biglietti, 94
bills of exchange, 29, 35
bills of lading, 33
biotechnology, 264
Black, F., 231
Black Tuesday (1929), 232
blue skies laws, 200
Blunt, John, 104
Board of Trade (Great Britain), 89, 90n3,
106, 140, 141, 185, 323; and balance of
trade, 93; and corporate monitoring, 161

Bologna, 37
Bonaparte, Napoleon, 121
Bonbright & Company, 175
Borg–Warner Company, 290
Boston, 135, 137, 163, 193
Boston Tea Party of 1773, 85
bottomry (ship loans), 73, 316
bounded rationality, 13
Brady, Nicholas, 270
Brandeis, Louis D., 154
Brazil, 55, 270
Brescia, 37
Bretton Woods Agreement of 1944, 220,
261
brewing industry, 171
Bridgewater, duke of, 122
Briggs, Henry, 93
Briloff, Abraham J., 281
Britain, *see* Great Britain
Brookmire Economic Service, 186
Bruges, 33, 37, 41, 42, 89; factors leading
to decline of, 95
Bubble Act of 1720 (Great Britain), 111,
118, 121, 130, 140
bullionists, 78
Burdett's Official Intelligence, 143
Bureau of the Census (U.S.), 215
Bureau of Corporations (U.S.), 186
Burgundy, dukes of, 95, 96
Burgundy, fairs of, 32
business education: shortcomings in the
1950s, 10; reform of, 226
business organization: *compagnia,* 38, 40,
41–42; *societas,* 38; *accommanda* (limited partnership), 44 (*see also* Medici
Bank); *colleganzia* (limited partnership),
48; *fraterna* (family partnership), 48;
maona (fleet contract), 50–51; regulated
company, 58–59; joint-stock company,
58–62; joint-stock company in oceanic
discovery, 55–57; railroads and canals,
127–66; industrial and utility corporations, 167–209; center firms, 213–27,
309–10; congolmerates, 258–83, 301–
302, 310; LBOs, 213, 259, 267, 289–
301, 310; *Hausbanks,* 324, 327; *Keiretsu,* 325, 327
Business Roundtable, 294
Business Week, 230
Byzantine Empire, 32, 35–36, 47

cable television, 298
Cabot, Sebastian, 55, 60
Cabral, Pedro Alvares, 55
Calais, 45, 59, 95

Clark, Kim B., 240
Cleveland, Frederick A., 144, 189
Clitherow, Christopher (Sir), 65
cloves, 64
coal, 308
coffee, 64
coinage, 29; in Carolingean era, 34; and
  gold, 34; and vellom, 34; English silver
  penny, 34; debasement and reminting in
  England, 103; in France before John
  Law, 106; louis d'or, 106; in ancient
  Greece, 315–16
coal mining, 273
Colbert, Jean, 93, 106, 106, 226
collegantia, 48; *see also colleganzia*
colleganzia: partnership form used at Venice, 48; limited liability, 49; features designed to reduce agent opportunities, 49;
  displaced by commission agencies, 49–
  50; challenges to limited liability, 49;
  profit measurement difficulties, 50
Cologne, 37, 60
Colorado Springs, Colo., 8
Colt Industries, 274
Columbia University, 9, 144, 186
Columbus, Christopher, 55
Combination Act (Great Britain), 130
Coming of Managerial Capitalism, The
  (Chandler and Tedlow), 274
commenda, 48; *see also colleganzia*
Commerce, Department of (U.S.), 186
Commerce and Labor, Department of
  (U.S.), 186
Commerical and Financial Chronicle, 144
commercial paper, 94, 243
Commines, Philippe de, seigneur D'Argen-
  ton, 40
commission agencies, 49–50
Committee on Accounting Procedure *see*
  American Institute of Accountants
Committee on Economic Research (Harvard University), 186
Common Market, 221
common stock finance: and rise of managerial capitalism, 167–209; and electric
  power growth, 170–71; and internal
  combustion engine, 170–71; economies
  of scale in industry, 171–72; economies
  of scope in industry, 171–73; new forms
  of industrial management, 173–74; electrical utility industry finance and organization, 174–75; influenced by example
  of partnerships, 177–79; par values and
  common stock, 179–82; book value and
  public accountants, 183–89; economic
  reporting and market risk assessment,

186–87; common stock valuation and industrial securities, 189–97; dividends
  and valuation, 190–94; rise of industrial
  common shares, 194; early mergers and
  economies of scale and scope, 194; U.S.
  industrial payout ratios, 195; common
  stock and financial intermediaries in
  1920s, 196–97, 206–207; drive for
  greater transparency in corporate affairs,
  197–204; *see also* equity
Commonwealth Edison Company, 174
communications, 264
compagnia: use in Florence, 38, 40, 41–42;
  lack of extensive use in Venice, 48
Compagnie des Indes (a.k.a. Mississippi
  Company), 114n55, 123, 124; role in
  John Law's plan to retire French indebtedness, 107–108; factors causing share
  price decline, 111
Companies Act of 1844 (Great Britain),
  184
Companies Act of 1856 (Great Britain),
  130
Companies Act of 1862 (Great Britain),
  185
Companies Act of 1879 (Great Britain),
  141
Companies Act of 1900 (Great Britain),
  185
Companies Act of 1928 (Great Britain),
  185
Companies Clauses Consolidations Act of
  1845 (Great Britain), 140
compensation, agent, *see* contracting
comprere (public debt, Genoa), 60
computational capacities: and research in
  modern finance, 9–10; discounts in Middle Ages, 34; time value of money in
  Middle Ages, 34
computer industry, 264, 329
computer technology, 275
Conde, de, Prince, 111
Congress (U.S.), 183, 202, 203, 270, 323
conglomerates, 25, 213, 310; rationalization for their formation, 258–59, 275;
  economic background to their development, 260–73; impact on U.S. business
  sector, 273–75; and portfolio theory,
  275, 299; purported sources of synergism, 275–76; accounting policies and
  growth, 276; taxes and share- financed
  acquisitions, 276; factors encouraging
  debenture finance, 278; restrictions on
  acquired tax attributes, 279–80; adverse
  effect of accounting reforms, 280–82;
  mounting political opposition, 282;

INDEX

Morgan, J. P., and Company, 138, 175, 176, 251
Morgan Guaranty Trust Company, 283
Moss, John (Representative), 229
Motor Carrier Act of 1980 (U.S.), 266
movable type, 93
Moxham, Arthur, 238–39
Mullins, David W., Jr., 295
Muslim world, 34, 35
Myers, Stewart C., 21, 255
Mylar, 238, 253

Nancy, Battle of, 46
Napier, John, 93
Naples, 37, 41
Naples, Kingdom of, 42, 47
Napoleon, see Bonaparte, Napoleon
Napoleonic Wars, 123
NASDAQ, 266
National City Bank, 196
National City Corporation, 196
National Cordage Company, 194
National Recovery Act of 1933 (U.S.), 207–208, 222
National Student Marketing, 229, 283
National Transportation Act of 1920 (U.S.), 146
Navigation Acts, 85, 99
Near East, 137
Neale, Thomas, 105
Necker, Jacques, 115
negligence, 200; see also law
neoclassical economic theory, 10–11
neoprene rubber, 238, 253
Netherlands, 96
New Deal, 197, 224: securities market reforms, 201–203; professions and corporate governance, 202; public opinion and corporate oversight, 203; risk perceptions and banking reform, 203–204; financial market benefits and securities reforms, 206–207; economic disadvantages and federal regulation, 207–208; regulation and post–World War II economy, 222, 263
New East India Company, see East India Company, New
New England, 137, 148
New York Central Railroad Company, 149, 164
New York City, 137, 209, 306
New York State, 142, 160
New York Stock Exchange, 167, 187, 199, 200, 201, 232, 265, 266, 272–73
Newcomen, Thomas, 128
Newton, Isaac, 93

nexus of contracts, 259
Neyman, Jerzy, 9
Nine Years' War, 81
nitrocellulose chemicals, 173, 238
Nixon, Richard M. (President), 261
Nobel Prize, 3
Noncomformists, 119
North, Douglass, C., 4, 298
Northwest Industries, 274
notaries, 33–34, 70
nuclear energy, 308
nutmeg, 64
NWA Inc., 290
nylon, 173, 238, 253

Objectives of Financial Reporting, 228
ocean shipping, 273
Office of Thrift Supervision (U.S.), 271
Ogden Industries, 274
oil, 278; see also petroleum
oligopolies, 131
On Deterioration of Railway Plant and Road (Huish), 144
Oncogene Science Corporation, 329
opportunism, see agency problems
options: used on the Amsterdam bourse, 98; development of Black–Scholes pricing model, 231; for shares and indices in the U.S., 265
Orient, 71
organizations, 4, 29
Orlon, 238, 253
Other People's Money and How the Bankers Use It (Brandeis), 154
Owens–Illinois Company, 290

Pacific Stock Exchange, 265
Pacioli, Lucca, 33
padrone (fleet voyage manager), 50
paints and lacquers, 171
Palermo, 37
papacy, 36, 39
Papillon, Thomas: as leader of dissidents to Child's administration, 78; undermining Child's recapitalization, 79; formation of New East India Company, 80; failure to displace English East India Company, 81–82, 84; see also Child, Josiah; East India Company, New; East India Company, English; East India Company, English, administration and organization; East India Company, English, financial structure
Paramount Communications, 273, 285, 298; see also Gulf and Western Industries
parcenvoli (coventurer), 50–51

a

345

Railroad Gazette, 144
Railroad Promotion and Capitalization in the United States (Cleveland and Powell), 144
Railroad Transportation: Its History and Its Laws (Hadley), 144
railroading, 273
railroads, finance, 25, 127–57, 307, 308; quasi-public appearance, 132–34; economies of scale and scope and interregional system, 134–45; informational asymmetry and debt, 134–35; investment bankers and railroad finance, 135–36, 138; and investor learning, 137–38; and management techniques, 138; and limited liability, 138–42; and specialized publications, 142–43; and accounting, 142–43; limitations of accounting, 145; debt and informational asymmetry, 146–57; and governmental assistance, 148–49; debenture financing, 154; bankruptcy risk in the nineteenth century, 154–55; income bonds, 155–56; preferred stock financing, 155–57; dividend policies in UK and U.S., 192–93
Railroads: Their Origins and Problems (Adams), 144
Railway Economy (Lardner), 143
Railway Monitor, 143
Railway Morals and Public Policy (Spencer), 144
Railway World, 144
rayon, 173, 238
real estate market collapse of the 1980s, 270
recording industry, 298
Red Sea, 64, 65
Reformation, 61
Registrar of Companies (Great Britain), 161
regulated company: and foreign trade, 58–59; guildlike characteristics, 58; similarities to joint-stock companies, 58–59; advantages of this form in trade, 58–59; example of the Staple of London, 59; and Dutch East India Company, 96
Regulation Q, 224, 244
Regulation of Railways Act of 1868, 141; Regulation T, 204
Reich, Robert, 301–302
Renaissance, 24, 184
rentes, 94, 96
Report on the Question of Depreciation and on the Policy of Establishing a Reserve Fund (Laing), 144
representative firm (Marshall), 310

Republic Steel Company, 285
research and development, 275
research federally sponsored, 264
Resolution Trust Corporation (U.S.), 271
Restoration (of Stuart monarchy), 78
retail brokerage firms, 196, 206, 209
Revolution of 1688, 78, 79, 89–90, 91, 92; *see also* Glorious Revolution of 1688
Revolutions of 1848, 136
Rhine River, 33
Rhone River, 33
Ricardo, David, 127, 129
ricordi, 42
rights issues, 178
Ripley, William Z., 144, 149, 197
RJR Nabisco, 290, 293
Rock, Kevin, 21
Rockefeller, John D., 171, 308
Rohm & Haas Chemical Company, 238
Roman Empire, 30, 31, 318–19, 320–21
Rome, 319
Roosevelt, Franklin Delano, 197, 203
Roosevelt, Theodore, 176, 186
Rothschild, House of, 136
Rothschild, Nathan Meyer, Baron, 308
Rotterdam, 70
Rouen, 37
Rousseau, Jean-Jacques, 92
Royal African Company, 56
Royal Exchange (London), 96
Royal Exchange Assurance, 117
royal loans, 42–47, 62; *see also* political risk
rubber, 171
rubber industry, 173, 215
Rumelt, Richard P., 279
Russia, 221
Russia Company, 56, 60
Ryswick, Treaty of, 104

Safeway Stores, 290
St. John, Henry, chancellor of the Exchequer, 104
salt, 36
San Francisco, 266
Sarenic invasion, 30
satins, 64
satisficing, 13
savings and loan industry, 267, 271, 292, 295
Schiller, Robert J., 14
Scholes, Myron S., 231
Schumpeter, Joseph A., 1–2, 9, 311; and process of creative destruction, 254
Schwab & Company, Charles, 266